CULTURAL DIVERSITY IN SCHOOLS

CULTURAL DIVERSITY
— in —
SCHOOLS

▼

FROM

RHETORIC

TO

PRACTICE

▲

Edited by
Robert A. DeVillar,
Christian J. Faltis,
James P. Cummins

STATE UNIVERSITY OF NEW YORK PRESS

Published by
State University of New York Press, Albany

© 1994 State University of New York

For information, address the State University of New York Press,
State University Plaza, Albany, NY 12246

Production by Bernadine Dawes
Marketing by Dana Yanulavich

Library of Congress Cataloging-in-Publication Data

Cultural diversity in schools: from rhetoric to practice / Robert A.
   DeVillar, Christian J. Faltis, James P. Cummins, editors.
      p.   cm.
   Includes bibliographical references and index.
   ISBN 0-7914-1673-9. — ISBN 0-7914-1674-7 (pbk.)
   1. Multicultural education—United States.   2. Educational
equalization—United States.   3. Education—Social aspects—United
States.   4. Classroom management—United States.   5. Educational
technology—United States.   I. DeVillar, Robert A.   II. Faltis,
Christian, 1950- .   III. Cummins, Jim, 1949- .
LC1099.3.C82   1994
370.19'6'0973—dc20   93-24309
                                                                 CIP

   2   3   4   5   6   7   8   9   10

▼ Contents ▼

INTRODUCTION   1
    Reconciling Cultural Diversity and Quality Schooling:
    Paradigmatic Elements of a Socioacademic Framework
    ROBERT A. DEVILLAR and
    CHRISTIAN J. FALTIS

PART I: CULTURAL DIVERSITY AND SCHOOLING

1   The Rhetoric and Practice of Cultural Diversity   25
    in U.S. Schools: Socialization, Resocialization,
    and Quality Schooling
    ROBERT A. DeVILLAR

2   Cooperative Learning in the Culturally   57
    Diverse Classroom
    DAVID W. JOHNSON and ROGER T. JOHNSON

3   Building Bridges for the Future: 75
    Anthropological Contributions to
    Diversity and Classroom Practices
    STEVEN F. ARVIZU

PART II: CULTURAL DIVERSITY AND
          TEACHER EDUCATION

4   Responding Successfully to Cultural Diversity   101
    in Our Schools: The Teacher Connection
    ROBERT D. MILK

5   Mentoring, Peer Coaching, and Support   117
    Systems for First-Year Minority/
    Bilingual Teachers
    MARGARITA CALDERON

PART III: CULTURAL DIVERSITY IN
THE CLASSROOM

6   Cooperative Learning for Language-Minority   145
     Students
     RICHARD P. DURAN

7   Influences of L1 Writing Proficiency on L2   161
     Writing Proficiency
     ROBERT S. CARLISLE

8   Promoting Positive Cross-Cultural Attitudes   189
     and Perceived Competence in Culturally and
     Linguistically Diverse Classrooms
     KATHRYN J. LINDHOLM

9   Managing Behavior in the Culturally   207
     Diverse Classroom
     SAUNDRA SCOTT SPARLING

10   Effectiveness of Bilingual Education: 233
     A Comparison of Various Approaches
     in an Elementary School District
     LINDA GONZALES

PART IV: CULTURAL DIVERSITY
AND TECHNOLOGY

11   A Communicative Computer Environment   263
     for the Acquisition of ESL
     NIDIA GONZALEZ-EDFELDT

12   Bilingual Team-Teaching Partnerships Over   299
     Long Distances: A Technology-Mediated
     Context for Intragroup Language
     Attitude Change
     DENNIS SAYERS

13   Teaching Teachers about Computers and   333
     Collaborative Problem-Solving
     HOWARD BUDIN

14   Pedagogical and Research Uses of Computer-   349
      Mediated Conferencing
      ARMANDO A. ARIAS, JR., and BERYL BELLMAN

CONCLUSION   363
      The Socioacademic Achievement Model
      in the Context of Coercive and
      Collaborative Relations of Power
      JIM CUMMINS

Author Index   391

Subject Index   398

▼ Introduction ▼
Reconciling Cultural Diversity and Quality Schooling: Paradigmatic Elements of a Socioacademic Framework

ROBERT A. DeVILLAR
and
CHRISTIAN J. FALTIS

Schooling: The Realization of Access, the Need for Equity

Schools in the United States are generally characterized by policies and practices that are antithetical to meeting our nation's purported goal of delivering a comparable education to its culturally and racially diverse populace (see DeVillar this volume). The negative effects of these policies and practices on the elementary and secondary schooling outcomes of African-Americans, Hispanic-Americans, and other designated minority-group students are clear, widespread, and growing in scope and complexity (cf. Arias 1986; Calathes 1991; Catterall and Cota-Robles 1988; Cohen and Arias 1988; Fernández and Shu 1988; Fordham 1988; Goldenberg and Gallimore 1991; Levin 1985; Moore and Pachón 1985; Navarro 1986). Recent demographic data with respect to the disproportionately large birth and immigration rates of minority populations relative to their majority-population counterparts, their significantly younger age rates, and their rates of increasing poverty and low-income status compound the bleakness of their educational futures and add to the mounting pressure for institutional change (cf. Borjas and Tienda 1987; Bouvier and Gardner 1986; Calathes 1991; Commission on Work, Family, and Citizenship 1988; Davis, Haub, and Willette 1983; Orfield and Ashkinaze 1991; William T. Grant Foundation 1988; O'Hare 1988).

School Access as an Indicator
of Equality and Integration

School administrators, staff, and teachers are arguably in the best professional position to be the most effective change agents in our national challenge to achieve congruence between our educational rhetoric and educational practices, notwithstanding substantial historical and current evidence to the contrary (cf. Bennett and LeCompte 1990; Cuban 1984; Goodlad 1984, 1990; The Holmes Group 1990; Ramírez and Merino 1990). In moving toward this prospective balance between rhetoric and practice, however, we must ensure that the results of educators' anticipated concerted efforts are not too narrowly defined with respect to what constitutes student equality and social integration. Specifically, future achievements must extend beyond traditional notions of what is meant by having attained consonance between educational rhetoric and practice in these two areas of our societal development.

There is little doubt, for example, that the United States already practices its rhetoric with respect to providing universal access to schooling for virtually all children within its national borders without regard to, among other factors, citizenship, economic status, race, ethnicity, or primary language spoken. Implementing a universal policy of access to schooling within this context of national heterogeneity is in itself a formidable achievement, particularly when compared to or contrasted with policies and outcomes of universal access to schooling in other advanced industrialized nations (Kirst 1984), including those with relatively homogeneous (at least with respect to national self-perception) populations (cf. White 1991) and those experiencing recent major influxes of culturally and linguistically diverse immigrant groups (cf. Bruce 1991). However, as highlighted in a later chapter (DeVillar), our national dilemma is decidedly not one of universal schooling but one of universal quality schooling. Thus, universal school access is an insufficient mechanism by which to attain a unified, informed, productive, and creative populace, or through which to reap the related developmental, economic, political, and other advantages associated with such a national profile. The focus, then, of our national attention must be more encompassing, fixing itself upon students' quality of educational experiences once in school and the derivative social and academic outcomes that result for them. Universal quality schooling, rather than universal access to schooling, is necessary for our desired national profile and its intended benefits to occur.

Educational Equity: Refining the Indicators of Integration and Equality

Access is a necessary, but not sufficient, element within the quality schooling equation. Hence, access by itself, whether as policy or practice, will not translate into the advantages which are expected to accrue at the individual, group, and national levels. For advantages to occur at these levels, access must become part of a more encompassing notion, one that includes student participation and the benifits derived from that participation (Brookover and Lezotte 1981, cited in Lipkin 1983). These three critical elements—access, participation, and benefit—are of fundamental importance in two interrelated ways. First, as a group they provide the foundation for our view of educational equity (DeVillar 1986; DeVillar and Faltis 1987, 1991), that is, the notion that all groups of students can have comparable access to quality schooling, that they can have comparable participation in the schooling enterprise once they are there, and that they will derive comparable educational benefits from their participation. Second, they serve as more appropriate criteria by which to gauge whether and to what degree quality schooling is actually made available to all groups of students and experienced positively by them. This judgment, in turn, enables us to determine the extent to which our rhetoric of schooling relates to our practices in terms of equality and social integration.

Integration, Communication, and Cooperation: The Roots of Unity

DeVillar and Faltis (1991) have developed a socioacademic achievement framework that incorporates the notion of equity as described above. Additionally, it identifies, defines, and interrelates three key elements required to attain equity within culturally and linguistically heterogeneous school settings and, by extension, universal quality schooling in the United

States. These three essential elements—*integration, communication,* and *cooperation*—also have served as key components within preexisting conceptual frameworks. The principal of integration reflects the work of Allport (1954) in the area of contact theory, particularly with respect to successful performance and equal-status relationships within heterogeneously comprised human groupings. The principle of communication relates to the work of Vygotsky (1978) in the area of social learning theory, with particular emphasis upon the fundamental role of communication with others as a means to individual learning and transformation. The principle of cooperation reflects the works of educational researchers such as Johnson and Johnson (1981, 1984, 1986, this volume) and others in the area of cooperative learning, especially with respect to the role of structured cooperation in realizing enhanced social relationships and academic gains at the individual and group levels within heterogeneous classroom contexts. The following synthesis of their socioacademic framework represents its essence and serves to theoretically anchor and guide the reader relative to the contents of this volume and its array of contributions, which address substantive issues of quality schooling across elementary, secondary, and university settings within our culturally diverse notion.

Current Teaching and Learning Practices in U.S. Classrooms: The Need for an Alternative Framework

There are three major social and physical contexts in which communicative exchanges that support student learning occur: (1) teacher-led whole class instruction, (2) teacher-led small group teaching, and (3) teacher-delegated small group-work in which students work together on their own.

   Although increasing numbers of teachers are incorporating small group teaching and small group learning strategies into their instructional repertoire, teacher-led whole class instruction continues to be the most widespread strategy of organizing for instruction. Currently, then, teachers remain reluctant to incorporate small group teaching and learning as integral parts of their students' daily learning experiences. Kliebard (1989) offers an explanation of this reluctance when he speaks of teachers' need to control with whom students talk, as well as to control when and how much they talk:

> The teacher as a question-asker and the student as responder
> is a way of ensuring teacher dominance in the classroom sit-
> uation. If students asked the questions or if they addressed
> one another rather than the teacher or if they engaged inde-
> pendently in discovery practices, the risk of disorder would be
> introduced, and the structure of school organization will not
> tolerate that kind of risk. (10)

This prevailing need to control student talk, and hence student learning, can also be seen in the frequent companion to
whole class teaching, individualized instruction. In this type of
instruction, students work alone on problems ostensibly related to information presented to the whole class. Calling the
practice "individualized" is largely a misnomer, however, since
teachers rarely customize learning materials for individual
seatwork, and all tasks assigned to students for individual
completion are essentially identical (Goodlad 1984). In fact,
individualized instruction amounts to little more than seatwork in which students complete prefabricated worksheets on
their own.

Just how widespread is teacher-dominated whole class
teaching? Sirotnik (1983) conducted a nationwide study involving 129 elementary school all-English classrooms and
found that students spent about 70 percent of their time in
class listening to the teacher, who taught mostly to the class as
a whole group. Verbal interaction with students within this
setting most frequently entailed asking and answering factual
questions about known information. Nearly all of the classrooms had a combination of fixed and moveable chairs, but
students were almost never observed talking or working together on learning tasks. Fewer than half of the classrooms
had separate learning centers that had been arranged by the
teacher. Summarizing the findings, Sirotnik offered the following dismal image of the typical elementary school classroom:

> Consider again the model classroom picture presented here:
> a lot of teacher talk and a lot of student listening, unless
> students are responding to teachers' questions or working
> on written assignments; almost invariably closed and fact-
> ual questions; little corrective feedback and no guidance;
> and predominately total class instructional configurations
> around traditional activities—all in a virtually affectless en-
> vironment. (29)

More recently, Ramírez and Merino (1990) investigated the nature of classroom interaction in three types of bilingual education program models: (a) structured English immersion, (b) early-exit transitional bilingual, and (c) late-exit transitional bilingual. (Note that the first program type could perhaps more appropriately be termed an English-only program and the last program type a developmental-maintenance bilingual program.) Using a systematic observation instrument, they observed social interaction in 103 first- and second-grade classrooms at eight sites in California, Florida, New Jersey, New York, and Texas. They found that instruction was conducted mainly in large groups, typically to the whole class. Teachers generated two to three times more talk than students, and when students did talk, it was most often in the form of short responses to teacher questions. These findings are virtually indistinguishable from the patterns of teacher-controlled talk that Sirotnik (1983) reported for all-English mainstream classrooms. Earlier findings (Dawe 1934; Furst and Amidon 1962; Pankratz 1967; Sirotnik 1981; Cuban 1984) reported in DeVillar and Faltis (1991) provide comparable evidence that this current instructional profile reflects our historical practice since at least the 1880s and remains intact across all subject-matter areas and grade levels.

In summary, the majority of both mainstream and bilingual/ESL classrooms are fundamentally teacher-controlled whole classroom learning environments. In essence, students are silenced (Fine 1987). They are provided with minimal opportunities to use their own ideas for verbal exchanges with the teacher, and they are not allowed to engage in conversations with their peers. Ironically, as DeVillar and Faltis (1991) point out, "as students grow increasingly able to expand their vocabularies and to manipulate and articulate complex language and thoughts, the opportunities to engage in meaningful classroom conversations which would develop these skills decrease" (7).

Thus, teachers rely on the whole class as the chief social context for teaching, virtually excluding the contexts of teacher-led small group teaching and small group learning from their pedagogical repertoire.

There are serious problems associated with the fact that our nation's classrooms have been and continue to be structured in such a way that students are denied access to communication both with their teacher and their peers. First, students are not seen as capable of contributing to and developing knowledge. Second, knowledge itself is reduced to the rote acquisition of existing facts. Third, classroom learning under these conditions, in essence, does not reflect the way that students learn in their social contexts outside of school or, albeit rarely, in student-centered learning settings within the school, particularly in small group contexts where the teacher and peers talk and work together toward a common goal. Fourth, whole class instruction followed by individualized instruction socially isolates and segregates students. Taken together, these four problems point to a need for a fundamental change in the way that teachers organize for instruction, in order for social integration and interaction, equality of educational opportunity, and enhanced academic achievement to occur within culturally diverse, and otherwise heterogeneous, classroom contexts.

It should come as no surprise, then, that students cannot develop and exchange ideas through talk or learn to work together cooperatively in classrooms dominated by whole class instruction and driven by the operating assumptions that only teachers have knowledge, that only they can transmit it, and that students cannot learn from one another. Thus, in addition to generating the four problem areas listed above, the silencing of students also violates a fundamental maxim of our socioacademic framework:

> Schooling will foster an educational context conducive to enhanced academic achievement by all students to the extent that it models the creation and implementation of an equitable and socially integrated society where individual and group voices, actions, and talents are explicitly valued, nurtured, and incorporated within the learning environment.

Hence, the social context of learning and academic outcomes are intimately linked. Thus, to achieve our universal quality-schooling goals, students must not only hear and learn indirectly about our democratic society and the potential benefits derived from it, they must experience democracy and its workings continually within the very socialization institutions that proclaim its merits and by so doing directly derive benefit from their participatory efforts.

Successful Schooling in a Culturally Diverse Society: Applying and Integrating the Socioacademic Principles

Classroom instruction that disallows communication, that segregates students, and that encourages competition hinders successful teaching and learning in the culturally diverse classroom. As mentioned previously, the socioacademic view of teaching and learning integrates important principles from the works of Lev Vygotsky concerning the social role of interaction, particularly communicative, for individual learning; the works of Gordon Allport in terms of contact theory, especially relative to the successful integration of members of distinct groups in reaching common goals in a shared and equitable manner; and the works of David and Roger Johnson, and others, concerned with promoting cooperative learning to enhance academic outcomes and prosocial behavior in culturally heterogeneous classroom settings. Descriptions of these principles and illustrations relating to their integration in culturally diverse classroom settings follow.

The Principle of Communication

The socioacademic framework is in theoretical alignment with Vygotsky's notion that classroom learning is first and foremost a social event mediated through communication between the students and the teacher, and among students as they converse with more capable peers. One of Vygotsky's major principles is that teaching and learning entail a two-phase process that first requires the student to receive assistance through social interaction with the teacher or more capable peers before individual learning can take place (Vygotsky 1978). A more capable peer is a student who, similar to the teacher, possesses certain skill preparation that is particularly appropriate to assisting a fellow student in the completion of a task (DeVillar and Faltis 1991). By talking through a problem with the teacher or a more capable peer and then practicing it, for example, the student ultimately internalizes the ability to solve similar problems unassisted. It is important to note that the student does not merely internalize the teacher's or more capable peer's higher level of ability; rather, the student reconceptualizes it into a novel form of understanding. That is, the student gains a unique, internally organized method of responding to and solving problems of the type with which he or she initially needed the assistance of the teacher or more capable peer (Díaz, Neal, and Amay-Williams 1990). In effect, this socially interactive communicative process, in combination with the student's own internal foundations, enables the cognitive transformation of the student. Moreover, novel forms of understanding in one area tend to transfer to other areas of cognition. Vygotsky (1978) refers to this language mediated, two-phase process as moving from other-regulated to self-regulated learning.

Another of Vygotsky's social learning principles is that jointly constructed social interaction must fall within the student's *zone of proximal development*. When students talk and work in collaboration with their teacher and among their peers, they gain access to new areas of learning potential beyond those they are able to accomplish alone. These areas of learning potential comprise each student's zone of proximal development; that is, the difference between a student's actual level of ability and his or her immediate potential for development. It is fundamentally important to underscore that a student's immediate potential for development can be realized only with assistance through joint interaction (Tudge 1990).

Vygotsky's social learning principles thus provide a theoretical frame of reference that gives communication a pivotal role in socioacademic achievement. With its emphasis on social interaction through assisted performance in the zone of proximal development, the Vygotskian perspective supports the socioacademic principle that students must have opportunities to communicate and exchange ideas both among themselves and with their teachers. A classroom must be a place where students are able to talk with one another about ideas and have the ideas make sense to them so that they can reconceptualize them into their own system of knowledge.

The *experience-text-relationship* (ETR) method (Au 1979; Au and Mason 1981; Au and Kawakami 1984, 1985; cited in DeVillar and Faltis 1991) provides an illustration of how Vygotskian principles may be adapted to culturally diverse learning settings. In ETR lessons, the teacher models and guide students through the process of applying background knowledge to understand and interpret text. In the experience (E) phase, the teacher elicits the students' personal experiences relevant to the topic of the text to be read, then passes to the text (T) phase, where the students silently read a section of the text in order to locate specific information (e.g., characters and setting) before discussing the details of the text as a class and generating hypotheses regarding the story. In the relationship (R) phase, the teacher uses assessment and assistance questions to help the students generate relationships between their own experiences and the text immediately read. The object of the ETR strategy is to gradually transfer the students from their relative dependence on teacher assistance at each phase to relative student independence across all phases. Au and Kawakami's (1984, cited in DeVillar and Faltis 1991) study of five Hawaiian children in the Kamehameha Early Education Program in Honolulu, Hawaii, demonstrates the value of adult and peer assistance in leading students from an other-regulated to a self-regulated learning stage. Their research found that successful teachers in the program generally

1. Instructed within the students' zone of proximal development, sustaining interaction by balancing the student's background knowledge with new knowledge available within their socially assisted grasp
2. Enabled students to arrive at their own generation of new knowledge through waiting for alternative responses after incorrect responses, ignoring the incorrect response, or asking an assisting question after the incorrect response
3. Engaged students in quantitatively more complex verbal interactions than simple verbal interactions, but used simple verbal interactions to check comprehension and establish simple propositions required for understanding information presented in the text
4. Consistently reinforced appropriate student responses, modeled comprehension processes, and, through discussion, focused students' attention on critical textual information
5. Facilitated and integrated into the lesson student-generated topics for discussion that were not directly elicited by a teacher-generated question.

The research cited below (and elaborated upon in DeVillar and Faltis 1991) provides additional support for the application of Vygotskian social learning principles to enhance individual learning and performance outcomes of students, particularly those within nontraditional classroom settings (e.g., culturally diverse, low-income, racially or ethnically segregated). The strategy of reciprocal teaching, for example, has resulted in improved reading skills for designated poor readers through teacher-assisted small group settings (Palincsar, Brown, and Campione 1989; Palincsar 1986; Palincsar and Brown 1984; Brown and Palincsar 1986). With respect to the role of peers in a student's learning development and content area outcomes, Bruce, Michaels, and Watson-Gegeo (1985) found that students in a low-income, urban school improved their writing and developed a sharp sense of audience through working together, in this particular case at computers, to compose critical reviews of events within a variety show. Bruce et al. also found that students' interest in their tasks was heightened and extended to their informal as well as formal learning settings. Informally, students paid attention to each other's writing and shared comments about it when not at the computer; formally, when working together at the computer, they generated discussion about the immediate task. Additional research findings in support of the use of peer interaction within culturally diverse learning settings as a positive means to successful task completion and individual cognitive development—fundamental features in Vygotskian social learning theory—include Weisner, Gallimore, and Jordan (1988), relative to Hawaiian American students; and García (1990) and Moll (1988), with respect to Hispanic-American students among others (see DeVillar and Faltis 1991).

Communication Principles and Second-Language Acquisition

A related and no less important schooling outcome that we, as a nation, desire our students to achieve is the ability to speak, read, write, and understand English, particularly in the context-reduced sense that Cummins (1981, 1989) associates with being required to succeed in school. The socioacademic elements of social integration, communication, and cooperation each, and in combination with the others, are present in the socially and verbally interactive communicative settings required for both native-like second-language development and, we propose, enhanced academic outcomes. DeVillar and Faltis (1991), in their analysis of selected research related to peer interaction and second-language acquisition, reported advantages for second-language learners interacting with native speakers (e.g., Hawkins 1988), and less than satisfactory outcomes in native-like second-language acquisition in the case of students being segregated from native-speaking school contexts (e.g., Swain 1985). The benefits derived by second-language speakers from their access and participation in authentic communicative contexts with native-language speakers, especially with peers, are compelling in their support for integration and cooperation (Gaies 1985; McGroarty 1989; Wong-Fillmore 1985), as are the disadvantages wrought from second language schooling contexts where segregation and communicative artifice prevail, whether by design or accident. (Milk 1980; Neves 1984).

Socioacademic Success: Communication, Integration, and Cooperation

The principles that comprise the socioacademic framework are in an interdependent relationship with one another. It is through their combined presence that the *minimal necessary conditions for universal quality schooling* can be met. Allport (1959), for example, both explicitly understood the nature of his focus to be *integration* and the relationship of *communication* to that focus:

> If the prejudiced style of life can be learned—and certainly it is not innate—then surely . . . in Gandhi's terms, the "equiminded" outlook can also be acquired. In schools, I suggest, we discard [aspects] of the present content and replace it with suitably chosen instruction and experience in the *principle of integration....*[Humans'] choices can be only among sequences they have known, and so our problem of training involves also the giving of experience, especially in childhood, that will enlarge the cognitive style and turn the mind automatically toward the *integrative mode of handling conflict.* (Emphasis added; 14–149)

Addressing the relationship of communication to integration, Allport added:

> The successful resolution of *social* conflict proceeds always along the same lines. Take the issue of desegregation, a problem of the first magnitude not only in this country but in the

world at large. On the social level . . . [and on] the personal level . . . the principle of inclusion fails. At the moment this particular problem is most acute in the United States and South Africa. . . . The policy of [exclusion] extends to housing, transportation, schools, public assemblies, recreation, and politics, so that there is no . . . opportunity to become acquainted. And needless to say the precondition of all normative compatibility is communication. (Original emphasis; 142)

Vygotsky (1962) also clearly understood the interdependent relationship of the principles of integration, cooperation and communication, which he identifies and applies throughout his social learning theory, although not necessarily from a cross-cultural or interracial perspective. Nevertheless, like Allport (1954), his writings reflect the interdependence between equimindedness among participants (an integrative and cooperative feature) and successful communication, most notably in the contrastive examples he supplies using a passage from Tolstoy's *Anna Karenina* and an uncredited poem about three hearing-impaired men in court. In the former case, for Tolstoy's characters, Kitty and Levin, to understand each other's declaration of love required nothing more (at the concrete, decoding level) than writing the initial letter of each of the words one wished to express to the other, regardless of the complexity of their syntax. Thus, the strings of letters

W y a: i c n b, d y m t o n; I c n a o t; s t y m f a f w h; and *I h n t f a f. I n c l y,*

absolutely void of meaning for all others, expressed an emotionally charged, even passionate declaration of unrequited love between Kitty and Levin (as it did in real life for Tolstoy and his future wife) due to their ideal degree of equimindedness (see Vygotsky 1962: 140–41). Vygotsky then presents the following doggerel verse to exemplify the effects on communication when an insufficient degree of equimindedness exists:

Before the judge who's deaf two men bow.
One deaf man cries: "He led away my cow."
"Beg pardon," says the other in reply,
"That meadow was my father's land in days gone by."
The judge decides: "For you to fight each other is a shame.
Nor one nor t'other, but the girl's to blame." (141)

Although ostensibly referring to the participants' lack of the necessary auditory tools with which to communicate, Vygotsky purposely used the doggerel analogously to illustrate the inevitable "total misunderstanding, even with full speech, [that occurs between] any two people who give a different meaning to the same word or who hold divergent views" (141).

Applying the Socioacademic Framework in Schools: Future Prospects, Present Limitations

The following illustration of the interdependent relationship among the principles of integration, communication, and cooperation within a culturally heterogeneous classroom context will address concerns of teachers and other educators with respect to applying the socioacademic framework.

As each student may have a different zone of proximal development, it would be difficult for a teacher to adjust his or her interaction to the learning needs of a broad range of students at the same time. In light of the present teacher-student ratio, and that of the foreseeable future, the two most promising contexts for the effective application of social learning principles appear to be teaching in small groups (e.g., reciprocal teaching and ETR methods illustrated earlier) and learning in small groups, particularly in the form of cooperative learning. In both contexts, students of different language and cultural backgrounds exchange and develop ideas, and otherwise collaborate with one another cooperatively, participating in formally structured cooperative learning methods such as *Student Teams-Achievement Divisions* (STAD), *Teams-Game-Tournament* (TGT), *Teams-Assisted Individualization* (TAI), *Jigsaw I and II,* and *Group Investigation,* as well as methods associated with Johnson and Johnson, Weigel, and others (see Slavin 1985, and summary of same in DeVillar and Faltis 1991).

As stated earlier, physically integrating students of diverse language, ethnic, and racial backgrounds by assigning them to "work together" in small groups will not generally lead them to cooperate with one another. For multiple reasons, students do not automatically feel bound through talk and past experiences to their fellow students (Johnson, Johnson, and Holubec 1986). The principle of cooperation, then, must be complemented by the concurrent application of additional principles—specifically, communication and integration—to ensure that all students are contributing through talk and action to the group effort. The four elements identified by Johnson, Johnson, and Holubec (1986) as supporting equitable participation in cooperative group work are particularly compatible with the accompanying two tenets comprising the socioacademic framework. These elements, which are interconnected and mutually supportive, are (1) preparation in interpersonal and small group skills; (2) face-to-face interaction; (3) positive interdependence; and (4) individual accountability for learning the concepts and information germane to the task.

Cooperative learning activities that are built upon these elements are critical to the socioacademic framework because they theoretically satisfy several of the conditions that favor successful social integration and social interaction. Additionally, there is widespread agreement among cooperative learning adherents (cf. DeVillar and Faltis 1991; Kohn 1986) that cooperative learning methods must adhere to the criteria associated with Allport (1954) to achieve effective integration of interracial/interethnic groups, specifically: (a) equal status among participants, (b) individual attributes that successfully challenge the negative minority stereotype, (c) mutual interdependence, (d) promotion of individual perception, and (e) promotion of egalitarian norms.

Thus, to promote successful social integration at the classroom level, students must assign equal status to themselves and others, exhibit attributes that successfully challenge negative stereotypes, see themselves as mutually responsible for their own learning, and adhere to egalitarian norms of interaction.

In addition, successful social integration in the heterogeneous classroom requires the institutional promotion of supportive policies and practices among administrators, parents, and students alike. Schools need to openly advocate and celebrate the importance of intergroup contact through communication and cooperation. In combination, these efforts help schools to transcend ethnic, linguistic, and social divisions, and at the same time set the stage for successful cooperation, the social context for learning that best facilitates social integration and communication.

Implementing principles of the socioacademic framework means that considerably more instructional time will have to be allotted to small group teaching and cooperative learning. These two social contexts, however, will not automatically lead to equal status among participants or to prosocial behavior, particularly in the form of, but not limited to, new friendship patterns. Brief examples from DeVillar and Faltis (1991) relative to these two areas will lend evidence to this claim.

Friendship Patterns and Other Prosocial Behaviors

Research in desegregated junior and senior high school settings by Weigel et al. (1975), found that Anglo-American students' attitudes toward Mexican-American students improved, but not their attitudes toward African-Americans; likewise, the Mexican-American students' attitudes toward African-American and Anglo-American students did not improve, nor did those of the African-American students toward Anglo-American students (Slavin 1985). Thus, DeVillar and Faltis (1991) describe improved friendship pattern outcomes as potentially characterized by one-way and two-way improvement. The one-way pattern reflects a nonreciprocal friendship pattern improvement, where the attitude improvement on the part of one group (Anglo-American students in the above instance) is not balanced by an improved attitude on the part of the other group (African-American students). A two-way pattern would reflect a reciprocal friendship pattern improvement, where both groups would demonstrate improved attitudes toward each other. Research by Johnson and Johnson (1981) serves to illustrate this condition. Again, as DeVillar and Faltis (1991) point out, caution must be applied when interpreting research results too generally since, in this case, the increased interaction patterns between racially different students were greater only at free time rather than throughout the students' general school day or during any content-area class within that day, where no improvement was evidenced. Other studies indicate that cooperative learning effects among heterogeneous groupings vary with respect to the type of cooperative learning method utilized and whether or not the cooperative task was successfully completed. For example, *competition* between cooperatively-structured teams can neutralize some of the positive gains made through cooperation at the intrateam level; further, cooperative assignments resulting in task failure can diminish intergroup appeal (cf. Miller, Brewer and Edwards 1985). Thus, while there are distinct prosocial advantages associated with cooperative learning, there remains much to be done at the process level to develop student experiences in a manner that will result in both widespread cross-racial and cross-ethnic social integration at the two-way level, prosocial behaviors, and enhanced academic performance.

Equal Status among Participants

Equal status among peers will not automatically ensue from grouping strategies. Allport (1954) clearly noted the conditions under which equal-status misperceptions by a dominant group toward a perceived subordinate group were changeable: where the minority group members, *already equal* in skill level to their majority member counterparts, are *misperceived* as having less than equal skills, and subsequently demonstrate their equality in situations where both groups strive together toward a common goal. Further, Allport (1954) was clear in the need for explicit institutional support by management in the form of setting policies and implementing practices that communicated to members within the institution that social integration and equal status were valued:

> To hire [minority members] with minimum friction it seems advisable for management to lead the way in breaking down discrimination at the top level. Likewise a firm policy ruling will probably offset the initial protests that are likely to occur. . . . In short, equal-status contact may lead to a dissociated, or highly specific, attitude, and may not affect the individual's customary perceptions and habits. (263–64)

Hence, educational sites (at federal, state, county, district, school, and classroom levels) must take a long-term leadership role in setting concrete policies and engaging in visible practices that actively and articulately demonstrate integration.

Also, as we noted earlier, competitive learning contexts, classroom organizational contexts which physically segregate learners from one another, and teacher-centered instructional delivery systems that value a knowledge-dispensing philosophy over one that encourages discovery learning, continue to work against social integration in schools and in classrooms. Evidence presented here and elsewhere (DeVillar and Faltis 1991) supports the notion that students will continue to be segregated interactionally at the classroom level, *even though they are physically integrated in groupwork*, unless a conscious effort is made to attend to the features that are most likely to bring about successful social integration.

An effective socioacademic context results when students perceive themselves and are perceived by their peers and their teachers as resources for learning, without regard to their language, ethnic, or other background variables; and when administrators, teachers, and parents actively endorse communicative, prosocial, and integrative endeavors. In current classroom life, cooperative learning methods that attend to the constraints of intergroup communication have the potential to bring students of diverse background together to collaborate on problems and to interact in ways that other social classroom contexts we have described cannot offer. The socioacademic framework, with its attention to communication, integration, and cooperation, can lead to the social harmony and academic achievement that we are seeking for all students, can align our national practice within the context of the school more closely with our national rhetoric, and can move us as a nation toward metacultural unity (see DeVillar this volume).

Conclusion

A summary of the rationale for the socioacademic framework has been presented together with an illustration of the types of contributions it could make toward school success and, ultimately, national cohesion. Since all of our nation's children experience formal schooling as part of their socialization into adulthood, schools have an extraordinarily significant role to play in leading students to metacultural unity through equitable and socially responsible teaching practices and learning experiences. In so doing, they will have enabled students to internalize through concrete experiences values that promote respect for multicultural understanding. Such values, in turn, are a critical means to secure, sustain, and enhance metacultural unity at the national level. Thus, students who emerge from socioacademically-based schooling will be better prepared to live, work, and coexist amicably with one another in the 21st century (Cummins 1991). The final advantage to implementing the socioacademic framework is of utmost importance: In their future roles as socialization agents, students will be in the historically singular position to model for succeeding generations both the rhetoric that embodies our national image and the inclusionary practices that enable us to realize it.

References

Allport, G. (1954). *The nature of prejudice.* (1958 ed.) Garden City, N.Y.: Doubleday Anchor.

———. (1959). Normative compatibility in the light of social science. In A. H. Maslow (Ed.), *New knowledge in human values* (1970 ed.). Chicago: Henry Regnery Company, 137–50.

Arias, M. B. (1986). The context of education of Hispanic students: An overview. In "The education of Hispanic Americans: A challenge for the future," *American Journal of Education, 97*(1), 26–57.

Bennett, K. P. and M. D. LeCompte (1990). *How schools work, a sociological analysis of education.* White Plains, N.Y.: Longman.

Borjas, G. J. and M. Tienda (1987). The economic consequences of immigration. *Science, 235,* 645–51.

Bouvier, L. F. and R. W. Gardner (1986). Immigration to the U.S.: The unfinished story. *Population Bulletin, 41*(4). Washington, D.C.: Population Reference Bureau.

Bruce, M. G. (1991). The standards debate across the Atlantic. *Educational Leadership, 48*(5), 31–3.

Calathes, W. (1991). Perpetuating social inequalities. *Thought & Action, The NEA Higher Education Journal, vii*(2), 137–54.

Catterall, J. and E. Cota-Robles. (1988). The educationally at-risk: What the numbers mean [summary]. *Accelerating the Education of At-risk Students, Conference Papers* (Stanford University, November 17–18, 1988), 6–7.

Cohen, E. and M. B. Arias (1988). Limited-English students can benefit from accelerated classes [summary]. *Accelerating the Education of At-risk Students, Conference Papers* (Stanford University, November 17–18, 1988), 24–5.

Commission on Work, Family and Citizenship (1988). *The forgotten half: Pathways to success for America's youth and young families.* Washington, D.C.: William T. Grant Foundation.

Cuban, L. (1984). *How teachers taught, Constancy and change in American classrooms, 1890–1980.* White Plains, N.Y.: Longman.

Cummins, J. (1981). The role of primary language development in promoting educational success for language minority students. In California State Department of Education, *Schooling and language minority students: A theoretical framework.* Los Angeles: Evaluation, Dissemination and Assessment Center, California State University, Los Angeles, 3–49.

———. (1989). *Empowering minority students.* Sacramento, Calif.: California Association for Bilingual Education.

————. (1991). Foreword. In R. A. DeVillar and C. J. Faltis, *Computers and Cultural Diversity* (pp. vii–ix). Albany, New York: State University of New York Press.

Cziko, G. A. (1992). The evaluation of bilingual education, From necessity and probability to possibility. *Educational Researcher,* 21(2), 10–15.

Davis, C., C. Haub, and J. Willette. (1983) U.S. Hispanics: Changing the face of America. *Population Bulletin, 38*(3), June 1983.

DeVillar, R. A. (1986, March). Computers and educational equity within the United States: An overview and examination of computer uses in education. Stanford-UNESCO Symposium on Computers and Education, Stanford University.

DeVillar, R. A., and C. J. Faltis. (1991). *Computers and cultural diversity.* Albany, N.Y.: State University of New York Press.

————. (1987). Computers and educational equity in American public schools. In *Capstone Journal of Education, viii*(4), 1–8.

Díaz, R., C. Neal, and M. Amaya-Williams. (1990). The social origins of self-regulation. In L. Moll (Ed.), *Vygotsky and Education* (pp. 127–154). Cambridge: Cambridge University Press.

Fernández, R. R. and G. Shu. (1988). School dropouts: New approaches to an enduring problem. *Education and Urban Society,* 20(4), 363–86.,

Fine, M. (1987). Silencing in public schools. *Language Arts, 64*(2), 157–74.

Fordham, S. (1988). Racelessness as a factor in Black students' success: Pragmatic strategy or Pyrrhic victory? *Harvard Educational Review, 58*(1), 54–84.

Goldenberg, C. and R. Gallimore. (1991). Local knowledge, research knowledge, and educational change: A case study of early Spanish reading improvement. *Educational Researcher, 20*(8), 2–14.

Goodlad, J. I. (1990). Better teachers for our nation's schools. *Phi Delta Kappan, 72*(3), 184–94.

————. (1984). *A place call school: Prospects for the future.* New York: McGraw-Hill.

The Holmes Group (1990). *Tomorrow's schools: Principles for the design of professional development schools.* East Lansing, Mich. The Holmes Group.

Johnson, D. W. and R. T. Johnson (1981). Effects of cooperative and individualistic learning experiences on interethnic interaction. In *Journal of Educational Psychology, 73*(3), 444–49.

Johnson, D. W., R. T. Johnson, and E. Johnson Holubec (1984). *Circles of learning, Cooperation in the Classroom.* Alexandria, Virginia: Association for Supervision and Curriculum Development.

Johnson, R. T., D. W. Johnson, and M. B. Stanne (1986). Comparison of computer-assisted cooperative, competitive, and individualistic learning. *American Educational Research Journal, 23*(3), 382–92.

Kirst, M. W. (1984). *Who controls our schools? American values in conflict.* New York: W. H. Freeman.

Kliebard, H. (1989). Success and failure in educational reform: Are there historical 'lessons?'. Occasional paper. East Lansing, Mich.: The Holmes Group.

Kohn, A. (1986). *No contest: The case against competition.* Boston: Houghton Mifflin.

Levin, H. J. (1985). *The educationally disadvantaged: A national crisis* (Prog. Rep. No. 85–B1). Stanford: School of Education, Stanford University, Institute for Research on Education Finance and Governance.

Lipkin, J. (1983). *Equity and microcomputer use in American public education.* ECS Working papers. Denver, Colorado: Education Commission of the States.

Miller, N., M. B. Brewer, and K. Edwards. (1985). Cooperative interaction in desegregated settings: A laboratory analogue. *Journal of Social Issues, 41*(3), 63–79.

Moore, J. and H. Pachón. (1985). *Hispanics in the United States.* Englewood Cliffs, N.J.: Prentice-Hall.

Navarro, R. A. (1986). A silent scream: An essay review of *"Make something happen:" Hispanics and urban high school reform* (2 vols.). In *Metropolitan Education, 1* Spring, 119–26.

O'Hare, W. P. (1988). *The rise of poverty in rural America.* Occasional paper, Population Trends and Public Policy. Washington, D.C.: Population Reference Bureau, Inc. (July).

Orfield, G. and Ashkinaze, C. (1991). *The closing door: Conservative policy and black opportunity.* Chicago: The University of Chicago Press.

Ramírez, J. D. and B. Merino. (1990). Classroom talk in English immersion, early-exit and late-exit bilingual education programs. In R. Jacobson and C. Faltis (Eds.), *Language distribution issues in bilingual schooling.* Clevedon, England: Multilingual Matters Ltd., 61–103.

Sirotnik, K. (1983). What you see is what you get—consistency, persistency, and mediocrity in classrooms. *Harvard Educational Review, 53*(1), 16–31.

Slavin, R. E. (1985). Cooperative learning: Applying contact theory in desegregated schools. In *Journal of Social Issues, 41*(3), 45–62.

Tudge, J. (1990). Vygotsky, the zone of proximal development, and peer collaboration: Implications for classroom practice. In L. Moll

(Ed.), *Vygotsky* and Education (155–174). Cambridge: Cambridge University Press.

Vygotsky, L. S. (1962). *Thought and language* (originally published in 1934, in Russian). Cambridge, Mass. M.I.T. Press.

———. (1978). *Mind in society: The development of higher psychological processes.* Cambridge, Mass.: Harvard University Press.

White, M. I. (1991). Higher education: A comparative examination. *Thought and Action, The NEA Higher Education Journal, vii*(2), 5–18.

William T. Grant Commission on Work, Family and Citizenship (1988). The forgotten half: Pathways to success for America's youth and young families. *Phi Delta Kappan, 70*(4), 280–89.

▼ Part I ▼
Cultural Diversity and Schooling

The Rhetoric and Practice of Cultural Diversity in U.S. Schools: Socialization, Resocialization, and Quality Schooling

ROBERT A. DeVILLAR

Cultural Diversity: The Roles of Rhetoric and Socialization

The United States is traditionally viewed, popularly and institutionally, as a nation that from its inception has embraced differences and in so doing has strengthened itself nationally. The Declaration of Independence, the Constitution, the Bill of Rights, and Emma Lazarus's poetic paean boasting of the miraculous national alchemy that transforms all immigrants into Americans, serve as the foremost legal and spiritual metaphors that embody this national self-image of a unified and distinct people resulting from a synergetic intergroup amalgamation. Its national seal, *E pluribus unum,* or 'one composed of many,' has supported this national self-image, as has the term popularized in Israel Zangwill's 1909 play of the same name, 'melting pot'.

This image of one united people, culture, and nation resulting from the creative admixture of many different peoples and cultures inhabiting the same geographic setting represents the very essence of our national rhetoric. It also embodies the ideal toward which we imagine ourselves constantly progressing as a nation, in ever-refined increments across generations. Accordingly, we formally attempt to pass on this national image to each succeeding generation through our institutions, particularly the school. Thus, our national rhetoric—that is, the language and symbols that characterize how we think and feel about ourselves collectively as Americans, and that ideally

serve as the basis for national policies and actions—is transmitted through the vehicle of socialization to maintain and re-
fine our national image.

Rhetoric and Socialization:
The Need and Basis for Assessment

The importance of the role of rhetoric in developing and sustaining our perceived national identity cannot be denied. However, it must be evaluated in terms of national practice. In this
way, the degree to which national rhetoric reflects the common
historical and current national circumstance of the different
racial and ethnic groups residing in the United States may be
critically assessed. An initial examination of the relationship
between national rhetoric and practice involves two questions:
To what degree do the distinct groups that comprise the United
States form part of the national rhetoric, and to what degree do
these groups share in the practices that reflect that rhetoric?

Perhaps the axiom that enjoys greatest currency within our
national rhetoric relates to equality, specifically the notion that
as Americans we are all equal. For our purposes, then, the
rhetoric and practice of equality in schooling for particular racial and ethnic groups will provide the context for addressing
these two questions and the yardstick for measuring the relative extent of the rhetoric–practice relationship among particular groups. This critical assessment may lend insight to the
phenomenon of differential individual and group outcomes,
particularly in relationship to school performance.

The rhetoric of equality assumes by definition that all
Americans have equal chances to succeed regardless of their
actual station or circumstance in life. Simply stated, if you are
in the United States, then you can succeed. Thus, the internalized logic associated with our national rhetoric of equality im-
pels us to believe that individual or group attainment is due to
the efforts of the individual or group. The converse is also held
as a truism: failure is essentially associated with the individual's or group's lack of effort.

As we enter the last decade of this millennium, longstanding social, economic, political, and educational disparities are
increasingly evident among U.S. racial, ethnic, and language
minority groups, particularly when comparing African-American, Asian-American, Hispanic-American, Native-American,
and Pacific-Island–American groups to their European-

American counterparts.[1] These disparities are at times masked and at other times glaring, depending upon many factors, including the particular group, context, period, and variables under examination. To offer an indication of the differences and commonalities among designated minority groups vis-à-vis their European-American counterpart group, the following section will examine the rhetoric—practice relationship, generally within the context of schooling, with specific respect to African-Americans, Hispanic-Americans, and Asian-Americans.

Race, Rhetoric, and Practice: The Myth of the Melting Pot, the Reality of Exclusion

Obvious historical inconsistencies exist with respect to our national rhetoric and our national practice where racial diversity is concerned. The influence of race, however ambiguous the notion, is paramount in understanding the degree of differential integration and achievement across time of racially (and, as we shall see, ethnically) diverse groups in the U.S.

The Notion and Social Consequences of Race

There is broad consensus within the social and physical science communities that the concept of race continues to lack a scientifically robust typology able to categorize human biophysical variation (cf. Dobzhansky 1962; Montagu 1964; Scruton 1982; Trueba, in Fernández 1988), particularly by such flawed identifiers as pigment, hair texture, and other surface features. That is, the notion of race cannot with scientific plausibility be applied to accurately categorize particular human groups in concrete ways that essentially differentiate them biologically from other human groups. Furthermore, there is no evidence that variations in the form of superficial surface characteristics physically present among human groups equate to each or any of these groups belonging to a separate human species (see Banton 1979 for a concise and lucid essay on this topic).

Throughout our past and present, however, the notion of race has been perniciously applied in social, legal, economic, political, and religious contexts to support antagonistic popular and elite sentiment toward non-Caucasian racial groups, whether they be indigenous, native-born, naturalized, or immigrant. Similarly, this national practice also has been applied toward Caucasian ethnic groups whose physical attributes are considered generally unreflective of "whiteness." Statements for example, regarding the unfitness of African-Americans for equal participatory status by George Washington, Thomas Jefferson, and Abraham Lincoln are well-documented (cf. Franklin in *Daedalus* 1965), as are those by Benjamin Franklin with respect to any group other than the ones he narrowly defined as "white" (cf. Daniels 1990).

This racially based exclusionary philosophy has served to sanctify the perceived superiority of the group with the inappropriate but popularly accepted color-bound label of *White*. Superior race status, together with its inferior race status conceptual counterpart, have justified exclusionary race policies and practices toward individuals and groups whose pigmentation, other physical features, or "blood" were deemed other than White. Belief in this notion, for example, has not only justified slavery and its corollary, institutional segregation— although these are abhorrent enough in themselves—but, as we shall see, continues in various forms even today to support educationally related perspectives and practices espoused by prominent figures within the social science community and by reputable institutions of higher learning. The following components in this section illustrate the exclusionary, long-term norms that have resulted as a consequence of racial and ethnic diversity for groups designated as minorities and the effects of these norms, particularly in the realm of schooling.

The African-American Experience in U.S. Schools

The South, Slavery, and Schooling

Slavery was a state and national practice that permeated our society from 1700 to 1870, even though the slave trade (as opposed to slavery) was officially banned by Congress in 1810 (Daniels 1990). Africans were, of course, involuntary immigrants bereft of rights, including those we consider primordial: life, liberty, and the pursuit of happiness (cf. Daniels 1990; Myrdal 1944). Schooling African-Americans in bondage, expressly teaching them how to read and write, was virtually forbidden throughout the southern states (Myrdal 1944).

The North and African-American Schooling

Schooling in the North evinced a reciprocal desire by African-Americans and European-Americans for segregated schooling, albeit for different but related reasons. Schools, for example, were physically integrated as early as the 1640s in parts of Massachusetts. Nonetheless, they were characterized by social hostility in the form of "mistreatment and racial insults" toward African-Americans by their European-American teachers and student counterparts, practices which led organized groups of African-Americans to clamor for segregated schooling after the Revolutionary War (Brooks 1990). The issue of segregated schools, however, was not solely based on the need African-Americans perceived for a quality and discrimination-free learning setting. A concomitant racially based rationale for school segregation, presented by the School Committee of Boston, reasoned that racial difference

> [which] no legislature, no social customs, can efface renders a promiscuous intermingling in the public schools disadvantageous both to them and to the whites. (Franklin 1965:902)

These types of attitudes, policies and practices would ensure that Boston schools would remain officially segregated until 1855 and that educational quality for African-American students would remain elusive and, to the extent that it did exist, unequal.

Other factors relating to African-Americans' quality of life in this period and area illustrate its restrictive and segregated nature. Daniels (1990:107), for example, reminds us that the behavior of the 1,300 African-Americans residing in Massachusetts in 1710 (about 2 percent of the population) was already legally regulated, restricting slaves, servants, and mulattoes through curfews and prohibition of interracial marriage of related intimate behaviors; even so-called "free Negroes" could not shelter or fraternize with African-American servants "in their homes without the consent of the latter's masters."

The West and Schooling

The above types of attitudes, policies, and practices were prevalent throughout the United States, following European-

American settler patterns. In California in 1852, for example,
legislation also regulated the freedoms of the 2,206 African-
Americans (2 percent of the population) who resided there, including the return of fugitive slaves to their southern
locations, even though California had abolished slavery in
1849 (Wollenberg 1978). Moreover, interracial marriages were
forbidden, "and people with as little as 'one-sixth African blood'
were denied the right to vote, hold public office, and testify in
court against white persons" (Wollenberg: 9).

Furthermore, by 1855, African-Americans were legally
barred from attending Californian schools with Whites and,
four years later, were finally allowed by the State Superintendent of Public Instruction to attend segregated schools with
"Mongolians and Indians" on the grounds that "the great mass
of our citizens will not associate in terms of equality with these
inferior races; nor will they consent that their children do so"
(Wollenberg: 13).

The Nation and Schooling

Under the above types of widespread, legally sanctioned, unequal, and hostile living and schooling conditions, the tradition of quality schooling for African-Americans in the United
States was stillborn and grotesquely shrouded in European-
American prejudice and discrimination. From 1896 to 1954,
the oxymoronic separate-but-equal doctrine, sanctioned by the
Supreme Court's decision in *Plessy v. Ferguson* (1896), continued this disparate treatment of African-Americans within our
schools. Despite the Supreme Court's decision in *Brown v.
Board of Education* (1954) to desegregate U.S. schools, segregated schools remain the norm, and the quality of schooling for
the majority of Americans of African descent continues to be
decidedly lower than that of American students of European
descent along those indicators required for sustained and general academic performance leading even to a credible high
school diploma (cf. DeVillar and Faltis 1991).

Schooling's historical and contemporary profile, therefore,
is poignantly sharp and remarkably consistent with respect to
its degree of accommodation to the educational needs of
African-American students: Whether segregated or integrated,
whether in the North, South, or other geographical setting,
whether pre–Civil War or after, whether pre– or post–Civil
Rights, schooling for African-Americans has remained signifi-

cantly inferior to that provided European-American students. Educational disparity based on race, then, is a legacy that dates from the beginning of European immigration and has remained with us until the present day.

Race, Ethnicity, and Intellectual Ability: The Defense and Practice of Hispanic-American Exclusion and Failure in U.S. Schools

Groups labeled as *non-White, non-Anglo,* and variations thereof in the United States differ amongst themselves, each having its own particular immigrant history, degree to which it has experienced racially based prejudice and discrimination, and types of prejudice and discrimination encountered. Also, each group has generated a unique set of cultural response formulations to the perceived context (this applies to Native-Americans also, who are indigenous to this geographical setting). Regardless of these cross-group differences, the commonality that all groups have shared is based on their general pigmentation and perhaps other surface features not being the same or similar enough to what is popularly referred to as "White."

Confusing Race and Ethnicity:
The Effect on Schooling Segregation

The popular misperception of race has also spilled over into the area designated as *ethnicity,* where human differences are deemed as more culturally based than racially. In the particular case of Hispanic-Americans, for example, there has been continued insistence on the part of the media, academia, the judicial system, schools, and the general populace to question or ignore their Caucasian, or White, racial designation in favor of their perceived non-White status. Ironically, the official classificatory status of Americans of Mexican descent as Caucasians has also been used by school districts, albeit unsuccessfully, as a mechanism to legally enable European-American students from having to attend schools with African-Americans. In 1970, for example, sixteen years after the Supreme Court's ruling in *Brown v. Board of Education,* schools in Texas were still placing Mexican-American students in segregated schools with African-American students on grounds that, as Mexican-

American students were Caucasian, this practice met the Court's desegregation mandate. In 1970, this insidious practice was successfully challenged in *Cisneros v. Corpus Christi Independent School District* (Salinas 1973).

This purposeful racial–ethnic ambiguity has been used as a segregation device throughout Hispanic-American students' educational experience and has been consistently challenged by Hispanic-Americans. In California, *Roberto Alvarez v. the Board of Trustees of the Lemon Grove School District* (1931) successfully challenged the notion that Mexican-American students could be legally segregated from their Anglo-American peers and, in the same year, the Bliss Bill, which attempted to have Mexican-Americans designated as Indians and thereby subject to legal school segregation, was defeated (Trueba 1988). In 1947, yet another court case in California, *Mendez v. Westminster*, ended the State's de jure segregation for Mexican-Americans, with Texas and Arizona following suit in 1948 and 1950, respectively (Wollenberg 1978). De facto segregation, however, still persists, its numbers having increased even beyond those under de jure segregation (Arias 1986).

Defending Exclusion and School Failure

The practice of segregation historically rested upon euphemistic notions of "racial" inferiority and the general unsuitableness of Mexican-Americans, and other Hispanic-Americans, for integration into American institutions. The general response to a 1920 survey conducted in the Imperial Valley, for example, reasoned that segregation was justified due to "a consciousness of racial difference" (Wollenberg 1978: 111), a rationale not unlike that used in Boston 50 years earlier with respect to African-Americans.

The long-term attempt to characterize students from actual or perceived non-White/non-Anglo-American backgrounds, such as African-Americans and Hispanic-Americans, as intellectually and culturally inferior is another persistent manifestation of racially based/ethnically based arguments (cf. Dunn 1987, quoted in Fernández 1988; Dunn 1988; Jensen 1969, 1980, 1981). A monograph written in 1987 by Lloyd Dunn, the senior author of the *Peabody Picture Vocabulary Test Series*, for example, characterizes Puerto Rican and Mexican-American children in the U.S. as experiencing poor performance in school due to "inferior Spanish language skills"

(Dunn 1987, quoted in Fernández 1988, p. 183). Moreover, Dunn presents an ethnically based, metacultural deficit perspective to explain low school performance *at the group level:*

> Because of their lack of intellectual, scholastic, and language aptitude, but also for many other reasons . . . , it is clear that these children are not, as a group, able to cope with the confusion of two languages. . . . (183–84)

For Dunn, then, the mere fact of being Hispanic-American serves to explain school failure, for according to his logic, Hispanic-American is synonymous with a general lack of intellectual, language, or academic aptitude.

Dunn continues displaying predictable elements within his deficit model, in this case absolving the school of significant responsibility for instruction and outcomes, and targeting responsibility for school success on the children's parents:

> For too long, analyses of the lack of school success of this fastest-growing minority group have emphasized the failure of the educational system to serve them. . . . It would be more correct to point out that these Hispanic pupils and parents have also failed the schools and society, because they have not been motivated and dedicated enough to make the system work for them. (186–187)

The notion of racial inferiority also surfaces as an element in poor school performance. Dunn associates African-American and Native-American students' scores on intelligence tests, and how they lag behind those of Anglos and "Orientals," with Hispanic ethnicity encompassing racially mixed groupings (Quoted in Willig 1988:225):

> Race, as a contributing factor, cannot be ignored. It is recalled . . . that most Mexican immigrants to the U.S. are brown-skinned people, a mix of American Indian and Spanish blood, while many Puerto Ricans are dark-skinned, a mix of Spanish, black, and some Indian. Blacks and American Indians have repeatedly scored about 15 points behind Anglos and Orientals on individual tests of intelligence.

This type of rhetoric was prevalent almost seventy years earlier in the United States. In the 1920s, intelligence tests administered to Mexican-American students and other groups resulted

in "findings" that "Mexicans scored lower than 'Americans,'
'English,' 'Hebrews,' and 'Chinese,' but higher than 'Indians,'
'Slavish,' 'Italians,' and 'Negroes' (Wollenberg 1978:115).

Wollenberg also reports that interpretations given by researchers with respect to Hispanic ingroup variation on intelligence tests were racially based. One university professor, for
example, who administered the National Intelligence Test to
more than a thousand students of Mexican origin, explained
that the score of 142 obtained by one student was due to the
student being a "Spanish American" and therefore more
"white" than his Mexican-American counterparts, whose average score was 78.1.

Finally, Dunn applies the 'they did it, why can't you' argu-
ment, alluding to the academic differences between Asian-
American, on the one hand, and Puerto Rican and Mexican-
American students, on the other:

> [The system] has functioned extremely well for most of the
> children of this nation, including recent Asian-American im-
> migrants. . . . The major source for overcoming the lack of
> school success of Hispanics rests squarely with the people
> themselves, and more specifically with the parents. In my
> view, [nothing] will succeed unless there are dramatic
> changes in the child-rearing practices of Hispanic mothers
> and fathers. Hispanic parents have much to learn from Asian-
> American parents. . . . [Valuing education] is a tradition that
> Hispanics in general do not appear to have. . . . It is time for
> the Hispanic people to stop blaming teachers for their own
> lack of school success and other troubles, and set about work-
> ing harder to obtain a quality education for their children.
> (Dunn 1987, quoted in Fernández 1988:186–87, 189–90)

Dunn's monograph represents a consolidation of the array
of arguments voiced throughout the second half of this century
by educators and researchers of educational contexts as to the
reasons that Hispanic-American and other minority students
underachieve in school. Walker (1987) cites the genetic defi-
ciency position of Jensen (1971), the language-deficit perspective of Deutsch (1963), the dysfunctional family and cultural
systems paradigm of Moynihan (1967), the field-sensitive
learning style orientation of Ramírez and Castañeda (1974),
and the low-self-concept model articulated by various researchers (see also DeVillar and Faltis 1991) as earlier examples of

studies that attributed major, if not sole, responsibility for school performance to minority student learners.

The history of Hispanic-American students within U.S. schools is as unequivocal in its clarity as it is unequal in its content and character. Hispanic-Americans have traditionally been excluded from schooling contexts in which they would be on an equal educational footing with their European-American counterparts and have consistently had to challenge official school policy through the courts to attain access to integrated and quality schooling. In spite of this persistent conflict, the quality of their schooling has continued to generally reflect that of their African-American student peers, particularly in the form of predictably low academic outcomes and disproportionately low rates of school completion.

Even within integrated classroom contexts, Hispanic-American students' school performance is generally not on an equal footing with that of European-American students. Perceptions within the school and the influence they exert account for some of the difference. There is, for example, evidence of differential, negative pedagogical treatment of Hispanic-American students by their teachers within integrated classrooms at the *intercultural* level (Schinke-Llano 1983; Suárez-Orozco 1987), which can affect students' motivation and participation and the benefit derived from the classroom experience. Issues of quality of schooling and academic outcomes are further compounded by the extent of *intracultural* variation among Hispanic students from the same descent-group. Matute-Bianchi (1986), for example, categorized Mexican-descent students at a California high school into five categories: recent Mexican immigrant, Mexican-oriented, Mexican-American, Chicano, and *Cholo*. Her research dramatically demonstrates the palpable influence that can be exerted by intracultural variation upon students' perceptions toward school, academic and social programs, grades, their futures, themselves, and others, and upon teachers' perceptions and attitudes toward the different categories of Mexican-descent students. (For excellent analyses of related phenomena within the African-American schooling experience and West Indian immigrant schooling experience in England, see Fordham 1988 and Weinreich 1979, respectively). Access to integrated and quality schooling, then, is necessary, but insufficient to the successful educational experience of Hispanic-American and other minority-group students. Access, therefore, must be complemented by significant and meaningful participation within the context of quality schooling and by deriving benefit from it (Cf. DeVillar and Faltis 1987, 1991).

A dual irony results from our traditional exclusionary rhetoric and practice that may be generalized beyond the Hispanic-American grouping. First, this combination of rhetoric and practice keeps us, as a nation, ignorant of the dynamic sociocultural features characterizing a national group and promotes a sustained, uneasy, at best functional, relationship between the Hispanic-American group and European-American society. At the same time, Hispanic-American culture in the United States continues to develop in increasingly complex ways. Impelled by the centrifugal and centripetal social forces accompanying segregation—historically de jure and now principally de facto—Hispanic-American culture moves away from the language and cultural expressions and dynamics of mainstream America, forging and reinforcing its own language and cultural alternatives.

These language and cultural alternatives, broadly speaking, take two forms, occurring as a *macrocultural* phenomenon (e.g., Hispanic-Americans as a total group; Mexican-Americans as a total group) and, through significant intracultural variation, as *microcultural* phenomena (e.g., differentiated microgroupings within the Mexican-American macrogroup). Therefore, attempts to identify, understand, and reconcile differences and to establish constructive, unifying national policies between the larger society and Hispanic-Americans will be seriously flawed and inevitably fettered. Such flaws and constraints will flow naturally from our increasingly invalid perceptions, information, strategies, and tactics with respect to the issues. These latter elements, in turn, will result from our historically sustained and continually compounded collective ignorance of the intergroup and intragroup dynamics that spring from the segregated cultural realities characterizing our nation. The threatening consequences of segregation, then, reach far beyond mere physical distance, as the Supreme Court justices so sagaciously perceived in their *Brown v. Board of Education* ruling in 1954. Segregation thwarts accurate perceptions, authentic communication, and cooperation at the intergroup and intragroup levels (DeVillar and Faltis 1991). It has been and remains a significant disabling agent in our society, which we can ill afford to value in rhetoric or practice.

Language and Schooling

Quality of schooling and educational outcomes are also highly influenced by the learner's ability to receive instruction in a language comprehensible to him or her. Spanish is, of course, spoken as a first or dominant language by hundreds of thousands of students in the United States (cf. Moore and Pachón 1985; Veltman 1988). Yet, we have remained stubbornly remiss, for what is now a quarter of a century, in acknowledging and promoting the role of a student's primary language in successful academic performance and second-language acquisition.

The lack of sound pedagogical rhetoric regarding the role of a language other than English and the relationship of that language to culture and schooling outcomes has predictably translated into a comparable lack of sound pedagogical practice. Thus, we have failed to provide sustained, pedagogically sound mechanisms to enable Hispanic-American students to effectively learn subject matter in their own language as they learn to speak and otherwise command English as a second language. Instead, as a nation, we have made bilingual education a political issue, choosing to deny its pedagogical value in favor of reinforcing exclusionary attitudes and practices toward this particular ethnic group and their primary or heritage language.

The types of pedagogical practices that our national rhetoric has emphasized since 1968 are essentially in the form of transitional bilingual education and English-immersion programs. These programs have served at best as an uneasy compromise between language-minority groups' demand for primary-language instruction for their children's educational benefit and our national rhetoric that all instruction should be in English since anything else diminishes rather than enhances a student's chances for educational and economic survival. Furthermore, this reluctant compromise remains unsettling at the national level precisely because it continues to grate against our traditional value that the only road to schooling, professional, and societal success is through a one language, one culture model. (As mentioned earlier, at the rhetorical level we have traditionally referred to this model as that of the melting pot; later in this chapter we shall see how the model we have actually practiced is indeed quite different.) Moreover, these programs also reinforce by their presence our revered national myth that all immigrants have had to go through the same English-language-immersion experience and have done so successfully without pleading for special consideration as a group. Thus, transitional and immersion programs, although apparently in receipt of our nation's legislative imprimatur since 1968, have remained suspect from the outset because they conflict with these fundamental rhetorical elements—one language, one culture; inevitable immigrant acculturation; and lifting one's self by one's own bootstraps—that are viewed as forming essential aspects of our national image.

The irony associated with this uneasy compromise is that legislative policy has not led to school practice. Thus, transitional and immersion educational programs continue to fail our nation's students of Hispanic origin requiring primary-language instruction, not because Spanish is spoken in the classrooms, but because the use of English in early instruction dominates at the expense of Spanish. In spite of the strong research evidence clearly substantiating the value of sustained content area instruction in the primary language as students learn English (cf. Ramírez et al. 1991; Willig 1985), the dismal but highly predictable result of this transitional/immersion policy is clear: After twenty-five years of money, studies, and practices, we as a nation have not afforded ourselves, our schools, our teacher education institutions, our students, or our economy the opportunity to objectively or creatively explore, develop, or benefit from the possibilities of bilingual education and a well-educated bilingual citizenry. In short, what we officially have termed 'bilingual education' have remained virtually English-language-dominant programs. It matters little whether students in need of primary-language content instruction complemented by ESL immediately find themselves in an academic sink-or-swim schooling context (as in the case of English-immersion/submersion programs), or whether they wade out to the deep end after a brief period of false encouragement in their native language (as in the case of early-exit transitional programs), since the results are the same: persistent academic and social underachievement in school, and failure to complete the K–12 schooling cycle successfully.

Assessing Shifts in Rhetoric

Our official rhetoric toward bilingual education has shifted orientation of late and now reflects the "minority" perspective of yesteryear. The language associated with the Bilingual Education Act (Title VII—Bilingual Education Programs, Bilingual Education Act, Public Law 100–297–April 28, 1988), for example, commits our nation to the policy and funding of bilingual education in recognition

> (5) that the Federal Government has a special and continuing obligation to assist language minority students to acquire the English language proficiency that will enable them to become full and productive members of society; (6) that the instructional use and development of a child's non-English native language promotes student self-esteem, subject matter achievement, and English-language acquisition; (7) that a primary means by which a child learns is through the use of such child's native language and cultural heritage. . . . (Bilingual Education Act, 102 STAT. 274)

At the national level, then, we now have a rhetoric that more appropriately embraces the needs and desires of our general citizenry, both actual and prospective, in that it tangibly acknowledges the relationship between a student's primary language and his or her educational achievement. Nevertheless, we remain in the same dilemma we were in prior to this shift in rhetoric because our practices have failed to sharply reflect our rhetoric. There is no encouraging evidence within colleges and universities that prepare our teachers for instructing within bilingual and culturally heterogeneous classrooms that linguistically and culturally appropriate instructional practices *on a national level*, or even a significant level, are being devised, learned, and integrated into our schools. This same lack of evidence extends to teachers and sites within the K–12 schooling spectrum itself.

Our instructional practices remain inadequate primarily due to national political positions taking priority over pedagogical ones during the past two and a half decades. This practice continues to override our new national rhetoric respecting education, however abstractly sensible or inclusive. More disturbing are the long-term effects of this lopsided political conflict. Essentially, it has prevented sound, long-term investments in (a) culturally and linguistically educating postsecondary and K–12 teachers to meet the basic communication and cultural requirements of their students; (b) revamping our schools of education to lead the way with the faculty, research, publications, and practices required to educate teachers and administrators for teaching and leading effectively within a culturally diverse context; (c) restructuring schools at the K–12 level to respond with creative appropriateness to their culturally diverse and otherwise heterogeneous student populations; and (d) developing pedagogically appropriate curriculum materials reflecting the languages, cultures, and experiences of *heterogeneous group life in America*. Due to this fundamental absence, we have failed as a nation in our commitment to universal and quality schooling for our students, those native-English-speaking and those dominant in a language other than English alike. Tired as the cliché must sound, its restatement serves to guide those who will listen: Students represent our most valuable national resource. Yet, students' potential to realize their indispensable and unified role to achieve sustained, productive nationhood remains stymied by educational practices that neither reflect our historically egalitarian nor our nouveau official rhetoric.

And there is precious little room for optimism that change is in the offing. Innovative programs in bilingual education remain underfunded, particularly when compared to transitional bilingual education programs. Developmental bilingual education (DBE) programs, for example, are those that offer a "full-time program of instruction in elementary and secondary schools which provides . . . structured English language instruction and instruction in a second language. Such programs will be designed to help children achieve competence in English and a second language, while mastering subject matter skills" (Bilingual Education Act, 1988, 102 STAT. 277).

To meet specified federal funding priorities, the above passage is generally interpreted to mean programs that "help limited English (LEP) children and children whose native language is English achieve competence in English and a second language, while mastering challenging subject matter" (*Federal Register*, vol. 57, No. 20, Jan. 30, 1992).

Thus, DBE programs differ fundamentally from structured immersion and transitional programs generally in two ways. First, students whose native language is English begin studying subject matter in a second language with students for whom the language of instruction is a primary language. English as a language of instruction would gradually be introduced to both groups and ultimately share equally with the other language of instruction. For example, students would study subject matter almost entirely in Spanish at the beginning of their DBE program and receive incremental exposure to English, appropriately integrated in terms of grade level and curriculum, until English as a language of instruction were to be used at least 50 percent of the time. Second, DBE programs are typically designed to last as long as six years. Transitional and structured immersion programs, on the other hand, generally advocate short-term exposure (2–3 years) and minimal use of a primary language (twenty minutes to one hour per day) in the early elementary school grades.

There is one type of bilingual education program that may be viewed as either transitional or developmental, and as a result has been referred to as both in the literature: the late-exit bilingual program. Ramírez et al., for example, define a late-exit program as "a developmental primary language . . . transitional bilingual education program" (1991, 1:38). Although the popular view is that such programs inhibit the learning and use of English, students within developmental bilingual education programs theoretically receive 40 percent of their instruction in English by the fourth grade and 60 percent by the sixth grade. Ramírez et al., however, found that while Spanish was used in practice by the teachers in grades K through four in accordance with the program criteria, late-exit fifth-grade teachers used English as the language of instruction two-thirds of the time and late-exit sixth-grade teachers used it 84 percent of the time. Still, this recent large-scale, long-term research at the national level indicated decisive advantages to students within these programs when compared to their counterparts in English-immersion and transitional bilingual education programs. Cziko (1992) concisely summarizes the impact of the findings relating to late-exit bilingual education programs:

> [Late-exit students] showed the greatest growth in mathematics, English language skills, and English reading. Indeed, the late-exit bilingual students' rates of growth in these three areas were noticeably higher than those of the tests' norming population. (12)

Nevertheless, the federal allocation for developmental bilingual education programs for the 1991–92 academic year totalled $2,800,000, and was expected to average $175,000 to an anticipated eighteen recipients. On the other hand, funding for transitional bilingual education programs, the vast major-

ity of which are early-exit, during this same period totalled
$8,925,000, and was expected to average $175,000 to an anticipated fifty-one recipients. This pattern of funding allocation mirrors prior politically-motivated policies despite the
recent shift in rhetoric, and signals the maintenance of
English-dominant instructional practices, despite their documented relative inefficacy.

Adjusting the Rhetoric–Practice Imbalance

Adjusting schooling policies and practices to accurately accom-
modate the newly adopted official rhetoric will itself require a
major shift at the national level, away from the negative light in
which the Spanish language and Hispanic-Americans have
been generally perceived in the United States. Additionally, it
will require an acted-upon set of beliefs that languages other
than English have an inherent value to our nation, that those
students who need to receive instruction in their primary language will be afforded a higher probability of academic success
and school longevity, and that learning in one's primary language will ultimately enhance, rather than detract from, the
acquisition of English. Furthermore, our national policy and
practice will need to emphasize massive long-term, rather than
marginal short-term, investment in areas *a–d* mentioned
earlier.

Asian-Americans:
Disproportionate Overachievement
as a Barrier to Schooling and Employment

The presentation of Asian-Americans as a "model minority"
based on academic achievement of course ignores the consequence of race and its relationship to meaningful integration
in our society. From the mid-nineteenth century to the
present, the belief in racial superiority has also been the flag-
ship of our practices that demean, stigmatize, restrict, and ex-
clude Asian immigrants and native-born Americans of Asian
descent from full access, participation, and benefit as members of U.S. society. Ironically, the belief in racial superiority
need not rely exclusively on the subsidiary belief of intellectual
superiority. Rather, it may alternately be based on the perceived fundamental right "White" Americans have over "non-

White" Americans to preferential access to and increased participation in labor and professional preparation opportunities in America, as well as to derive superordinate benefit from these opportunities. Recent examples of racial preference practices include job ceilings that limit non-Whites who are as competent or more competent than their Anglo-American peers from competing for and obtaining desired professional levels; higher pay for White Americans having lower educational qualifications than their non-White peers; and discriminatory university admissions policies at our most esteemed universities favoring less-qualified Anglo-American students (cf. Chan 1991; Takaki 1989). These practices ensure that more highly qualified racial minority Americans (in this case, Asian-Americans) are denied opportunity in favor of less qualified Anglo-Americans.

Clearly, other-that-White racial and related ethnic designations in the U.S. continue to reflect a historical unacceptance by White society, the effects of which have been deleterious to the specific group and, ultimately, to the nation at large. Chan (1991) divides institutional and isolated hostility toward Asian-Americans in the U.S. into seven categories, the first six of which may be extended to include all racial and ethnic minorities: (1) prejudice, (2) economic discrimination, (3) political disenfranchisement, (4) physical violence, (5) immigration exclusion, (6) social segregation, and (7) incarceration. Investigators from various disciplines have provided documentation and analyses of past and present hostility in these areas with respect to one or more racial or ethnic minority groups (cf. Chan 1991), Kitano and Daniels 1988, Takaki 1989, and Tenhula 1991 in the area of Asian-American studies; Daniels 1990 in the area of general immigration, including African-Americans, to the U.S.; Wollenberg 1978, Acosta-Belén and Sjostrom 1988, Barrera 1979, Moore and Pachón 1985 in the area of Hispanic-American studies; Brooks 1990, *Daedalus* 1965, Myrdal 1944 in the area of African-Americans).

Toward Meta-Cultural Unity: Distinguishing between Socialization Models of Rhetoric and Practice

> The great Melting Pot where all races . . . are melting and re-forming! . . . The real American has not yet arrived. He is only in

the Crucible. . . . He will be the fusion of races, perhaps the coming superman. . . . Ah, what a stirring and a seething! Celt and
Latin, Slav and Teuton, Greek and Syrian,—black and yellow—
. . . the glory of America, where all races and nations come to la-
bour and look forward! (Zangwill, *The Melting Pot*, 1916: 33, 34,
184, 185)

[E]thnics were stamped "inferior" because of racist views sharp-
ened for the occasion. The sickness of America was another source
of resentment they received. For America is a land in which pride
in the English heritage gradually became pride in the Anglo-
Saxon–Teutonic heritage, and the latter was all too near to pride
in the Nordic race. The ethnics were victims of "white racism." The
immigrants who arrived after 1880 struck the American imagina-
tion as a dark, swarthy, inferior race. . . . Their habits of life, their
mores, their passions were what condemned them. (Novak, *The
Rise of the Unmeltable Ethnics*, 1973:95)

   The perceived non-White racial status of a group and its individual members remains an inordinately significant factor in
all institutional interactions and relationships with European
origin (and more specifically with what historically has been
termed Anglo-Saxon) America. The historical and contemporary importance of color cannot be overstated, for from this
single trait have sprung all the legal, academic, occupational,
and social determinants that ultimately characterize the degree to which a group can capitalize upon schooling and other
opportunities in the U.S., and the degree to which a group is
accepted as being "American." This obsession with race and
color is a critical weakness in our national quest for metacultural unity and a contradiction in our national ethos, both of
which are of veritable fatal proportions if left unchecked. Moreover, our national development continues to be stifled because
of the credence given to this binary color trait perspective,
(White, non-White) a perspective that imposes limits on the
value, rights, and achievements of particular groups. This perspective also overshadows positive individual and group attributes, while suppressing the knowledge and significance of
a group's actual societal and global contributions and those
which could result for our nation.
   Progress of course has occurred within this racially based
societal model, not only in our conversion from slavery as a national institution to non-slavery, but from a de jure to de facto
social context for racial and ethnic minority groups in areas
such as schooling, employment, housing, and politics. Nevertheless, the overview presented here describes the halting and

incomplete nature of that progress. Our national unity model *at the rhetorical level* may indeed still be the melting pot, regardless of the efforts of academicians and other professionals over the past three decades to reveal and transmit its historical limitations and inappropriateness (cf. Gordon 1964). The fact that this model survives in our populace and in our institutions is not the main problem to be addressed. A greater problem is that *national rhetoric* with respect to integration and equality is confused with *national practice*. Furthermore, this confusion is compounded in intensity by the consequent invisibility of actual national practice among the populace and our institutions.

Thus, we do not differentiate as a nation between the *e. pluribus unum* rhetoric reflective of the melting pot model and the persistent selective reality of the *Anglo-American conformity* model of national identity and integration. The ideal embodied in the notion of the melting pot is elegant in its simplicity: Our American identity is at once the melded result of the contributions made by the separate immigrant (and Native-American) groups that amalgamated within the context of our borders, yet at the same time greater than the sum of all of the amalgamated features. This is our *e pluribus unum*, our one from the many. And it remains a noble and appropriate *national identity image* to describe Americans within the United States.

The problem has been that we confuse the national ideal toward which we should always strive (the melting pot model) with actually having achieved this state, when indeed we operate as a nation in accordance with the principles reflected in the Anglo-American conformity model. If this is indeed the case, then how does the Anglo-American conformity model differ from the melting pot national identity image? Essentially, the Anglo-American conformity model is exclusive rather than inclusive, and group selection has been perennially and inexorably tied to color.

Within the melting pot model, which represents our national rhetoric, the United States is seen as a democratic nation: that is, a nation where every group has the same freedoms and ultimate access to opportunities and achievement, and participates in the nation-building process at politically, economically, and socially significant levels (see Figure 1). This is, of course, naive and inaccurate, both historically and currently. Figure 2 illustrates how selective practices within the Anglo-American conformity model foster and sustain inclusionary and exclusionary practices at the group level. It also illustrates how particular minority individuals can form part of the acculturated mainstream without threatening the status quo aspects of the Anglo-American conformity model.

Workings of the Anglo-American Conformity Model: Socialization and Resocialization

The socialization process through which native-born Americans are to pass in the Anglo-American conformity model may be termed "developmental-conformist": developmental because the socialization process should always result in each new generation modeling and achieving to an even greater extent the norms, values, and expectations of prior generations; conformist because refinements are viewed as essential modifications to the existing model rather than as leading to a new model of national identity and development. Socialization traditionally has been attained through the family and through the schools, as well as through organizations such as churches, organized youth activities in areas of community service (Cub Scouts, Boy Scouts, Brownies, Girl Scouts), organized sports (Little League, soccer leagues), and the like.

Enculturation is the term used here to describe the expected result of the socialization process, and which ultimately sustains and refines the model of national identity and the cultural elements embodied within it. Acculturation ostensibly refers to the socialization process through which nonnative aspiring members of U.S. society pass in becoming "American." We have seen, however, that both historically and currently, acculturation of immigrants has been highly selective, and consequently that freedoms and access to opportunities have been severely restricted by law, custom, and practice.

The notion of socialization implies, then, the process of social adaptation through which whole groups of individuals pass. In our history, enculturation as the result of the native-born socialization process has been essentially reserved for those native-born individuals from groups labeled as *White*, while acculturation has been reserved for foreign-born individuals from groups with this same racial designation. Thus, both enculturation and acculturation processes have been highly selective and racially based.

A few individuals from racially or ethnically non-White groups also are always represented within the selective acculturation model, but never to the degree that the whole group or even significant numbers from the whole group are represented. It is important to note that these individuals may be native born as well as foreign born and that the process through which they pass reflects the acculturation process rather than the enculturation process. That they have become part of the "mainstream" *as an individual* reflects that the group they represent, whether native born or foreign born, does not form part of the nation's enculturation process. Thus, a further irony relating to the Anglo-American conformity model is that native-born, historically nonintegrated groups, such as African-Americans, Hispanic-Americans, and others, continue to be viewed as in need of acculturation rather than enculturation regardless of their actual historical presence in the United States.

The alternative to socialization that non-White (whether perceived or actual) racial and ethnic groups are presented within the Anglo-American conformity model is resocialization. Unlike the developmental–conformist character of the socialization model, resocialization is a remedial–deviant model of societal integration: remedial in that the group is considered in need of alteration prior to engaging in the socialization process; deviant in that the group's behaviors are considered antithetical to the nation's well-being. Prisons and other forms of incarceration contexts are examples of resocialization institutions with which we are generally familiar. In the case of prison, for example, an individual must have committed an explicit legal transgression for which the punishment, upon being found guilty, entailed the individual's incarceration for a predetermined period. Theoretically, the individual is to be rehabilitated during that period in order to exit as a socially responsible member of our society.

Resocialization for racial and ethnic minority groups can be compared and contrasted to the principles espoused and mechanisms present within the rehabilitation model. These groups, principally based on color, have been historically judged as not having the language, cultural, moral, or intellectual traits necessary to engage in the enculturation or selective acculturation process. The transgressions, therefore, that the groups were perceived to have committed were racial or cul-

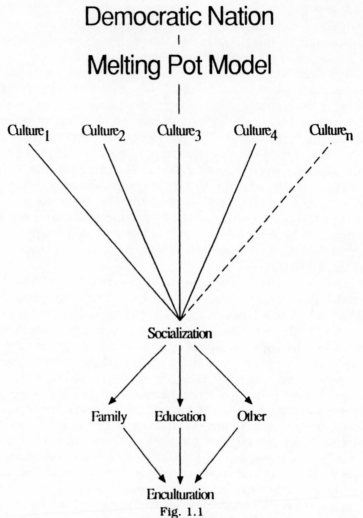

Democratic Nation
|
Melting Pot Model
|

Culture$_1$ Culture$_2$ Culture$_3$ Culture$_4$ Culture$_n$

Socialization

Family   Education   Other

Enculturation

Fig. 1.1
National Rhetoric: Melting Pot Model

tural in origin. Our comfort level in identifying these traits as
unfavorable to the well-being of our society has changed over
the years from being explicitly present in our institutions to being implicitly present. Nevertheless, the result is similar: rele-
gation of whole groups to institutions that ultimately serve as
restrictive acculturation contexts. Thus, schooling, whether at
the pre-school, elementary, secondary, or even postsecondary
level, generally attempts to change the original language and

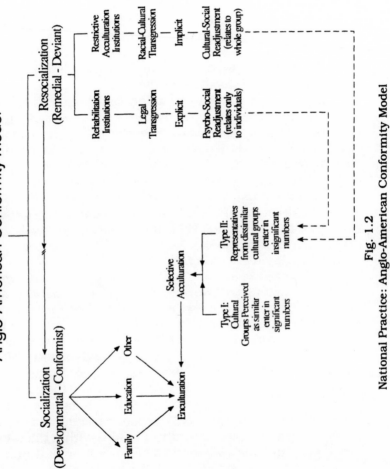

Democratic Nation

Anglo-American Conformity Model

Socialization
(Developmental - Conformist)

Family　　Education　　Other

Enculturation

Selective
Acculturation

Type I:
Cultural
Groups Perceived
as similar
enter in
significant
numbers

Type II:
Representatives
from dissimilar
cultural groups
enter in
insignificant
numbers

Resocialization
(Remedial - Deviant)

Rehabilitation
Institutions

Restrictive
Acculturation
Institutions

Legal
Transgression

Racial-Cultural
Transgression

Explicit

Implicit

Psycho-Social
Readjustment
(relates only
to individuals)

Cultural-Social
Readjustment
(relates to
whole group)

Fig. 1.2
National Practice: Anglo-American Conformity Model

culture of the group in favor of the language and culture re
flected within the Anglo-American—conformity model, in many
cases even before content instruction can take place. There are
variations now on this pattern, but its essential character remains intact: What the student brings to the classroom is insufficient, even antithetical, to the requirements that the
school has set out for being ready to learn.

As in the case of prisons intended to serve as meaningful
contexts for rehabilitation and as significant deterrents to re-
cidivism, so, too, are schools that function as restrictive acculturation institutions doomed to fail their students. The
signalling to students that wholescale sociocultural adjustment is necessary before they can be looked upon as American
is of course nonsense, particularly when "American" in this
case means "Anglo-American." The probability for school success and for these students moving *as a group* from a remedial-
deviant resocialization schooling context to an enculturation
or acculturation socialization context (depending on their
native-born status) is further and significantly diminished
when long-term racial and ethnic prejudice and discrimination
have been the rule rather than the exception, as has been the
case in the United States.

The Anglo-American conformity model, then, is itself antithetical to meeting our national identity goal so aptly symbol-
ized by the melting pot. We must above all and before all else be
American (I am referring to the term in its national sense and
not its extended international sense which would include Canadian Americans and Latin Americans). But that means accepting all groups, whether native or foreign born, as free,
equal, and contributing members of the United States;
through acceptance, there is unity. It is clear that the Anglo-
American conformity model embodies the philosophy and practices that prevent *integration, authentic communication,* and
cooperation among the diversity of groups within the common
geographic and spiritual borders of our nation and that reinforce *segregation, communicative semblance,* and *competition* among us. These latter practices will continue to rend our
national fabric and impede attainment of the educational, social, and political goals by particular groups of Americans.

We must now for the common good relieve ourselves of this
model in favor of an alternative national model that balances
the egalitarian principles so richly embedded within our rhetoric with egalitarian practices at the educational, social, and

political levels, which up to now have eluded us as a nation. In so doing, we will be in a socially viable position to move toward those collective goals our national rhetoric deems fundamental for true equality and national progress. Adherence to these principles and practices would certainly yield a more encouraging national educational and productivity scenario than has been possible to date. Figure 1.3 illustrates a multicultural national context where each cultural group participates significantly within the democratic context. To the extent that cultures exist in a persistent subordinated status within a national context, all cultures within that context, whether dominant or subordinate, are distant from an actual democratic context. The metaphor of stellar cohesion allows for cultural integrity and national unity. Assessment of the relationship between rhetoric and practice will of course remain fundamental to our national development.

For the foreseeable future, assessment must emphasize the quality and rate of movement along the paths of education, economics, and politics by significant numbers of individuals from all racial, ethnic, cultural, and linguistic backgrounds—for, clearly, this Janus-like indicator represents both the bleakest threat and the greatest promise to realizing our democratic national image. The road is ours to choose.

Notes

1. The use of terms based on race, ethnicity, and color to identify particular groups within the United States reflects persistent, fundamental, and unfortunate aspects of our national system of values and practice, specifically our historical belief in and practice of segregation and limited rights for groups based on those same three elements.

Why color designations as opposed to another designation? The answer of course relates to the historical inequalities legally and socially sanctioned toward "non-Whites" by the dominant society, usually characterized as Anglo-American, who thought of themselves as "White" and others as "Colored." Based on these historical foundations of color-based discrimination, we must question the logic of a national practice that continues to differentiate among its citizens by color, regardless of the group applying the labeling.

Labeling groups is a necessarily awkward process. For example, it invites contention: Categorizing groups highlights issues of inequality associated with our particular historical and contemporary national circumstance that continues to be the basis of extraordinary contention at political, other institutional, and popular levels. Too,

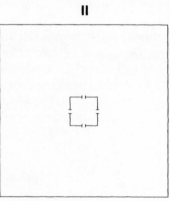

I. Multicultural National Context

- Group Heterogeneity
- Network of Interrelated Groupings
- Fragile National Foundation

+

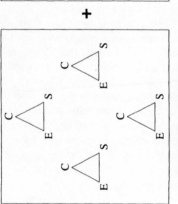

II. Democratic Framework

- Group-Wide Cohesive Agent
- Common Value: Group-Wide Equitable Engagement

=

III. Stellar Cohesion of Cultures

- Cultural Group Heterogeneity
- National Homogeneity
- Solid National Foundation
- Stellar core is a participatory democratic context.

KEY

C = Cultural Survival
S = Socialization
E = Enculturation

Fig. 1.3

Proposed National Metaphor: Stellar Cohesion of Cultures

the categories tend to be too general, failing to do descriptive or ana lytic justice to the individual groups within each category. The category "Asian-American," for example, is too broad to sufficiently characterize or interpret the intracategory groups it represents, namely, Chinese-Americans, Indian-Americans, Korean-Americans, Japanese-Americans, Philippino-Americans, and the multitude of other groups within this category.

The same of course applies to Hispanic-Americans, a group designation which includes Basque-Americans (of Spanish origin), Cuban-Americans, Mexican-Americans, Puerto Ricans/Puerto-Rican–Americans, Spanish-Americans, and groups representing Central and South America (excepting Brazil). Moreover, the U.S. national presupposition and practice of denying the European origin (predominantly from Spain) of Hispanic-Americans, together with its sustained and extensive influence, is erroneous with respect to their ethnicity culture, language, religion, and self-image. It reflects our woefully vast and lamentable cultural ignorance and insensitivity toward Hispanics in general and Hispanic-Americans in particular.

Acknowledging these and other limitations, for purposes of this analysis I will nonetheless use the following terms to identify particular groups and trust the text to disassociate the terms from any offensive connotations: African-American, Anglo-American, Asian-American, European-American, Hispanic-American, and Native-American.

References

Acosta-Belén, E. and B. R. Sjostrom (Eds.). (1988). *The Hispanic experience in the United States, Contemporary issues and perspectives.* New York: Praeger.

Arias, M. B. (1986). The context of education for Hispanic students: An overview. In "The education of Hispanic Americans: A challenge for the future," *American Journal of Education, 97*(1), 26–57.

Banton, M. (1979). The idea of race and the concept of race. In G. K. Verma and C. Bagley (Eds.), *Race, education and identity.* New York: St. Martin's Press, 15–30.

Barrera, M. (1979). *Race and class in the Southwest, A theory of racial inequality.* Notre Dame, Ind.: University of Notre Dame.

Brooks, R. L. (1990). *Rethinking the American race problem.* Berkeley: University of California.

Brown v. Board of Education, 347 U.S. 483 (1954).

Chan, S. (1991). *Asian Americans, An interpretive history.* Boston: Twayne Publishers.

Cziko, G. A. (1992). The evaluation of bilingual education, From necessity and probability to possibility. *Educational Researcher,* *21*(2), 10–15.

Daniels, R. (1990). *Coming to America, A history of immigration and ethnicity in American life.* New York: Harper Collins.

DeVillar, R. A. and Faltis, C. J. (1987). Computers and educational equity in American public schools. *Capstone Journal of Education,* viii(4), 1–8.

———. (1991). *Computers and cultural diversity.* Albany, N.Y.: State University of New York Press.

Dobzhansky, T. (1962). *Mankind evolving, The evolution of the human species.* New Haven, Conn.: Yale University.

Dunn, L. (1988). Has Dunn's monograph been shot down in flames—Author reactions to the preceding critiques of it. *Hispanic Journal of Behavioral Sciences, 10*(3), 301–323.

Fernández, R. R. (Ed.) (1988). Achievement testing: Science vs ideology. Special Issue. *Hispanic Journal of Behavioral Sciences, 10*(3).

———. (1988). Introduction. In *Hispanic Journal of Behavioral Sciences, 10*(3), 179–198.

Fordham, S. (1988). Racelessness as a factor in Black students' success: Pragmatic strategy of Pyrrhic victory? *Harvard Educational Review, 58*(1), 54–84.

Franklin, J. H. (1965). The two worlds of race: A historical view. *DAEDALUS, Journal of the American Academy of Arts and Sciences, 94*(4), 899–920.

Gordon, M. M. (1964). *Assimilation in American life, The role of race, religion, and national origins.* New York: Oxford University Press.

Jensen, A. R. (1969). How much can we boost IQ and scholastic achievement? *Harvard Educational Review, 39*(1), 1–23.

———. (1980). *Bias in mental testing.* New York: The Free Press.

———. (1981). *Straight talk about mental tests.* New York: The Free Press.

Kitano, H. H. L. and R. Daniels. (1988). *Asian Americans, Emerging minorities.* Englewoods Cliffs, N.J.: Prentice Hall.

Matute-Bianchi, M. E. (1986). Ethnic identities and patterns of school success and failure among Mexican-descent and Japanese-American students in a California high school: An ethnographic analysis. *American Journal of Education, 97*(1), 233–255.

Montagu, A. (1964). *The concept of race.* New York: Collier Books.

Moore, J. and H. Pachon. (1985). *Hispanics in the United States.* Englewood Cliffs, N.J.: Prentice-Hall.

Myrdal, G. (1944). *An American dilemma, The Negro problem and modern democracy.* New York: Harper & Brothers.

Novak, M. (1973). *The rise of the unmeltable ethnics.* New York: Macmillan Publishing Co., Inc.

Plessy v. Ferguson, 163 U.S. 3 (1896).

Ramírez, J. D., S. D. Yuen, D. R. Ramey, and D. J. Pasta. (1991). *Final report: Longitudinal study of structured English immersion strategy, early-exit and late-exit transitional bilingual education programs for language-minority children,* Volume I (Contract No. 300–87–0156, U.S. Department of Education, Washington, D.C.). San Mateo, Calif.: Aguirre International.

Ramírez, J. D., D. J. Pasta, S. D. Yuen, D. K. Billings, and D. R. Ramey. (1991). *Final report: Longitudinal study of structured English immersion strategy, early-exit and late-exit transitional bilingual education programs for language-minority children,* Volume II (Contract No. 300–87–0156, U.S. Department of Education, Washington, D.C.). San Mateo, Calif.: Aguirre International.

Salinas, G. (1973). Mexican Americans and the desegregation of schools in the Southwest. In O. I. Romano-V (Ed.), *Voices, Readings from El Grito* (second edition). Berkeley: Quinto Sol, 366–399.

Schinke-Llano, L. A. (1983). Foreigner talk in content classrooms. In H. Seliger & M. Long (Eds.), *Classroom oriented research in second language acquisition* (pp. 146–164). Rowley, MA: Newbury House.

Scruton, R. (1982). *A Dictionary of Political Thought.* New York: Hill and Wang.

Suárez-Orozco, M. M. (1987). Towards a psychosocial understanding of Hispanic adaptation to American schooling. In Trueba, H. T. (Ed.), *Success or Failure? Learning & the Language Minority Student.* Cambridge, Mass.: Newbury House Publishers, 156–168.

Takaki, R. (1989). *Strangers from a different shore: A history of Asian Americans.* Boston: Little, Brown and Company.

Tenhula, J. (1991). *Voices from Southeast Asia, The refugee experience in the United States.* New York: Holmes & Meier.

Trueba, H. (1988). Comments on L. M. Dunn's bilingual Hispanic children on the U.S. mainland: A review of research on their cognitive, linguistic, and scholastic development. In *Hispanic Journal of Behavioral Sciences, 10*(3), 253–262.

Veltman, C. (1988). *The future of the Spanish language in the United States.* New York: Hispanic Policy Development Project.

Walker, C. L. (1987). Hispanic achievement: Old views and new perspectives. In Trueba, H. T. (Ed.), *Success or failure? Learning & the language minority student.* Cambridge, Mass.: Newbury House Publishers, 15–32.

Weinreich, P. (1979). Cross-ethnic identification and self-rejection in a
    Black adolescent. In G. K. Verma and C. Bagley (Eds.), *Race, ed-
    ucation and identity.* New York: St. Martin's Press, 157–175.

Willig, A. C. (1988). A case of blaming the victim: The Dunn mono-
    graph on bilingual Hispanic children on the U.S. mainland. In
    Fernández, R. R. (Ed.), Achievement Testing: Science vs Ideology.
    Special Issue. *Hispanic Journal of Behavioral Sciences, 10*(3),
    219–236.

————. (1985). A meta-analysis of selected studies on the effectiveness
    of bilingual education. *Review of Educational Research, 55*(3),
    269–317.

Wollenberg, C. M. (1978). *All deliberate speed, Segregation and ex-
    clusion in California schools, 1855–1975.* Berkeley: University of
    California.

Zangwill, I. (1916). *The melting pot.* New York: The Macmillan
    Company.

▼ 2 ▼

Cooperative Learning in the Culturally Diverse Classroom

DAVID W. JOHNSON
and
ROGER T. JOHNSON

Diversity: Promise Or Problem?

The United States has always been a nation of many cultures, races, languages, and religions. In the last eight years alone, over 7.8 million people journeying from over 150 different countries and speaking dozens of different languages came to make the United States their new home. America's pluralism and diversity has many positive values. It contributes to our vitality as a society. It is a source of energy and creativity. Diversity among collaborators has been found to contribute to achievement and productivity, creative problem solving, growth in cognitive and moral reasoning, increased perspective-taking ability, and general sophistication in interacting and working with peers from a variety of cultural and ethnic backgrounds (Johnson and Johnson 1989a). Such positive outcomes, however, do not automatically come from placing diverse people in close proximity with each other.

Diversity among people can either be a valued resource generating energy, vitality, and creativity, or it can be a source of divisiveness, racism, and prejudice. Diversity among individuals creates an opportunity, but like all opportunities, there are potentially either positive or negative outcomes. Whether the outcomes are positive or negative depends on (a) whether or not diverse individuals come into contact with each other and (b) how social interdependence is structured within the situation.

The primary place in which diverse students from different cultural, ethnic, social class, and language backgrounds come

57

together is in schools. Sometimes the results are positive and students get to know each other, come to appreciate and value the vitality of diversity, learn how to use diversity for creative problem solving and enhanced productivity, and internalize a common American heritage that binds them together. Sometimes the results are negative and students become more ethnocentric and racist. If the diversity inherent in the history and future of the United States is to be a source of creativity and energy that few other countries have, learning situations and schools must be structured so that students learn to value and seek out diversity rather than fear and reject it. The very fabric of school life needs to enhance the valuing and utilization of diversity for increased learning.

Once diverse children are brought together in the same school and classroom, whether the diversity among students results in positive or negative outcomes depends largely on how student–student interaction within learning situations is structured: competitively, individualistically, or cooperatively. This chapter focuses on the use of cooperative learning to promote strength through diversity. A broad overview of cooperative learning as a research-based school practice is presented. In order to use cooperative learning in the classroom it is necessary to understand the essential elements that differentiate (a) cooperative learning from traditional classroom grouping and (b) a well-implemented cooperative lesson from a poorly implemented one. The rationale for using cooperative learning is the strength of the research verifying its effectiveness. Much of this research has focused on students from diverse backgrounds learning together. Before social interdependence is discussed, the American tradition of diversity is discussed in more detail.

The American Tradition of Strength through Diversity

American culture is and always has been pluralistic. Our common culture has been formed by the interaction of subsidiary cultures, being influenced over time by a wide variety of willing (and sometimes unwilling) European, African, and Asian immigrants, as well as American Indians. American music, art, literature, language, food, and customs all show the effects of the integration of diverse cultures within one nation.

Historically, since the founding of our country, the United States has used compulsory education as the means for promoting strength through diversity. All children, no matter what their religious, ethnic, or cultural backgrounds, have been required to attend a common school. While the track record of our schools is uneven and spotty, it is within our schools that we lay the groundwork for creating a *unum* from our *pluribus*. This is done in four basic steps. First, students are encouraged to develop an appreciation for their religious, ethnic, or cultural background. Students' identity with the culture and homeland of their ancestors is valued and recognized. The assumption is that respect for one's cultural heritage will translate into self-respect.

Second, students are encouraged to develop an appreciation for the religious, ethnic, and cultural backgrounds of other students. A critical aspect of developing an ethnic and cultural identity is whether ethnocentricity is inherent in one's definition of oneself. An ingroup identity must be developed in a way that does not lead to rejection of outgroups. There are many times when being a member of one group requires the rejection of other groups. There are also many times when being a member of one group requires the valuing of and respect for other groups. Outgroups need to be seen as collaborators and resources rather than competitors and threats. The degree to which one's ingroup identity leads to respect for and valuing of outgroups depends on whether one develops a superordinate identity that subsumes both one's own group and all other groups within America and throughout the world.

Third, students are encouraged to develop a strong superordinate identity as "Americans." Being American is creedal rather than racial or ancestral. The United States is a nation that unites as one people the descendants of many cultures, races, religions, and ethnic groups through an identification with America and democracy. America is one of the few successful examples of a pluralistic society where different groups clashed but ultimately learned to live together through achieving a sense of common nationhood. In our diversity, there has always been a broad recognition that we are one people. Whatever our origins, we are all Americans.

Fourth, students are taught a pluralistic set of values concerning democracy, freedom, liberty, equality, justice, the rights of individuals, and the responsibilities of citizenship. It is these values that form the American creed. We respect basic human rights, listen to dissenters instead of jailing them, and have a multiparty political system, a free press, freedom of speech, freedom of religion, and freedom of assembly. These values were shaped by millions of people from many different backgrounds. Americans are a multicultural people knitted together by a common set of political and moral values that are primarily taught by the schools.

In order to educate diverse students so that they learn about and take pride in their cultural and ethnic heritage, understand and appreciate the cultural and ethnic heritage of others, develop a superordinate identity as "Americans," and learn and internalize the democratic values expressed in our Constitution and Bill of Rights, cooperative efforts are required among students, among faculty, and among administrators. Diverse students must be brought together in the same classroom, the teacher must use cooperative learning procedures the majority of the time, the principal must organize teachers into collegial support groups aimed at increasing their expertise in using cooperative learning, and the superintendent must organize administrators into collegial support groups aimed at increasing their expertise in leading a cooperative school. Cooperative efforts are the heart of a basic change in organizational structure from a competitive–individualistic "mass manufacturing" model of organizing to a high-performance team-based organizational structure (Johnson and Johnson 1989b).

The Nature of Cooperative Learning

> Two are better than one, because they have a good reward for toil. For if they fall, one will lift up his fellow; but woe to him who is alone when he falls and has not another to lift him up. . . . And though a man might prevail against one who is alone, two will withstand him. A threefold cord is not quickly broken.
>
> —Ecclesiastes 4:9–12

Cooperative learning is an old idea. The Talmud clearly states that in order to learn you must have a learning partner. In the first century, Quintillion argued that students could benefit from teaching one another. The Roman philosopher Seneca advocated cooperative learning through such maxims as *qui docet discet* ('when you teach, you learn twice'). Johann Amos Comenius (1592–1679) believed that students would benefit both by teaching and by being taught by other students. In the late 1700s Joseph Lancaster and Andrew Bell made extensive use of cooperative learning groups in England, and the idea was brought to America when a Lancastrian school was opened in New York City in 1806. Within the Common School Movement in the United States in the early 1800s there was a strong emphasis on cooperative learning. In the last three decades of the nineteenth century, Colonel Francis Parker brought to his advocacy of cooperative learning enthusiasm, idealism, practicality, and an intense devotion to freedom, democracy, and individuality in the public schools. His fame and success rested on his power to create a classroom atmosphere that was truly cooperative and democratic. Parker's advocacy of cooperation among students dominated American education through the turn of the century. Following Parker, John Dewey promoted the use of cooperative learning groups as part of his famous project method in instruction. In the late 1930s, however, interpersonal competition began to be emphasized in schools. In the late 1960s, individualistic learning began to be used extensively. After forty years of exploring competitive and individualistic learning, and after numerous research studies demonstrating the efficacy of cooperative learning, American schools are returning to their traditional use of cooperative learning.

Cooperation is working together to accomplish shared goals. Within cooperative activities individuals seek outcomes that are beneficial to themselves *and* to all other group members. *Cooperative learning* is the instructional use of small groups so that students work together to maximize their own and each other's learning (Johnson, Johnson, and Holubec 1990). Within cooperative learning groups, students are given two responsibilities: to learn the assigned material and to make sure that all other members of their group do likewise. In cooperative learning situations, students perceive that they can reach their learning goals only if the other students in the learning group also do so. Students discuss the material to be learned with each other, help and assist each other to understand it, and encourage each other to work hard.

Cooperative learning groups may be used to teach specific content (formal cooperative learning groups), to ensure active cognitive processing of information during a lecture (informal cooperative learning groups), and to provide long-term support and assistance for academic progress (cooperative base groups)

in the classroom (Johnson, Johnson, and Holubec 1990). Any
assignment in any curriculum for any age student can be done
cooperatively. Formal cooperative learning groups are created
to complete specific tasks and assignments, such as solving
math problems, writing reports or themes, conducting experiments, and reading stories, plays, or books. The teacher
introduces the lesson, assigns students to groups (two to five
members), gives students the materials they need to complete
the assignment, and assigns students roles. The teacher ex-
plains the task, teaches any concepts or procedures the students need in order to complete the assignment, and structures
the cooperation among students. Students work on the assignment until all group members have successfully understood
and completed it. While the students work together the teacher
moves from group to group systematically monitoring their interaction. The teacher intervenes when students do not understand the academic task or when there are problems in
working together. After the assignment is completed the
teacher evaluates the academic success of each student and
has the groups process how well they functioned as a team. In
working cooperatively, students realize they have a stake in
each other's success. They become mutually responsible for
each other's learning. Informal cooperative learning groups are
temporary, ad hoc groups used as part of lecturing and direct
teaching to focus student attention on the material to be
learned, create an expectation set and mood conducive to
learning, ensure students cognitively process the material being taught, and provide closure to an instructional session. Finally, cooperative base groups are long-term groups (lasting for
one semester or year) with stable membership, whose primary
responsibility is to give each member the support, encouragement, and assistance he or she needs to make academic
progress.

Basic Elements of Cooperative Efforts

Many teachers believe that they are implementing cooperative
learning when in fact they are missing its essence. Putting students into groups to learn is not the same thing as structuring
cooperation among students. Cooperation is not (1) having
students sit side by side at the same table and talk with each
other as they do their individual assignments, (2) having stu-

dents do a task individually with instructions that the ones who finish first are to help the slower students, (3) assigning a report to a group where one student does all the work and others put their name on it. Cooperation is much more than being physically near other students, discussing material with other students, helping other students, or sharing materials with other students, although each of these is important in cooperative learning.

In order for a lesson to be cooperative, five basic elements are essential and need to be included (Johnson, Johnson; and Holubec 1990). In a math class, for example, a teacher assigns her students a set of math story problems to solve. Students are placed in groups of three. The instructional task is for the students to solve each story problem correctly and understand the correct strategy for doing so. The teacher must now implement the five basic elements. The first element of a cooperative lesson to be included is *positive interdependence*. Students must believe that they are linked with others in such a way that one cannot succeed unless the other members of the group succeed (and vice versa). In other words, students must perceive that they "sink or swim together." Within the math story problems lesson, positive interdependence is structured by group members (1) agreeing on the answer and the strategies for solving each problem (goal interdependence) and (2) fulfilling assigned role responsibilities (role interdependence). Each group is given a set of story problems (one copy for each student) and a set of three role cards. Each group member is assigned one of the roles. The *reader* reads the problems aloud to the group. The *checker* makes sure that all members can explain how to solve each problem correctly. The *encourager* in a friendly way encourages all members of the group to participate in the discussion, sharing their ideas and feelings. Other ways of structuring positive interdependence include having common rewards, being dependent on each other's resources, or dividing the labor.

The second element of a cooperative lesson is *face-to-face promotive interaction* among students. This exists when students orally explain to each other how to solve problems, discuss with each other the nature of the concepts and strategies being learned, teach their knowledge to classmates, and explain to each other the connections between present and past learning. This face-to-face interaction is "promotive" in the sense that students help, assist, encourage, and support each other's efforts to learn. In the math lesson, the teacher must provide the time and encouragement for students to exchange ideas and help each other learn.

The third element is *individual accountability*. The teacher needs to ensure that the performance of each individual student is assessed and the results given back to the group and the individual. It is important that the group knows who needs more assistance in completing the assignment, and it is important that group members know they cannot "hitchhike" on the work of others. Common ways to structure individual accountability include giving an individual test to each student and randomly selecting one student's work to represent the entire group. In the math lesson, since group members certify that all members (1) have the correct answer written on their answer sheets and (2) can correctly explain how to solve each problem, individual accountability is structured by having the teacher pick one answer sheet at random to score for the group and randomly asking one group member to explain how to solve one of the problems.

The fourth element is *social skills*. Groups cannot function effectively if students do not have and use the needed leadership, decision-making, trust-building, communication, and conflict-management skills. These skills have to be taught just as purposefully and precisely as academic skills. Many students have never worked cooperatively in learning situations and, therefore, lack the needed social skills for doing so. Today, the math teacher is emphasizing the skill of "making sure everyone understands." When the teacher sees students engaging in the skill, she verbally praises the group and puts a star on the group's paper. Procedures and strategies for teaching students social skills may be found in Johnson (1990, 1991), Johnson and F. Johnson (1991), and Johnson, Johnson, and Holubec (1990).

Finally, the teacher must ensure that *groups process* how well they are achieving their goals and maintaining effective working relationships among members. At the end of the math period the groups process their functioning by answering two questions: (1) What is something each member did that was helpful for the group? and (2) What is something each member could do to make the group even better tomorrow? Such processing enables learning groups to focus on group maintenance, facilitates the learning of collaborative skills, ensures that members receive feedback on their participation, and reminds students to practice collaborative skills consistently. Some of the keys to successful processing are allowing sufficient time for it to take place, making it specific rather than vague, maintaining student involvement in processing, reminding students to use their collaborative skills while they process, and ensuring that clear expectations of the purpose of processing have been communicated.

What Do We Know about Cooperative Efforts?

> Everyone has to work together; if we can't get everybody working toward common goals, nothing is going to happen.
> —Harold K. Sperlich, President
> Chrysler Corporation

Learning together to complete assignments can have profound effects on students. A great deal of research has been conducted comparing the relative effects of cooperative, competitive, and individualistic efforts on instructional outcomes. These research studies began in the late 1800s but the field did not gain momentum until the 1940s when Morton Deutsch, building on the theorizing of Kurt Lewin, proposed a theory of cooperation and competition. His theory has served as the primary foundation on which subsequent research and discussion of cooperative learning has been based. During the past ninety years, over 550 experimental and 100 correlational studies have been conducted by a wide variety of researchers in different decades with different age subjects, in different subject areas, and in different settings (see Johnson and Johnson 1989a for a complete listing and review of these studies).

Building on the theorizing of Kurt Lewin and Morton Deutsch, the premise may be made that the type of interdependence structured among students determines how they interact with each other, which in turn largely determines instructional outcomes. Structuring situations cooperatively results in students interacting in ways that promote each other's success; structuring situations competitively results in students interacting in ways that oppose each other's success; and structuring situations individualistically results in no interaction among students. Students can help, assist, support, and encourage each other's efforts to learn. Students can obstruct

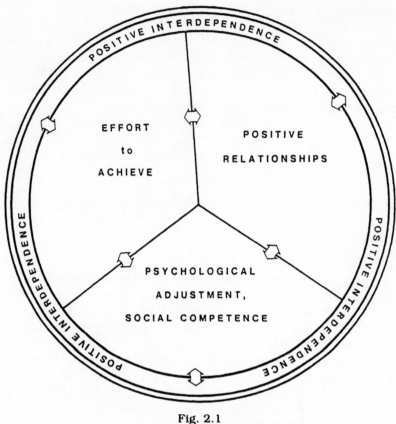

Fig. 2.1
Outcomes of Cooperation

and block each other's efforts to learn. Or students can ignore each other and work alone. These interaction patterns affect numerous variables, which may be subsumed within the three broad and interrelated outcomes of (a) effort exerted to achieve, (b) quality of relationships among participants, and (c) participants' psychological adjustment and social competence (see figure 2.1) (Johnson and Johnson 1989a).

Achievement

Over 375 studies have been conducted over the past ninety years to determine how successful competitive, individualistic, and cooperative efforts are in promoting productivity and achievement (see table 2.1) (Johnson and Johnson 1989a).

TABLE 2.1 MEAN EFFECT SIZES FOR IMPACT OF SOCIAL
INTERDEPENDENCE ON DEPENDENT VARIABLES

	Achieve	*Inter A*	*Support*	*S-Esteem*
Total Studies				
Coop vs. Comp	0.67	0.67	0.62	0.58
Coop vs. Ind	0.64	0.60	0.70	0.44
Comp vs. Ind	0.30	0.08	−0.13	−0.23
High Quality Studies				
Coop vs. Comp	0.88	0.82	0.83	0.67
Coop vs. Ind	0.61	0.62	0.72	0.45
Comp vs. Ind	0.07	0.27	−0.13	−0.25
Mixed Operationalizations				
Coop vs. Comp	0.40	0.46	0.45	0.33
Coop vs. Ind	0.42	0.36	0.02	0.22
Pure Operationalizations				
Coop vs. Comp	0.71	0.79	0.73	0.74
Coop vs. Ind	0.65	0.66	0.77	0.51

Note: Coop = Cooperation, Comp = Competition, Ind = Individualistic,
Achieve = Achievement, InterA = Interpersonal Attraction,
Support = Social Support, S-Esteem = Self-Esteem
For complete description of effect sizes and the data see Johnson and
Johnson (1989a).

*Working together to achieve a common goal produces higher
achievement and greater productivity than does working
alone.* This is so well confirmed by so much research that it
stands as one of the strongest principles of social and organizational psychology. Cooperative learning, furthermore, results in more higher-level reasoning, more frequent generation
of new ideas and solutions (i.e., process gain), and greater
transfer of what is learned within one situation to another (i.e.,
group to individual transfer) than does competitive or individualistic learning. The more conceptual the task, the more
problem solving required; the more desirable higher-level reasoning and critical thinking, the more creativity required; and
the greater the application required of what is being learned to
the real world, the greater the superiority of cooperative over
competitive and individualistic efforts.

Interpersonal Relationships

A faithful friend is a strong defense, and he that hath found him,
hath found a treasure.
—Ecclesiastes 6:14

Individuals care more about each other and are more committed to each other's success and well-being when they work together to get the job done than when they compete to see who
is best or work independently from each other. This is true
when individuals are homogeneous and it is also true when individuals differ in intellectual ability, handicapping conditions, ethnic membership, social class, and gender. When
individuals are heterogeneous, cooperating on a task results in
more realistic and positive views of each other. As relationships
become more positive, there are corresponding increases in
productivity, in feelings of personal commitment and responsibility to do the assigned work, in willingness to take on and
persist in completing difficult tasks, in morale, and in commitment to peer's success and growth. Absenteeism and turnover
of membership decrease.

There are 180 studies that have been conducted since the
1940s on the relative impact of cooperative, competitive, and
individualistic experiences on interpersonal attraction
(Johnson and Johnson 1989a). The data indicate that cooperative experiences promote greater interpersonal attraction
than do competitive or individualistic ones (effect sizes = 0.66
and 0.62 respectively). The higher the quality of the study and
the more pure the operationalization of cooperation, the stronger the impact of cooperation on interpersonal attraction. The
positive relationships formed continue into voluntary choice
situations. Even when individuals initially dislike each other,
cooperative experiences have been found to promote liking.

Much of the research on interpersonal relationships has
been conducted on relationships between white and minority students and between nonhandicapped and handicapped
students (Johnson and Johnson 1989a). There have been over
forty experimental studies comparing some combination of
cooperative, competitive, and individualistic experiences on
cross-ethnic relationships, and over forty similar studies on
mainstreaming of handicapped students (Johnson and Johnson 1989a). Their results are consistent: Learning cooperatively creates far more positive relationships among diverse
and heterogeneous students than does learning competitively
or individualistically.

Once the relationship is established, the next question becomes why. The social judgments individuals make about each
other increase or decrease the liking they feel towards each
other. Such social judgments are the result of either *a process*

of acceptance or *a process of rejection* (Johnson and Johnson 1989a). The process of acceptance is based on the individuals promoting mutual goal accomplishment as a result of their perceived positive interdependence. The promotive interaction tends to result in frequent, accurate, and open communication; accurate understanding of each other's perspective; inducibility; differentiated, dynamic, and realistic views of each other; high self-esteem; success and productivity; and expectations for positive and productive future interaction. The process of rejection results from oppositional or no interaction based on perceptions of negative or no interdependence. Both lead to no or inaccurate communication; egocentricism; resistance to influence; monopolistic, stereotyped, and static views of others; low self-esteem; failure; and expectations of distasteful and unpleasant interaction with others. The processes of acceptance and rejection are self-perpetuating. Any part of the process tends to elicit all the other parts of the process.

Psychological Health and Social Competencies

Working cooperatively with peers, and valuing cooperation, results in greater psychological health and higher self-esteem than does competing with peers or working independently. Personal ego-strength, self-confidence, and autonomy are all promoted by being involved in cooperative efforts with caring people who are committed to each other's success and well-being and who respect each other as separate and unique individuals. When individuals work together to complete assignments, they interact (mastering social skills and competencies), they promote each other's success (gaining self-worth), and they form personal as well as professional relationships (creating the basis for healthy social development). Individuals' psychological adjustment and health tend to increase when schools are dominated by cooperative efforts. The more individuals work cooperatively with others, then the more they see themselves as worthwhile and as having value, the greater their productivity, the greater their acceptance and support of others, and the greater their autonomy and independence. A positive self-identity is developed within supportive, caring, cooperative relationships, while a negative self-identity is developed within competitive, rejecting, or uncaring relationships. Children who are isolated usually develop the most self-rejecting identities. Cooperative experiences are not a luxury.

They are an absolute necessity for the healthy social and psychological development of individuals who can function independently.

Reciprocal Relationships among Outcomes

There are multidirectional relationships among efforts to achieve, quality of relationships, and psychological health (Johnson and Johnson 1989a). Each influences the others. First, caring and committed friendships come from a sense of mutual accomplishment, mutual pride in joint work, and the bonding that results from joint efforts. The more students care about each other, on the other hand, the harder they will work to achieve mutual learning goals. Second, joint efforts to achieve mutual goals promote higher self-esteem, self-efficacy, personal control, and confidence in their competencies. The healthier individuals are psychologically, on the other hand, the better able they are to work with others to achieve mutual goals. Third, psychological health is built on the internalization of the caring and respect received from loved ones. Friendships are developmental advantages that promote self-esteem, self-efficacy, and general psychological adjustment. The healthier people are psychologically (i.e., free of psychological pathology such as depression, paranoia, anxiety, fear of failure, repressed anger, hopelessness, and meaninglessness), on the other hand, the more caring and committed are their relationships. Since each outcome can induce the others, they are likely to be found together. They are a package, with each outcome a door into all three. And together they induce positive interdependence and promotive interaction.

Implications for Diversity

The three outcomes of cooperative efforts all play a part in developing an appreciation for one's own and others' cultural heritages and in forming an identity as an American. First, developing an identity and adopting a set of democratic values are learning processes and, therefore, are subject to all the dynamics found within all other learning situations. Just as achievement in math or reading will be higher if students work cooperatively, students will learn more about themselves, their cultural and ethnic heritage, the cultural and ethnic heritage of classmates, values such as liberty and equality, and their su-

perordinate identity as 'American' when they work cooperatively. Second, learning is not enough. There must also be
interaction with individuals different from oneself. Cooperative
learning is both necessary and sufficient for promoting constructive interaction among diverse students. If students from
different cultures, races, languages, religions, genders, and
ability levels are to interact with each other constructively, to
get to know each other on a personal and professional level, to
exchange information about their cultures and perspectives,
and to build positive and caring personal relationships, then
they must work together cooperatively. Third, having a set of
identities is not enough. They must be positive identities. Positive self-attitudes are developed within cooperative relationships with others. In addition, working with diverse peers
results in increased competencies in working with individuals
from cultural and ethnic backgrounds different from one's
own. Finally, to develop an identity as an American based on
beliefs in democracy, liberty, freedom, and equality, students
must participate in cooperative groups with classmates who
believe in democracy and democratic values. Cooperative efforts more closely match the realities of living in a democracy
than do competitive or individualistic efforts. Being part of a
community of shared values enhances one's identity as an
American.

Summary

In order to educate diverse students so that they learn about
and take pride in their cultural and ethnic heritage, understand and appreciate the cultural and ethnic heritage of others, develop a superordinate identity as 'Americans,' and learn
and internalize the democratic values expressed in our Constitution and Bill of Rights, cooperative learning is required.

Cooperative learning is the instructional use of small
groups so that students work together to maximize their own
and each other's learning. Cooperative learning experiences
are based on students' perceiving that they sink or swim together and that they must provide face-to-face help and support, do their fair share of the work, provide leadership and
resolve conflicts constructively, and periodically process how
to improve the effectiveness of the group.

In order to learn information and conceptual frameworks
concerning the cultural heritage of self and others, and in or-

der to learn about the American Constitution and Bill of Rights, cooperative learning is required. There is considerable evidence that students will learn more, use higher level reasoning strategies more frequently, build more complete and complex conceptual structures, and retain learned information more accurately when they learn within cooperative groups than when they study competitively or individualistically.

Much of the information about different cultural and ethnic heritages cannot be attained through reading books. Only through knowing, working with, and interacting personally with members of diverse groups can students really learn to value diversity, use it for creative problem solving, and develop an ability to work effectively with diverse peers. While information alone helps, it is only through direct and personal interaction among diverse individuals who develop personal as well as professional relationships with each other that such outcomes are realized. Understanding the perspective of others from different ethnic and cultural backgrounds requires more than information. It requires the personal sharing of viewpoints and mutual processing of situations. In addition, in order to identify with the values inherent in the American Constitution and Bill of Rights, students must work cooperatively with others, build personal and committed relationships with peers who are committed to a superordinate identity as Americans and who believe in democracy, liberty, justice, and freedom for all. There is considerable evidence that cooperative experiences, as compared to competitive and individualistic ones, promote more positive, committed, and caring relationships regardless of ethnic, cultural, language, social class, gender, ability, or other differences.

Finally, if the discords of diverse students meeting in the school are to be transformed into a symphony, students need positive self-images, the psychological health to face conflict and challenge, and the social competencies required to work effectively with diverse peers. Personal and superordinate identities are developed through group processes. It takes membership in cooperative groups to develop a personal identity, an ethnic identity, an identity as an American, and an identity as a world citizen. There is considerable evidence that working cooperatively increases students' self-esteem and psychological health, their ability to act independently and exert their autonomy, their interpersonal and small-group skills, and their understanding of interdependence and cooperative efforts.

Diversity can fulfill its promise rather than be a problem when learning situations and schools are structured cooperatively. This begins with diverse students being brought together in the same classroom, the teacher using cooperative learning procedures the majority of the time, the principal organizing teachers into collegial support groups aimed at increasing their expertise in using cooperative learning and working together as a team, and the superintendent organizing administrators into collegial support groups aimed at increasing their expertise in leading a cooperative school and working together as a team. Such a cooperative organizational structure will result in learning enhanced by diversity, and will create a shared superordinate identity as Americans and, at an even higher level, world citizens.

References

Deutsch, M. (1962). Cooperation and trust: Some theoretical notes. In M. Jones (Ed.), *Nebraska symposium on motivation* (pp. 275–319). Lincoln, Neb.: University of Nebraska Press.

Johnson, D. W. (1990). *Reaching out: Interpersonal effectiveness and self-actualization.* Englewood Cliffs, N.J.: Prentice Hall.

———. (1991). *Human relations and your career.* Englewood Cliffs, N.J.: Prentice-Hall.

Johnson, D. W. and F. Johnson (1991). *Joining together: Group theory and group skills.* Englewood Cliffs, N.J.: Prentice-Hall.

Johnson, D. W., and R. Johnson (1989a). *Cooperation and competition: Theory and research.* Edina, Minn.: Interaction Book Company.

———. (1989b). *Leading the cooperative school.* Edina, Minn.: Interaction Book Company.

Johnson, D. W., R. Johnson and E. Holubec (1990). *Circles of learning.* Edina, Minn.: Interaction Book Company.

▼ 3 ▼
Building Bridges for the Future: Anthropological Contributions to Diversity and Classroom Practices

STEVEN F. ARVIZU

This chapter, which consists of four segments, presents material on the anthropological contributions to futuristic classroom practices, and explores the significant elements of the DeVillar/Faltis (1991, this volume) framework (communication integration, cooperation) and other ideas related to diversity and educational futures. The first segment presents an introduction and definition of terms; the second offers a historical overview of anthropological contributions to education; the third describes methodological contributions to diversity efforts in education by providing some specific examples of the use of life history and other ethnographic fieldwork techniques; and the fourth discusses cross-cultural leadership, the creation of special projects, and the operationalizing of pluralism in educational settings.

Definitions

For purposes of this paper it is important to define such key terms as *culture, diversity, anthropology, ethnography, cross-cultural literacy, cross-cultural leadership,* and *pluralism.* They are either so common that they have multiple meanings, or are so specific to an anthropological perspective that they may not be used in traditional educational literature.

Culture is what guides people in their thinking, feeling, and acting, and serves as an emotional road map or plan of action in their struggle for survival. Culture is a state of being—a process—rather than a person, place, or thing; a verb rather than a noun. Because of the culture-creating capacity of people

through the exercise of free will, and because of the complicated influences of cultural transmission and transformation
across generations, cultural change is an ever-present reality
for all groups, whether through or without contact with other
groups. Culture gives meaning to peoples' lives and is symbol-
ically represented through language and interaction.[1]

Diversity is a term whose meaning varies with the background, concerns, theoretical framework, and context in
which it is discussed. For example, in a political and public policy sense, diversity has been interpreted by Secretary of Education Lamar Alexander as relating to quotas and affirmative
action in the accreditation controversy involving the Middle Atlantic States Accreditation Association (Chronicle of Higher
Education 1991). An accreditation-based definition of diversity
is included in the *Western Association of Schools and Colleges
(WASC) Handbook,* under Standard 1B, as integrity and respect for persons that fosters educational diversity (1988). A
draft Commission Policy on Diversity also provides multiple
meanings for diversity in overlapping institutional efforts that
go beyond matters of representation to consider goals, attitudes,
and practices; curricular adaptation; pedagogical improvements; giving voice to new arrivals; expansion of scholarship
in women's and ethnic studies; and assessment of diversity efforts (Caughlin 1991). Diversity applied to learner population
is also explained in cultural contexts in *Cross Cultural Literacy Ethnographies of Communication in Multiethnic Classrooms* (Saravia-Shore and Arvizu 1992).

An anthropological approach to diversity focuses upon culture and includes a cross-cultural perspective (Arvizu and
Saravia-Shore 1990). For purposes of this chapter, it means
recognition of variation among people related to their cultural
heritages, racial and ethnic identities, and gender and class experiences. The concept communicates the need to understand
universals and differences in the human species, as well as the
translation of understanding into behavior respectful of people
and their many forms of interacting. Diversity is relevant to a
cultural approach to learning in that learning and motivational styles and cross-cultural pedagogical strategies assume
attention to diversity in learner populations and pluralistic
learning outcomes.

Anthropology, the scientific study of peoples and cultures,
is a discipline that explores human diversity on a worldwide
basis in historical, contemporary, and futuristic contexts
through its major branches, which include archeology, linguis-

tics, physical anthropology, and cultural anthropology. As anthropology has been applied to the discovery of alternative sources of knowledge and to the explanation of commonalities and differences among cultural groups, such subfields as medical, psychological, political, and educational anthropology have developed. An anthropological approach encompasses attention to culture, a comparative perspective that enables the understanding of particular groups in the context of all human groups, a holistic orientation, the use of cultural relativity to avoid prejudgment of groups, and the use of fieldwork and ethnography—methodologies that require long term contact and cultural description and analysis.

Ethnography is the process of systematic inquiry to discover, describe, and analyze a culture or group of cultures, and is the major method used by anthropologists in conducting fieldwork. Ethnography is the way that anthropologists and others from culture X learn about people from culture Y by gaining access to and having long-term, continuous contact with people, and by using such techniques as participant observation, interviewing, event and network analysis, life history, and projective and other qualitative means for collecting and analyzing data. Ethnography, done through an anthropological approach, centers on the human and interactive element in research with attention to culture, comparative perspective, insider views, and the balance between the independent pursuit of truth and accountability to those studied. Ethnography is a method that distinguishes anthropologists from other behavioral scientists and from most educational researchers (Wolcott 1976). Didactic ethnography involves learning about self in the systematic study and learning about others. "Blitzkrieg" ethnography is the use of ethnographic techniques without an anthropological approach, as in short term site visits and "quickie" evaluation contracts (Fetterman, 1984).

Cross-cultural literacy (Saravia-Shore and Arvizu 1992) is the use of an anthropological approach to develop diversity and pluralism and to improve our ability to adapt, survive, and relate to one another in a respectful and fulfilling manner. It includes understanding critical issues that involve diverse cultural groups in a holistic context, and encompasses the recognition of cultural differences in learning populations, the integration of new arrivals into our schools and society, and the teaching of American cultural heritage(s). It embraces the development of a cross-cultural perspective among teachers, stu-

dents, and adults in the home environment, and it enables one
to connect and transcend cultures in study and action.

Cross-cultural leadership is leadership characterized by
skill, art, and influence in cross-cultural problem-solving and
pluralistic community building.

Pluralism is the consideration of more than one way of life
in the conceptualization and operation of curricula, programs,
policies, and institutions of society such as schools and religious, political, and governmental entities. According to Carlos
Cortes, *E pluribus unum* ('of many we are one') is a motto that
represents diversity and unity as inherently related concepts in
the United States as a democratic society (Cortes 1990). Pluralism is also a concept that organizes reform efforts in education
to integrate equity with quality in learning environments
(Saravia-Shore and Arvizu 1992).

Historical Overview

From its inception, anthropology has dealt with the explanation of cultural similarities and differences. Early efforts at describing differences in evolutionary terms gave attention to the
origins and nature of people by contrasting their technology,
social organization, and stages of progress. The social Darwin-
istic theories that arose supposed that culture was biologically
and environmentally based and not necessarily diffused or independently invented. The historical particularists, under the
leadership of Franz Boas, developed the notion of cultural relativity and were meticulous in advocating fieldwork, the learning and describing of each language and culture in the context
of its own history and sense of continuity. Many of these studies involved the study of socialization (teaching/learning of societal knowledge and proficiency) and enculturation (teaching/
learning of knowledge and proficiency of a particular cultural
community) at work informally within these societies, and
some described the various means by which teaching occurred
between generations in nonschooling contexts. For example,
Whiting and Child investigated the cultural influences of socialization in cross-cultural child-rearing studies (Whiting and
Child 1953), and Margaret Mead studied cultural differences in
enculturation in American Samoa and other non-Western societies (Mead 1928, 1935). The culture-area and culture-
and-personality theorists studied cultural transmission,

borrowing, and diffusion as means of understanding acculturation (culture change) and as typical or modal developmental processes for people within cultural communities and cultural contact situations in the development of personality and identity. Many life histories and autobiographies of American Indian leaders/survivors typify an era (1920–1950) commonly referred to as salvage anthropology, where endangered and disappearing cultures were reconstructed and measured through qualitative presentation of the lives of key informants. These later anthropological studies gave great emphasis to understanding the role of schooling as a means of modernizing indigenous populations, as well as a means of understanding missionary and trade influences on the shifts in values and behavior of people. Functional and structural theorists attempted to study small portions of daily life and behaviors to infer the nature of culture and the meaningful relationships among people—for example, the role and function of schools in integrating new arrivals into the United States mainstream.[2]

Educational anthropology is a field of specialization that has evolved over the past forty years, even though attention to acquisition of language and culture through formal and informal learning has historically been a part of traditional anthropological studies. Educational anthropology grew in popularity and gained attention in academia in the mid-fifties through conferences organized and chaired by Dr. George Spindler of Stanford, which resulted in several major books explaining the relationship between anthropology and education. Over the next several decades, the series *Case Studies in Anthropology and Education* was published by Holt, Rinehart, and Winston, providing simple ethnographies that addressed cultural transmission and formal and informal learning in different cultures. Several key universities concurrently developed doctoral programs in educational anthropology.

The development of the Council on Anthropology and Education (CAE), an affiliate organization of the American Anthropology Association (AAA), over the past three decades serves as a milestone in the organization of anthropological efforts in education. Anthropologists and educators aggressively created an active committee structure within this organization to apply anthropology to education. This professional organization publishes a newsletter and a journal, the *Anthropology and Education Quarterly*, as well as co-sponsors special publications. Additionally, it has sustained support for sponsored symposia and sessions involving bilingual and cross-cultural education at such professional meetings as the annual meetings of the American Anthropology Association (AAA), the Society for Applied Anthropology (SFAA), and the American Educational Research Association (AERA). The CAE leadership also supported development of the Society for Black Anthropologists and the Association for Latina-Latino Anthropologists.

Over a critical decade of debate, the CAE leadership engaged its members, as well as those of the SFAA and AAA, in developing professional positions in support of bilingual and cross-cultural education through the adoption of three key resolutions. The Mexico City Resolution, passed by the CAE in 1974, supports respect for cultural differences, acknowledges bilingualism and biculturalism as worldwide phenomena, and adapts basic principles of educational rights to services in the native language, respect for the cultures of the local community and the larger community, and the participation and accountability in development of programs. This resolution was cosponsored by teachers from Latin America who also participated in the meetings. The Resolution for Action on Culture, introduced by anthropologists Steven Arvizu and Margaret Gibson, passed by the CAE, SFAA, and AAA in 1978, provides the following operational definition of culture within a cross-cultural context:

1. Culture is intimately related to language and the development of basic communication, computation, and social skills.
2. Culture is an important part of the dynamics of the teaching-learning process in all classrooms, both bilingual and monolingual.
3. Culture affects the organization of learning and pedagogical practice, evaluative procedures, and rules of schools, as well as instructional activities and curriculum.
4. Attention to the cultural dimensions of education has widespread potential utility in resolving performance dysfunctions and interpersonal and group conflicts in schools and society.
5. Culture is more than the heritage of a people through dance, food, holidays, and history. Culture is more than

a component of bilingual education programs. It is a dynamic, creative, and continuous process that includes behaviors, values, and substances shared by people and that guides them in their struggle for survival and gives meaning to their lives. As a vital process, it needs to be understood by more people in the United States, a multiple society which has many interacting cultural groups.

6. Public institutions, such as schools, should facilitate the cross-cultural learning of their clients as a basic tool for effective citizenry and economic, political, and psychological existence.

7. It is the responsibility of all educational agencies—federal, state, and local—to give attention to culture in their programs.

8. All those involved in the educational process—policy makers, program officials, school personnel, and students—are cultural beings, products of and producers of culture, influenced in decision making by their cultural background and orientation. Therefore, it is imperative that all personnel responsible for educational decisions be conscious of the cultural factors that shape their actions and also, that they analyze the social/cultural impact of their actions with regard to the realization of quality education and equity of educational opportunity for all students.

(Los Angeles, December 1978)

The Cross-Cultural Approach Resolution was passed by CAE in 1981 and defines a cross-cultural approach as:

1. Teaching American culture to assist newcomers to learn about and integrate into United States life

2. Facilitating the teaching/learning process by recognizing and integrating the cultural background of the student in programs that are linguistically and culturally compatible and enriching

3. Teaching about the multiple cultural communities within the American culture heritage to stimulate understanding and social cohesiveness within and between groups

4. Linking school staff with culturally and linguistically different parents as mutual resources for cultural expectations and patterns of behavior

5. Preparing students for the future with communicative and cross-cultural competencies necessary for an ecologically and economically interdependent world

(Los Angeles, December 1981)

The following summary gives some key examples of development and applications of anthropology to education over several decades and demonstrates the variety of activity among educational anthropologists in the CAE.

The Kamehameha Project in Hawaii serves as a classic example of several decades of applied research being used to impact educational reform. Hawaiian children were studied out of school in home settings to discover learning styles and to engineer culturally relevant classroom lessons. Educational practices derived from this research resulted in improved attendance, engagement in learning, and academic achievement (Gallimore et al. 1974). The Mexican-American Education Project (MAEP) and the Cross-Cultural Resource Center (CCRC) at California State University, Sacramento, similarly integrated anthropology into teacher training and technical assistance efforts in the western United States and Micronesia. The MAEP was a large multiple-year fellowship program that trained approximately two hundred educators on how to use anthropology to improve linkages between schools and the Mexican American community, how to design culturally relevant curricula and programs, and how to change the culture of schools (Arvizu 1974). Jules Henry's "Cross Cultural Outline of Education" (1960) provides a listing of learning modalities in different cultures around the world, illustrating by comparison how learning approaches in the United States are limited. John Gumperz and Dell Hymes brought the use of ethnographic methods for the study languages and communication processes to the attention of sociolinguists and education researchers with their article on "The Ethnography of Communication" (Gumperz and Hymes 1964). Elizabeth Eddy wrote an applied article on teacher training in *Human Organization* (Eddy 1968) and an anthropological volume on becoming a teacher (Eddy 1969), to illuminate the process of teacher training and the cultural pressures on first-year teachers. Henry

Wolcott did several studies on teachers and administrators, including a classic ethnography entitled *The Man in the Principal's Office* (Wolcott 1973). To illustrate the power of ethnographic tools in qualitative cultural studies of schools and communities, John Ogbu's very influential case study, *The Next Generation*, analyzed the structural problems between schools and minority communities (Ogbu 1974) suggesting a social and structural framework for explaining differential achievement among minority students. Doug Foley's *From Peones to Politicos* is an ethnography of educational and political change in South Texas that used qualitative interviews, participant observation, and historical reconstruction to explain insider and outsider views of cultural and power shifts in schools, city government, and regional political structures (Foley, 1977).

Methodological Contributions to Educational Practice

To understand the future potential of anthropology to impact educational practice, it is important to state briefly its historical role in educational research methodology and its contributions to pedagogy and training.

The contributions of anthropology to educational reform efforts have dealt with language and communication, socialization and social interaction, and cooperation and conflict between and among cultural groups. These contributions have come from a wide variety of theoretical orientations over the past century, primarily through the use of the ethnographic method. One particular technique in traditional anthropological studies—life history technique—is just beginning to be used as a research and training tool in education. Even though anthropology has been used to study schooling, there are several areas where contributions from anthropological literature have been applied to impact the quality and nature of educational practice. Anthropological literature, for example, has impacted the content of curriculum in history and the social sciences, and also has influenced the development of ethno-pedogogical practices in learning contexts. Moreover, it has been used in staff development and training efforts to improve educational practices among diverse learner populations and to improve parental involvement in education.

Life History in Educational
Anthropology Research

In this segment, ethnography is discussed as a method of discovery, as well as in terms of its fieldwork techniques, particularly life history, for didactic and pedagogical application in
the development of classroom practices and educational programs. Life history technique is an important tool for understanding educational problems. Even though life history has
not been used as a research or pedagogical technique in major
early works in educational anthropology, it is beginning to be
used more frequently in the movement to strengthen qualitative research and evaluation, and in applied education anthropology. In this context, some examples are presented of
strategic use of life history technique in school-related areas
such as research and evaluation, teacher training, curriculum,
staff development, parent participation, and community involvement in schools, together with the development of cross-
cultural competencies among counselors and special
educators, and in the preparation of mentors from the private
sector who work with dropouts.

Anthropological studies of schools and education exhibit a
great range of theory and methodology. Unfortunately, they
also vary considerably in quality, due to the type and quality of
the training of the investigators, the funding sources, the purposes of the study, and the nature of and time dedicated to the
fieldwork. Conspicuously lacking in these naturalistic studies
of schools is the use of life history techniques. Major figures in
the development of educational anthropology and in the study
of schools for the most part have utilized participant observation, event analysis, a variety of interviews, and such specialized measurement instruments as videotape microanalysis,
instrumental activities inventories, and ethnographic filming.
Participant observation and interviewing have been techniques most open to misunderstanding and abuse, particularly by those not adequately trained in the ethnographic
method in an anthropological context.

A review of anthropological literature, or a perusal of research articles or dissertations, reveals the lack of any widespread attention given to life history technique. As an
illustration, the following well-known ethnographers have had
a particularly significant impact on educational anthropology,
but their major work makes little or no use of life history tech-

nique: George Spindler, John Ogbu, Harry Wolcott, Jaquetta Hill-Burnett, Fredrick Erickson, and Henry Trueba.

The use of life history technique is probably not well suited for research where quantitative methods are the major approaches, unless a complementary qualitative dimension or description or analysis is also needed. Life history is also very costly in terms of time and resources. In addition, some research, by its very nature, is more concerned with issues and conditions that are incompatible with life history technique. However, the general trends and contributions of educational anthropology argue for cultural explanation, the use of fieldwork techniques, a comparative method, and a holistic orientation. With very few exceptions, the use of life history technique in cross-cultural education and in educational anthropology has been very limited. By contrast, there are many instances in which life history technique can be strategically used in educational anthropology.

Strategic Uses of Life History

For this author, life history has been the most concrete technique for enabling educators to learn about themselves and others culturally. During the past eighteen years, this author has had many occasions to use life history technique in the conduct of his work as an educational anthropologist. The examples that follow illustrate the value and, in some instances, the strategic use of this particular technique where it is almost uniquely suited for application. Life history also has been used in research and evaluation, in teacher training, in curriculum development, and in the development of cross-cultural understanding and competencies in conflict situations. Life history has proved invaluable in the process of teaching anthropology and in the process of applying anthropological tools to problem solving in educational settings.

It is common for educational anthropologists to parallel the training of anthropologists in the training of educators. One reason for this is the similarities in process of learning a language and a culture different from one's own. Another is the knowledge that learning about others and learning about self are interrelated. In fact, becoming conscious of culture in one's self is important to becoming conscious of culture at work in others. Thus, overcoming ethnocentrism (the belief that one's own culture is superior to others') and the development of a culturally relative perspective are complicated processes that involve self-discovery and the study of others, the use of an insider and an outsider frame of analysis, and an appreciation of multiple cultural realities in the world.

Life history can be used as a starting point to get people to begin introspection and presentation of self in cultural terms and as a means of getting a diverse group of educators to get to know one another's values and way of life. This author has used life history to show teachers how they can model disclosure of cultural information about self with students. Life history also has been used to show teachers how they can use students, adults, and themselves as relatively low-cost learning resources in the classroom.

At CSU Sacramento, life history was used as a technique in the Mexican-American Education Project (MAEP), in the Cross-Cultural Resource Center, and in a variety of training and educational projects. The MAEP trained approximately 200 educators at the BA and MA levels in cross-cultural education and the use of anthropological theory and methods to solve educational problems involving minority learners. Life history and fieldwork experience were invaluable to individual development of participants and in the development of cross-cultural competencies. In fact, the live-in experiment was cited repeatedly over a five-year period as one of the most significant learning experiences of the students (Valencia 1972). The MAEP fieldwork experience often used life history and ethnographic journal techniques to develop cultural self-analysis, as well as a cross-cultural perspective among trainees. Many of the graduates of this project became leaders in bilingual/cross-cultural education contexts as project directors, principals and superintendents, teacher trainers, and curriculum developers.

Ethnographic films were also developed to facilitate cross-cultural teacher training. *Demystifying Culture* is a film that introduces conceptual tools for studying culture to non-anthropology audiences. *Día de los Muertos, Estilo Chicano* is an ethnographic film that gives an insider (emic) view of how and why Chicanos in the Sacramento community celebrate a Mexican holiday, modifying the celebration for their own purposes as a means of community building among different age groups. *Kamadipw: Ponapean Feasting* is an ethnographic film that reconstructs and preserves community feasts in Micronesian islands where a community struggles to protect itself from outside influences while also borrowing from the outside to modernize. *Alejandra's Story: Life History Technique* is an ethnographic film that shows how Hispanic parents can be a powerful hidden resource in the education of their children. Alejandra's life history is collected and told on film in her own words through simple use of strategic interview and life history technique. All of these films are available through the Cross-Cultural Resource Center in Sacramento or through the author at CSU Bakersfield.

In a workshop in Palau (now the Nation of Belau), seventy-five elders, parents, and educators went through two weeks of training in cross-cultural problem-solving. The traditional leaders were very excited about the use of life history technique, about the telling of their stories of the past, about struggles involving competing values, and about developing relevant curriculum for Palauan students consistent with the goals of their nation and schools. They collected group life histories and, with translation and assistance, developed interesting learning units subsequently integrated into learning materials.

Similar experiences occurred in summer institutes at the University of Guam, in Ponape, the Marshall Islands, and other places when a variety of cultural communities were interested in cultural relevance in their schools. Workshops presented anthropological theory, ethnographic method, and fieldwork techniques in direct application to program development, staff training, curriculum, and evaluation efforts, and to build stronger parental involvement and home—school linkages. In fact, in Hawaii, at the Pacific leadership Institute at Kamehameha School, life history technique was used as a means of conducting program evaluations, analyzing economic and educational development, increasing parent participation and community involvement, and coordinating staff development among leadership teams from throughout the American Flag Territories among Samoran, Chamoro, Marshalese, Trukese, Ponean, Yapese, and Palauan, and Southeast Asian reference groups.

Through the Cross-Cultural Resource Center, Micronesian, Polynesian, and Native-American personnel were trained to develop, direct, and evaluate their own educational programs. Over a ten-year period, between 1975 and 1985, students obtained master's degrees, as well as experience in applied educational anthropology, to mount major efforts in cross-cultural education resulting in the creation of multiple-year projects and in a shift in administrative leadership from outside control to inside control. These indigenous graduates became leaders and CEOs for their Nation–States' educational systems.

More recently, in Bakersfield, life history has been used in three ways: first, in the training of special-education graduate students to discover sociolinguistic and cultural contexts for working with exceptional learners; second, in preparing graduate students in counseling for the Marriage and Family Counseling Certificate sequence by teaching them cross-cultural values and mores; and third, in the use of life history technique with potential high school dropouts and private-sector mentors to enable them to learn about one another in cross-cultural mentoring situations. This program, the Career Beginnings Project, funded by the MacArthur Foundation, also uses Arnold Van Gennep's framework of *rites of passage* to help students to transcend conceptually the world of family, school, and work in graduating from high school and going on to college.

In this author's research on educational change, comparative life histories of activists are used as a means of explaining the process and cultural dynamics of innovation and problem-solving in educational and community settings (Arvizu 1992). The psychocultural adaptation strategies of these individuals and, in particular, their explanation of how they overcame discrimination and became committed to working for educational change would not have been possible without the use of life history technique. Similarly, life history was useful in related research on exemplary bilingual educational programs in Parlier, California, and Milwaukee, Wisconsin, in a comparative study of schools and communities (Arvizu 1992).

The Future

Even though anthropology has used life history technique and many other ethnographic techniques to describe and explain cultural variation among peoples in the world, educational anthropology and cross-cultural education as specialized fields have just begun to use ethnography in educational practice settings. Particular examples have been given of the strategic use of life history technique. For life history and ethnography to be used more often in future educational classroom studies and practices will require attention to several obstacles. Teacher training and advanced graduate study curricula will need to integrate educational anthropology and ethnography into course-work, especially in qualitative research and evaluation and pedagogical courses. The cost for diachronic and qualitative research will need to be viewed in terms of long-term benefits to school effectiveness, perhaps through comparative studies of costs of school failure. Training materials on ethnographic method and life history technique will need to be developed and disseminated and given more attention in professional journal and book publications and in conference presenta-tions. Educational anthropologists need to apply life history technique strategically to educational and classroom settings beyond psychological units of analysis to share how such tech-niques can be used to improve teacher–student and student–student interactions, to develop healthy and whole identities among diverse populations, to develop cross-cultural literacy and leadership, and to create pluralistic schools.

Cross-Cultural Leadership

For purposes of this chapter, *cross-cultural leadership* is de-fined as action influencing others to spread cross-cultural understanding, behavior respectful of cultural diversity, and relevant cultural change in environments and organizations. A *cross-cultural leader* is defined as one who is knowledgeable and comfortable with self, who clearly identifies with a partic-ular cultural community, and who relates well with others from the same and other cultural communities. A cross-cultural leader is also conscious of cultural, sociopolitical, and struc-tural variables and relationships, as well as proficient in pro-cesses of change.

To a great degree, the future is predictably unpredictable because of technology, natural disaster, and human-caused catastrophe. Nevertheless, planning for the future remains a necessary and common practice. Within this context of pre-dictability, our educational future is viewed as being especially impacted by the quality of leadership available to schools. Cross-cultural leadership is therefore a valuable asset to our fu-ture because it provides an understanding of cultural change from within and across cultural communities. It also assists in the development of better means of communicating in a world complicated by miscommunication due to people's relative in-ability to cope with multilingualism, multiculturalism, and multiple identity.

Effective cross-cultural leaders seem to evince the courage to disagree with their own ethnic groups, as well as with powerful decision makers within universities and schools, in support of a greater principle. Cross-cultural leaders also work at earning the respect of others by dealing with complex, controversial situations day after day. They exhibit special sensitivities, abilities, and strengths in critical conflict situations and special events. Reputations and past achievement are not enough to sustain long-term leadership. Rather, working through others and continuing to perform effectively seem necessary for sustained leadership. Cross-cultural leaders strategically use support systems that ensure continuity of their efforts, and build "communities-of-interest."

Implications for Future Theory and Classroom Practice

The framework by DeVillar and Faltis (1991, this volume) focuses attention on three areas of critical importance to classroom interactions—communication, integration, and cooperation. Their three concepts form an important framework for understanding the classroom and especially for reform of classroom practices. Other theories also will develop from the study of practice settings, which means that anthropology and educational anthropologists, as well as educational researchers, by using anthropological approaches have a strategic position to explore the qualitative explanation of the "schooling" experience.

The DeVillar/Faltis framework is logical in providing attention to communication, integration, and cooperation in analyzing classroom practices, particularly in a reform context. Anthropology and ethnographic method, particularly life history technique, can contribute to a better understanding of what occurs in schools and communities and what works and why. Cross-cultural leadership that evolves from ethnography of successful attempts to deal with communication, integration, and cooperation across cultures probably will become a more visible tool and competency to impact classroom practices in the future.

The bilingual education movement has primarily been embedded in the communication arena, with decades of experimentation using varying combinations of home language and majority language to facilitate communication in the classroom. The major efforts of language-minority communities have been to reform the schools in order to make them more compatible to the populations they serve, as evidenced by attention to innovative program design, curricular and staff development reform, and parental involvement. The United States government and status quo power interests have pursued the bilingual education movement as a means to integrate and assimilate language-minority learners and their communities into United States society *sans* home language and home culture. Numerous attacks on bilingual legislation have attempted to eliminate the program, cut its budget, or modify its goal and procedures under the rationale that de-emphasis on home language and home culture will improve English acquisition and mainstreaming even if both are premature to overall educational development of students.

Ethnography and ethnographic techniques such as life history technique serve as a major available alternative for researchers and practitioners in studying schools and attempting reforms. As a qualitative method of the science of the study of people, ethnography has already contributed an invaluable understanding of both the social structure of United States society and United States schools and the many varied educational contexts at work in a multiple and heterogeneous society. Ogbu's (1974) work in Stockton contributed greatly to the understanding of school failure among minority students in settings where the world outside of school communicates a powerful message of stratification on issues of communication, integration, and cooperation. In Ogbu's world the smart students figure it out early and drop out of a system that they perceive is not working in their immediate and long-term interests. But he discovered these realities through ethnography, long-term fieldwork, and continuous contact with the people central to the problem. If he had used life history technique with successful and nonsuccessful students, even in an environment structured by lack of opportunity, he might also have uncovered the key to educational reform, a problem with which he and his proteges struggle even today. They can say what is wrong from their theoretical perspective, but they cannot guide the rest of us through the process of how to fix it. A power struggle is implied as underlying Ogbu's structural world of stratification, but he does not deal with identity or power in this power struggle nor in the resolution of related problems.

Ethnography is playing an absolutely essential role in the work of the social-context-of-learning theorists; it also is helping them discover experimental designs for how to improve schools. Witness the Kamehameha Project in Hawaii, now past its second decade in experimenting with the study of Hawaiian children at home to create more harmonious learning and pedagogical practices in the non-Hawaiian classroom. The project has gathered a monumental body of data that show that schools can transmit and transform culture if they are smarter about how they communicate, integrate, and cooperate. Life history technique could enhance the evaluation of the project by giving in-depth insider information on the impact of such approaches as those used in the project. In addition, it could have given great insight into the quality of cross-cultural leadership needed to build bridges between the home and school. But here again, these theorists have neglected the role of identity in the behavior of students, teachers, and parents and the power dynamics of educational decision making with regard to language, culture, and school organization.

Ethnography of innovative pedagogy will probably be our most effective means of understanding successful experimentation, and an essential step in the diffusion of innovation to broader audiences, especially through qualitative study of experiments and strategic life histories. There are probably already developed new practices created by decades of experimentation in Headstart, compensatory education, migrant education, and bilingual education that have not been carefully documented by qualitative methodology nor individually based technologies. Perhaps in the future?

Operationalizing Pluralism

It is proposed that pluralism is a concept and that cross-cultural literacy a competency which together are instrumental to diversity and classroom practices for the twenty-first century. Further, how we integrate these concepts and competencies requires the use of anthropological methods and techniques to ensure cultural relevancy, a necessary comparative perspective on culture, identity, and groups, as well as procedures for facilitating learning and acquiring cross-cultural competencies and for developing cross-cultural leadership. Pluralism as a goal will become operationalized through creative efforts by cross-cultural leaders who are able to relate communication issues to cooperation and integration.

One important factor for the future of diversity and the development of cross-cultural competency and pluralism is the quality and quantity of cross-cultural leadership. Cross-cultural leadership requires considerable vision and important process skills for working with diverse constituencies in a positive and proactive manner. In a pluralistic society, a particular cultural or ethnic community cannot become fully empowered without the sacrifice of power by a few individuals or without the support of other communities. For example, in many urban settings ethnic groups begin organizing around self-interest issues and eventually have to form coalitions with other groups to gain significant increases in power, if they are not already members of the power elite. In heterogeneous communities, elected officials must obtain political support from a broad spectrum or a strategic set of communities to obtain and keep power over time. Cross-cultural leadership is an important quality for mobilizing and organizing groups as well as for bridge-building and coalition-building to influence one's surroundings and long-term relationships.

For leaders of disenfranchised communities, occasional strategic help from outsiders is sometimes necessary for them to achieve their objectives, even though the long-term ideal is interdependence or freedom from dependence on outsiders. Again, cross-cultural leadership is instrumental to becoming a successful broker and leader within and among cultural communities. Many ethnic and racial group leaders are successful within their groups but less successful with other groups because they lack cross-cultural competencies or cross-cultural leadership abilities. The imperfections of being human also cause leaders to err in their strategies even though their followers idolize and idealize them as role models. Those leaders who can manage effectively as cross-cultural leaders find that some of their skills can sometimes transfer to other, noncultural areas of leadership; for example, in economic or creative areas. Within organizations that are bureaucratic and structural, it is rare to find cross-cultural leaders within the established structure, and more common to find cross-cultural leaders in the margins and "soft money management" areas; for example, in innovative educational projects oriented toward pilot or demonstration efforts. Cross-cultural leadership is relatively unstudied in the anthropological and educational research literature. Even though there is considerable material on indigenous or minority managers and leaders, it is mostly focused upon within-group interactions and limited in cross-cultural analysis.

Futuristic practices in education will be greatly impacted either by the presence or absence of cross-cultural leadership, especially in areas of empowerment of historically underrepresented and disenfranchised groups. Without cross-cultural leadership factionalism, separation, and inter-ethnic conflict will increase. With cross-cultural leadership, within-group and between-group cooperation will increase. However, cross-cultural leadership will not develop efficiently without clear sustained support from diverse constituencies, especially from power elites who through enlightened self-interest will see the necessity of cross-cultural leadership for long-term stability of established world systems. In some instances, the empowerment of the underclass will threaten those in power or those motivated by upward mobility, and those threatened will resist such empowerment efforts.

Education and Empowerment

Education is one ideal mechanism for opening opportunity to the "have-nots" in United States society. However, opportunity for low-income and powerless groups is currently affected by such conditions as fewer resources; personnel quality; overcrowdedness; inadequate curricula, facilities, and equipment; insufficient financial assistance; and the lack of cross-cultural leadership in our educational institutions. In the continued absence of cross-cultural leadership, education will continue to function as a socializing agency for the undereducated, even though it may have a value-added character for some.

Cross-cultural leadership and empowerment are interconnected concepts affecting the quality of life of many communities in our world. Where there is increasing contact, conflict, and change between groups, there will be inevitable creative tension and struggle among individuals and groups around vested self-interest. In such situations, sensitive mediators, innovators, and leaders are in high demand and (at least currently) in short supply. Identity and power will be key concepts that impact communication, cooperation, and integration.

The role of educational anthropology and cross-cultural education in the dialogue on diversity will depend upon several important factors. The ability to demonstrate conceptual and programmatic utility to educational problem solving will likely determine the relevance of conceptual and methodological contributions. However, it is in the training and development of personnel that the field will be mostly tested. Successful development of the field will require development of cross-cultural leadership. This will require recruitment and training of the best and brightest from powerless communities, enabling them to work within their own communities and those of others. It will also mandate the development of cross-cultural competencies among more of our educators and community leaders. It will require providing support to existing professionals at risk for conducting unpopular research and developing new ideas for creative action. It will require becoming more proactive about cross-cultural leadership among ourselves and among various segments of the educational world.

Our future in education will require more bridge-builders and more tools for bridge-building than in the past. DeVillar and Faltis frame how we should explain and organize response to diversity, and anthropology offers added concepts and methods for understanding and action to create pluralistic learning environments.

Notes

1. A more detailed explanation of culture as applied to education is provided in a Monograph Series by Arvizu et.al (1977–1981) entitled *Demystifying the Concept of Culture*, which includes (1) *Conceptual Tools*, (2) *Methodological Tools*, (3) *Cultura Chicana*, (4) *Anthropological Study of Play and Games*, and (5) *Home School Linkages*, available through the Cross Cultural Resource Center, California State University, Sacramento. In educational anthropology, early research described cultural influences on child rearing and in formal and informal schooling. Later research described the culture of schools in contrast to the cultures of service populations and analyzed socio-cultural influences on learning, particularly within diverse linguistic and cultural learner populations. In business contexts the concept of organizational culture has been used to describe differences in values and in management approaches in order to study productivity and change.

2. Marvin Harris, in *The Rise of Anthropological Theory*, gives a detailed analysis of the historical developments of particular theoretical schools, along with their methodological characteristics (Harris 1968). More recent theories in American anthropology are being developed through ethnographic studies of schools and communities in the tradition of educational anthropology, as can be synthesized through key articles and debates in the Council on Anthropology and Education Quarterly.

References

Arvizu, S. et.al (1977–1981). Monograph series. *Demystifying the concept of culture: Number one: Conceptual tools; Number two: Methodological tools; Number three: Cultura Chicana; Number four: Anthropological study of play and games; Number five: Home school linkages.* Sacramento, CA: Cross-Culture Resource Center, CSU, Sacramento,

Arvizu, S. F. (1993). *Putting something back: Comparative life histories of Chicano activists.* Manuscript accepted for publication, University of Texas Press.

———. (1992). Cross-cultural leadership. Paper presented at the American Anthropological Association Annual Meeting, San Francisco, California.

———. (1988). Cross-cultural leadership and empowerment. Paper presented at the American Anthropology Association Annual Meeting, Phoenix, Arizona.

———. (1974). One plus one equals three. Masters Thesis, Department of Anthropology, Sanford University.

Cortes, C. (1990). Pluribus, Unium, and the American future. *Today,* 15 (3), 8–10.

DeVillar, R. A. and Faltis, C. J. (1991). *Computers and cultural diversity.* Albany: SUNY Press.

Foley, D. (1977). *From peones to politicos.* Austin: University of Texas Press.

Gallimore, R., J. Boggs and C. Jordan (1974). *Culture behavior and education: A study of Hawaiian-Americans.* Beverly Hills, CA: Sage.

Gumperz, J, and D. Hymes (1964). Ethnography of communication. *American Anthropologist, 66* (6), 1–34.

Harris, M. (1968). *The rise of anthropological theory.* New York: Thomas Y. Crowell Company.

Henry, J. (1960). A cross cultural outline of education. *Current Anthropology, 1* (4), 267–305.

Mead, M. (1928). *Coming of age in Samoa.* New York: Morrow.

———. (1935a). *Sex and temperment in three primitive societies.* New York: Morrow.

———. (1974). *The next generation: Ethnography in an urban neighborhood.* New York: Academic Press.

Saravia-Shore, M. and S. F. Arvizu, (1992). *Cross-cultural literacy: Ethnographies of communications in multiethnic classrooms.* New York: Garland Press.

Spindler, G. D. (1976). From omnibus to linkages: Cultural transmission models. In J. Roberts and S. Akinsanya (Eds.), *Educational patterns and cultural configurations: The anthropology of education.* New York: David McKay Company, Inc.

———. (Ed.)(1974). *Education and cultural process: Toward an anthropology of education.* New York: Holt, Rinehart and Winston, Inc.

———. (1973). *Burgbach: Urbanization and identity in a German village.* New York: Holt, Rinehart and Winston, Inc.

———. (Ed.)(1970). *Being an anthropologist: Fieldwork in eleven cultures.* New York: Holt, Rinehart, and Winston, Inc.

———. (Ed.)(1963). *The transmission of American culture. Education and cutlure.* New York: Holt, Rinehart, and Winston, Inc.

———. (Ed.)(1963). *Education and culture.* New York: Holt, Rinehart, and Winston, Inc.

———. (1959). *Transmission of American culture.* Cambridge, Mass: Harvard University Press.

———. (Ed.)(1955). *Education and anthropology.* Palo Alto, CA: Stanford University Press.

———. Education in transforming American culture. *Harvard Educational Review, 25,* 145–56.

Valencia, A. (1972). *The Mexican American education project: Evaluation report.* Sacramento: CSU.

Whiting, J. and I. Child (1953). *Child training and personality: A cross-cultural study.* New Haven: Yale University Press.

Wolcott, H. (1976). Criteria for an ethnographic approach to research in schools. In J. Roberts and S. Akinsanya, *Schooling in the cultural context.* New York: David McKay Company, Inc.

———. (1973). *The man in the principals office: An ethnography.* New York: Holt, Rinehart and Winston, Inc.

▼ Part II ▼
Cultural Diversity
and Teacher Education

▼ 4 ▼

Responding Successfully to Cultural Diversity in Our Schools: The Teacher Connection

ROBERT D. MILK

Challenges Posed by Cultural Diversity in the Schools

A great deal of focus has been directed over the past decade in the United States towards perceived inadequacies in the nation's educational system. A series of major studies have received national attention by documenting glaring areas of weakness in public schools and in the outcomes of public schooling, particularly in such specific curriculum areas as math, science, geography, and foreign languages. Some of the points raised in these reports are based on issues that are clearly debatable—for example, what is the best approach for teaching a particular subject area, or what are appropriate indicators for success/failure, or even what are reasonable expectations for success in a universal public education system in a nation as diverse as the United States?

Achievement Gaps in Minority Schooling

Regardless of where one stands on substantive issues related to curriculum and instruction in the public school setting, however, there are certain data related to educational outcomes of students in these schools that are incontrovertible. Specifically, it is clear that students from minority groups in the United States continue to fare poorly in the nation's schools, despite a number of educational reforms implemented with the express intention of addressing unsatisfactory achievement outcomes. High school completion rates are particularly revealing when broken down by race/ethnicity. According to 1989 fig-

101

ures from the Bureau of the Census, completion rates for the 18–24 age group during that year were 82.1 percent for whites, 78.1 percent for African-Americans, and 55.9 percent for Hispanics (Matthews 1991: 44). Similarly revealing are college participation rates, which for the same age group are reported as 38.8 percent for whites, 30.8 percent for African-Americans, and 28.7 percent, for Hispanics. Particularly disturbing are indications that the college participation rate for Hispanics is actually declining instead of increasing as one might expect: Between 1984 and 1989 the college participation rate for Hispanics from the 18–24 age group declined from 29.9 percent to 28.7 percent whereas for whites it increased from 33.7 percent to 38.8 percent, and for African-Americans it increased from 27.2 percent to 30.8 percent (Matthews 1991: 44). A report on the status of minorities in higher education released in January, 1991, by the American Council on Education finds that "Hispanics are grossly underrepresented at every rung of the educational ladder" and that "the degree of Hispanic under-representation increases at each successive educational level. . . . Although Hispanics are highly concentrated in the school-age population, they are less likely than non-Hispanics to have enrolled in preschool programs or to pursue either secondary or postsecondary education" (American Council on Education 1991: 3). Finally, only 6 percent of Hispanics in the 25–34 age group have completed four years or more of college, compared to 26 percent for non-Hispanics (Valdivieso 1990). In sum, it is apparent that educational outcomes for Hispanic and African-American students in the United States are at a substantially lower level than what is attained with respect to white students.

Inadequacy of Test-Driven Reform Efforts

The reasons for this relative lack of success are complex, and it is clear that a multitude of interacting factors contribute to unsatisfactory outcomes (Cortes 1986). A variety of state-initiated reform efforts have focused heavily on accountability measures, such as competency tests for teachers and basic skills tests for students. These initiatives are strongly driven by testing and, as a consequence, run the risk of heavily distorting the instructional process, since both teacher and administrator "success" come to be defined by a single set of test scores. Some researchers have suggested that, whatever the adverse "backwash" effects of test-driven educational reforms may be, they tend to impact most heavily on minority students in general, and on language-minority students in particular (Cummins 1984). This argument is based both on research evidence as well as on theoretical considerations that suggest that focusing on discrete elements of instruction serves to decontextualize learning in a manner that makes comprehension more difficult, particularly for language-minority students, who are often required to function in their second language.

National data from the 1980s suggest that there is genuine cause for alarm: rather than narrowing the achievement gap between minority and majority students, "there is rising concern that the school reform movement may serve to widen the already substantial gap between the achievement of majority students and those from minority groups unless special steps are taken" (McPartland and Slavin, cited in Rivera and Zehler 1990: 1). Fairly broad consensus appears to exist that this persistent achievement gap constitutes a critical national concern. The consensus ends, however, when discussions shift from the mere listing of problems to identification of proper courses of action that should be taken to remedy the situation. Since this is, at root, a political issue more than a pedagogical issue, it is not surprising that widespread consensus does not exist among the public at large on the logical next step for educational reform, although buzzwords such as *restructuring* and *empowerment* seem to represent prevalent notions that are currently being put forth in the arena of public debate on educational policy.

The Promise of Classroom-Centered Reforms

Regardless of what the cause of inadequate achievement outcomes for minority students may be, solutions will need to be multifaceted, addressing politically grounded structural reforms such as financing, equal access, and governance, in addition to instructional changes. Neither structural reforms nor curriculum/instructional initiatives alone can sustain the kind of steady change that must occur in the day-to-day educational experience of language-minority students—multiple reforms, working at different levels, each generating its own ripple effect, will need to take place in order for the formidable challenge posed by culturally diverse schooling to be effectively met.

One of the most hopeful signs emanating from current research efforts is a general consensus with respect to the kinds of classroom-based solutions that need to be implemented in order to achieve educational success for language-minority students. Judging from the professional literature, it appears evident that, among educational specialists focusing specifically on the instructional needs of language-minority students, a small core of central themes consistently emerge from a variety of different sources, each representing a contributing link to an effective plan for educational success. These themes include:

- With regard to instruction, focusing on *cooperation* and maximum *interaction*
- With regard to curriculum, working toward *integration* across subject areas
- With regard to administration, seeking increased *collaboration* between persons responsible for implementing policy, and those responsible for delivering instruction

Cutting across all three of these areas, the overall unifying theme is enhanced *communication*, proceeding from a *holistic* framework. This seems to be an appropriate cover theme, indeed, for framing discussions on educational improvement for language-minority students.

Reconceptualizing Instruction for Language-Minority Students

The basic premise guiding educational interventions for language-minority students has often, in the past, been one of compensation—compensation for perceived deficiencies on the part of students in critical domains of knowledge, as well as in language development. Educational practice for racial and ethnic minorities has been specifically tailored to overcome these perceived deficiencies, both in the realm of content as well as in terms of instructional strategies.

Two fundamental critiques can be made of this approach to the education of language minority children: (1) it is based on false premises with respect to the knowledge base of the child; and (2) the instructional procedures it employs are not only ineffective but self-defeating, since they actually make learning more difficult instead of easier, as intended.

The latter point is raised by a number of researchers, including Cummins (1984), who argues forcefully that breaking down concepts to their smallest component actually makes the learning task more difficult. Cummins's argument is based on evidence that a context-reduced learning environment actually presents a more difficult task for the learner than one that is contextually enriched. Instructional approaches that are based on breaking down instruction into small, discrete units, therefore, are probably increasing the difficulty level of the task (not to mention decreasing the motivational basis for attending to the activity) by depriving the learner of an adequate contextual environment for meaningful comprehension rather than aiding the learner by focusing narrowly on fundamental, basic skills (Cummins 1984: 140–141). Furthermore, for limited-English-proficiency (LEP) students, instructional approaches that are grounded in procedures requiring extensive two-way interaction are more likely to create the kind of context-embedded learning environment that provides maximal support for comprehension. One-way exchanges (for example, from teacher to learner) characterize the predominant interaction pattern of many conventional classrooms that rely heavily on direct teaching to transmit knowledge. LEP students working within these learning environments often find themselves engaged in tasks they do not fully comprehend. Teachers who follow instructional procedures that encourage two-way interaction (e.g., through cooperative learning and/or small-group problem-solving tasks) appear to be providing their students with a contextually rich environment that enhances understanding and that provides cognitive support for tasks that require higher cognitive involvement on the part of the learner. In addition to enhancing communication, therefore, these learning environments lead students into experiences that encourage a higher degree of cognitive functioning—ultimately a necessity for successful involvement in the curriculum in upper elementary school and beyond (DeVillar and Faltis 1991).

Deficit-based models for educational intervention are wrong for all minority children, but they are particularly wrong in the case of language-minority children because they do not lead to the kind of learning environment that facilitates second-language acquisition. They are also wrong, however, because they are founded on an erroneous conception of the child.

The points raised here are not merely polemical—they are at the heart of effective instructional practices for language-minority children. No educational approach can be successful over the long term if it is based on an erroneous and unflattering perception of the capabilities of learners, and if it is not grounded in a full respect for the student's home culture and community values. Perhaps the best way to illustrate this point is to describe an ethnographic research study that sets out to document the knowledge base existing in one specific bicultural community and then explores instructional options available that are grounded in the social and cultural *funds of knowledge* present in that community. The study, one of four included in the Innovative Approaches Research Project (IARP) funded through the U.S. Department of Education, is entitled "Community Knowledge and Classroom Practice: Combining Resources for Literacy Instruction." The goal of the study is to explore culturally appropriate means for immersing language-minority students in literacy activities, and the philosophy guiding the project is that "all communities contain a wealth of knowledge and skills which can be recognized and used by schools to facilitate instruction" (Moll, Vélez-Ibáñez, and Greenberg, cited in Rivera and Zehler 1990: 9). Based on this philosophy, a team of ethnographers set out to document the extensive funds of knowledge in a broad array of domains within the target community, and to classify these funds in a manner that makes them understandable and accessible to practitioners. Drawing on their findings, the researchers then met with classroom teachers to elaborate strategies that might take advantage of the vast reservoirs of knowledge that students possess, yet that under conventional approaches had been ignored by the school since they were neither part of the established curriculum nor known by the educators responsible for designing instruction for these learners. From this collaborative effort between researchers and teachers, two fundamental innovations were identified and implemented: First, classroom interaction patterns were altered away from teacher-centered interaction to more student-centered patterns; and second, the funds of knowledge available in the students' homes were utilized as a basis for curriculum content (Rivera and Zehler 1990: 11). The outcomes of these modifications are still being investigated, but preliminary results appear to be extremely encouraging (Moll 1990).

This study provides a particularly useful backdrop for discussing reconceptualization of instruction for language-minority students, because it illustrates a number of themes that are prevalent in studies focusing on effective instructional practices for this group. The guiding assumption of the study is that enhanced comprehension afforded by incorporation by the community's funds of knowledge into curriculum design will lead to increased achievement outcomes. Instructional practices are characterized by increased student–student interaction, and are grounded in closer collaboration between teachers and parents in the educational enterprise. In order to effectively incorporate the students' funds of knowledge into the instructional process, artificial boundaries between subject areas (for example, science, math, social studies, reading, writing) are broken down as the instructional activities themselves provide a basis for learning across content areas, following an integrated approach to the curriculum. Preliminary results suggest enhanced communication at all levels: between teacher and parents, among students in the classroom as they work cooperatively on common goals, and most importantly, between individual students and the learning process they are engaged in.

The instructional process described in the above study implies a different kind of teaching role than what has commonly been assumed in conventional teacher education programs. It is unlikely that standard university coursework can deliver that kind of preparation that is needed to implement this educational approach; hence, the question that remains is how teacher education programs might restructure their process to better prepare future teachers for these altered instructional roles.

Preparing Teachers for Culturally Diverse Schools

Despite the optimism and excitement posed by our advancing state of knowledge with respect to more fully meeting the educational needs of language-minority students, there is reason to believe that the nation's schools are ill-prepared to deal with the increasing diversity of students. Although it is difficult to obtain direct evidence to support this assertion, there is substantial indirect evidence to indicate that neither teachers who are currently teaching in the schools nor those who are currently being trained as our future teachers have been adequately prepared to deal with substantial cultural diversity in the classroom. According to a recent report on the state of Hispanic education, only 2.9 percent of public school teachers in the United States are Hispanic, based on 1990 data (National Council of La Raza 1990). Critical shortages of bilingual teachers have been consistently reported throughout the nation for many years, and it is estimated that fewer than 10 percent of children who could benefit from bilingual instruction actually receive it (Faltis, 1991, p. B2). In the Los Angeles Unified School District, where the student body is 80 percent minority, the teaching staff is 70 percent white (Center for Bilingual Education & Research 1990: 1).

Although these data provide only indirect evidence of inadequate institutional response to the needs of minority children in general, and language-minority children in particular, when these figures are paired with the extremely poor outcomes described at the outset of this chapter, a pattern of educational neglect appears quite evident. Behind this pattern lies a whole history of undereducation for marked groups within our society, as well as institutionalized obstacles to educational access for racial and ethnic minority groups in this country. Given these societal factors for differential educational outcomes that exist between majority and minority groups, it may be unreasonable to expect that classroom teachers alone can significantly alter achievement results. Yet anecdotal evidence suggests that individual schools and, indeed, individual teachers who implement effective strategies can be rewarded with exemplary results.

Dealing with Cultural Diversity in Teacher Education

The question of how best to prepare teachers to deal effectively with education in pluralistic schools is a very complicated one, particularly given the constraints imposed by universities on teacher education programs. Nevertheless, one thing is clear: Coursework, in and of itself, is insufficient to accomplish the desired goal, for future teachers are not likely to restructure their classrooms for increased interaction and for cooperative modes if they themselves have had no such experiences. Indeed, "it is counterproductive to lecture about group work in a teacher training course; training must itself provide ample opportunity to experience group work. It is unrealistic to hope that language teachers will help students sharpen their learning-to-learn strategies unless they themselves have had training in learning how to learn. . . . And it is foolish to believe that . . .teachers will be able to convey to students the need for active involvement with authentic materials drawn from many disciplines and sources unless in their teacher training program they have sampled a wide range of exciting, cross-disciplinary activities and materials" (Geddes, Sturtridge, Oxford, and Rax 1990: 85).

The relative ineffectiveness of theory alone, in the absence of concrete demonstrations and/or practice sessions, is supported by research on inservice teacher training. One study found that only 5 to 10 percent of teachers applied new skills in their classrooms that were presented by theory only, whereas 90 percent of teachers applied new skills that were presented through demonstration, practice, and individual coaching (Joyce and Showers 1982, cited in Kwiat 1988).

In conceptualizing teacher education strategies that might lead to an improved delivery system for meeting educational needs of language-minority students, it appears clear that both innovative coursework as well as additional training experiences outside the university are required in order to accomplish the desired results. At the University of Texas at San Antonio (UTSA), a number of alternatives have been explored over the past three years in an effort to implement a more experiential approach to bilingual and ESL teacher education. These changes can best be described within two broad categories: (1) innovations in university coursework, and (2) field experiences.

Coursework

University coursework can be quite effective, if properly conceived and delivered, in presenting theoretical frameworks and research principles that support innovative practices. In the specific case of language-minority students, it is possible to develop through coursework a powerful rationale for a whole set of effective practices for this target group, based on sound interpretation of current research and theory. Specifically, three areas in particular need to be stressed in order for future teachers to effectively participate in the kind of instructional innovations implied by contemporary research: *(a)* creating cooperative modes of learning in the classroom; *(b)* integrating the curriculum for cross-disciplinary learning activities; and *(c)* achieving high levels of two-way interaction in bilingual contexts that are characterized by differing levels of language proficiency among students. Each of these areas constitutes a fundamental element for reconceptualizing instruction along the lines described above, and each has a sound theoretical base. Yet each of these is difficult to describe apart from concrete examples, and none of the three is likely to be implemented in the absence of an experiential basis for understanding what is involved from a procedural standpoint.

In an effort to explore the potential benefits of an experiential approach to teacher education through formal university coursework, an experimental methods course was developed for bilingual and ESL teachers during the Spring of 1987. The key defining characteristics of this course are: (1) it is conducted almost fully in Spanish (despite the inclusion of ESL teachers with limited Spanish proficiency in the class); (2) it utilizes cooperative learning procedures, with students of high and low Spanish proficiency deliberately grouped together to work on common problem-solving tasks; (3) students spend significant amounts of time engaged in intensive small group problem-solving tasks in math, science, and social studies, drawn from the bilingual curriculum; and (4) students are required to keep a dialogue journal in Spanish of their learning experiences. One of the primary goals of the course is to expose students to the kinds of models they must implement in order to maximize two-way interaction and dual language development in the bilingual classroom—in particular, content-based second-language instruction (in this case, through Spanish), as well as small-group activities as a means for greatly increasing two-way interaction within a classroom. A concurrent goal is to address separate training needs with respect to language development for both bilingual and ESL teachers: for bilingual educators, the goal is to increase proficiency in academic Spanish as it relates to the three basic subject areas (math, science, and social studies); for ESL teachers the goal is to develop functional proficiency in Spanish, as well as to develop (experientially) an empathy for the difficulties encountered by LEP students when dealing with academic concepts through their weaker language, English. Finally, students are directly exposed (experientially, since they are actually doing it regularly as a part of the ongoing class activities) to major innovative practices that in previous courses they may have only read about—in particular, cooperative learning an dialogue journals. Data have been collected on this experimental course over a three-year period (Milk 1990), and results, based on both test data and participant reactions, have been quite favorable.

A more recent example of how prevalent themes encountered in the professional literature can be effectively illustrated through innovative course design at the university level is provided by a current externally funded project which seeks to substantially increase the level of educational leadership within bilingual education. The project, titled "Educational Leadership in Bilingual Education" and supported by funds from the U.S. Department of Education, is currently developing a three-course sequence for principals/administrators in schools with heavy LEP populations, together with graduate students specializing in bilingual education, designed to create model learning environments for language-minority students. In the first course, fundamental theory related to linguistic and cultural issues, as well as research on effective practices, is presented. The second course, offered during the summer in an intensive institute format, seeks to provide an experiential base for developing a cooperative learning approach to restructuring learning experiences in culturally pluralistic contexts. The third and final course in the sequence provides participants with an opportunity to develop a funding proposal for a model bilingual school, reconceptualized and restructured to reflect the innovations presented in the first two courses. One of the principal innovations of this project, from the perspective of prevailing university-based teacher education practices, is that administrators and bilingual education teachers are involved in the same set of courses over a twelve-month period, working toward a common goal: more effective educational outcomes for the LEP students who they commonly serve. Previous university programs (primarily oriented toward certification and degree requirements in completely different areas), have provided totally separate courses for administrators and teachers. The collaboration that will be required in local school districts between administrative and instructional components in order for current efforts in site-based management to function effectively is being experientially modeled through this project, and it is hoped that substantial interaction between administrators and teachers will lead to enhanced collaboration within the schools on issues related to effective practices for language-minority students. A research component has been incorporated into this training project in order to track the results (both intended and unintended) of these efforts.

Fieldwork

The effectiveness of university coursework as a training device can be increased by incorporating demonstrations as well as by employing experiential techniques such as simulation and role-playing. But there are limitations to what can be achieved within university classrooms, and field experiences are a necessary component of any fully developed training program that strives to truly create an innovative mindset among trainees. Although field experiences can provide models of good instruction, they are perhaps even more valuable in accomplishing other goals related to cultural awareness, as well as in exploring the need for close collaboration between school and home and highlighting the critical role played by parents in the educational enterprise. Two kinds of field experiences have been developed at UTSA in conjunction with the bilingual teacher education project: *(a)* participation in cultural events, and *(b)* involvement in a cooperating bilingual school.

Because many of the students preparing to become bilingual teachers do not fully share the cultural experiences of their future students (despite sharing their ethnicity), it has, for many years, been a requirement for participants in externally funded training projects to attend a broad variety of cultural events in the community. These events—which include such experiences as attending a bilingual play in the cultural arts center in the barrio or attending a *conjunto* music festival—often serve to enhance the university students' understanding of the history and culture of bilingual students and also serve as a window toward understanding more fully the world as seen through the eyes of the community they will serve.

A quite different kind of field experience is exemplified by student involvement, in a variety of different forms, in a cooperating bilingual school designated by the program. Currently, two schools with heavy concentrations of LEP students work closely with faculty and students in the teacher education program to provide a variety of opportunities for student involvement on an ongoing basis. In their early stages of professional development, students are assigned to a specific teacher and engage in classroom observation and after-school tutoring. As they become more experienced, they may function as teacher assistants and prepare lessons or working with small groups of students. Advanced trainees who choose to do so are encouraged to work with parents in special courses designed to respond to needs that are identified periodically through needs assessments. Currently, trainees conduct classes in ESL for parents, as well as small group sessions focusing on topics such as Spanish literacy, citizenship preparation, or concepts related to homework assignments that the children bring home from school. Based on trainees' evaluations, the field experiences encountered at the cooperating schools constitute one of the most meaningful requirements for participants in the UTSA teacher education project (Liberty 1989).

Conclusion

The teacher education profession has been under assault in recent years from a variety of quarters. The public at large, dissatisfied with the outcomes of public schooling, has questioned the efficacy of teacher education programs that prepare the educators responsible for public education in our nation. Policymakers, searching for politically acceptable themes in constructing educational reform legislation, have found teacher education to be a fairly safe target for directing concrete initiatives that appear to address concerns commonly held by observers from outside the field of education. These initiatives have addressed questions related to both quality as well as quantity. Exit tests required of teacher education graduates prior to receiving state certification relate to concerns about adequate standards, as well as other qualitative issues related to perceived lack of substance in teacher education courses. Alternative certification programs, on the other hand, respond to concerns about inadequate numbers of graduates being produced in areas of critical need, such as bilingual education, math, science, and special education.

In addition to these general questions about effectiveness and efficacy of teacher education as a whole, specific questions have emerged about the lack of vision in teacher education programs in responding adequately to the profound demographic shifts currently exhibited in public school enrollments throughout the country. Minority educators have long been critical of teacher education courses that appear to assume, in the presentation of educational theory and practice, the existence of some prototypical average middle-class child who is monolingual and who reflects the cultural values and worldview of the mainstream. This assumption is damaging to both teachers and students: it not only leads to poor preparation of teachers for the instructional settings they are likely to encounter, but it also contributes to an inadequate educational response to the needs of nonprototypical, nonmainstream students who, in many instances, will constitute a majority of the pupils that entry-level teachers are likely to find in their classrooms.

More recently, mainstream educators who are looking towards the future have begun to criticize teacher education for its lack of vision in responding to the changing realities of our nation's international posture. Specifically, there is a concern that our educational system does not prepare students for a world in which the ability to work cooperatively within groups and to collaborate with others who come from different backgrounds will be an essential skill in both public and private life. Nor does the curriculum of our public schools prepare students to incorporate and connect knowledge from a variety of sources, integrating skills and concepts in the construction of appropriate answers to complex questions. Moreover, our current teacher education programs do not deal realistically with issues of bilingualism and multiculturalism that currently exist in our society, nor do they provide our teachers with the learning experiences needed to effectively promote among their future students the kinds of skills, knowledge, and attitudes that relate to successful functioning in an interdependent, interconnected world. These goals can only be partially achieved through the redesign of teacher education coursework; they must inevitably include a substantial field component that requires future educators to experience directly the implications of living, learning, and working in a pluralistic society.

References

American Council on Education (1991). Hispanic educational attainment low, ACE status report shows. In *Higher Education & National Affairs, 40*(2), 3–8.

Center for Bilingual Education Research (1990). Minority teacher shortage. *El Portavoz, 2*(2), 1.

Cortes, C.E. (1986). The education of language minority students: A contextual interaction model. In *Beyond language: Social & cultural factors in schooling language minority students.* Los Angeles: Evaluation, Dissemination and Assessment Center at California State University, Los Angeles, 3–34.

Cummins, J. (1984). *Bilingualism and special education: Issues in Assessment and Pedagogy.* Avon, England: Multilingual Matters.

DeVillar, R. and C. Faltis. (1991). *Computers and cultural diversity: Restructuring for school success.* Albany, N.Y.: State University of New York Press.

Faltis, C. (1991). We need scholarships and other incentives to attract prospective schoolteachers into bilingual education. *The Chronicle of Higher Education, 37*(22), B2.

Geddes, M., G., Sturtridge, R.L. Oxford, and H. Raz (1990). Teacher training: Rationale and nine designs. In D. Crookall and R.L. Oxford (Eds.), *Simulation, Gaming, and Language Learning.* New York: Newbury House, 81–89.

Kwiat, J. (1988). Peer partnerships: Cooperative, collaborative learning for teachers of limited English proficiency students. *Linguathon, 4*(2), 1–2.

Liberty, P. (1989). Annual evaluation report: Academic year 1988–89. Report submitted to Bilingual Education Teacher Training Project, Division of Bicultural-Bilingual Studies, The University of Texas at San Antonio, November, 1989.

Matthews, F. (1991). Special report: Recruitment and retention. *Black Issues in Higher Education,* January 31, 1991, 8–47.

Milk, R. (1990). Preparing ESL and bilingual teachers for changing roles: Immersion for teachers of LEP children. *TESOL Quarterly, 24*(3), 407–426.

Moll, L. (1990). Community knowledge and classroom practice: Combining resources for literacy instruction. Presentation at 1990 Annual Meeting of the American Educational Research Association, Boston, April 18, 1990.

National Council of La Raza (1990). *Hispanic education: A statistical portrait 1990.* Washington, D.C.: National Council of La Raza.

Rivera, C. and A. Zehler (1990). Assuring the academic success of language minority students: Collaboration in teaching and learning. Report of The Innovative Approaches Research Project. Arlington, Virginia: Development Associates.

Valdivieso, R. (1990). Demographic trends of the Mexican-American population: Implications for schools. *ERIC Digest,* EDO-RC-90-10, September, 1990. Charleston, W.V.: Appalachia Educational Laboratory.

▼ 5 ▼

Mentoring, Peer Coaching, and Support Systems for First-Year Minority/Bilingual Teachers

MARGARITA CALDERON

The continued shortage of teachers to meet the ever-increasing limited-English-proficient student population in the coming decade is clear. It is critical, then, for school districts with language-minority student populations to identify the most effective and efficient means to recruit, retain, and empower the required pool of minority and/or bilingual teachers. For this purpose, school districts can systematically establish staff development programs to train experienced support teachers, principals, and supervisors to assist beginning teachers during their first year of teaching.

The Theoretical Framework

The importance of minority teacher induction has been documented, and resources are being devoted to induction programs designed to assist novice teachers (Houston and Calderón 1990–91). A number of studies have contributed to the understanding of the concerns of beginning teachers (Bolam, Baker, McMahon, Davis and McCabbe 1977; Grant and Zeichner 1981; Howey and Bents 1979, Huling-Austin, Barnes and Smith 1985; Huling-Austin and Murphy 1987; McCaleb 1984; McDonald 1980; Newberry 1977; Ryan 1970; Tisher 1978; Veenman 1984; Zeichner, 1983). However, fewer studies have

The author would like to acknowledge and thank Dr. Susana Mata and Ms. Alicia Parra for their contributions to this article and to the direction, management and evaluation of the YISD Minority/Critical Shortage Beginning Teacher Project.

117

been documented that investigate the effects of specific induction interventions, and very little research has been initiated to test the cumulative effects of specific induction programs (Huling-Austin and Murphy 1987). Even fewer studies have looked at naturally occurring exchanges between mentors and teachers to study the effectiveness of communication about teaching (Little 1990). Most importantly, minimal attention has been given to study beginning minority teachers and/or beginning bilingual teachers (Calderón 1990).

Barriers to Successful Teaching

The first year of teaching is the most critical year for classroom teachers (Gálvez-Hjornevik 1985; Bush 1978). The conditions under which a teacher carries out the first year of teaching have a strong influence on the level of instructional effectiveness, on the attitudes that govern the teacher's behavior over a career, and on the decision whether or not to continue in the teaching profession. In this crucial year, beginning teachers engage in either a successful and rewarding experience or a painful, frustrating, and terminal one (Compton 1979: 23).

Lortie (1975) finds that teaching seems to be the only profession where "the beginner becomes fully responsible from the first working day and performs the same tasks as a 25-year veteran." This "sink-or-swim" situation can be demoralizing in a context where teachers are not encouraged to help each other or to form support groups for continuous growth. Generally, beginning teachers fear being thought incompetent if they request assistance from their more experienced peers (Newberry 1977). Unless a positive and collaborative ecology is created, even experienced teachers will hesitate to offer assistance to beginners for fear of appearing to interfere. This has been particularly evident where the mentor was not a minority (Calderón and Mata 1990). Majority teachers reported shying away from giving constructive technical feedback for fear of sounding paternalistic, too negative, or pushy.

Beginning minority teachers, particularly those in bilingual settings, are faced with additional challenges. Calderón and Marak (1988) found that their stress is greater because they are responsible for planning two preparations for each content area, conducting lessons in two languages, and maneuvering two or three reading series and sets of text books. Instructional management may become an insurmountable task. This preoccupation is accentuated by feelings of isolation and lack of self-confidence, and a fear of failure (Chapala, Brizzi, Calderón, Mata and Valadez).

In many school contexts, bilingual minority teachers must be able to effectively deal with adversity and lack of community/ society support and receptiveness to bilingual education (Clark and Milk 1983). According to Ada (1986), bilingual teachers are caught between the accepted, traditional classroom practices they are required to follow and the sound theories and research that often contradict those practices. Being members of minority groups that have experienced language oppression and racism, many bilingual teachers lack a sense of empowerment and the confidence that they can succeed as teachers (Cummins 1989).

Based upon the above findings and demographics, and recognizing that the beginning minority teacher is faced with many unique teaching challenges, the Ysleta Project in El Paso, Texas, was designed and implemented. The project also has a research component to address the question: "What induction and retention practices work best for minority/critical-shortage teachers and under what conditions?" The Ysleta Independent School District had a particularly strong interest in this study—over 50 percent of its teaching workforce in the next five years will consist of new teachers, of whom at least 50 percent will be minority. The overall goal of the project was to design an effective prototype for the education and retention of beginning minority/critical-shortage teachers. The project's design, training components, and two-year results are described in this chapter.

Program Design

The project was based upon studies of mentoring and beginning teacher induction programs, research on peer-coaching and effective schools, staff development programs, implementation of change, and the education of language-minority students. The project's goals were to

1. Design and implement a training program with follow-up support systems for mentor and novice teachers for the purpose of enhancing the quality and retention of first-year minority teachers

   2. Design and implement a support network and a dissem-
       ination system with seven other projects on mentoring
       that were funded by the Texas Education Agency
   3. Document and study the implementation of the training/
       follow-up support program, the effects of that program
       and its products on minority/critical-shortage novice
       teachers and their support teachers

Target Population

Twenty-five mentor and twenty-five first-year minority teachers
participated in the first year of the project. Thirty mentor and
thirty first-year minority teachers were added the second year.
The participants' role was to attend workshops totalling forty
hours and as many workshops as they needed on instructional
strategies; conduct peer observations and peer-coaching sessions; keep interactive journals; comply with all the project
requirements and activities, and comply with the project evaluation paperwork and video taping.

Methodology

The project utilized both quantitative and ethnographic approaches. The treatment groups of fifty (Year 1) and sixty (Year
2) had equivalent control groups of fifty and sixty not participating in the program. The quantitative data collection consisted of pre- and post-tests on instructional and coaching/
mentoring knowledge; teacher attitudes towards coaching;
background factors and experiences surveys; teachers pre- and
post-formal appraisals by principals and supervisors; teachers'
evaluations of all workshops and activities; and interviews and
retention data. This enabled a broader view of the project and
the organizational structures that enhanced or restricted implementation. These data were triangulated with evaluation
data gathered by the Intercultural Development Research Association, which conducted its own evaluation of each of the
eight mentor projects funded throughout the state.
   A more naturalistic study took place at the micro level. Video
recordings of mentors and novices teaching and coaching/
mentoring were analyzed for their interaction patterns and
content protocols. Interactive journals and partners' coaching
logs were also analyzed. These were complemented with teacher

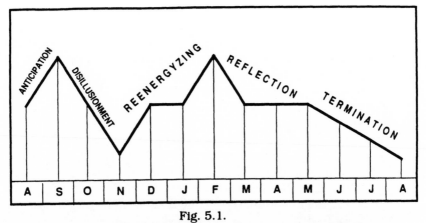

Fig. 5.1.
First year of teaching for teachers without support system.

interviews and ethnographic notes of the discussions at the workshop sessions.

Pairs of teachers were video taped in the following sequence: (1) the preconference; (2) the mentor teacher modeling the strategy in her/his classroom; (3) the beginning teacher conducting the same strategy in her/his own classroom; and (4) the postconference, where they analyzed each others coaching logs and set goals for the next cycle of peer-coaching.

Results

What Determines Termination or Looking Forward to the New School Year?

During the first year of teaching, beginning minority/bilingual teachers go through a typical pattern of unrealistic expectations, disillusionment, reflection, and reality checks that end in either termination or anticipation of the new school year. Figures 1 and 2 illustrate the ups and downs during critical times in the year. These fluctuations seem to dovetail with the patterns found in a study on experienced teachers attempting to implement new teaching strategies they had learned that summer (Calderón 1984). The fluctuations also seem to dovetail with events in the schools, enabling us to predict what is happening to the teachers, the types of problems they are encountering, and their mood swings as they attempt to cope. A typical pattern is illustrated below:

August. Beginning teachers come to the work place with great expectations and an anticipation of many positive things to come. For many, it is their first full-time job. It is a "professional" job, unlike the part-time menial jobs they held all through college in order to make it this far. They hold romantic notions of what teaching is and how they will impact upon the lives of their linguistic minority students and perhaps even the lives of their students' parents. They are ready to change the world. However, reality soon sets in with a multitude of problems. Many immediate problems have to do with classroom management, discipline, and other in-classroom factors. However, out-of-the-classroom problems seem to have a greater positive or negative impact. These are: the type of bilingual or pseudo-bilingual program at the school, administrative support for the program, peer status and amount of peer support, availability of instructional resources, and the type and combination of students assigned to the teacher (e.g., lower-level students, problem students, three or four reading levels). The most common problems identified by beginning teachers and their typical questions are further described in the Mentoring/ Coaching Topic section below.

September/October. When their problems are not resolved and their questions go unanswered, disillusionment sets in. First, some teachers are finding out that what they learned at the university is practically irrelevant. Other teachers feel that the school setting is one where the status quo predominates and works against student and teacher empowerment. They are now convinced that outmoded teaching practices are rewarded and creative, innovative teaching is threatening to their powerful colleagues. Second, kid germ-warfare has invaded and they themselves are fighting off all types of colds they never knew existed. Third, their first paycheck went to pay loans and buy materials for bulletin boards, so there is hardly any money left to last until the end of the month.

November/December. All aspects of a teacher's life have probably hit rock bottom around November. Report cards, holiday activities, parent conferences, standardized testing, inservice workshops and conferences—all converge to keep the novice from implementing lessons that take so long to prepare. Fortunately, Thanksgiving comes along and rest, recuperation, loved ones, and reflection help the teachers get back on their feet. Acknowledging that the semester is almost over, teachers find a surge of new energy and commitment. Christmas vacation helps even more.

January. Renewal and rebirth come in January. This is also the time when students surprise teachers. Out of the blue, Juanito starts speaking English, Tran can decode, Lisa knows how to multiply! All the teacher's efforts have finally paid off!

February. The euphoric state lasts probably until February, when it is replaced by fear and threat of incompetence. Insecurities set in again with talk of standardized testing coming up, teacher evaluations, end of the year accountability. Soon, "there aren't enough days in the week to teach everything my students haven't learned!"

March/April. All thoughts are turned inward and teacher stress increases markedly. Teachers begin to reflect upon the future. "Should I stay in this school?" "Would another grade level be better?" "Should I quit altogether?" "Should I just stop trying so hard?" "How do the other teachers get away with all this, anyway?"

May. By now the teacher has made a decision—to continue or to terminate. Termination can take one of several forms. Sometimes the least harmful form of termination is the physical termination from teaching when the teacher decides to leave the profession altogether. However, there are more harmful ways of terminating: 1) *stagnation*—where the teacher decides to stay at a level of homeostasis, guarded from any threats to his or her sense of well-being by becoming very passive in nature, totally obscure, and withdrawn; 2) *frustration*—where the teacher wants to quit one minute and stay the next ("If only. . . ." is a common phrase); and 3) *apathy*—where the teacher takes on a very negative view of teaching, of her or his students, and of the whole schooling system, and becomes a negative force in faculty meetings, workshops, and (worst of all) to her or his students.

While figure 5.1 plots the road to termination when teachers are left on their own, figure 5.2 plots the road for teachers participating in a quality support system. Although supported teachers experience the same hurdles and problems as any

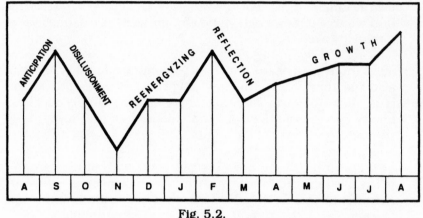

Fig. 5.2.
First year of teaching for teachers with support system.

other beginning teacher, the difference is that there is someone
to help them during those critical moments. Supported teachers tend to end their first year in positive anticipation toward
the next year.

The support system that the teachers with positive outcomes experienced consisted of a year-long series of workshops,
meetings, peer-coaching cycles, and school-based activities
that supported both beginning and mentor teachers. The key
elements of that support system and teachers' views are interwoven here, as they were in the development of this model.

The Training Process

The process for the training program consisted of the following
interrelated elements:

1. Presentations followed by the study of the theoretical basis or the rationale of effective school correlates, teaching methods, coaching, and reflective teaching
2. The observation and experiencing of demonstrations of
   effective instructional practices
3. Practice with feedback of new communicative strategies
   and teaching behaviors at the workshops
4. Reflection activities followed by discussion of application and formulation of action plans
5. Synthesis and debriefing at the end of each workshop

Cooperative learning techniques such as Jigsaws, team-building, dramatization, role-playing, team products, Group Investigation, Roundtable, Write-Around, Think-Pair-Share, and others were used to conduct the training sessions. Cooperative learning was selected for the staff development activities for the purpose of accelerating the acquisition of knowledge, team unity and cohesiveness, and the development of trusting relationships.

Training for Instructional Content

The topic "Educational Needs of Diverse Student Populations" guided one component of the training content. Specific topics dealing with instruction of language-minority students were presented through the district staff development program. Beginning teachers also had a choice of sessions on reading in the primary language, ESL, and many other related topics for further enhancing the teaching skills they needed.

The second component dealt with beginning teacher survival skills, the basic how to's: how to hold a parent conference, order materials, get an advance until the first paycheck arrives, make the first paycheck last until the end of the month, etc. These will be discussed further in the coaching section.

As required by the funding agency, the third component of the training content also had to include effective schools research and center on the following correlates:

1. Clear instructional focus
2. High expectations and standards
3. Safe and orderly climate
4. Frequent monitoring of student achievement
5. Active parent involvement
6. Principal as Instructional Leader

(Steller 1988)

Cooperative learning strategies were used at the workshops to present and help teachers learn and apply implications of effective schools correlates and effective instruction for language-minority students. After studying the content, teachers remained in groups for discussion of classroom application and problem solving. After each activity a debriefing session was help to process the cooperative structure that was used with them and to find relevance to their own classroom use. Thus, at each session, teachers were able to learn several things: (1) effective instruction for language-minority students, (2) effective school correlates, (3) how to use cooperative learning strategies in their classroom, and more importantly (4) how to reflect, debrief, and further enhance critical thinking.

Training for Peer Coaching and Mentoring

The coaching/support component was organized around the following premises: Coaching is a learned skill and subsumes the art of effective communication. "Coaching is at least as difficult as the introduction of new teaching practices, and both are more difficult than we would like to think" (Bird and Little 1983).

Mentoring/Coaching Topics

Mentoring and coaching topics were organized into two categories: instructional and personal/social (see figure 5.3). Little (1990) has found that relations between mentors and teachers generally stress matters of comfort over issues of competence. Mentors provide socioemotional support but appear to exert little influence on teachers' thinking or performance. When teachers and mentors are taught the importance of balancing both comfort and competence, and the structures are in place for them to observe and work on skill development, the quality of mentoring is greatly enhanced.

The Use of Cooperative Learning for Developing Collaborative and Social Skills

Teachers who have reached a high level of success as classroom teachers are the ones most likely to be selected as mentors or support teachers. However, expert classroom teachers may or may not be expert mentors or coaches of other teachers. The art of mentoring and/or peer-coaching requires certain social and collaborative skills. Yet, collaborative skills are not developed in isolation. If teachers have "grown professionally" in isolation for many years, the tasks and skills of working with peers need to be reviewed or developed.

MENTORING AND COACHING TOPICS FOR BEGINNING
MINORITY/BILINGUAL TEACHERS

The following lists containing self-identified areas for attention
and the most common questions asked by beginning teachers
were used to help mentor teachers focus on their mentee's
needs.

a. Instructional

1. Classroom Management/Organization of Instruction. I
   have problems getting classes started promptly, keeping
   students on task, giving suitable rewards, maintaining
   discipline, and establishing routines. I have LEP students, monolingual Spanish and monolingual English
   speaking students, how do I group them? I have two grade
   level combinations and some LEP students, what do I do?
   How do I set up my learning centers? When do I conduct
   ESL? How is the language arts block split between first
   and second language instruction? What is the best time
   allocation for each content area?

2. Delivery of Instruction. Do I present material clearly, in an
   organized and systematic fashion, with appropriate examples and instructional materials? Do I give attention to
   all or most of my students? Are the rest of the students on
   task when I am working with a small group? Is there a
   balance among instructional strategies? Are interests of
   students and cultural background taken into account
   during instruction? Are transitions smooth and rapid?
   Do I provide on-going feedback to students? Do I get the
   message across in both languages?

3. Time Management. I run out of time to accomplish everything planned for the class period. How do I handle paperwork and administrative detail efficiently? I spend too
   much time in the evenings and on weekends grading and
   keeping up with paperwork. I am physically and emotionally drained and very tired. Help me plan my life better.

4. Curriculum Planning. My lesson plans are unrealistic, my
   students finish too quickly (or never finish). Am I cover-
   ing the content accurately? Should I plan for a week or
   one day at a time? How do I modify this curriculum for the
   non-English speakers?

5. Instructional Materials. Do I have all the textbooks, curriculum guidelines, manipulatives, and other materials
   that the rest of the teachers have? I don't have enough
   materials in either language. Where do I obtain those?
   Which other teachers like to share materials? Which materials are best to use with x, y, z?

6. Relationships with Parents. What is the school's protocol in terms of parent conferences, informal contacts, and so forth? How do I conduct my first open-house session? What do I do when a parent is angry? How well do I communicate with non-English speaking parents? With parents from different cultural backgrounds? What should I do to get more parent volunteers? What messages should I send home with the students?

7. Evaluation, Grading, Reporting. Are my tests appropriate? How can I be sure of my students' progress? What are the grade-level expectations and the standards applied to student grades? What's the relationship between grading and evaluation? Am I giving too many grades or not enough? How do I interpret these grades to parents?

8. Teacher Appraisals. How do I prepare for my upcoming appraisal? What happens if . . .? Can I rehearse with you? What have you done before? Do I have to adhere to every item on the instrument?

B. Personal/Social Topics

1. Working with Colleagues. How do I get other teachers to collaborate with me? Who will be a positive influence on me? What is the principal like? What committees should I volunteer for? What formal or informal groups exist in our building? How can I develop a better professional/social relationship with other teachers?

2. Financial Management. What bank do you use? Which retirement plan should I buy into? Where do you shop? How do you make your paycheck last? Where can I get a loan? How much should I spend on classroom materials, student activities, student rewards?

3. Personal Comfort/Peace of Mind. How am I doing so far? What do other teachers say about me? The bilingual teachers? The principal? Will this ever get any easier? I just made the most horrible mistake, will I ever be forgiven? How can I make things better? Am I cut out to be a teacher? How do *you* cope with x, y, z? How can I better address the needs of my students?

Fig. 5.3

Our premise was that in order to know how to coach and provide peer support, collaborative skills had to be developed and transferred into the work place. If an effective coaching program was to take place, trust had to be developed among participating expert and beginning partners. Thus, in order to foster an environment of trust and skills for coaching, collaborative structures were orchestrated where partners worked and learned together at the workshops through activities that combined trust-building, joint experimentation, and appreciation for one another's talents.

Interdependence was built-in deliberately for each teacher-pair through simple activities such as asking them to keep an interactive journal. Only one binder was given to each pair and they were asked to jointly decorate the cover and use it for their journal. Partners were asked to make weekly entries into the interactive journal that was to be placed in the novice's classroom. Coaching logs, which are typically one-way events in most other projects (the mentors keep coaching logs on the novice), were to be filled by both support and beginning teacher during one another's observations. Both mentor and novice attended and role-played the coaching cycle, and practiced giving and requesting help and other important communication protocols.

The Use of Cooperative Learning for Self-Esteem

Typical staff development programs are sometimes so laden with the presenters' content that not enough teacher reflection and expression time is built in. Teachers, just as students, are not empty receptacles that are to be filled with knowledge. Our premise, based on the principle of self-esteem, was to avoid being only transmitters of knowledge and instead strive to become mediators of thinking and to show respect for each teacher's contribution and own ways of constructing meaning.

At the monthly workshops, partners were asked to sit in teams of four or six in order to share successes, problems, questions, and solutions and to learn from each other's experiences in the project. These shared experiences were then synthesized and graphically depicted in a final team product. These team products were shared with the rest of the groups. The products became visual representations of feelings, concerns, ideas, and their reflective thinking during each month. These contributions are the moments teachers learned to value significantly because they gave meaning to their efforts. The sessions also served to identify issues to share with us for readjusting our training sessions. Eventually, the growth of self-esteem and self-confidence in many became evident through the multiple opportunities for teacher reflection and self-expression.

Project Outcomes for Teachers

The first-year evaluation of the project identified outcomes for beginning teachers and mentor teachers. The project helped beginning teachers

- Develop more effective teaching styles
- Enhance their self-confidence in a new profession and continue teaching in the district
- Become better decision makers in their classroom
- Better understand and address children's cognitive, affective, learning and linguistic needs.
- Broaden and deepen their repertoire of teaching strategies and coping mechanisms
- Develop an openness to the continuous study of their craft, and a desire for continued personal and professional growth.

The outcomes reported for mentor teachers were

- Renewed energy for teaching
- Self-confidence and empowerment
- Improved instructional strategies and new teaching strategies
- Leaderships skills
- Mentoring skills
- Continued reflection, self-analysis, and professional growth

Beginning and mentor teachers reported that on a personal level they developed a high degree of trust, honesty, and confidence in each other. They reported that discussions and interactions were open. They learned to accept and receive constructive criticism from each other. Planning efforts were more productive. Overall they developed respect for each other and felt their obligation to each other was strong. Teachers shared their feelings about trust in the following manner:

My mentor pulled me out of a few sticky situations. I trusted her enough to confide my problems and between the two of us, we were able to find a solution.

My beginning teacher and I, both believe in the project. I believe that both of us accepted our responsibilities ungrudgingly! We accepted one another as we were. We relied and depended on each other.

I feel that we trust one another enough to be secure in what we say and do. To my knowledge neither one of us has broken a confidence, nor felt that our input was not valued.

What Teachers Learned from Each Other

It is the exception rather than the rule that beginning minority teachers have a positive mentoring relationship with a seasoned, experienced teacher. Most beginning teachers have a "sink-or-swim" experience where there is little, if any, support from other teachers. The project provided a unique opportunity to alter the experience for beginning teachers who participated.

Most beginning teachers said they primarily learned various teaching methods, how to organize instruction, how to handle discipline problems, and how to keep up with paperwork and district policies. Specific help was received in areas related to special students, cooperative learning strategies, school curricula, and testing procedures. They worked closely with their mentor teacher in making learning centers work for all students, setting up bulletin boards, reviewing and revising lessons, and getting a handle on time management. In addition to the biweekly observations, mentors were on call as needed.

I observed her during her daily routine. Often I went in upon her request at undesignated times, just to observe classroom climate, etc. I was available on a daily basis to provide support. We shared interactive journals. We shared classroom activities and rewards that were not necessarily documented.

Beginning teachers said they appreciated being reminded to be positive and keep students motivated. For example, one beginning teacher said her mentor teacher advised her frequently.

> To be enthusiastic and effective when you teach—it will show
> through and through. Your enthusiasm must be contagious
> to students.

At the same time they were cautioned to maintain a sense of
order and discipline. Some mentor teachers put notes or resources in the beginning teachers' mailboxes on a systematic
basis. One beginning teacher reported how helpful it was that
her mentor teacher advised her every time the seasoned teachers did their annual fall and spring cleaning.

While beginning teachers were learning the formal "tricks
of the trade" of instruction from their mentor teachers, they
were also receiving an informal, more humanistic perspective
on teaching. Mentor teachers were compassionate and understanding of the "trials and tribulations" of the first year of
teaching. The mentor teacher advised the beginning teacher to
have patience and be flexible.

Mentor teachers needs are not dissimilar to those of beginning teachers. They, like most teachers, feel alone and isolated.
The project in some ways forced or coerced mentor teachers
into a mentoring role and broke that isolation. What many
mentor teachers experienced was the development of a peer relationship with their beginning teacher. They found that the
beginning teachers helped *them* as much as they helped the
beginning teachers.

Informal Interactions

The topics beginning teachers and mentor teachers discussed
during and outside a coaching episode were markedly different. As mentioned earlier, their discussions during coaching
episodes focused on instructional matters related to teaching.
However, mentor teachers also provided beginning teachers
with practical, "nitty-gritty" advice on nonteaching tasks such
as grading, clerical tasks, who's who in the lounge, paperwork,
school policy, and working with parents.

Working as a team also created a safe place to talk about
other concerns and feelings. They talked about themselves,
their families, money matters, upcoming holidays or vacations,
or the number of weeks until the school year was over. Their
conversations were not always school related. Sometimes, both
beginning teachers and mentor teachers were under great
stress. During these difficult periods some beginning teachers

shared their deepest feelings and thoughts. They told their mentor teachers their frustrations, fears, and other personal problems. Not surprisingly, mentor teachers also responded with their own set of problems. Their relationship provided a much needed place to "vent" frustrations, fears, and anxieties. They "joked around" a lot when one or the other was feeling stressed.

Formal appraisals of teaching by school site administrators were particularly stressful for most beginning teachers. One beginning teacher (junior football coach) shared his feelings of apprehension and anxiety about his upcoming evaluation with his mentor teacher (head football coach). He was worried about whether he would receive a "good" appraisal. His mentor teacher responded in the following way:

> Evaluations are like getting ready for a big game. You've got to love the pressure of performing or it will blow your mind.

As the mentor teacher expected, the beginning teacher received a positive appraisal.

In summary, these difficult and stressful times further strengthened the bonds between beginning teachers and mentor teachers. They truly became colleagues who shared good times and bad times. Their experiences in many cases made them become the "best" of friends.

Feelings and Perceptions about Peer Coaching

Beginning teachers were asked about their experiences with their mentor teachers during the coaching process. Most beginning teachers were very positive. They felt it was a beneficial learning process. As one beginning teacher described the experience:

> It can be very beneficial. It's ideal to get feedback in a positive manner so that you can improve. Coaching is the interaction between a beginning teacher and an experienced teacher that builds a positive attitude and confidence in teaching strategies.

Most beginning teachers said that listening, guidance, and sharing were the most important elements of coaching. Most received feedback on teaching matters related to curriculum instruction, discipline, and management techniques. Two beginning teachers described their experiences with these coaching elements in the following ways:

> It must be a two-way street—listening and talking. Coaching is sharing and supporting, developing confidence in *me*.

> Coaching is a learning process that is very helpful. Coaching is when you give advice (good or bad) on teaching or handling the overall classroom.

Most beginning teachers reflected on the human dimension of coaching, saying that coaching was beneficial and offered constructive feedback, moral support, and a positive vote of confidence. For many mentor teachers, the entry into the mentoring role was uncertain and difficult. Yet different experiences with their beginning teachers changed them. As they became more involved in the coaching process, their skills, attitudes, and perspectives shifted in a positive way. They learned that the coaching process was complex and required commitment and time. Mentor teachers said effective communication was essential and that conferences (both pre- and post-) were critical.

Most mentor teachers spoke eloquently on the topic of coaching. They stated that coaching entailed helping, guiding the teaching of a lesson, and learning together. It also developed the self-confidence of beginning teachers through positive experiences with teaching and "listening and hearing". More importantly it was learning to give feedback in a nonjudgmental way. Several mentor teachers gave their definitions of coaching.

> Coaching is a way of helping without intimidating. Coaching is sharing.

> Coaching is the ability to listen and use previous experiences to enhance future experiences. Coaching is building a foundation.

> Coaching is providing helpful and constructive feedback. I learned that coaching should be pre-planned and aimed at specific areas.

> Coaching is being a trusting, supportive, and confident teacher and individual.

While for some mentor teachers mentoring or supporting comes quite naturally, others need to learn, step-by-step, how to do it with a modicum of success and quality. Two teachers reported that they wanted to be "left alone" to do things "their" way, without the coaching cycle. They felt it was a burden to observe other teachers. At the training sessions it was obvious that for these mentor teachers it was very difficult to be nurturing and supportive to other adults, even though they had great classroom expertise to share.

This led program developers to question whether the coaching model was incompatible with these mentor teachers who had a particular "personal style," or whether they needed more intensive training and guidance. One mentor teacher, for example, stated in her prequestionnaire that her biggest problem at the schools where she had worked was lack of emotional support and lack of opportunities to observe teaching demonstrations. It was obvious that years of feeling disempowered had taken their toll and she had very little left to give to others. Yet, she stayed with the program.

Interactive Journals

Although half of the teachers had trouble starting journals, by the end of the year all but two teachers had established an ongoing interactive communication link. There was a variety of interpretations and ways of interacting through the journals:

- Some wrote extensive narratives with no space between each other's entries; at a first glance, it was difficult determining where one teacher left off and the other picked up
- Some made beautiful full-page artistic pages, praising specific events or personal positive traits or characteristics of the other
- Some took pictures of their class activities and turned the journals more into joint scrapbooks with captions or narrative

In addition to technical discussions on instruction, classroom management and special student cases, some of the actual narratives were as follows. The comments found in brackets are the author's.

Today I felt very restless. I would do anything to be at a beach somewhere in the Bahamas. I wouldn't mind going alone. I think it would be fun and adventurous. Maybe an island. [mentor teacher replies with a picture of an island and these words:] Sandra's Island—We all have days that we feel like this—Don't let it get you down. Go home, relax and do something that will take your mind off school. . . .

[One mentor teacher wrote the following utilizing the page horizontally so she could frame it with colored decorations:]

Wow! What can I say after reading something like that? I'm dumbfounded, speechless (hard to believe, huh?) If I'm all you say I am, it's because you were there every step of the way—no matter what—as a colleague and friend. You've made my 1st year so special! Yes, it's been a lot of work (for you as well) but it's all been worth it! I hope you know how very much I appreciate all you've done for me and as I've said so many times before, the best part of it all is that I've made such a good friend. I only hope that one day I will follow in the foot steps of one hell of a teacher! Thanks more than you know! [the mentor teacher replies with another elaborate decorated page]

[After long narrations between beginning teacher and mentor teacher on discipline problems and solutions, the beginning teacher sums up the interaction with:] You can say that this year has been a trial year. I don't really know how to say it, but it was like a test to see if I would stay or not. Well, I'm staying. They can throw anything at me and I won't be knocked down or out!

Because the approach for filling out a journal was very open-ended, there was a lot of room for creativity but also a feeling of ambiguity for the teachers that need more structure. Some teachers requested more direction the following year for writing in their journals.

Outcomes of Project Implementation for the District

Perhaps the greatest outcome for the district was a renewed sense of commitment to providing teacher support. Ysleta I.S.D. has a tradition of supporting and "pampering" its teachers, particularly bilingual teachers. This project served to collect those energies into a systematized approach. More important, an ecology for peer-coaching, mentoring, and teacher support systems at the schools and central office has been established. Specific outcomes were listed by the project evaluators as follows:

- A better understanding of the coaching process
- A model for assisting minority/critical-shortage beginning teachers
- A model for assisting any beginning teachers
- A model for the forthcoming induction programs
- A network of collaborative institutions and agencies
- Products such as training materials on mentoring and coaching; brochures and video tapes
- A cadre of in-district trainers

Conclusion

The picture of teacher development that emerges from this study is in accordance with research on students' active learning. That is, students learn more effectively through participation in meaningful joint activities in which their performance is assisted by a more capable peer (Vygotsky 1978; Tharp and Gallimore 1989).

It is also natural for adults to learn together and expand what Vygotsky called their "zone of proximal development." By the mere fact that we put teachers together in cooperative teams, they developed a quicker understanding of the content. What is more important is that they developed an ecology conducive to continued personal and professional growth. Mentor teachers reported that they had learned as much as the beginning teachers. Both partners were experts at something. Mentor teachers had the seasoned experiences of years of teaching and problem solving. Beginning teachers had current knowledge of new teaching strategies and approaches. Each one took turns becoming the "more capable peer." This assisted performance built self-respect and respect for other colleagues.

Although the first year of the project was limited to a five-month implementation period, we came to the realization that, had we used individualized learning or total group lecturing with questions and answers, we would have had problems with coaching. Effective peer-coaching presupposes an established relationship. If that does not exist, the role of the staff developer is to construct the context for meaningful relationships to flourish. Cooperative learning brought teachers closer together even in a short amount of time. It also set the tone for the Year 2 new recruits.

The second-year plan was to add a more sophisticated cooperative learning method called "group investigation" (Hertz-Lazarowitz 1980). Through group investigation, as well as the other cooperative structures, we hope to empower teachers to become continuous researchers, where exchange among peers and cooperative inquiry can be sustained while novice and master teachers study the art of teaching. Group investigation is now being used as a resource for achieving understanding and as a means for communicating both inside and outside the workshop and school setting. The essentially social nature of teaching and learning is being emphasized, along with its power to facilitate thinking. We anticipate that by participating in such interactions, sometimes as an equal member and sometimes as the coach, the mentor teacher can model and explain how to engage in teaching in ways appropriate to the purpose at hand. Capitalizing on Year 1 and Year 2 experiences, Year 3 workshops will begin by sharing teacher reports on the project and video recordings of this year's teachers' coaching cycles; and by having partners share about their relationship, which, as several reported, "will last throughout the years!"

This project demonstrated that both beginning minority teachers and experienced teachers, whether minority or not, can benefit from a planned program of teacher support. For the beginning teacher, the guesswork and pain are relieved by the experienced teacher. For the experienced teacher, a refreshing new look at teaching and a more careful look at language-minority students are vicariously created by the new teacher.

These partnerships are particularly important as more student-centered teaching, such as cooperative learning and whole language, is introduced into schools. Sometimes experienced teachers have great difficulty motivating each other to explore new ways of teaching. As teachers move away from "teacher-proof" materials to more reflective teaching, both new and experienced teachers can give each other support and motivation. The dichotomy of their experiences and views of teaching potentially generate more in-depth discussion, elaboration, and joint exploration than with pairs of experienced teachers who may restrict their divergent thinking because they have both "done it this way" for so many years.

Building a Caring Community of Teachers

The expectation that schools can create successful experiences for minority students without creating successful experiences for minority teachers will be very difficult to accomplish. Schools in general need to work on better goals for the benefit of a teacher's life. Schools need to create a new environment where collaborative inquiry leads to continued growth and learning about minority issues. The conditions, contexts, and purpose for coaching and mentoring at the schools need to be sensitive to the needs of beginning minority teachers. Just pairing teachers together and asking them to coach or mentor will not work. Another thing that surely will not work is to cut back on the training and on the time teachers need to spend together. Another waste of resources and energy is the assignment of one mentor teacher to a group of beginning teachers. One mentor to five or ten or even three beginning teachers will not enable the type of goals, mutual growth, interaction, closeness, and trust that the pairs of teachers in this project accomplished.

The rapidly growing popularity of mentor programs has left implementors with few guidelines and a small body of research as to how to orchestrate these programs. None focus on minority teachers' needs. Many have condescending tones and structures. All are lacking in a mutual benefit, mutual empowerment philosophy and framework. While this project focused on Hispanic minority and Hispanic bilingual teachers, its basic elements cut across cultures. The empowerment of teachers from diverse cultural backgrounds should serve as a worthy point of departure for further research and implementation.

References

Aaronson, E. (1978) *The jigsaw classroom.* Beverly Hills, CA: Sage Publications.

Ada, A.F. (1986) Creative education for bilingual teachers. *Harvard Educational Review, 56,* No.(4), 386–94.

Bolam, R. Baker, K., McMahon, A., Davis, J., and McCabbe, C. (1977). *The 1977 National Conference on Teacher Education.* Bristol, England: University of Bristol, School of Education.

Bush, R. (1978). *The formative years. In the real world of the beginning teacher.* Washington, D.C.: National Education Agency.

Calderón, M. (1984) *Training bilingual trainers: An ethnographic study of caching and its impact on the transfer of training.* Doctoral dissertation, Claremont Graduate School, Claremont, CA.

Calderón, M. & Marsh, D. (1988) Applying research on effective bilingual instruction in a teacher training program. The Journal of the National Association for Teacher Education. *12,* (2), 133–52.

———. (1990) Enhancing the quality and retention of beginning minority and critical shortage teachers. San Antonio, TX: Intercultural Development Research Association.

———. (1990–91) Cooperative learning builds communities of teachers. In *Teacher Education and Practice.* Fall/Winter, *6,* (2), 75–8.

Calderón, M. & Mata, S. (1990) *Beginning teachers evaluation report.* Report submitted to the Texas Education Agency.

Clark, E. and Milk, R. (1983) Training bilingual teachers: A look at the Title VII graduate in the field. *National Association for Bilingual Educators Journal, 8,* (1), 41–53.

Chapala, C., Brizzi, E., Calderón, M., Mata, S., & Valadez, C. (in press). *Options for meeting the bilingual teacher demand.* Sacramento: California State Department of Education.

Compton, R.S. (1979). The beginning high school teachers . . . Apprentice or professional? *American Secondary Education,* 9, 23–29.

Cummins, J. (1989) *Empowering minority students.* California: California Association for Bilingual Education.

Gálvez, D.-Hjornevik (1985). *Teacher mentors: A review of the literature.* Research & Development Center for Teacher Education. The University of Texas at Austin.

Grant, C., and Zeichner, K. (1981). Inservice Support for First-Year Teachers: the State of the Scene. *Journal of Research and Development in Education, 14* (2), 99–111.

Hertz-Lazarowitz, R. (1989). Cooperation and helping in the classroom: A contextual approach. *International Journal of Research in Education,* 13, 1, 113–119.

Houston, W.R. & Calderón, M. (1990–91) Preparing an ethnically diverse teaching force. In *Teacher Education and Practice.* Fall/Winter Vol. 6, No.2, pp. 43–48.

Howey, K.R., & Bents, R.H. (Eds.). (1979) *Toward meeting the needs of the beginning teacher.* Minneapolis, MN: Midwest Teacher Corps Network.

Huling-Austin, L., Murphy, S.C. (1987). *Assessing the impact of teacher induction programs: Implications for program development.* Paper presented at the Annual Meeting of the American Educational Research Association, Washington, D.C.

Huling-Austin, L., Barnes, S., and Smith, J., (1985). *A research based staff development program for beginning teachers.* Paper presented at the Annual Meeting of the American Educational Research Association, Chicago, Il.

Johnson, D.W. and Johnson, R.T. (1986). *Learning together and alone.* 2nd Ed. Inglewood Cliffs, N.J.: Prentice Hall.

Little, L.W. (1990) The mentor phenomenon. In Cazden, C.B. (ed.) *Review of Research in Education.* Washington, D.C.: American Educational Research Association.

Lortie, D. (1975). *School teacher.* Chicago: University of Chicago press.

McCaleb, J.L. (1984) *An Investigation of On-the-Job Performance of First Year Teachers.* College Park, MD: University of Maryland at College Park, Department of Curriculum and Instruction.

McDonald, F., (1980). *The Problems of Beginning Teachers: A Crisis in training (Vol. 1). Study of Induction Programs for Beginning Teachers.* Paper presented at the Annual Meeting of the American Educational Research Association, Washington, D.C.

Newberry, J.M. (1977, April). *The First Year of Experience: Influences on Beginning Teachers.* Paper presented at the Annual Meeting of The American Educational Research Association, New York.

Purkey, S.C. & M.S. Smith. (1983). Effective schools: A review. *The Elementary School Journal,* 83, 4, March, 427–452.

Ryan, K. (ed). (1970). *Don't Smile Until Christmas: Accounts of the First Year of Teaching.* Chicago, Il: The University of Chicago Press.

Steller, A.W. (1988) *Effective schools research: Practice and promise,* Bloomington, Ind.: Phi Delta Kappa Education Foundation.

Tharp, R.G., and R. Gallimore. (1989). *Rousing Minds to Life: Teaching, Learning, and Schooling in Social Context.* Cambridge: Cambridge University Press.

Tisher, R., (ed). (1978). *The Introduction of Beginning Teachers in Australia.* Melbourne, Australia: Monash University.

Trueba, H.T. (1987). *Success or failure? Learning and the language minority student.* New York: Newbury House.

Veenman, S. (1984). Perceived problems of beginning teachers. *Review of Educational Research.* 54 (2), 143–178.

Vygotsky, L.S. (1978). *Mind in Society.* Cambridge, Mass.: Harvard University Press.

Zeichner, K. (1983). Individual and institutional factors related to the socialization of teaching. In G. Griffin and H. Hukill (Eds.), *First year of teaching: What are the pertinent issues?* Austin: The U.T. at Austin, R & D Center for Teacher Education.

▼ Part III ▼
Cultural Diversity in the Classroom

▼ 6 ▼
Cooperative Learning for
Language-Minority Students

RICHARD P. DURAN

Cooperative learning is widely believed to be an intervention capable of improving the socioacademic achievement of all students, including language-minority students (DeVillar and Faltis, 1991, this volume). Research studies indicate that cooperative learning improves the achievement test scores, social integration, and self-esteem of students from a variety of ethnic and racial backgrounds (Kagan 1986). Relatively few studies, however, have focused on language-minority students who are likely to be limited in English language proficiency (Slavin 1990). This paper explores some philosophical, theoretical, and implementation issues arising from using cooperative learning with students from language-minority backgrounds. The views expressed draw from an ongoing empirical study implementing and evaluating a curriculum known as Cooperative Integrated Reading and Composition, or CIRC. This curriculum involves language-minority school children who are enrolled in bilingual education programs in El Paso, Texas, and in the community of Goleta, California, adjacent to Santa Barbara (Prado-Olmos, Durán, and García 1991; Calderón, Hertz-Lazarowitz, and Tinajero 1991).

Cooperative learning involves groups or teams of students jointly carrying out academic learning tasks in a structured manner (Kagan 1985; Johnson, Johnson, and Holubek 1987; Slavin 1990). There is no single model for conduct of cooperative learning, but the method is distinguished from "collaborative learning," which refers in general to students working in

*This research was made possible through a grant from the Center for Research on Effective Schooling for Disadvantaged Students, Johns Hopkins University

small groups. Cooperative learning is a specialized form of collaborative learning that requires students to fulfill academic task goals following a specified plan for student productivity and student interaction. The success of the group in attaining its task goals depends upon group members helping each other perform a task, and upon each member's development of requisite expertise to contribute to the group. Most cooperative learning methods provide extrinsic rewards, such as certificates of accomplishment to teams attaining goals. Individual student accountability is also acknowledged based on evaluation of independent learning performance, such as scores earned on tests.

Research on the effectiveness of cooperative learning in raising students' achievement test scores identifies group goals and individual student accountability as the most powerful factors affecting achievement, though alternative models to explain the success of cooperative learning have been proposed (Slavin 1989). Alternative models underlying implementation of cooperative learning would seem especially relevant in understanding why and how to implement cooperative learning with language-minority children. An alternative model needs to be grounded in sound educational practices tailored to the linguistic and cultural needs of students, but first it must be grounded in an understanding of the role of schooling in the education of language-minority students.

Cooperative learning alone will not resolve the educational challenges facing language-minority students. It is important for educators to analyze the nature of schooling as an institution and the ways in which schooling assists or attenuates curriculum improvements for language-minority students. Analyses should include attention to important social changes potentially affecting the conduct and quality of education. The rapid increase of language-minority students in classrooms is but one realization of a dramatic shift towards multiculturalism and cultural fusion that is occurring at present in the United States. Rather than becoming more culturally homogeneous, the United States is becoming more heterogeneous as its neighborhoods, community institutions, and schools fill more and more with children from non-European backgrounds. And while it seems contradictory, this increased cultural heterogeneity is spontaneously giving rise to new cultural orientations that synthesize and fuse together elements of diverse cultural heritages, whether of non-European origin or not. We are witnessing a dramatic shift in U.S. society that has tremendous implications for schooling and for making schooling relevant to our children's preparation for life and livelihood in our changing society.

Comparative international studies of education and studies of the success or failure of ethnic minority children in the United States call attention to economic and social power relations that affect the schooling chances of language-minority students (Ogbu and Matute-Bianchi 1986). Increased cultural heterogeneity and cultural fusion do not necessarily translate into economic, political, and social empowerment for language minority groups. With the exception of African-Americans, non European immigrant children and families are more likely than most other U.S. residents to live in poverty and to be socially stigmatized and discriminated against (Report on Education Research 1991). Improving societal conditions of language minority group members cannot be accomplished solely by improving the educational outcomes of language-minority students. However, improved educational outcomes can be helpful—especially if the educational context is attuned to developing students' capacity to view learning as a tool for extended personal and social development.

Cooperative learning can help raise the academic achievement of language-minority children, while at the same time assisting children in developing critical literacy skills that will empower them to increase their participation in schooling. Most importantly, it can help these children discover ways in which schooling and the curriculum are of value in making sense of the everyday world that they encounter out of the classroom. Fundamentally, effective cooperative learning for language-minority students must be more than a set of strategies for efficient management of students' behaviors solely for the purpose of completing discrete academic assignments. Rather, a cooperative learning curriculum must strive to develop the capacities of children to take charge of their own learning as it relates to making sense of their world. One way to strive for this goal is to understand more fully the desired goals of a cooperative learning curriculum. The views that follow explore this goal with regard to cooperative learning in the language arts.

Literacy and Cooperative Language Arts for Language-Minority Students

The putative goal of language arts (and reading) classes for elementary school children is to teach them reading and writing.

Traditionally, "literacy" has been taken to refer to knowledge of how to read and write in a language. Research in sociolinguistics, ethnography of communication, classroom discourse behavior, and bilingual education over the past twenty years has come to question such a narrow view of literacy. This research has spawned development of a broader view of literacy that has important implications for designing a cooperative learning curriculum in language arts and reading. From this perspective, literacy has come to be associated with the notion of *communicative competence*.

Hymes (1972) used the term 'communicative competence' to refer to the full range of social, cognitive, and linguistic skills that underlie knowing how to communicate. A competent speaker, writer, listener, and reader must know a great deal about the grammar and other structural features of a language. Yet this knowledge is insufficient to be able to communicate effectively. The competent user of a language must be able to connect knowledge about language form with interpretation of how to behave and act in real world settings and events. This knowledge of how to behave and act through language is tied to individuals interpreting the *who, what, where, when,* and *why* of the communicative activities they are involved in.

Literacy inherently involves communicative competence. Researchers such as Scribner and Cole (1981) have found that a person's acquisition and use of reading and writing skills are tied to his or her socialization into the cultural activities requiring reading and writing for specific purposes. Reading and writing, therefore, do not exist in isolation from real world events that cast a purpose and social value to their use. From a contemporary perspective on literacy, when students write they presume an audience and shared knowledge with this audience. When students read they attempt to construct ideas and information encoded in writing by other social beings. The term 'discourse community' is used to refer to any social network of persons able to share ideas and meaning through everyday language (Gutiérrez, in press). Discourse communities do more than share language: through the medium of language and through interaction they share in a broad range of understandings about how to interpret experience and how to cope with the world. Members of the same discourse community share (to varying degrees) belief systems about society and culture, and about the roles of community members within society and culture. When students read and write in classrooms, they participate in multiple discourse communities, which shape the meaning they make of the world as they use language. Most importantly, students' reading and writing activities in the classroom shape students' perception of education in their lives (Guttiérez, in press).

Discourse Communities and Paradigms for Teaching, Learning, and Testing

The most immediate discourse community in the classroom is the network of students and teaching staff present in the classroom. This community interacts in activities that are managed by the teacher and that have certain learning objectives. Cooperative learning groups functioning as discourse communities that aid students' learning is the topic of the next section of this paper. Before proceeding to this topic, it is helpful to discuss other discourse communities that affect the teaching and learning of reading and writing in a classroom. It will also be helpful to discuss assumptions made about teaching, learning, and testing that emanate from the society's powerful discourse communities, affecting prevalent educational practices. As will be shown, cooperative learning can represent an alternative paradigm for instruction that can draw on current theory and research overturning previous assumptions about the nature of teaching and learning. This shift has important consequences for educating language-minority students because it can draw more fully on the linguistic and cultural resources that students bring to the classroom.

As students participate in classroom learning activities, they are influenced by discourse communities that set the context for education in the classroom. Teachers themselves have received training that leads them to talk with students about teaching, learning, and testing in specific ways. The use of such terms as 'IQ', 'smart', 'grades', 'worksheets', etc., was learned by teachers through their participation in discourse communities such as teacher training programs empowering teachers as professionals. Other discourse communities encountered by teachers in their previous experiences create beliefs about the capabilities and social characteristics of students from different cultural and linguistic backgrounds. These beliefs come to the fore in the way teachers praise or show recognition of students' classroom performance based on perceptions of students' background. Some teachers have been found to be less responsive to Hispanic children who speak accented English than to Hispanic students who speak unaccented English (Ramírez 1981).

Additional discourse communities affect the climate of instruction in the classroom. School administrators, textbook authors/publishers, legislators, school policy-makers, and classroom curriculum developers create ways of thinking and talking about schooling that become evident both in the way teachers structure classroom activities and how teachers and students communicate to each other in the classroom. One of the most prevalent conceptions of teaching and learning presumed by teachers (and public discourse communities at large) is that good teaching constitutes clearly "transmitting" new knowledge to students who learn by passively receiving and understanding this knowledge (Goodlad 1984; Cuban 1984). According to this view, teachers evaluate students' learning by administering pencil-and-paper tests periodically to assess students' memory and problem-solving knowledge. If students fail to learn under this paradigm, it is because they are academically behind and lack skills that the better prepared and intelligent children already have. Deficits in achievement are considered a *characteristic of children*, not shortcomings in the education system.

Cummins (1986) has attacked this commonly perceived instructional paradigm, citing ways in which it impedes the educational progress of language-minority students. As an alternative, Cummins proposes that language-minority children's instruction emphasize validation of children's background and community, use of constructive learning techniques, and use of assessments to better guide children's true learning needs. The views of Cummins are consistent with teaching and learning as seen from a Vygotskian or sociohistoric perspective.

Sociohistoric Analysis of Teaching and Learning Activities, Discourse Communities, and Cooperative Learning

The sociohistoric school of learning and cognitive development provides a conceptual framework supporting the use of cooperative learning with language-minority students. One important contribution of this approach is that it supports designing language arts and reading instruction so that they empower the learner to benefit from the expertise not only of the teacher but of other students. At the same time, the learner acquires increased control over his or her own learning. In cooperative learning activities, when a teacher is not present it is not always clear which student is viewed by others as the 'expert' to evaluate and guide a groups' problem solving performance (Ford 1991). Cooperative learning groups, as discourse communities in the classroom, need to evolve communication and interaction practices that allow students to analyze and negotiate ways to help each other when there is no clear expert immediately present. Related to this need, students have to develop an ability to revise their learning performances as new feedback on previous learning performance becomes available.

According to the sociohistoric approach, all higher order thinking skills, all language capabilities, are learned through social experience. In the initial stages of learning, the apprentice learner is guided by a more-capable other or teacher who demonstrates competent performance within a target learning activity. The apprentice's *zone of proximal development* (ZPD) represents the ability of the apprentice to demonstrate competent performance with help on a learning task that could not otherwise be performed successfully without help. The more-capable other *mediates* or assists the performance of the apprentice learner by monitoring the progress of the apprentice and by providing hints and cues on problem solving. The ability of the apprentice to successfully perform a task first arises through shared communication with the more-capable other. As the apprentice progresses through his or her ZPD for a task, the apprentice increasingly *internalizes* the hints and cues previously provided by the more capable other. The talk between the more-capable other and the apprentice learner becomes a form of inner speech within the apprentice that gradually comes to be activated without the immediate presence of the more capable other. Eventually, the apprentice develops the ability to perform competently on a problem solving task without need for an appeal to this inner speech. When this stage is reached, learning performance becomes automated.

There is no unique way in which to describe interaction that arises between an apprentice learner and a more-capable other. One such descriptive system drawing on the sociohistoric perspective is presented by Tharp and Gallimore (1988).

They identify a number of strategies that a more-capable other or teacher uses in assisting a student. The strategies can be used to describe ways that a student (or teacher) may help other students in a cooperative learning activity. The helping strategies include

1. *Modeling:* offering behavior for imitation
2. *Contingency management:* arranging rewards or punishments depending upon whether behavior is desired
3. *Feeding back:* providing information on the suitability of behavior relative to a performance standard
4. *Instructing:* telling of information relevant to accomplishing a task; directing a student on how to perform a task
5. *Questioning:* asking for information activating more competent task behavior
6. *Cognitive structuring:* providing explanatory and belief structures that organize and justify problem representation and solution

To these categories we may add a seventh category representing a teacher or more-capable other sharing new information with a learner in a manner that may be distinguished from modeling of a behavior per se:

7. *Informing:* giving of information to a student

The aforementioned categories of teaching strategies provide a useful framework for characterizing ways in which students (or the teacher) may offer aid to other students in a cooperative learning activity. However, students are learners and not just teachers in this activity. Thus it make sense to ask: How do students solicit explicit or implicit help in learning, and how do they signal the receipt of help? The following five strategies exemplify some ways in which students may show such behavior (Durán 1992):

1. *Asking for help:* a student asks a question of other students or a teacher as a means of aiding his or her own problem solving
2. *Demonstrating knowledge:* a student states a knowledge claim or enacts a behavior that he or she judges and signals as appropriate to a problem-solving activity

3. *Testing a hypothesis:* a student states a knowledge claim or enacts a behavior that signals tentativeness
4. *Challenging:* a student expresses a belief that a knowledge claim or behavior by another student or the teacher is inappropriate or questionable
5. *Acknowledging information and feedback:* a student verbally or paralinguistically signals either receipt or uncertainty about assistance provided by other learners or a teacher

Durán (1992) has interpreted students' interaction in CIRC cooperative question/answer activities in terms of the teaching and learning strategies described. In these activities students discuss and negotiate answers to questions based on a story they are reading. After they have negotiated possible answers, students write down their own answer. Questions are designed to require inferences on the part of students, and some questions may be answered in more than one way depending on the student's viewpoint. While it is possible to interpret sequences of turns among students negotiating answers in terms of occurrences of the teaching and learning strategies described above, there are conceptual problems with the approach that need to be considered. Foremost among these problems is that there is often no clear separation of teacher versus learner roles as students interact. The participation structure in the cooperative learning activity more resembles a conversation than a scaffolded, tutorial interaction where an expert guides the performance of a novice learner.

In our implementation of CIRC, students become sensitive to key steps in answering questions that have been *modeled* and *instructed* by a teacher. All teachers teach students that their written answers will need to be complete sentences and that in order to answer a question students first have to agree upon the linguistic form of the initial clause of the answer. The initial clause of the answer response is supposed to repeat the body of the question followed by a transition expression or connector that will be linked to the answer portion of the response. Students, indeed, tend to follow this procedure. Once the beginning of the clause is negotiated, they proceed to discuss answer possibilities. On the whole, students tend to accept the first suitable answer arising in their discussions. Only occasionally do students engage in extended discussions marked by spontaneous *restructuring* or *challenging,* or by extended exploration of a topic. We consider this a weakness in our current implementation of CIRC. This kind of finding, however, is not uncommon in studies of students' small group interaction (Rueda, Goldenberg, and Gallimore 1991).

Cooperative learning activities are likely to involve context-specific participation structures. That is to say, students will follow interaction patterns that have evolved within the particular culture of a classroom, in addition to the way a teacher has set up expectations for the students' interaction. Our experiences with cooperative learning have been that it is possible for students to adhere to the roles and "surface" requirements for behavior in cooperative activities. This adherence can benefit students immediately, but it also may leave room for improvement. One important and very evident immediate benefit is that the students in a cooperative group tend to assume responsibility for their own learning at an early stage in the implementation of cooperative learning. Another early-stage benefit is that cooperative activities are readily seen as scaffolds ensuring attention to certain learning behaviors that are required by the activity and that prove easy for students to learn—e.g., answering questions with complete sentences. The major limitation that we have encountered is that students may need considerable coaching from a teacher on the value of extended interaction. Students will not automatically show evidence of higher order thinking skills in cooperative learning interaction just because the structure of an activity invites use of such skills. A lot of work is required on the part of teachers to show children how to assume appropriate styles and strategies for interactions of this sort.

Topics Arising in
Cooperative Learning Interaction

When students do interact extensively in cooperative learning activities, the conversational orientation of their interactions can enhance their ability to focus individually and collectively on a wide range of cognitive and linguistic issues arising in a learning activity. In our work with CIRC question answering, we have observed students asking for and giving help on a wide range of topics relevant to question answering. As students proceed through the activity they are free to raise points for discussion that emerge and that need clarification or resolution before a question response is finalized. We have found that students spontaneously raise and negotiate such task-relevant topics as:

- The meaning of a question
- The content of a good answer to a question
- Where to look in a text for answer-relevant information
- The kind of story being read and its relation to a question
- The meaning of particular words, phrases, and sentences in a story or question
- Grammatical and other surface features of words, phrases, and sentences
- The relationship of story content to background knowledge of the world
- Progress on completing questions

The above list was derived from topics arising in CIRC question answering and was affected by students' interpretation of how to enact CIRC. Other kinds of cooperative learning curricula and student participation structures would lead to other topics for group negotiation. The important point is that cooperative learning, when effectively pursued by students, can enable students to pursue learning in a flexible manner that is tailored to specific learning needs linked to the main goal of an activity. Further, in bringing up and exploring a topic, students gain practice in verbalizing their own metacognition. They often need to explain and justify why an issue is important to a group's activity, and they have to develop an ability to gauge other group members' understanding of and position on an issue.

Even if students do actively engage each other regarding a variety of learning topics in cooperative activities, there is no guarantee that students in a cooperative learning activity are progressing through an "idealized" ZPD for the topic at hand. If the teacher happens to be present to guide a group, then there is more likelihood that students will get expert help, with a teacher using teaching/helping strategies such as those outlined earlier. In this case students are more likely to progress through their ZPD for the academic subtask at hand. Without the teacher, students have to "co-construct" an expert perspective based upon prior knowledge and familiarity with various teaching and learning strategies in order to guide the discussion. Students' resolution of an issue may or may not be appropriate given standards for knowledge that a teacher or expert would apply. In some instances this may be especially problematic for language-minority children, as when children are attempting to decode or encode an English word or structure needed in their assignment. If 'comprehensible input' from a fluent English speaker is not available, students may not learn from each other efficiently and may make errors in language use (Wong-Fillmore 1985).

The problem of providing timely, accurate feedback to students in cooperative learning activities may be alleviated, though never absolutely resolvable. Students working collectively on their own without adequate teacher mediation may co-construct expertise and answer problems inappropriately. In our CIRC research, we have found that teachers develop supplemental activities to permit students to review and revise some of their misunderstandings. For example, some teachers use a 'numbered heads' activity to help students evaluate their previous answers to story questions. In this procedure, after student groups have completed question answering, they are questioned on a team-by-team basis before the whole class. Students within a team are asked to number off: one, two three, four, or five. The teacher instructs students that he or she will randomly ask students with a given number to read their answer to a question before the entire class. Students within a team are then required to review the appropriateness of an answer to a question. Subsequently, the teacher begins to call on students with a target assigned number to deliver their answer. After the response of a student, the teacher immediately and publicly gives *feedback* to the student and uses additional teaching strategies to guide the student to an appropriate answer. The entire sequence of interaction between the teacher and students can help *instruct* and *model* appropriate responding for students across all teams.

Concluding Comments

Undertaking development and implementation of a cooperative learning curriculum with language-minority students raises concerns beyond those covered in this paper. These include, for example, strategies for transitioning students from non-English to English instruction, and strategies for maintenance of first-language skills. We believe that cooperative learning activities may be especially helpful in the transition from first- to second- language instruction, provided that the activities activate meaning-making in students and can act as scaffolds for thinking. We have observed CIRC students who have been transitioned into English discuss in Spanish what they wish to say in English. Familiarity with how to approach and answer comprehension questions can transfer across languages. Students understand the cognitive and semantic characteristics of a good answer in Spanish and they discuss how to attempt such an answer in English. They discuss in Spanish what they wish to say in English and they test out ways to create the corresponding English statements.

Another area relevant to implementing cooperative learning with language-minority students that deserves study is the social and cultural perceptions that students maintain about appropriate behavior in the classroom. External observers of our CIRC implementation remark that it is somewhat of a shock to see students interacting with such casual informality as they proceed through their group activities. Students at times laugh and joke as they speak to each other, and they may introduce asides that appear to be off-task comments made among friends in playful settings. External observers and our own observations suggest, however, that a climate of informality strengthens students' enthusiasm for learning. The students gain recognition from the teacher and peers about their being in charge of their own learning, and they develop a responsibility to complete their tasks and to coordinate their behaviors and interactions.

In conclusion, there appear to be a number of potential benefits of cooperative learning for language-minority students. Many of the ideas raised in this paper are not yet fully supported by research. Discussion and evaluation of such ideas can be helpful in deciding directions for research. Previous research on cooperative learning has emphasized quantitative-achievement-test-socre evidence that cooperative learning works. Straightforward pursuit of this goal in the case of language-minority students would be a mistake. The social and cultural context of schooling and literacy for language-minority students needs to be taken into account, though we have barely scratched the surface of issues to examine. Some of the most important teaching, learning, and thinking skills that students acquire through cooperative learning may be evident only in authentic learning activities where students have the opportunity to guide their own learning. These forms of learning may never be captured by an artificial testing context that at best assesses what students can recall from memory.

References

Calderón, M., R. Hertz-Lazarowitz, and Tinajero, J. (in press). Bilingual students in CIRC (Cooperative Integrated Reading and Composition): Moving from traditional to cooperative classrooms. In J. Williamson. *Cooperative learning: International perspectives*, London: Fulton.

Cuban, L. (1984). *How teachers taught: Constancy and change in American classrooms, 1890–1980*. New York: Longman.

Cummins, J. (1986). Empowering minority students: A framework for intervention. *Harvard Educational Review, 56* (1), 18–36.

DeVillar, R. A. and C. J. Faltis. *Computers and Cultural Diversity*. New York: State University of New York Press.

Durán, R. P. (1992). Clinical assessment of instructional performance in cooperative learning. In K. Geisinger. (Ed.) *Psychological testing of Hispanics*, Washington, DC: American Psychological Association, 137–156.

Ford, E. (1991). Criteria for developing an observation scheme for cooperative language learning. *The Canadian Modern Language Review, 48* (1), 45–60.

Goodlad, J. I. (1984). *A place called school: Prospects for the future.* New York: McGraw-Hill.

Gutiérrez, K. (in press). Unpackaging academic literacy. *UCLA Journal of Education*. Los Angeles: Graduate School of Education, University of California.

Hymes, D. (1972). Models of the interactions of language and social life. In J. J. Gumperz and D. Hymes. (Eds.), *Directions in sociolinguistics; The ethnography of communication*. New York: Holt, Rinehart and Winston, 35–71.

Johnson, R. T., D. W. Johnson, and E. J. Holubec (1987). *Structuring cooperative learning: Lesson plans for teachers*. Edina, MN: Interaction Book Company.

Kagan, S. (1986). Cooperative learning and sociological factors in schooling. In *Beyond language: Social and cultural factors in schooling language minority students*. Los Angeles: California State University, Evaluation, Dissemination and Assessment Center, 231–298.

Kagan, S. (1985). *Cooperative learning resources for teachers*. Riverside, C. A.: University of California.

New faces at school: How changing demographics reshape American education [Special issue]. (1991). *Report on Education Research, 23* (15).

Ogbu, J. U. and M. E. Matute-Bianchi (1986). Understanding sociocultural factors: Knowledge, identity, and school adjustment. In *Beyond language: Social & cultural factors in schooling language minority students*. Los Angeles: California State University, Evaluation, Dissemination, and Assessment Center, 73–142.

Prado-Olmos, P., R. García, and R. Durán (1991, April). Cooperative learning for bilingual students: A case study of a CIRC implementation. Paper presented at the Annual Meeting of the American Educational Research Association, Chicago.

Ramírez, A. G. (1981). Language attitudes and the speech of Spanish-English bilingual pupils. In R. P. Durán (Ed.) *Latino language and communicative behavior*. Norwood, N.J.: Ablex, 217–235.

Rueda, R., C. Goldenberg, and R. Gallimore, (1991, April). When is an instructional conversation? In R. Gallimore (Chair), *Instruction through conversation: The description and analysis of instructional conversations*. Symposium conducted at the Annual Meeting of the American Educational Research Association, Chicago.

Scribner, S. and M. Cole (1981). Unpackaging literacy. In M. Farr Whiteman (Ed.); *Writing: The nature, development, and teaching of written communication*. Hillsdale, N.J.: Lawrence Erlbaum, 71–87.

Slavin, R. E. (1990). *Cooperative learning: Theory, research, and practice*. Englewood Cliffs, N.J.: Prentice Hall.

Slavin, R. E. (1987). Developments and motivational perspectives on cooperative learning: A reconciliation. *Child Development, 58,* 1161–1167.

Slavin R. E. (1989). *When and why does cooperative learning increase achievement? Theoretical and empirical perspectives*. (OERI No. G-86-0006). Baltimore: Johns Hopkins University, Center for Research on Elementary and Middle Schools.

Stevens, R. J., Slavin, R. E., and Farnish, A. M. (1991). The effects of cooperative learning and direct instruction in reading comprehension strategies on main idea identification. *Journal of Educational Psychology, 83* (1), 8–16.

Tharp, R. G. and Gallimore, R. (1988). *Rousing minds to life*. Cambridge: Cambridge University Press.

Wong-Fillmore, L. (1985). When does teacher talk work as input? In S. Glass and C. Madden (Eds.) *Input in second language acquisition*, Rowley, MA: Newbury House, 17–50.

▼ 7 ▼

Influences of L1 Writing Proficiency on L2 Writing Proficiency*

ROBERT S. CARLISLE

Even though most educators recognize writing as a decontextualized language skill important for the transmission of information, academic success, and social advancement, few realize that it may also be a much better means of learning and retaining information than just reading. A number of studies have revealed that students learn and retain information better if they write on a topic rather than if they just read about it (see Langer and Applebee 1987 for a review of some of these studies). Some evidence even suggests that experience with certain types of writing tasks may promote the development of specific cognitive skills (Scribner and Cole 1981a, 1981b).

Other research has revealed that there are crucial differences between the writing processes of more-proficient and less-proficient adult writers composing in their first language.[1] More-proficient writers tend to spend more time on prewriting activities (Pianko 1979; Stallard 1974), construct global plans that they reevaluate during the process of transcribing, reread large chunks of text both to evaluate plans and to plan from that point on (Flower and Hayes 1980), readily make global revisions (Faigley and Witte 1981; Sommers 1980), and generally save the revision of local errors until last (Faigley and Witte 1981; Sommers 1980). Less-proficient writers in turn spend less time in prewriting activities including planning (Pianko 1979; Stallard 1974), create less flexible plans (Rose 1980), reread small chunks of text (which prohibits them from evaluating over plans) (Faigley and Witte 1981; Flower and Hayes 1981; Perl 1979; Sommers 1980), correct locally rather than globally

---

*Based on a paper presented at TESOL 1991, New York City, March 24–28 1991.

161

(Faigley and Witte 1981; Perl 1980; Sommers 1980), and demonstrate too much concern for local errors early in the composing process (Faigley and Witte 1981; Perl 1980; Sommers 1980).

Researchers in second-language writing have observed that the process of writing in the second language greatly resembles that of writing in the first language (Jones and Tetroe 1987; Zamel 1982, 1983). Proficient L2 writers demonstrate many of the same composing behaviors of proficient L1 writers (Zamel 1982, 1983), but less-proficient L2 writers, though similar to less-proficient L1 writers, are less homogeneous in their behavior than are the less-proficient L1 writers (Raimes 1985).

For more than a decade, specialists in the teaching of writing to both native English speakers and to ESL students have been urging a process approach to the teaching of writing rather than a product approach (Woods 1984). The latter could be characterized as the traditional approach to the teaching of writing. At its worst, the product approach to writing consists of the following linear steps: Teachers generally assign the same topic to all students with the intent of determining if the students have mastered certain content rather than to determine if they can use writing to explore a topic. Students then may write an outline of the paper, reflecting the philosophy that all writing plans must be known to writers even before they touch pencil to paper. In some cases the instructors even stipulate a required length or specific structure for the writing.[2] Students then usually turn in the papers to the instructor—the one recognized audience of the paper—who marks their mechanical flaws and assigns final grades. The students then receive the graded papers back and either are not allowed to revise them or are required to edit mechanical problems. Such teaching practices produce writers with the characteristics of poor writers described above. If students are given topics, instructed to make outlines, and prohibited from revising content, they will pay little attention to planning or to the discovery of meaning. The product approach to the teaching of composition and its effects are still evident in American schools, as revealed in recent assessments of the writing of American students from the elementary grades through high school (Applebee, Langer, and Mullis 1986).

In contrast to the product approach, an ideal process approach to writing would not have students record prefabricated ideas but rather allow them to discover and explore ideas through their writing. In a process approach, students are often allowed and even encouraged to choose their own topics

under the realization that they write more developed and rhe-
torically effective papers (Perl 1980). Adherents of this approach also encourage paired and small-group activities, such
as brainstorming and peer review. They also encourage multiple drafts of a paper, conduct conferences with students, and
regard editing as a final polishing activity.

It is easy to determine how the process approach to the instruction of writing is related to the three sound educational
principles of communication, cooperation, and integration formulated by DeVillar and Faltis (1991) and stressed throughout
this text. If students are allowed to choose their own topics for
composing, they then become responsible for its communicative effectiveness, as they are now the "expert" on their own
topic. In other words, the students are no longer writing to an
audience, the instructor, who is presumed to know more about
the topic than the students; in such writing, the students
merely have to craft a response demonstrating that they have
acquired sufficient information. But when students choose
their own topics, such an assumption is no longer valid. The
students may still be writing the paper for the instructor, but
now the instructor has the role of general audience, and the
students must provide crucial background information that
the general reader may not share, and must organize coher-
ently if the writing is to be communicatively effective.

Cooperation and integration also naturally result from
the process approach, especially in small-group activities with
fellow students and conferences with the instructor. If instructors have heterogeneous classrooms, they can integrate students from different backgrounds into the same small groups.
Such integration would be especially valuable to language-
minority students, as they would be exposed to meaningful English. And in the small groups, especially in brainstorming
and peer review, cooperation is essential if students are to assist others in generating further content and in organizing
that content. In addition, by allowing students to choose their
own topics and then encouraging group discussions of topics,
especially in linguistically heterogeneous groups, teachers provide students with a meaningful experience to learn to function in the written culture through the medium of the oral
culture associated with the students' home and community
(Cook-Gumperz and Gumperz 1981).

Because of the apparent educational, cognitive, and integrative benefits of the process approach to the teaching of
writing, researchers and teacher educators have proposed that

bilingual teachers be taught to use this method in bilingual classrooms (Edelsky 1986; Hudelson 1989). Apparently, the process approach can be quite successful for language-minority children. Ammon (1985) examined the writing development of language-minority third graders in thirteen different classrooms. The students in two of those classrooms (one regular classroom and one bilingual classroom) has made notable progress in their English composition skills from the beginning to the end of the year. An analysis of the writing instruction in those classrooms revealed that the instructors had the students write frequently and allowed the students to choose their own topics and participate in prewriting activities, including small-group discussion. The instructors also read for content, conducted student–teacher writing conferences, published students' writing, and addressed editing as the final subprocess of writing.

The following paper has two general purposes. The first is to review what is known about the influence of L1 writing on L2 writing. Specific emphasis will be placed upon the few available studies that have compared students who learned to write in their L1 before learning to write in their L2 with those students who learned to write only in their L2 or with native speakers. Because of this comparative approach, much interesting research on the writing process of LEP children, their written products, and the influence of sociocultural background on writing development both in school and out of school will not be discussed (see, however, Amastae 1981; Cronnell 1982; Edelsky 1981, 1982, 1983; Gipps and Ewen 1974; Hudelson 1984; Philips 1975; Potter 1981; Samway 1987; Urzúa 1987; Valdez 1981). The second purpose of the paper is to determine if teachers in different educational programs used different instructional methods for the teaching of writing. Such information is vital to evaluate any possible differences in writing proficiency among the groups of students cited in the review. For example, if it were demonstrated that bilingual-program students were more proficient in writing English than were submersion-program students, the natural assumption might be that the bilingual program is superior to the submersion program. However, if it were also demonstrated that the bilingual-program instructors were using a process approach and the submersion-program instructors were using a product approach, a confounding variable would now be introduced, and it would not be possible to ascertain whether the bilingual students' superior writing proficiency was attributable to the bilingual program itself and the concomitant effects of L1 literacy or to the instructional approach used by the bilingual instructors or even to a complicated interaction between the two.

Comparative Studies

Three studies in the 1970s compared diverse groups of linguistically different students on syntactic maturity, error frequency, or both. Rodrigues (1974) examined written compositions by Spanish/English bilinguals who had been in a bilingual program for three years and native English speakers in the fourth grade in Las Vegas, New Mexico. Rodrigues examined three measures of syntactic maturity (the average number of words per T-unit, the average number of clauses per T-unit, and the average number of words per clause) and one measure of error frequency (the average number of morphological and syntactic deviations from "Standard English" per one hundred written words). Rodrigues found no significant differences on either the syntactic maturity measures or on the error frequency measure.[3]

A second study examining the syntactic maturity of bilingual subjects and monolingual native English speakers was conducted by Braun and Klassen (1973). Their subjects consisted of forty-eight German/English bilinguals, forty-eight French/English bilinguals, and forty-eight English monolinguals studying in the fourth and sixth grades at various elementary schools in Manitoba. The results of the study revealed that the the bilingual subjects wrote significantly shorter T-units than did the monolingual subjects. Thus, this study seems to contradict the findings of Rodrigues for syntactic maturity. However, the study by Braun and Klassen has some serious problems with subject identification and description. Apparently, bilingual subjects were identified solely by the community they came from—two bilingual communities (German/English and French/English) and one monolingual English community. The educational backgrounds of the subjects were not discussed at all, and it is not known if the bilingual subjects had ever attended a bilingual program or even if they were literate in their L1. This lack of educational information renders this study useless as an example of the influence of

L1 writing proficiency on L2 writing proficiency, though to study such an influence was not the original intent of the researchers.

Another study from Canada examined the writing proficiency of forty Anglophone third graders in a French immersion program and compared it to that of twenty-four other Anglophones in the regular program (Swain 1976).[4] In the immersion program the students were taught exclusively in French during kindergarten and grade one. Starting in the first grade the immersion students received an hour of English language arts every day from an instructor who was a native speaker of English. Each group wrote two stories in English based upon pictures that the students were shown. The students were measured on a number of factors including the number of words per sentence, the number of sentences per story, the number of words per story, vocabulary variety as measured by a type-token ratio, morphological and lexical errors, mechanical errors (punctuation, capitalization, and spelling), types of sentences (simple, compound, complex, compound-complex, and fragments), syntactic errors, and creativity. In the analysis of the data, Swain chose to use descriptive statistics rather than tests of statistical significance, as the study was more concerned with general characteristics of writing rather than the magnitude of differences between the immersion students and the regular-program students. Comparing the English writing proficiency of the immersion students and the regular-program students, Swain found that the two groups of students were nearly identical on all measures with the exceptions that the immersion-program students wrote longer essays, made fewer lexical and morphological errors, and wrote proportionately more complex and compound/complex sentences. However, they did make more mechanical errors per essay.[5]

Two other studies have examined adolescent students who learned to write in their first language prior to learning to write in their second language. The first study compared the writing of bilingual-program students and submersion-program students in a primary school serving an Aboriginal community on Milingimbi, an island off the Northern Territory of Australia (Gale, McClay, Christie, and Harris 1981). During the years that students attended the bilingual program, they received about half of their entire schooling through their native language, Gupapuyngu; and they learned both to read and write in their native language before receiving instruction in English literacy. In contrast, the students in the submersion program received all of their education through English and did not develop literacy skills in their primary language. In the 1970s, both programs operated concurrently in the Milingimbi School, and students exclusively attended one or the other program from the first grade through the seventh grade, the last year of classes at the school.

When the students reached the seventh and last year of their schooling in the Milingimbi School, the researchers tested them on their writing ability in English by having them first watch a filmstrip and listen to a tape on Ferdinand the Bull. After viewing the filmstrip, the subjects wrote a narrative of the filmstrip that they had just watched. The papers of the fifteen subjects of the bilingual group and the twelve subjects of the submersion group were then rated on an eleven point scale by two independent evaluators. Statistical results indicated that the scores for the papers written by the bilingual subjects were significantly higher than those written by the submersion students. However, the researchers also noted that the quality of the papers written by both groups was distinctly below the national average. Unfortunately, the researchers failed to provide any details on the basis for this appraisal. In addition, no indication was given in the study as to the amount of class time devoted to the instruction of writing in either the native language or English. As a consequence, it is not possible to know if the Aboriginal students at Milingimbi School were receiving approximately the same opportunity to write as were students in non-Aboriginal schools. Because the amount of writing instruction is not known, it is not possible even to hypothesize why both the students in the bilingual and submersion programs in the Milingimbi School were writing well below the national average.

The second study examining the writing proficiency of adolescent students writing in their second language was conducted in the United States by Ferris and Politzer (1981), though they did not examine students in a bilingual program. The subjects were two groups of native Spanish speaking students enrolled in a junior high school in Santa Paula, California. The subjects in the first group (the immigrant group) were born in Mexico and had received elementary schooling either through the second or third grade in Mexican schools; of course, this education was through their native language, and the subjects had presumably become literate in Spanish to the second or third grade level. Following their immigration to the United States, the students received at least four years of schooling in a submersion program. The second group of subjects (the submersion group) consisted of native Spanish speakers who were born in the United States and who had received their entire elementary education in a submersion program; consequently, none of these students had had any formal schooling either in or through their native language. At the time of testing all of the subjects were in either the seventh or eighth grade. Each group contained thirty subjects.

The subjects provided a writing sample by watching a short film and then writing about its contents. Teams of raters evaluated the essays on three measures of holistic scores: paragraph development, sentence boundaries, and verb inflections; on three objective measures of syntactic maturity: the length of T-unit, the length of clause, and the number of clauses per T-unit; and on six measures of error frequency: fused sentences, period faults, verb tense, pronoun agreement, article agreement, and possessives. Analyses revealed that the submersion group had significantly better scores on the two measures of verb morphology—verb inflections and verb tense. There were no significant differences on any of the other ten measures. Of interest is that the immigrant group had received significantly higher grades in their English classes than had the submersion group, so even though the submersion program students displayed a slight superiority in verb inflections, the immigrant students were actually receiving better grades in their English classes.

One study has compared the writing of native English speakers in a regular program with that of native Spanish speakers in a bilingual program and a submersion program (Carlisle 1986; 1989). The study was cross-sectional and involved a total of sixty-two subjects, thirty-two in the fourth grade and thirty in the sixth grade. The bilingual program students had been in the bilingual program for at least two years, and those in the sixth grade had been out of the program for at least one year. In contrast, even though the submersion-program students had been identified as LEP by the school district, they had never been in the bilingual program, nor had they even had classes in ESL.[6]

Five variables were examined: (1) rhetorical effectiveness, the average score of five essays evaluated with primary trait scoring; (2) overall quality of writing, the average score of two essays evaluated with general impression scoring; (3) productivity, the total number of words written on the seven essays; (4) syntactic maturity, the average number of words per T-unit; and (5) error frequency, the average number of errors per T-unit. The data for these variables were examined first by grade and then by program.

By grade, the results of the study revealed that the sixth graders as a whole had significantly higher scores on rhetorical effectiveness and overall quality of writing than did the fourth graders. The sixth graders also wrote significantly longer papers and T-units. Only on error frequency was there no significant difference between the two grades.

By program, more statistical differences were evident in the comparisons among the three groups. The regular-program students had significantly higher scores on both rhetorical effectiveness and overall quality than did the bilingual-program students and the submersion-program students. They also had significantly fewer errors than did the bilingual-program students. However, there was a significant interactive effect which revealed that the significant difference was only in the fourth grade; by the sixth grade no statistical differences were evident among the three program groups on errors frequency. The last two significant differences were in productivity and syntactic maturity: the bilingual-program students wrote significantly longer papers and T-units than did the submersion-program students. In neither case was there a significant interactive effect, meaning that the patterns of difference were the same for both the fourth and sixth grade.

Carlisle (1989) examined the holistic scores on all seven individual writing tasks and found that the averaged scores for rhetorical effectiveness and overall quality of writing had actually obscured some pertinent findings. The students in the regular program had significantly higher scores than did the bilingual-program students on two of the seven essays, but they had significantly higher scores than did the submersion-program students on five of the seven essays. It thus appears that the bilingual-program students were closer to the norms of the native English speakers than were the submersion-program students, even though there was not a single significant difference on the seven essays between those two program groups.

Carlisle's original study may have inadvertently discriminated against the bilingual-program students on the measure of error frequency. In the original plan for the study, Carlisle used the measure of the number of errors per T-unit because other research had demonstrated that of several measures of error frequency, it correlated most highly with holistic measures of writing quality (Perkins 1980). However, whereas such a measure of error frequency is valid if used to correlate error with holistic scores, it may be inadequate if used to determine differences among groups that have significantly different lengths of T-unit. This is due to the fact that longer T-units have more potential for error—especially error in punctuation—as writers are subordinating more and using more clause-internal coordination. In addition, more subordinate clauses means more verb groups, and second-language learners are notorious for deleting verb inflectional morphemes, as they essentially carry redundant information. A more appropriate measure would be one that controlled for length, such as the number of errors per 100 words, as has been used by Rodrigues (1974) and most recently by Gilbert and Grabe (1991).

Such a reanalysis was performed on these data with grade and program as the independent variables. By grade, the mean number of errors per 100 words for fourth graders was 25.6 and 18.3 for sixth graders, a significant difference: $F(1, 56) = 7.78$, $p < .008$. By program, the means were 14.72 for the regular-program students, 24.04 for the submersion-program students, and 26.80 for the bilingual-program students, differences which were significant: $F(2, 56) = 11.07$, $p < .0001$. Tukey analyses revealed that the regular-program students made significantly fewer errors than did the students from the other two programs. However, as was true of the first study, there was a significant interaction effect between grade and program: $F(2, 56) = 6.33$, $p < .005$. This significant interaction indicates a difference in the pattern of error frequency among the three programs according to grade. To uncover this difference it became necessary to compare the frequency of errors for programs for both the fourth and sixth grades in separate analyses. In the fourth grade, the regular-program students made 14.5 errors per 100 words, the submersion-program students 24.9 errors, and the bilingual-program students 34.6 errors. These means were significantly different: $F(2, 29) = 10.82$, $p < .0005$. Tukey analyses demonstrated that the bilingual-program students made significantly more errors than did the regular-program students; no other differences among program groups in the fourth grade reached significance (see table 7.1).

TABLE 7.1. PAIRWISE COMPARISONS OF ERROR
FREQUENCY FOR PROGRAMS IN THE FOURTH GRADE:
ERRORS PER 100 WORDS

	Programs		
Grades	Regular	Submersion	Bilingual
Fourth	14.5	24.9	34.6

Means not sharing a bar are significantly different from each other at .05.

In the sixth grade, the regular-program students made 14.9 errors as opposed to 22.8 and 18.2 errors for the submersion-program students and the bilingual-program students respectively. These means were also significantly different: $F(2, 27) = 3.36$, $p < .05$. Tukey analyses revealed that the submersion-program students made significantly more errors than did the regular-program students. There was no difference between the bilingual-program students and the regular-program students or between the bilingual program-students and the submersion-program students (see table 7.2). Thus, even though the bilingual-program students had made significantly more errors than had the native English speakers in the fourth grade, they reached the norms of the native English speakers in the sixth grade; whereas the submersion-program students were now making significantly more errors than were the native English speakers. In other words, by the sixth grade the bilingual-program students reached the norms of the native English speaking control group on the measure of error frequency even though they had had less experience writing in English than had the submersion-program students.

These results clearly indicate that the bilingual-program students were writing at least as well as the submersion-

TABLE 7.2 PAIRWISE COMPARISONS OF ERROR
FREQUENCY FOR PROGRAMS IN THE SIXTH GRADE:
ERRORS PER 100 WORDS

	Programs		
Grades	Regular	Bilingual	Submersion
Sixth	14.9	18.2	22.8

Means not sharing a bar are significantly different from each other at .05.

program students (even better on two measures) and were closer to the norms of the native English speakers than were the submersion-program students. And the bilingual-program students achieved these results even though their families used significantly less English in the home, had significantly less reading material in the home, had lived in the country less time (Carlisle 1989), and were from a significantly lower socio-economic class (SEC of course being an important predictor of academic achievement).[7] What is amazing about these findings is that this particular bilingual program is an example of early-exit programs, which have been demonstrated to be less effective than late-exit programs (Ramírez, Yuen, and Ramey 1991).

From these studies on writing, it is possible to make a number of generalizations.[8] From the studies that compared students in bilingual programs with native English speakers (Rodrigues 1974; Carlisle 1986, 1989), it appears that students in bilingual programs can reach native-language norms in syntactic maturity and productivity by the fourth grade. They may also reach native-language norms in error frequency by the fourth grade (Rodrigues 1974), though Carlisle's results indicated that the bilingual students may need until the sixth grade; the differences in results may be attributable to differences in defining error or in differences in the programs. According to measures of overall writing quality, students in bilingual programs write some essays just as well as native English speakers even by the fourth grade (Carlisle 1989). However, they do appear significantly weaker than native English speakers on other essays, an observation also made by Gale et al. (1981) even though they included no documentation to support their claim.

The combined results of these studies certainly support Cummins's Interdependence Hypothesis (Cummins 1979, 1981, 1989), which essentially postulates a common underlying proficiency between academic skills in the L1 and the L2. In other words, native Spanish speakers who learn to write in Spanish are developing composition skills that will enable them to acquire English composition skills, provided that they have sufficient opportunity to compose in English. Evidence for this common underlying proficiency has been presented from all of the studies reviewed above, which either compare immigrant students literate in their L1 with submersion-program students, or bilingual-program students with submersion students. In all cases, the L1 literate group did as well as, if not better than, the L2-only literate group. And they did so despite having much less composition instruction in the L2 and much less opportunity to write in the L2.

The results of the studies reviewed in this paper also provide evidence against critics of bilingual education such as Porter (1990) and Walberg (1990), who overtly claim that "time on task" is the most important variable for L2 acquisition in children. Of course, time on task is a recognized variable for learning in general, but it is a troublesome concept for L2 acquisition. Children normally learn language in a context or situation in which language is used for authentic communicative purposes and in which the children receive comprehensible input. The linguistically heterogeneous classroom hardly provides such a context of situation. Teachers monopolize speaking in most classroom contexts, even in language classes (Long and Porter 1985); discourage student interaction and the verbal exploration of ideas by relying too heavily on whole-class instruction (Forman and Cazden 1985); and ask questions that all of the students realize the teachers already know the answer to (Ramírez and Merino 1990). Such questions of course are quite different than those asked in authentic communicative contexts.

At a minimum, the goal of any program for language-minority students must be not only to teach them English but also to assure that they acquire academic skills through the medium of English. An effective bilingual program will achieve this goal by developing academic skills in the primary language and reinforcing the development of those skills in English through the implementation of meaningful and comprehensible ESL instruction and interaction with native English speakers. In fact, research on effective programs for language-minority children has revealed that teachers in such programs encourage the use of language for authentic communicative purposes (García 1990). "Time on task" in such a situation has substance because linguistic input is comprehensible. In a submersion program, however, neither the oral nor the written linguistic input has to be meaningful. If teachers "speak to the group," those with limited proficiency may not consistently receive comprehensible input. Researchers in L2 acquisition realize that children acquire their L2 best when when they are presented with language that is within the their psycholinguistic range (Pienemann 1984) and when they are allowed to use language for authentic communicative purposes (Wong Fillmore 1985). In the linguistically heterogeneous elementary classroom, children will have diverse levels of linguistic competence in the language of the class. Unfortunately, some research suggests that teachers interact most frequently with those students who are more fluent in the language of the class rather than with those who are less fluent (Schinke-Llano 1983). Consequently, those in most need of comprehensible input and opportunities to use language for authentic communicative purposes are the ones most likely to be disenfranchised from meaningful linguistic interaction.

Obviously, a situation that precludes minority students from meaningful communication, either between teacher and student, student and student, or even student and text cannot claim to be an appropriate "time on task" experience either for the development of the L2 or academic skills. Even instructors in programs that claim to teach English in a meaningful and appropriate manner, such as "structured immersion" programs, provide poor environments for second-language acquisition (Ramírez et al. 1991).

Instructional Practices of Teachers

The question that remains to be asked now is whether the results of these studies can be attributed solely to the influence of L1 literacy on L2 literacy, or to differences in writing instruction methodologies in the programs themselves; specifically, we would want to know if one program is using a product approach whereas the other is using a process approach, an approach that, if well implemented, incorporates the educationally sound concepts of communication, integration, and cooperation as discussed previously.

Unfortunately, most studies that have compared bilingual programs with other types of programs have usually supplied at least some background information on the two types of programs, but not on instructional methodologies within the programs. The assumption seems to be that such differences are either nonexistent or irrelevant, a very dangerous assumption, as has been demonstrated by Ammon (1985), who found that students who received process-oriented writing instruction tended to do better than those who did not, regardless of instructional program.

The study by Rodrigues (1974), which compared the writing of native English speakers and bilingual-program students in the fourth grade, provided no details about the types of writing instruction that the students received in the two programs. However, given the date of the study, essentially the time that research on the process of writing was just beginning, it is probably safe to assume that the students in both programs were receiving the same type of product-based instruction.

The same assumption can be made for the immigrant group and the submersion group in the study by Ferris and Politzer (1981): as was true of the Rodrigues study, no information was provided on the actual methodologies used by teachers to instruct writing. However, both groups of students were in the same junior high school at the time of data gathering, and some of them may have even had the same English instructors, though the authors did not provide information on that point.

Even though Gale et al. (1981) did not provide any information on the actual writing instruction of the teachers in the bilingual and submersion program, they did note that literacy instruction in Gupapuyngu was conducted by a partially trained or even untrained Aboriginal teacher, whereas English literacy training (presumably for both the bilingual and submersion programs) was conducted by fully trained non-Aboriginal instructors. There is no way of knowing how the results of this study would have been affected if the Aboriginal instructors had been fully qualified.

The only study, other than the one by Ammon previously discussed, that attempted to examine the actual writing methodologies used by teachers in different programs containing language-minority students was conducted by Carlisle (1986). Carlisle asked each of the sixteen teachers involved in the study to fill out a questionnaire consisting of twenty questions about their training in the teaching of composition and about their actual classroom practices in the teaching of composition. Unfortunately, only ten of sixteen instructors actually filled out the questionnaire either on their own or with the researcher. Most of the teachers who did not fill out the questionnaire were sixth-grade teachers. Consequently, the following discussion is based solely upon the responses of the fourth-grade instructors.

Four of the fourth-grade teachers who filled out the questionnaire taught in the regular program and had all nine of the native English speakers in their classes (the entire sample of this group) and six of the submersion-program students. These four teachers had a great deal of instructional experience among them, an average of nearly nine years. Though all of the teachers had taught another grade for at least one year, most of their experience was with the fourth grade. In their training to be teachers, none of them could remember ever having taken a class specifically about the teaching of writing, though they did state that writing was a minor topic in some of the language-arts classes that they had taken for their teaching certificates.

In their actual teaching practices the four teachers were very similar. Three of the four did not have any special time set aside for writing; the fourth, however, did try to reserve a forty-minute slot every week just for writing, but oftentimes the reserved time was used for something else. For all of these teachers writing was not viewed as a separate subject but as a skill to be used in conjunction with other subjects. Specifically, writing was used to indicate that the students had learned certain material or to demonstrate that exercises had been completed. For example, most of the writing that the students engaged in was the writing of answers to content questions found in their text books for reading, social studies, science, and health. These answers were often only a sentence in length and never longer than two short paragraphs. Because these answers constituted the majority of the writing that the students did, the students of course had very little say in what they would write about. Even when the students were required to write short papers, they were tightly controlled. For instance, the teachers sometimes gave the students prepared pages, which the teachers referred to as "starters." Starters contain a title—the topic to be written about—and part of the first sentence. The students then had to complete the first sentence and write several others; the page given to the students had only four lines for them to write on. Even research projects were tightly controlled. In social studies, the students sometimes wrote one-page reports; however, the teachers picked the topics and passed out printed instructions informing the students what points to include. An example of this type of task was called the "Dinosaur Report." The students were given the topic of describing any dinosaur that they wanted to describe; however, the report had to contain eight specific points about the dinosaur, each to be presented in a single sentence. Finally, the teachers mentioned two other writing exercises their students did in class—spelling tests and sentence-completion exercises.

The four fourth-grade teachers who had native English speakers and submersion students in their classes were also similar in the manner in which they evaluated writing, all four putting emphasis on mechanical correctness, including spelling, punctuation, and grammar. However, they stated that the accuracy of the content was also important because most of the writing consisted of answering content questions from the texts. For the most part the teachers did not hold individual conferences with their students on their writing; they reported that the only time they discussed writing with individual students was when a paper or written exercises contained what the teachers felt to be an unacceptable number of grammatical and mechanical errors. At times the teachers did require students to edit their writing, mostly for mechanical errors, but at other times students were also required to revise content, especially if students wrote completely incorrect answers to content questions in their texts.

Usually the teacher was the only audience for the students' writing, but the fourth-grade social science instructor at one school did require students to read each other's answers to the questions in the social studies text. The teacher did this so that students could make sure that they had found the correct answers to the questions. If two students disagreed, they had to work together to find the correct answer. All of the teachers did hang up short papers occasionally or pin them up on a board for others to read. However, such publication of student writing was not a regular part of any class and seemed to be spontaneous rather than a planned activity.

The three teachers in the bilingual program who completed the questionnaire were similar in training and teaching practices to the teachers in the regular and submersion programs. The bilingual teachers taught at two different schools. At the first school, one of the bilingual teachers taught native Spanish speakers from the second through the sixth grades and was responsible for instruction in both Spanish and in English as a second language. The bilingual teacher at the second school taught students in the same grades as the teacher in the first school; however, unlike the teacher in the first school, the one in the second had an assistant to teach the component of English as a second language. These three teachers did not have as much experience as those in the regular program and the submersion program discussed above. The two bilingual teachers had four and seven years of experience, and the ESL instructor was in her first year of teaching. None of the three instructors had had any specific training in the teaching of composition, a feature they shared with the teachers in the regular and submersion programs.

In their teaching of writing and in their use of it in the classroom, the three teachers in the bilingual program were similar to one another and to the other teachers previously discussed. To begin with, none of the teachers in the bilingual program had specific times for the students to write. Instead, students wrote in conjunction with the content subjects, as was true of students in the regular and submersion programs. This writing essentially consisted of students writing answers to the content questions found in their texts. The students in the bilingual program also wrote two short book reports every semester in Spanish. Because the bilingual students answered questions in their texts and because the book reports were highly structured, they had very little opportunity to choose topics to write about or to write for an audience other than the teacher.

As did the teachers in the regular and the submersion programs, the teachers in the bilingual program evaluated the mechanics and the grammar of writing. The ESL instructor placed primary emphasis on evaluating mechanics and grammar, as her assignments were generally designed to test students' knowledge of these features. Although the bilingual teachers also evaluated mechanics and grammar, they graded for content. If students answered questions correctly from their text, they would receive a high grade from either of the bilingual teachers. However, if the students answered incorrectly or committed too many mechanical or grammatical errors, they were required to do the assignment again. These types of revisions were the only ones that the bilingual students were required to make on the written answers to questions in the texts. However, at times the students did write short papers, and the teachers required them to correct content if there were inclarities in the papers.

Finally, as was true of the teachers in the regular and submersion programs, the teachers in the bilingual program tended to be the sole audience for the writing of their students. At times papers were placed on the walls, usually when the students were doing a special topic, such as a brief report in social studies. Also, as did the teachers in the other two programs, those in the bilingual program had their students read each other's written responses to the questions in the texts so that the students could check for themselves whether they had the correct answers.

The bilingual teachers did differ in one way from the teachers in the regular program and the submersion program. All three of the teachers held short conferences with their students in which they explained to the students how to revise those written exercises or papers that needed improvements. The benefit of such conferences was that they increased interaction and communication between instructors and students. However, these particular conferences were also quite limited in that they were not designed to allow for the exploration of ideas in students' original compositions but rather to assist students with finding more acceptable answers to questions in textbooks.

From this brief analysis of the teaching practices of the teachers in the three programs, it is possible to ascertain that writing served a very limited purpose in the classroom. The primary purpose of writing in all of the classes was to demonstrate mastery of a topic, a purpose that was very obvious from the major type of writing that the students were required to do: writing down answers to questions in texts, a task that did not require students to synthesize information from a number of sources or to use writing as a means of discovering meaning. Even the writing of papers was so structured that students did not have to retrieve information from long-term memory or organize information into a structure that they could claim was unique to themselves. For example, when students had to write a book report, all they had to do was follow an instruction sheet and put down the information that was asked for by each question on that sheet, reducing a book report to no more than a list in paragraph form. The students did not have to develop any sort of a thesis, search for a point of view, or organize the paper according to that thesis. As a consequence of this type of writing, the students were never required to examine, develop, or extend their knowledge of a given topic. In addition, because the teacher is the only audience, an audience that probably knows more about the topic than the students do themselves, the students were never forced to look for or provide the background information they would normally have to if they were writing for an audience who knew less about the topic than they did. Consequently, students were not using writing either to discover new meaning or to impart new meaning, which are two primary functions of writing.

Nothing that the teachers were doing would seem to explain the findings of Carlisle's research: Even though the bilingual-program students had considerably less exposure to English and fewer opportunities to write in that language, they did not differ significantly from the submersion-program group on holistic measures and on error frequency, and they wrote significantly longer papers and T-units. Given the close similarities between the teachers, it appears that both the similarities and the differences between the groups must be explained by the bilingual students' learning to write in their primary language before learning to write in English. It thus appears that the development of L1 composition skills is related to the development of L2 composition skills as hypothesized by Cumins. The results for writing development emulate those for reading achievement, which have demonstrated that students who learn to read in their L1 before learning to read in their L2 come to read in their L2 as well as, or even better than, students who learn to read only in their L2 (Modiano 1973; Ramírez et al. 1991; Rosier and Farella 1976; Rosier and Holm 1980; Troike 1978).

Conclusion

Because writing is a means of both discovering and creating meaning, the development of effective writing skills is crucial for the cognitive development of students and their eventual academic success. However, writing does not automatically become the means for such exploration and expansion: Students must be encouraged and taught to have their writing serve in these capacities rather than just as a passive means for restating previously acquired information. When a process approach rather than a product approach to writing is encouraged in the schools, the enabling benefits of writing emerge, and students who do receive it write better than those who do not. Unfortunately, however, the process approach is little used in schools, as revealed in national assessments of writing an in research. The absence of the process approach is not peculiar to any one educational program, student population, or age group; it is absent from mainstream programs as well as such programs for language minorities as bilingual education and structured submersion. As a consequence, most American students are disallowed from discovering meaning or exploring content through their writing and are essentially academically disabled by a national educational philosophy that favors teacher-centered instruction over meaningful integrative communication and teacher control over student cooperation. In addition, the lack of the process approach is pernicious to the oral language development of language-minority children, as they are not encouraged to explore their ideas, comment on the writing of others, or respond to those comments. Clearly, because the process approach embodies the educational precepts of integration, cooperation, and communication and leads to the development of enabling writing skills and improved oral language proficiency, it should especially be incorporated into the bilingual classroom.

Notes

1. The terms 'more proficient' and 'less proficient' are of course relative terms and are used as superordinate terms to cover the different populations of subjects observed in the studies cited in this section.

2. If this seems extreme to some readers, I can cite the practices of a local high school district, which has an essay examination that all students must pass before graduating. Students are specifically urged to write a five-paragraph theme to successfully complete the task, which is almost always on the same topic—the writer's favorite season. If students fail this test more than once, they are required to take a "writing" class, which essentially teaches the test. Approximately thirty seniors a year, usually minority students, fail the test and are denied participation in commencement ceremonies and graduation until they can pass the test after taking a writing class during the summer. Obviously, such a testing procedure disables students from using writing as a means to discover meaning and explore content.

3. In his study, Rodrigues also examined the writing of bilingual ninth graders, but even though they were bilingual, none of them ever attended a bilingual program and may have been illiterate in their primary language. These students could have been literate in Spanish if they had been immigrants, but Rodrigues has nothing to say on that point.

4. Actually, Swain performed a second contrast, one between the French-immersion students' writing proficiency in English and

French. This second comparison revealed that in general the students' writing proficiency in English was superior to that in French even though the students had had much more academic training in French than in English.

5. Spelling in English seems to be a consistently difficult skill to master for students in French immersion programs, at least in the early years. Swain notes that the French immersion students in her study also did less well on the spelling section of the Metropolitan Achievement Test than did the students in the regular program, even though they did as well on other areas of English language arts. Swain also cites a study by Genesee (1974) which compared the English writing proficiency of French immersion students and regular-program students in the fourth grade. Genesee found that the two groups demonstrated very few differences, though the immersion students did make more spelling errors.

6. This particular program identified students as LEP by actually observing their performance in the regular program. If non-native-English-speaking children were having difficulty in the regular classroom, their parents were informed, and they had the option of placing their children in the bilingual program. However, only about half of the parents chose to do so. According to the director of the bilingual program, parents presented two reasons for not selecting the bilingual program. Some parents thought that their children could be more successful in the regular program, and other parents did not want their children bussed. In this particular school district all of the bilingual classrooms were in schools outside of the neighborhoods where most of the Hispanics resided.

7. Ferris and Politzer (1981) also found that their immigrant group came from a significantly lower socioeconomic class, was more dominant in Spanish, and traveled more frequently to Mexico. A finding that has become typical in studies of Mexican-Americans is that more recent immigrants are of a lower socioeconomic class than immigrants who arrived at an earlier time (Baral 1977).

8. The results of two previously discussed studies will not be included in this section. Swain's (1976) study will be excluded because studies of Canadian French immersion programs really examine the influence of L2 literacy development on L1 literacy development. Also excluded is the study by Braun and Klassen (1973), as their study did not explain whether the "bilingual" groups were actually literate in their L1.

References

Amastae, J. (1981). The writing needs of Hispanic students. In B. Cronnell (Ed.), *The writing needs of linguistically different students.* Los Alamitos, Calif.: SWRL Educational Research and Development, 99–127.

Ammon, P. (1985). Helping children learn to write in English as a second language: some observations and some hypotheses. In S. W. Freedman (Ed.), *The acquisition of written language* (pp. 65–84). Norwood, NJ: Ablex.

Applebee, A., J. Langer and I. Mullis (1986). *The writing report card: Writing Achievement in American Schools.* Princeton, N.J.: Educational Testing Services.

Baral, D. P. (1977). *Achievement levels among foreign-born and native-born Mexican American students.* San Francisco: R & E Research Associates, Inc.

Braun, C., & Klassen, B. (1973). A transformational analysis of written structures of children representing varying ethno-linguistic communities. *Research in the teaching of English, 7,* 312–23.

Carlisle, R. S. (1986). The writing of Anglo and Hispanic fourth and sixth graders in regular, submersion, and bilingual programs. Unpublished doctoral dissertation, University of Illinois.

———. (1989). The writing of Anglo and Hispanic elementary students in bilingual, submersion, and regular programs. *Studies in Second Language Acquisition, 11,* 257–80.

Cohen, A., A. Fathman and B. Merino (1976). The Redwood City bilingual project, 1971–1974: Spanish and English proficiency, mathematics, and language use over time. *Working Papers on Bilingualism, 8,* 1–29.

Cook-Gumperz, J., J. J. Gumperz (1981). From oral to written culture: The transition to literacy. In M. F. Whiteman (Ed.), *Writing: The nature development, and teaching of written communication: Vol. 1. Variation in writing: Functional and linguistic-cultural differences. Hillsdale, N.J.: Lawrence Erlbaum Associates,* 89–109.

Cronnell, B. (1982). *A preliminary study of language influences in the English writing of third- and sixth-grade Chicano students.* (Report No. TN 2–82/13). Los Alamitos, Calif.: Southwest Regional Laboratory.

Cummins, J. (1979). Linguistic interdependence and the educational development of bilingual children. *Review of Educational Research, 49,* 222–51.

———. (1981). The role of primary language development in promoting educational success for language minority students. In California State Department of Education (Ed.), *Schooling and language minority students: A theoretical framework.* Los Angeles: National Dissemination and Assessment Center, 3–49.

———. (1989). *Empowering minority students.* Sacramento, Calif.: California Association for Bilingual Education.

DeVillar, R., and C. Faltis (1991). *Computers and cultural diversity: Restructuring for school success.* New York: State University of New York Press.

Edelsky, C. (1981). From "jimosalsco" to "7 narangas se calleron y el arbol-est-triste en lagrymas": Writing development in a bilingual classroom. In B. Cronnell (Ed.), *The writing needs of linguistically different students*. Los Alamitos, CA: SWRL Educational Research and development, 63–98.

———. (1982). Writing in a bilingual program: The relation of L1 and L2 texts. *TESOL Quarterly, 16*, 211–28.

———. (1983). Segmentation and punctuation: Developmental data from young writers in a bilingual programme. *Research in the Teaching of English 17*, 135–156.

———. (1986). *Writing in a bilingual program*.Norwood, N.J.: Ablex.

Faigley, L., and S. Witte (1981). Analyzing revision. *College composition and Communication, 32*, 400–14.

Ferris, M. R. and R. L. Politzer (1981). Effects of early and delayed second language acquisition: English composition skills of Spanish-speaking junior high school students. *TESOL Quarterly, 15*, 263–74.

Flower, L., and J. Hayes (1980). The cognition of discovery: Defining a rhetorical problem. *College composition and Communication, 31*, 21–32.

———. (1981). A cognitive process theory of writing. *College Composition and Communication, 32*, 365–87.

Forman, E., and C. Cazden (1985). Exploring Vygotskian perspectives in education: The cognitive value of peer interaction. In J. Wertsch (Ed.), *Culture, communication, and cognition: Vygotskian perspectives. Cambridge: Cambridge University Press, 323–47*.

Gale, K., D. McClay, M. Christie and S. Harris (1981). Academic achievement in the Milingimbi bilingual program. *TESOL Quarterly, 15*, 297–314.

García, E. (1990). Instructional discourse in "effective" Hispanic classrooms. In R. Jacobson, & C. Faltis (Eds.), *Language distribution issues in bilingual schooling*. Clevedon, England: Multilingual Matters, 104–20.

Gilbert, R. and W. Grabe (1991). Error patterns in fifth grade English L1 and L2 writing. Paper presented at the Twenty-Fifth Annual TESOL Convention in New York City.

Gipps, C. and E. Ewen (1974). Scoring written work in English as a second language: The use of the T-unit. *Educational Research, 16*, 121–25.

Hudelson, S. (1984). Kan yu ret and rayt en ingles: Children become literate in English as a second language. *TESOL Quarterly, 18*, 221–38.

———. (1989). *Write on: Children writing in ESL*. Englewood Cliffs, NJ: Prentice Hall.

Jones, S., and Tetroe, J. (1987). Composing in a second language. In A. Matsuhashi (Ed.), *Writing in real time*. Norwood, N.J.: Ablex, 34–57.

Langer, J., and A. Applebee (1987). *How writing shapes thinking*. Urbana, IL: National Council of Teachers of English.

Long, M., and P. Porter (1985). Group work, interlanguage talk, and second language acquisition. *TESOL Quarterly, 19*, 207–28.

Modiano, N. (1973). *Indian education in the Chiapas Highlands*. New York: Holt, Rinehart and Winston, Inc.

Perkins, K. (1980). Using objective methods of attained writing proficiency to discriminate among holistic evaluations. *TESOL Quarterly, 14*, 61–9.

Perl, S. (1979). The composing processes of unskilled college writers. *Research in the Teaching of English, 13*, 317–36.

———. (1980). A look at basic writers in the process of composing. In L. Kasden and D. Hoeber (Eds.), *Basic writing*. Urbana, Ill.: National Council of Teachers of English, 13–22.

Philips. S. U. (1975). Literacy as a mode of communication on the Warm Springs Indian Reservation. In E. H. Lenneberg, & E. Lenneberg (Eds.), *Foundations of language development: A multidisciplinary approach. Vol. 2*, New York: Academic Press, 367–82.

Pianko, S. (1979). A description of the composing processes of college freshmen writers. *Research in the Teaching of English, 13*, 5–22.

Pienemann, M. (1984). Psychological constraints on the teachability of languages. *Studies in Second Language Acquisition, 6*, 186-214.

Politzer, R. L. and A. G. Ramírez (1973). An error analysis of the spoken English of Mexican American pupils in a bilingual school and a monolingual school. *Language Learning, 23*, 39–62.

Porter, R. (1990). *Forked tongue: The politics of bilingual education*. New York: Basic Books.

Potter, L. (1981). American Indian children and writing: An introduction to some issues. In B. Cronnell (Ed.), *The writing needs of linguistically different students*. Los Alamitos, Calif. SWRL Educational Research and Development, 129–60.

Raimes, A. (1979). *Language in education: Theory and practice: 14. Problems and teaching strategies in ESL composition*. Arlington, Virginia: Center for Applied Linguistics.

———. (1985). What unskilled ESL students do as they write: A classroom study of composing. *TESOL Quarterly, 19*, 229–58.

———. (1987). Language proficiency, writing ability and composing strategies: A study of ESL college student writers. *Language Learning, 37*, 439–68.

Ramírez, D., and B. Merino (1990). Classroom talk in English immersion, early-exit, and late-exit transitional bilingual education programs. In R. Jacobson & C. Faltis (Eds.), *Language distribution issues in bilingual schooling.* Clevedon, England: Multilingual Matters, 61–103.

Ramírez, D., S. Yuen and D. Ramey (1991). *Executive Summary: Final Report: Longitudinal study of structured English immersion strategy, early-exit and late-exit transitional bilingual education programs for language-minority children.* San Mateo, Calif.: Aguirre International.

Reynolds, R., M. Taylor, M. Steffensen, L. Shirey, and R. Anderson (1982). Cultural schemata and reading comprehension. *Reading Research Quarterly, 17,* 353–66.

Rodrigues, R. (1974). *A comparison of the written and oral English syntax of Mexican American bilingual and Anglo American monolingual fourth and ninth grade students.* Unpublished doctoral dissertation, University of New Mexico.

Rose, M. (1980). Rigid rules, inflexible plans, and the stifling of language: A cognitivist analysis of writer's block. *College composition and Communication, 31,* 389–400.

Rosier, P., and M. Farella (1976). Bilingual education at Rock Point: Some early results. *TESOL Quarterly, 10,* 379–88.

Rosier, P., and W. Holm, (1980). *Bilingual education series: 8, The Rock Point experience: A longitudinal study of a Navajo school program.* Washington, D.C.: Center for Applied Linguistics.

Samway, K. (1987). Children's composing in English as a nonnative language. Unpublished doctoral dissertation, State University of New York at Rochester.

Schinke-Llano, L. (1983). Foreigner talk in content classrooms. In H. Seliger, and M. Long (Eds.), *Classroom oriented research in language acquisition.* Rowley: Newbury House, 146–64.

Scribner, S., and M. Cole (1981a). Unpackaging literacy. In M. F. Whiteman, (Ed.), *Writing: The nature, development, and teaching of written communication: Vol. 1. Variation in writing: Functional and linguistic-cultural differences.* Hillsdale, NJ: Lawrence Erlbaum Associates, 71–87.

———. (1981b). *The psychology of literacy.* Cambridge, MA: Harvard University Press.

Sommers, N. (1980). Revision strategies of student writers and experienced adult writers. *College Composition and Communication, 31,* 378–88.

Stallard, C. (1974). An analysis of the writing behavior of good student writers. *Research in the Teaching of English, 8,* 206–18.

Swain, M. (1976). Writing skills of grade 3 immersion pupils. In M. Swain, and H. Barik (Eds.), *Five years of primary French immersion*. Toronto: The Ontario Institute for Studies in Education, 10–30.

Troike, R. C. (1978). Research evidence for the effectiveness of bilingual education. *NABE Journal, 3,* 13–24.

Urzúa, C. (1987). "You stopped too soon": Second language children composing and revising. *TESOL Quarterly, 21,* 279–304.

Valdez, C. M. (1981): Identity, power and writing skills: The case of the Hispanic bilingual student. In M. F. Whiteman (Ed.), *Writing: The nature, development, and teaching of written communication: vol. 1. Variation in writing: Linguistic-cultural differences*. Hillsdale, NJ: Lawrence Erlbaum Associates, 167–78.

Walberg, H. (1990). Promoting English literacy. In G. Imhoff (Ed.), *Learning in two languages*. New Brunswick, NJ: Transaction Publishers, 139–61.

Wong-Fillmore, L. (1985). When does teacher talk work as input? In S. Gass and C. Madden (Eds.), *Input in second language acquisition*. Rowley: Newbury House, 17–50.

Woods, D. (1984). A process orientation in ESL writing. In L. Young (Ed.), *Carleton papers in applied language studies, 1* Ottawa: Carleton University, 101–38.

Zamel, V. (1982). Writing: The process of discovering meaning. *TESOL Quarterly, 16,* 195–209.

———. (1983). The composing processes of advanced ESL students: Six case histories. *TESOL Quarterly, 17,* 165–187.

▼ 8 ▼
Promoting Positive Cross-Cultural Attitudes and Perceived Competence in Culturally and Linguistically Diverse Classrooms

KATHRYN J. LINDHOLM

In the past few years we have seen renewed interest by educators in the psychosocial competence of children. At the state level, for example, a commission was recently established in California for studying self-esteem, and staff development sessions were provided on self-esteem enhancement. In addition, as a consequence of the ever changing U.S. demographics, national goals have begun to prioritize cross-cultural attitudes as a significant educational concern. Yet, while cultural and linguistic diversity within U.S. classrooms is becoming the norm, empirically-based research has not adequately addressed the issue of how to promote more positive cross-cultural attitudes and perceived psychosocial competence in addition to academic achievement for all students within the context of classrooms that are both culturally and linguistically diverse.

This chapter discusses theoretical issues relevant to the literature on the social context of language education, including the concepts of integration, cooperative learning, and two-way communication. Within this context, I will describe the bilingual/immersion educational model (at the elementary-school level), which integrates language-minority and language-majority children for instruction in two languages. Among the goals of bilingual/immersion are that students will demonstrate positive cross-cultural attitudes and moderate to high levels of perceived psychosocial competence. I will then present

*Portions of this paper were presented at the California Association for Bilingual Education Conference, Anaheim, California, February, 1991.

the results of evaluations of two different school sites that have
been implementing the bilingual/immersion model. Specifically, I will focus on the cross-cultural attitudes and perceived
psychosocial competence of third- and fourth-grade students.
Finally, I will briefly analyze the results from the perspective of
understanding how classroom practices need to consider the
cultural *and* linguistic diversity of students in the classroom
and offer both theoretically based and practitioner-oriented ra-
tionales for why the bilingual/immersion model is an effective
model for promoting successful cultural diversity.

Social Context of Language Education

Language-education theorists and practitioners have discussed the social context of language learning in terms of the
additive/subtractive bilingualism dichotomy. Additive bilingualism is a form of enrichment in which "children can add
one or more foreign languages to their accumulating skills and
profit immensely from the experience—cognitively, socially, educationally, and even economically" (Lambert 1984: 19). Additive bilingualism is associated with high levels of proficiency in
the two languages, adequate self-esteem, and positive cross-
cultural attitudes (Lambert 1984, 1987).

In stark contrast, subtractive bilingualism refers to the
situation in which children are "forced to put aside or subtract out their ethnic languages for a more necessary, useful, and prestigious national language" (Lambert 1984: 19).
Subtractive bilingualism is associated with lower levels of
second-language attainment scholastic underachievement,
and psychosocial disorders (Lambert 1984). The reasoning behind these negative consequences is tied to the relationship
between language and thought. When children are pressured
to learn English as quickly as possible and to set aside their
home language, they lose the critical linguistic foundation
upon which their early conceptual development is based, and
their psychosocial competence may be diminished.

Perceived psychosocial competence takes on increased significance in this context. Considerable early literature suggested that ethnic-minority children showed lower levels of
self-esteem than Anglo children (for reviews, see Rosenberg
1979; Wylie 1979), a finding contested on several methodological and conceptual grounds (Wylie 1979). More recent research

has proposed that ethnic-minority students may evaluate themselves differentially along two major domains. In a study of college students, Martínez and Dukes (1987) found that the self-esteem ratings of Hispanics were higher than those of Anglos along a culture-specific, or self-worth, domain. In the public domain of intelligence, which is measured in terms of the majority culture, Hispanic students rated themselves lower than Anglo students. If the results hold for younger students, this research would suggest that young children might show ethnic differences in ratings of their scholastic competence, but not in their ratings of global self-worth.

Some researchers have suggested that bilingual education programs promote children's self-esteem (Hernández-Chávez 1984). According to the rationale for this proposition, self-esteem is enhanced because the children feel that their language and culture are an important part of the classroom; this rationale would suggest that global self-worth would be facilitated. At the same time, evaluations of high-quality bilingual-education programs (i.e., programs that have experienced bilingual teachers who use the children's native language for curriculum instruction for a significant amount of the school day) also show that such programs promote academic achievement in the participants (Willig 1985). In addition, research suggests that achievement influences students' perceptions of their scholastic competence (Harter 1983). Accordingly, perceptions of students' competence should be high, and there should not be any ethnic differences in their ratings.

Positive cross-cultural attitudes are important for harmonious functioning in our society. Despite the relevance of cross-cultural attitudes in our society and in educational settings, little research has focused specifically on cross-cultural attitudes in children. Although numerous studies have assessed issues surrounding ethnic socialization in children (see Spencer & Markstrom-Adams 1990), most studies have centered on children's development of ethnic identity rather than the development of cross-cultural attitudes.

The majority of well-designed studies on cross-cultural attitudes have been conducted with adolescents, and much of this research has examined the influence of educational interventions on children's development of cross-cultural attitudes (e.g., Gardner & Lambert 1972). The few studies that have assessed cross-cultural attitudes in children as a result of educational interventions (Slavin 1983) have been important in demonstrating the positive influence of such interventions on both majority and ethnic-minority children's cross-cultural attitudes and achievement (e.g., Kagan 1986).

Student expectations toward each other are very important in how children begin to form perceptions of their own competence and in forming cross-cultural attitudes. Allowing only unplanned or incidental contact between majority and minority students may reinforce negative expectations on the part of classmates. In his highly influential work on peer relations and school desegregation, Allport (1954) proposed four factors that are the core conditions for improving intergroup relations and maximizing the achievement of minority and majority students. When minority and majority students have *equal status* in the classroom, *work interdependently* on tasks with common objectives, and have *opportunities to interact with each other as individuals*, student expectations and attitudes toward each other become more positive. Allport also pointed out that the effect of these contacts will be greatly enhanced if the contacts are *supported by teachers* and other authority figures. Other researchers have provided evidence to support Allport's basic premises by demonstrating that instructional treatments that explicitly promote positive interdependence between minority and majority students result in positive outcomes in terms of an increased number of cross-racial friendships and greater self-esteem and academic achievement (Lambert 1984, 1987). It is particularly during the early school years that children are malleable in their cross-cultural attitudes. Children educated in immersion programs from early elementary school develop more positive cross-cultural attitudes than their non-immersion-program peers (Lambert 1987).

Cooperative learning methods, which incorporate Allport's four factors, use heterogeneous grouping and shared group leadership with activities that require the students to work interdependently, with clear individual and group accountability for the achievement of all group members (Johnson, Johnson, and Holubec 1986; Kagan 1986; Slavin 1983). Research demonstrates unequivocal support for cooperative learning in achievement, ethnic relations, and self-esteem (Slavin 1983; see Kagan 1986 for a review of this literature). When students work in ethnically mixed cooperative learning groups, they gain in cross-ethnic friendships. Most research also shows positive effects of cooperative learning on achievement. Strong achievement gains have been found with minority and typically low-achieving students, with little or no effect for White (non-Hispanic) and higher-achieving students. However, the gains of minority and low-achieving students are not made at the expense of majority or high-achieving students, as these students also made gains at least as great as, if not greater than, in traditional classrooms. Thus, cooperative learning methods, while closing the achievement gap between minority and majority students, also have positive effects on the self-esteem and cross-cultural attitudes of both minority and majority children.

Bilingual/Immersion Education Model

Two-way bilingual/immersion education programs are equally concerned with the language and academic development of both language-minority and language-majority children (Lindholm 1990a). The students are integrated for all content instruction in a high-quality curriculum equivalent to the curriculum taught in mainstream classes. The major difference is that the language of instruction is the native language for the language-minority students (e.g., Spanish) and a second language for language-majority students (e.g., Spanish). (See Lindholm 1990a for a description of two-way bilingual/immersion programs.)

Variations in community and administrative needs mean that schools have varying goals for implementing two-way programs. However, three major goals of most programs include: (1) students will develop high levels of proficiency in two languages, (2) students will demonstrate normal to superior academic performance measured in both languages, and (3) students will show high levels of psychosocial competence and positive cross-cultural attitudes.

The definition encompasses four criterial features: (1) the program essentially involves some form of dual language instruction, where the non-English language is used for a significant portion of the students' instructional day; (2) the program involves periods of instruction during which only one language is used; (3) both native English speakers and nonnative English speakers (preferably in balanced numbers) are participants; and (4) the students are integrated for most content instruction.

There are also a number of key instructional features, which are empirically and theoretically based (Lindholm

1990). Some of these strategies that are relevant to the discussion here include:

- *Additive bilingual environment.* All students are provided the opportunity to acquire a second language at no cost to their home language and culture.
- *Positive and reciprocal interactive instructional climate.* Promotion of positive two-way communication between teachers and students and between language-minority and majority student peers is an important instructional objective, including methods of cooperative learning.
- *Classroom composition.* To maintain an environment of educational and linguistic equity in the classroom and to promote two-way communication among native and non-native English speakers, the most desirable overall program ratio is 50 percent English speakers to 50 percent nonnative English speakers.

Bilingual/immersion education, then, is built on providing the student with the most positive social context in which to develop bilingual and psychosocial competence, a context in which both linguistic minority and majority students can benefit from an additive bilingualism environment; in which students develop in a social context where both languages and cultures are equally valued and all students are treated equally; and in which students are integrated in a natural fashion to promote positive cross-cultural attitudes and psychosocial development, and higher levels of second language development and academic achievement.

Research Questions

This study examined the perceived psychosocial competence and cross-cultural attitudes of third- and fourth-grade native English and Spanish speakers in two bilingual/immersion programs. The major research questions were: (1) What are the levels of perceived psychosocial competence of bilingual/immersion students? (2) How positive are the cross-cultural attitudes of students in bilingual immersion programs? and (3) Are there differences between the native Spanish and English speakers in their attitudes or perceived psychosocial competence?

Methods

A total of 177 third- and fourth-grade students participated in the study; 148 were native Spanish speakers and 29 were native English speakers enrolled in a bilingual/immersion program at one of two schools in California. There were three samples of students: (1) 31 Spanish and English speakers from School 1; (2) 35 Spanish and 11 English speakers from School 2 in Year 1; and (3) 82 Spanish and 12 English speakers from School 2 in Year 2. Approximately equal numbers of boys and girls were represented among the English and Spanish speakers.

At both schools, teachers had been trained to use cooperative learning methods. Classroom observations confirmed that the teachers were effectively using cooperative learning for instruction in different subject matter areas; that students were grouped in ways to promote two-way communication; and that the Spanish language and Hispanic heritage were important components in the classroom (Lindholm and Cuevas 1991). Thus, these classroom environments promoted social equity and two-way communication among students and between teacher and student.

One rating instrument filled out by the children and teachers was the Self-Perception Profile for Children (Harter 1983), which measures the child's sense of competence across six domains (academic, social, athletic, physical appearance, conduct, self-worth). Each domain is composed of a separate subscale of six items. For each of the items, the student selects from among two dichotomous alternatives which better describes the student. For that alternative, the student decides whether that descriptor is "Not very true" or "Really true." This format provides a range from 1 to 4; 1 indicates low competence and 4 indicates high competence. Students completed the ratings in four domains: academic competence, social competence, appearance, and global self-worth. [Teachers also completed a Teacher's Rating version of this scale, in the domains of academic and social competence and appearance. These ratings are discussed elsewhere (Lindholm 1990b) and only briefly referred to in this study.]

The second instrument completed by the students was the Cross-Cultural Language/Attitudes Scale (CLAS) developed by the author. This scale consists of three subscales and assesses: (1) *integrative motivation,* or the motivation to learn a second language in order to interact with other people (Gardner 1981); (2) *instrumental motivation*, or the motivation to learn a language in order to enhance one's opportunities in life (Gardner 1981); and (3) *cross-cultural attitudes*, or the significance of physical features in determining friendship patterns. The format of this instrument is similar to that of the Self-Perception Profile for Children; that is, for each of the items, the student selects from among two dichotomous alternatives that which better describe the student. For that alternative, the student decides whether that descriptor is "Not very true" or "Really true." This format provides a range from 1 to 4; 1 indicates less-positive attitudes and 4 indicates more-positive attitudes.

Both these instruments were completed by the students in their language of preference (i.e., Spanish or English).

Results and Discussion

The first set of analyses examined grade-level differences in the perceived competence scale. Results from these analyses demonstrated no significant grade-level effects for any of the four subscales. Thus, the third- and fourth-grade levels were collapsed for further analyses.

Table 8.1 presents the means and standard deviations for the three samples for perceived psychosocial competence. The first major column of the table is labeled "ACADEMIC" and represents the children's perception of their level of academic competence. In this category, students rated their competence according to the following criteria (the items were not worded in this way):

1. Good at school work
2. Smart as others
3. Do school work quickly
4. Remember easily
5. Do well at classwork
6. Figure out answers

As stated earlier, the scale ranges from 1 (low) to 4 (high), with 2.5 as the midpoint. Attention to table 8.1 shows that the means for the Spanish and English speakers at School 1 were 3.0 and 2.7, respectively, which was not a statistically significant group difference. At School 2 in Year 1, the means for

TABLE 8.1 MEANS AND STANDARD DEVIATIONS FOR ACADEMIC, SOCIAL, APPEARANCE, AND SELF WORTH PERCEPTIONS BY SCHOOL AND LANGUAGE BACKGROUND

	ACADEMIC		SOCIAL		APPEARANCE		SELF WORTH	
	M	*SD*	*M*	*SD*	*M*	*SD*	*M*	*SD*
SCHOOL 1								
Spanish	3.0	.55	2.9	.57	3.0	.58	3.0	.80
English	2.7	.37	2.8	.54	3.0	.53	3.2	.38
SCHOOL 2								
Year 1								
Spanish	2.9	.65	3.1	.59	2.9	.59	3.2	.60
English	3.0	.76	3.2	.69	3.0	.76	3.3	.85
SCHOOL 2								
Year 2								
Spanish	2.8	.65	2.9	.60	2.8	.63	2.9	.63
English	3.3	.58	3.2	.53	3.3	.78	3.2	.75

Spanish and English speakers were again quite comparable ($M = 2.9$ and $M = 3.0$). In Year 2, though, the English speakers ($M = 3.3$) scored significantly higher than the Spanish speakers ($M = 2.8$), $F (1, 54) = 6.71$, $p < .05$.

The mean scores for both Spanish and English speakers at both schools and for both years were above the midpoint of the scale (midpoint = 2.5). In addition, the mean scores across the different samples were remarkable similar.

The second perceived competence subscale on which children rated themselves was social competence. In this subscale, students assessed their level of perceived competence according to the following criteria:

1. Easy to make friends
2. Have a lot of friends
3. Easy to like
4. Do things with a lot of kids
5. Most kids like them
6. Popular with others same age

The second column of Table 1 presents the means and standard deviations for social competence. At School 1, the Spanish and English speaking students' mean scores were 2.9 and 2.8, respectively. At School 2, the mean scores for Spanish and English speakers were 3.1 and 3.2 for Year 1, and 2.9 and 3.2 for Year 2. There were no significant group differences in any of the three samples.

As with academic subscale, all the means for the students were well above the scale's midpoint. In addition, the means across the three samples were comparable.

The third perceived-competence subscale on which students rated themselves was appearance. For this subscale, the following criteria were used:

1. Happy with way they look
2. Happy with height and weight
3. Like body way it is
4. Like physical appearance way it is
5. Like face and hair way they are
6. Good looking

Attention to the third column of Table 1 shows that the Spanish and English speakers at School 1 had equivalent mean scores ($M = 3.0$). At School 2, the mean scores for Spanish and English speakers were also quite similar, at 2.9 and 3.0, respectively. In the Year 2 sample, however, the English speakers rated themselves higher on the appearance subscale ($M = 3.3$) than did the Spanish speakers ($M = 2.8$), $F(1, 54) = 5.15, p < .05$.

As Table 1 indicates, all the means were well above the scale's midpoint. The English speakers in Sample 3 rated themselves higher in appearance than any of the other groups; the remaining groups rated themselves comparably ($M = 2.8–3.0$).

The last perceived-competence subscale was self worth. For this subscale, students responded to the following types of items:

1. Happy with self
2. Like way life is
3. Happy with self as person
4. Like kind of person they are
5. Happy with way they are
6. Way they do things is fine

As table 8.1 shows, Spanish and English speakers at School 1 obtained mean scores of 3.0 and 3.2 respectively. At

School 2, there were also no statistically significant differences in either Year 1 (Spanish $M = 3.2$ and English $M = 3.3$) or Year 2 (Spanish $M = 2.9$ and English $M = 3.2$).

As in each of the other subscales, the mean scores were above the midpoint and were comparable for the different groups.

Overall, looking across the subscales, it is apparent that students' ratings did not vary much across the subscales, from academic to self worth. Overall, there were few differences between Spanish and English speaking students, which is quite exciting. Furthermore, the students' mean ratings were also comparable to those reported in other studies (e.g., Harter 1983). In Harter's sample of California middle- to upper-class third graders, the mean scores were around 3.0. Despite the social-class gap between the Harter (middle to upper class) and current (working class to middle class) samples, the means are strikingly similar. These results are very important because they show the significance of a positive and equitable social environment in stimulating children's psychosocial competence and in seeing themselves as academically competent, socially adept, and physically attractive.

Table 8.2 presents the correlations between the different perceived-competence subscales (as well as the cross-cultural subscales, which will be discussed in the next section). While students' scores were rather similar across the different subscales, the subscales were not necessarily highly correlated. Attention to Table 2 shows that academic competence was positively correlated with social competence (.16), but the correlation was quite low. On the other hand, academic competence was highly correlated with both appearance ($r = .44$, $p < .001$) and self-worth ($r = .54$, $p < .001$). Social competence was also highly correlated with both appearance ($r = .41$, $p < .001$) and self-worth ($r = .45$, $p < .001$). Appearance and self-worth were also highly related ($r = .56$, $p < .001$).

Another set of correlations worth reporting were the correlations between the children's ratings of their academic and social competence and their appearance, and the teachers' ratings of the children's academic and social competence and their appearance. All the correlations were low and nonsignificant: children's ratings of their own academic competence with teachers' ratings of the children's academic competence ($r = .22$); children's ratings of their own social competence with teachers' ratings of the children's social competence

TABLE 8.2 CORRELATIONS AMONG THE PERCEIVED COMPETENCE AND CROSS-CULTURAL LANGUAGE/ATTITUDES SUBSCALES

	ACADEMIC	SOCIAL	APPEAR	SELF	INTEG	INSTRU	ATTIT
Academic	—						
Social	.16	—					
Appearance	.44***	.41**	—				
Self Worth	.54***	.45***	.56***	—			
Integrative	.27*	.03	.31*	.43**	—		
Instrumental	.37**	.34**	.43**	.41**	.36**	—	
Attitudes	.06	.08	.16	.33**	.57***	.46***	—

* p < .05
** p < .01
*** p < .001

($r = -.11$); and children's ratings of their own appearance with teachers' ratings of their appearance ($r = .22$). (For further information about the teacher ratings, see Lindholm 1991b.) Clearly, the children and teachers hold different perceptions of the children's academic and social competence, as well as their appearance.

Children's appearance is clearly an important issue, as it is significantly correlated with all of the other subscales. Its high correlation with academic competence and self-worth are particularly noteworthy. Because the ratings reflect the children's perceptions of their appearance, these results are encouraging in that they demonstrate that the Hispanic children were being socialized to feel good about their general physical appearance. In addition, it may be that the integration of their language (Spanish) and their culture into the curriculum has indeed led to increases in their self-esteem and in their feelings of competence in general, as other bilingual education researchers have discussed (Hernández-Chávez 1984; Lambert 1987). Also, the positive portrayal of Hispanic children and adults in the Spanish literature and textbooks to which these children were exposed may have helped to promote the children's positive feelings about their own appearance.

Cross-Cultural Language Attitudes

The next set of analyses examined grade level differences in the cross-cultural language attitudes of the students. As with the perceived competence scale, scores could range from 1 (low) to 4 (high), with 2.5 as the midpoint. Analyses examining grade-level differences revealed no significant grade-level main effects for any of the subscales. Thus, the third- and fourth-grade levels were collapsed for further analyses.

Table 3 presents the means and standard deviations for these three samples. In the first column of Table 3 are the means and standard deviations for the Instrumental subscale of the cross-cultural language/attitudes scale. Items in this scale included the following concepts:

1. Learning two languages makes them smarter
2. Learning two languages helps them do better in school
3. Learning two languages helps them to get a better job
4. Learning two languages helps them get better grades

The Spanish speakers scored only slightly higher than the English speakers in Sample 1 (M = 3.7 and M = 3.4) and in Sample 2 (M = 3.3 and M = 3.2). In Sample 3, the English speakers scored slightly higher (M = 3.6) than the Spanish speakers (M = 3.4). However, none of the group differences even approached statistical significance. All the groups scored well above the midpoint, and all above 3.0, with small standard deviations indicating little variation in the scores.

In the second subscale, Integrative motivation, there were four items related to students' motivation to engage in second-language (nondominant societal language) learning to interact with other people:

1. Learn two languages to learn about other people
2. Enjoy meeting and listening to people who speak another language
3. Learning Spanish is important to talk to Spanish-speaking people
4. Learning Spanish is important so can meet and talk with different kinds of people

In each of the samples, there was no difference between the Spanish and English speakers, though Sample 1 (M = 3.6) scored slightly higher than Samples 2 (M = 3.3) and 3 (M = 3.4). Again, the scores were not only higher than the midpoint, but well above 3.0 as well. Thus, these scores clearly show positive attitudes toward a second language for the sake of meeting and interacting with other people.

The last subscale related to cross-cultural attitudes more specifically, with content addressed at:

1. Invite kids to their house regardless of skin color
2. Like to play with other kids no matter what they look like
3. Invite kids to house to play regardless of hair color

In this subscale, English speakers scored only slightly higher than Spanish speakers in Sample 1 (M = 3.8 and M = 3.6, respectively), Sample 2 (M = 3.8 and M = 3.3, respectively), and Sample 3 (M = 3.7 and M = 3.5, respectively). These differences did not approach statistical significance.

Again, the mean scores were well above the midpoint and close to the highest possible score (4.0).

Attention to Table 2 shows the correlations among the three cross-cultural attitudes/language subscales and the perceived competence subscales. As Table 2 indicates, instrumental motivation was significantly correlated with integrative motivation ($r = .36$, $p < .01$). Instrumental motivation was also highly related to cross-cultural attitudes ($r = .46$, $p < .001$). As one might expect of two socially-oriented scales, the correlation was higher for integrative motivation and cross-cultural attitudes ($r = .57$, $p < .001$).

Instrumental motivation was also correlated with academic competence ($r = .37$, $p < .01$), social competence ($r = .34$, $p < .01$), appearance ($r = .43$, $p < .01$), and self-worth ($r = .41$, $p < .01$). It is interesting that integrative motivation was not correlated with social competence ($r = .03$), though it was correlated with academic competence ($r = .27$, $p < .05$), appearance ($r = .31$, $p < .05$), and self-worth ($r = .43$, $p < .01$). Finally, cross-cultural attitudes was not correlated with academic competence ($r = .06$), social competence ($r = .08$), or appearance ($r = .16$), though it was significantly related to self-worth ($r = .33$, $p < .01$).

Overall, the students scored very high in all three subscales. The cross-cultural-attitudes subscale received slightly higher scores than the instrumental or integrative subscales, whose scores were comparable. There were no significant grade or language-group differences. Thus, these results show that the students held very positive attitudes toward other languages, people speaking other languages, and other students, regardless of skin or hair color. These results are comparable to other attitudinal studies of language-immersion programs in Canada with comparably aged children (for a review of this work, see Lambert 1987). Studies of children in immersion programs (one-way immersion in which English speakers are given instruction in French but not integrated with native French speakers) show that immersion children hold more positive cross-cultural attitudes than children in regular non-immersion classes. Other research with older students has shown that immersion students demonstrate higher levels of integrative and instrumental motivation than students in traditional foreign-language classes (Gardner 1981; Lindholm and Padilla 1990). Consistent with this prior research, students in the present study felt that learning two languages might give them some academic/occupational benefits.

Conclusions

These results clearly show that the children, regardless of their language background (English or Spanish), scored moderately high to high in academic competence, social competence, appearance, self-worth, instrumental motivation, integrative motivation, and cross-cultural attitudes. Such positive psychosocial findings add to an already impressive list of positive results associated with bilingual/immersion programs, such as high levels of bilingual proficiency and academic achievement in two languages (Lindholm 1990a, 1991; Lindholm and Aclán 1991).

Pedagogically, these results are encouraging for two reasons. One reason is that the findings could be interpreted to suggest that a high quality educational program that incorporates the language and culture of both groups in a truly integrative social (additive bilingual) environment can also enhance ethnic minority students' perception of their own academic competence, social competence, appearance, and self-worth. Another reason is that the results show that Anglo students who are in a classroom in which Spanish is the language of instruction and in which they are the minority in terms of the number of students in the class also demonstrate a level of academic competence and self-worth comparable to middle- and upper-class students who are in an English-only program. Thus, these results suggest that both Hispanic and Anglo students can benefit psychosocially from their integrated and equitable additive bilingual classroom experience.

References

Allport, G. (1954). *The nature of prejudice.* Cambridge, MA: Addison-Wesley.

Gardner, R. C. (1981). Second language learning. In R. C. Gardner and R. Kalin (Eds.), *A Canadian social psychology of ethnic relations.* Toronto: Methuen, 92–113.

Gardner, R. C., & Lambert, W. E. (1972). *Attitudes and motivation in second language learning.* Rowley, MA: Newbury House.

————. (1983). Developmental perspectives on the self-system. In E. M. Hetherington (Ed.), P. H. Mussen (Series Ed.), *Handbook of child psychology: Vol. 4. Socialization, personality, and social development.* New York: Wiley, 275–85.

Harter, S. and J. P. Connell (1982). A comparison of alternative models of the relationships between academic achievement and children's perceptions of competence, control, and motivational orientations. In J. Nicholls (Ed.), *The development of achievement-related cognitions and behaviors.* Greenwich, Conn.: J. A. I. Press.

Hernández-Chávez, E. (1984). The inadequacy of English immersion education as an educational approach for language minority students in the United States. In *Studies on immersion education: A collection for U.S. educators.* Sacramento: California State Department of Education, 144–83.

Johnson, D. W., R. T. Johnson, and E. J. Holubec (1986). *Circles of learning: Cooperation in the classroom.* Edina, Minn.: Interaction Book Company.

Kagan, S. (1986). Cooperative learning and sociocultural factors in schooling. In *Beyond language: Social and cultural factors in schooling language minority students.* California State University, Los Angeles: Evaluation, Dissemination, and Assessment Center.

Lambert, W. E. (1984). An overview of issues in immersion education. In *Studies in immersion education: A collection for U.S. educators.* Sacramento: California State Department of Education, 8–30.

———. (1987). The effects of bilingual and bicultural experiences on children's attitudes and social perspectives. In P. Homel, M. Palij, and D. Aaronson (Eds.), *Childhood bilingualism: Aspects of linguistic, cognitive and social development.* Hillsdale, N.J.: Lawrence Erlbaum Associates Publishers, 197–221.

Lindholm, K. J. (1990a). Bilingual immersion education: Criteria for program development. In A. M. Padilla, H. H. Fairchild, and C. Valadez (Eds.), *Bilingual Education: Issues and Strategies.* Beverly Hills, Calif.: Sage Publications.

———. (1990b). Perceived competence of Hispanic and Anglo third graders: Discrepancies between teacher and student ratings. Presented at the American Educational Research Association annual meeting, Boston, Massachusetts.

———. (1991). Theoretical assumptions and empirical evidence for academic achievement in two languages. *Hispanic Journal of Behavioral Sciences, 13*, 3–17.

Lindholm, K. J. and Z. Aclán (1991). Bilingual proficiency as a bridge to academic achievement: Results from bilingual/immersion programs. *Journal of Education, 173,* 99–113.

Lindholm, K. J. and J. Cuevas (1991). Teacher and student factors influencing English speaking and Spanish speaking children's achievement. Paper presented at the American Psychological Association annual meeting, San Francisco, California.

Lindholm, K. J. and A. M. Padilla (1990). The Mount Miguel high school partial immersion program. In A. M. Padilla, H. H. Fairchild, and C. Valadez (Eds.), *Foreign Language Education: Issues and Strategies.* Beverly Hills, CA: Sage Publications.

Martínez, R. and R. L. Dukes (1987). Race, gender, and self-esteem among youth. *Hispanic Journal of Behavioral Sciences, 9,* 427–43.

Rosenberg, M. (1979). *Conceiving the self.* New York: Basic Books.

Slavin, R. E. (1983). *Cooperative learning.* New York: Longman.

Spencer, M. B., & Markstrom-Adams, C. (1990). Identity processes among racial and ethnic minority children in America. *Child Development, 62,* 290–310.

Willig, A. (1985). A meta-analysis of selected studies on the effectiveness of bilingual education. *Review of Educational Research, 55,* 269–317.

Wylie, R. (1979). *The self-concept,* Volume 2. *Theory and research on selected topics.* Lincoln, Nebr.: University of Nebraska Press.

▼ 9 ▼
Managing Behavior in the Culturally Diverse Classroom

SAUNDRA SCOTT SPARLING

A student in an anger and aggression study I conducted reported the following to his classmates during one of the study's discussion group activities: "My name is Kal Kam.[1] A lot of you in this room call me Cal Can, you know, like the dog food. I hate that. You tease a lot of us Vietnamese kids about our names. You say we stick together and won't mix with you on the playground. That's why we keep to ourselves. When you tease us, we would rather not even work with you in class, but we have to. I can't do my work well when I'm upset and, when you tease me like that, it upsets me a lot."

DeVillar and Faltis (1991) have argued that, for instruction in culturally diverse classrooms to be effective, teachers must "be able to counter social forces that mitigate against culturally and linguistically diverse students talking together and solving problems cooperatively" (p 27). One such social force is evident in the types of discipline problems teachers in culturally diverse settings are called upon to deal with in the course of a normal teaching day. The vast majority of such problems involve students' minor to moderate disruptive behavior (e.g., behaviors ranging from talking out of turn to arguing), and a significant portion of these involve interpersonal anger and retaliatory aggressive acts such as passive withdrawal of participation (as indicated by the student above), excluding peers' participation, teasing, threatening, and calling peers names. These types of disruptions can be a particular problem in culturally diverse classrooms where peer exclusion, teasing, threats, and name-calling take on culturally and racially derisive overtones (Sparling 1988), overtones which contribute to patterns of self-segregation among various cultural and ethnic groups and limit the extent of classroom communication, integration, and cooperation across groups.

In an effort to reduce the frequency of such acts and to increase communication, cooperation, and integration among 105 fifth- and sixth-grade students in an integrated urban Los Angeles elementary school, I conducted a study which focused on getting the students to change the way they interpreted, or attributed, each other's behaviors. I hypothesized that, by getting students to attribute each other's behaviors more compassionately, they would feel less anger and would be motivated to make fewer retaliatory aggressive responses toward each other. The results of the study indicated that modifying students' attributions is an effective aggression intervention. Results also indicated that such an intervention influences students differently, depending upon their cultural background. These findings can be of great help to teachers, counselors, and administrators who are dealing with the complexities of anger-related disruptive behavior in their culturally diverse school settings. The goals in this chapter, therefore, are to (1) describe my study and its results, (2) describe several of the intervention procedures employed, (3) discuss the varying cultural group responses to the intervention procedures, and (4) draw on the study's implications to offer guidance to teachers, counselors, and administrators.

The Intervention Study
Modifying Attributions to
Reduce Student Anger and Aggression

Study Assumptions

In conducting this study, I assumed the truth of certain findings other researchers have made about anger and aggression. I believe it will be helpful to identify the key assumptions.

Assumption #1:
Changing attributions (interpretations)
can reduce anger

A number of researchers have determined that aggression is often motivated by anger and that it is our *interpretations* of things that happen to us that evoke our anger (Dodge 1981;

Feshbach 1984; Lochman, Nelson, and Sims 1984). In keeping with this finding, recent studies of adults and children offer evidence that particular kinds of interpretations called "attributions" are major determiners of both the occurrence and the intensity of anger (Pastore 1950; Weiner, Anderson, and Prawat 1983; Weiner, Graham, Stern, and Lawson 1982). Attributions are explanations for why a negative or surprising event has occurred. An observer, for example, might attribute the cause of a students' test failure as follows: "He didn't study as hard as usual"; "She never studies"; "He's not very smart"; or "She's just unlucky." Although an infinite number of casual attributions are possible for any given outcome, underlying connotative similarities among them have been identified. Weiner (1986) identified similarities along three dimensions: *internality, stability,* and *controllability.*

Internality refers to whether the cause of an outcome is attributed to something in the individual (internal) or in the environment (external). An attribution to bad luck is external. Attributions to low ability (e.g., not being very smart) and to typical or atypical effort (e.g., never studying or not studying as hard as usual) are internal. Internal attributions made to ability and or typical effort have been found to elicit differing expectations about future achievement. Low ability or typical effort often elicits expectations of low future achievement. Low effort that is atypical often elicits expectations of higher future achievement. This difference in expectations indicates an additional dimension. That dimension is stability.

Stability refers to the perceived consistency/inconsistency or permanence/impermanence of an attributed cause. Weiner reports that ability and typical effort are perceived as permanent or consistent, while atypical effort is perceived as impermanent or inconsistent. Though ability, typical effort, and atypical effort fall similarly along the internality dimension, they differ on the stability dimension and, therefore, produce different responses.

A third dimension of particular relevance to anger has been labeled controllability. Controllability refers to whether an individual was or wasn't able to cause or prevent an event. Attributions differing along the controllability dimension elicit differing emotional responses. Weiner (1980a, 1980b), for example, observed that while subjects often felt sorry for a student for whom failure was attributed to low ability (an uncontrollable cause), they often felt angry with a student for whom failure was attributed to never studying (low typical effort, a controllable cause). Although low ability and low typical effort are both internal and stable, their difference along the controllability dimension generates differing responses. Controllability and stability are the anger-relevant dimensions. Children's attributions to controllability predict the occurrence of anger, while stability predicts it's intensity (Weiner 1986).

Assumption #2:
Reducing anger can reduce motivation to act aggressively

Kaplan (1984) and Korndant (1984) describe a type of aggression that is motivated by anger or rage and the desire to "even the score" or "get even." It is *hostile aggression* and, in this case, might be operationally defined as 'any passive, verbal, or physical act involving obvious and/or acknowledged anger and intent to retaliate against or harm persons and/or property'. Several researchers assert that reducing anger reduces hostile aggression (Dodge 1981; Feshbach 1984; Lochman et al 1981; Rule and Ferguson 1984). Rule and Ferguson propose that the likelihood one will perpetrate an act of hostile aggression increases as one's anger intensity increases, and that one's anger intensity increases in relationship to ones' attributions about the level of negative intention on the part of the person with whom one is angry.

   Rule and Ferguson categorize attribution somewhat differently than does Weiner (1979, 1984, 1986). They suggest that anger intensity varies from least to greatest for harmful outcomes attributed to: (1) unforeseeable accidental causes; (2) foreseeable but unintentional causes; (3) foreseeable and intentional but nonmalevolently intended causes; and (4) foreseeable, intentional, and malevolently intended causes. The Rule and Ferguson conceptualization suggests a direct relationship between anger and aggression.

Assumption #3:
Increasing empathy changes controllability attributions, thereby reducing anger and aggression

Theoretical approaches to aggression intervention in the classroom typically fall into two main categories: behavioral and cognitive. The behavioral approach assumes aggression to be determined by stimulus events, or events that come before aggressive behavior; and behavioral consequences, or reinforcing events that follow the behavior. Thus, behavioral researchers typically use behavior modification procedures to change stimulus events (e.g., by rewarding a child for teasing less often) and/or response consequences (e.g., by getting other children to ignore a child who teases).

Cognitive researchers, on the other hand, propose that aggression is determined by the way children cognitively process, or think about, events. There are several cognitive approaches in aggression intervention research. Empathy research is among these. Empathy theorists propose that anger and aggression result from a lack of ability to identify, understand, and respond to feelings in others (i.e., empathize). Empathy research efforts are focused on reducing anger and aggressive behavior by increasing subjects' empathetic responding (Feshbach 1983, 1984).

Feshbach (1984) has proposed a three-part empathy model, which includes the ability to do the following: (a) identify emotion in another; (b) understand the situation the way the other person understands it (cognitive perspective-taking); and (c) respond emotionally by experiencing or sharing the feelings of the other person (affective arousal). She employed this model in a study in which she compared the pre- and post-empathy training, placebo, and control-group aggression scores of ninety-eight male and female Black, Chicano, and Anglo third- and fourth-grade students. Subjects were identified as nonaggressive and aggressive. Measures of aggression compared teacher ratings of the children's social behavior in the classroom before and after the treatment. The empathy treatment featured opportunities for subjects' self-observation via video tape. The placebo group was trained in academic problem-solving skills. In comparison to the nontreatment controls, aggressive behavior decreased and prosocial behavior increased significantly in the empathy treatment group. These changes transferred to the classroom setting. Unfortunately, if there were cultural differences in responses to Feshbach's treatment, they were not discussed. However, results in her study do help to clarify the relationships among empathy, anger, and aggression.

Feshbach proposed that empathy influenced anger and aggression as follows:

Empathy would be expected to affect the antecedents of anger such as feelings of frustration, rejection, and unfairness. The

empathetic person, by virtue of understanding the other's
point of view is less likely to become angered through the mis-
interpretation of the other's behavior as arbitrary or unfair.
(194)

This explanation is very much in keeping with attribution
findings that have linked angry and hostile responses to attribution research about the causes of negative events. Attributing someone else's negative outcomes to controllable causes in
oneself (e.g., "I hurt you") has been shown to result in the experience of guilt (Weiner et al. 1982). Attributing someone
else's negative outcomes to causes uncontrollable by him or her
(e.g., "You accidentally hurt yourself") has been linked to pity,
sympathy, and motivation to help (compassionate responding).
Depending upon the source of the negative outcome (i.e.,
aggression-related pain and suffering caused either by oneself
or by others), either compassion or guilt and an accompanying
reduction of anger could result.

Compassion or guilt may be one source of the aggression
inhibition referred to by Feshbach (1984). Compassion and anger seem to be incompatible emotions. In her study,
perspective-taking seemed to modify the way children attributed causes in problem situations, thereby reducing the probability of their getting angry and being motivated to respond
aggressively. After empathy and perspective-taking activities in
which subjects acted aggressively and observed themselves,
they seemed to interpret those situations in ways that left them
feeling compassionate and motivated to help. Perspective-
taking activities may alter attributions from controllable
causes in others (one determinant of anger) to controllable
causes in oneself (one determinant of guilt) or to uncontrollable causes in others (one determinant of compassion). These
may, in turn, result in shifts from aggressive responses such as
withdrawal of help, teasing, fighting, etc., to prosocial responses such as helping.

In summary, I assumed in my study (1) that increasing
one's empathy through perspective-taking can change one's attributions (interpretations) to more compassionate ones, (2)
that changing attributions can reduce one's anger, and (3) that
reducing anger can reduce one's motivation to act aggressively.
In keeping with these assumptions, my study objective was to
test the effects of perspective-taking activities on children's
controllability attributions. I hypothesized (1) that children's

participation in perspective-taking activities would effectively change their interpretations of other children's behavior by reducing their controllability attributions and increasing their uncontrollability attributions; (2) that such changes in their interpretations would reduce their reported anger; and (3) their reduced anger would result in their reduced reported motivation to respond aggressively.

The Plan of the Study

One hundred five fifth- and sixth-grade students participated in perspective-taking activities designed to alter the way they interpreted the causes of negative events at school. Students from six classes were randomly assigned to one of two treatments: (1) perspective-taking and (2) read-for-directions art projects. Each group participated in six half-hour treatment sessions on six consecutive days. The art projects functioned as a placebo activity and provided a comparison for the perspective-taking intervention. The groups were reversed after the first six-session period so that the placebo group engaged in the perspective-taking activities and the perspective-taking group participated in the placebo activities.

Perspective-taking activities consisted of journal writing, role-playing, filling in cartoon dialogue, discussion circles, goal-setting, and overnight goal-implementation assignments. A major aspect of taking another person's perspective was addressed during each half-hour session. Placebo activities consisted of six different reading-for-directions art projects. Subjects could complete each project by reading and following a predrawn pattern to produce a given three-dimensional object.

At the beginning of the study and after each six-session intervention phase, subjects' responses to vignettes depicting familiar hypothetical negative outcomes were assessed. Their pre/post responses were analyzed for (1) shifts from controllability to uncontrollability attributions (i.e., their interpretations of why the perpetrator may have caused the event), (2) reductions in their reported anger, (3) reductions in the aggressive responses subjects said they wanted to make, and (4) reductions in the aggressive responses subjects predicted they would actually make. Subjects rated how likely they would be to respond in each of four categories of aggression. The aggression response categories reflected the following four primary types of aggression identified in the literature (Atkin 1957; Feshbach 1979; Goldstein, Apter, and Harootunian 1984; Lockman, Nelson, and Sims 1981): (1) Physical aggression against persons (e.g., hitting, pushing, kicking), (2) physical aggression against property (e.g., breaking, tearing, marking), (3) verbal aggression against persons (e.g., teasing, threatening, insulting), and (4) passive aggression (e.g., pouting, withdrawing friendship, refusing to participate).

The Sample

The sample consisted of 105 fifth- and sixth-grade pupils from an urban elementary school. There were 52 boys and 53 girls. Subjects' racial or ethnic backgrounds were as follows: 24 Asian-Americans, 5 African-Americans, 68 Hispanic-Americans, 2 Pacific Islanders, and 6 non-Hispanic whites. Twenty-eight subjects were identified as fluent English speaking (FEP), 25 as limited English speaking (LEP), 37 as English-only speakers (EO), and 1 as non-English-speaking. Language fluency information was not available for 14 students. All LEP students were receiving bilingual education services. The sample was assumed to be representative of the school population.

Subjects were drawn from a pool of 115 pupils. To be included, subjects had to have been identified by the school as EO, FEP, or LEP. They also had to have active consent from a parent or guardian and have consented to participate for themselves. One non-English-speaking student was excluded from the study. Nine students whose parents refused consent did not participate. During the study, excluded students did placebo activities during both six-day intervention periods and were not assessed.

The Instrument

To measure students' changes in attributions, levels of anger, and resultant motivation to commit aggressive acts, an instrument consisting of a collection vignettes to which students were to react was designed. Three forms of this instrument, the Negative Outcomes Response Assessment (NORA) were used. One was used for the preintervention and two for the postintervention assessments. Each form consisted of eight vignettes depicting one positive and seven negative outcomes that subjects might experience at school. In each negative vignette, the outcome was clearly caused by someone other than the subject but the controllability or uncontrollability of the cause was left ambiguous. One vignette, for example, read, "You are walking across the playground when you get bumped from behind. You turn to see the person who who bumped you walking away." In this case there is an obvious perpetrator but the reason for which s/he perpetrated the act is left ambiguous.

In two of the seven vignettes, the negative outcomes resulted from acts of personal aggression (e.g., being pushed, bumped, tripped), two from verbal aggression (e.g., teasing), and three from property aggression (e.g., hiding the person's notebook). Each native vignette was followed by nine 6-point likert scaled items for which the students gave likelihood ratings from 1 to 6 anchored as 1—not at all, 2—a tiny bit, 3—a little, 4—somewhat, 5—a lot, and 6—a whole lot. On the first four items the subjects rated the likelihood of four possible causal explanations for the outcome, as proposed by Weiner (1986). The explanations presented (1) a controllable-stable cause such as "This person is a bully," (2) a controllable-unstable cause such as "This person was just angry right then," (3) an uncontrollable-stable cause such as "This person is clumsy," and (4) an uncontrollable-unstable cause such as "This person did it by accident."

On the fifth item, subjects rated their level of anger over the event from one to six using the same anchors as for items one through four. On the sixth through the eighth items, they rated the likelihood that they would want to make any of four aggressive responses to the event. The aggressive response items reflected four primary types of aggression identified in the literature (Atkin 1957; Feshbach 1979; Goldstein, Apter, and Harootunian 1984; Lochman, Nelson, and Sims 1981). These were damaging property (e.g., breaking, tearing, marking); harming persons physically (e.g., hitting, kicking, pushing); harming persons verbally (e.g., teasing, threatening, insulting); and passively getting even other than by acts of property, verbal, or physical aggression (e.g., pouting, withdrawing friendship, refusing to participate). Once again the ratings for each aggressive item were the same as for items one through four. On the ninth item, subjects circled the letter of the response they predicted they could probably actually make regardless of what they felt they would want to do.

The eighth vignette was designed to nullify the negative affective focus which may have been elicited by the first seven vignettes. It depicted an unambiguous positive outcome. For example, one vignette read: "Toward the end of the school day you are called to the office. When you get there, you find that you have a phone call from your mother telling you that you are to wait after school to be picked up because you and the family are taking a surprise visitor to Disneyland." The positive outcome was always caused by another person. Subjects rated how happy they would have felt about the outcome (not at all happy, not very happy, a little happy, happy, very happy, and extremely happy). Subjects then rated how likely they would have been to make each of two negative and three positive behavioral responses. Ratings on all NORA items were combined to yield controllability and uncontrollability scores of 4 to 24 points, anger scores of 2 to 12, personal and verbal aggression scores of 8 to 48, and property aggression scores of 12 to 72. Probable actual responses scores for personal and verbal outcome causes were from 2 to 16 points, and for property aggression vignettes the scores were 3 to 24 points.

The Intervention Activities

The intervention activities were modifications of several games, demonstrations, and role-playing activities from the Responsibility Training used by Benson (1978, 1979) and Sparling (1986) to increase personal responsibility of students in an inner-city elementary school program. These activities were modified to incorporate Storms' (1973) attribution theory findings about perceived similarity (i.e., that when we see ourselves as others see us, we make similar attributions to theirs about our own behavior), the three parts of Feshbach's (1984) empathy model, and Higgins's (1984) suggestions about self-observation. Intervention sessions were designed to have subjects empathize with others (i.e., recognize the similarity between their own and others' feelings and responses) so that they would attribute their own and others' negative behaviors to more similar causes. Specifically, subjects were to practice interpreting others' behavior from the points of view that (1) like themselves, others frequently believed themselves to be aggressing in self-defense; (2) their own behavior was sometimes the cause when others responded aggressively; and (3) others' aggressive responses were similar to the responses subjects might have and probably had made in similar situations.

The six half-hour sessions were conducted on six consecutive days. Each day's activities built upon those of the previous day so that effects would occur gradually. The session activities consisted of role-playing in short skits, journal writing, filling in cartoon dialogue, discussion circles, goal-setting, and goal-implementation. These activities were used to promote perspective-taking (i.e., seeing oneself from different perspectives) and self-other identification (i.e., seeing similarities between oneself and others). At the end of each session, subjects were assigned an overnight experiment or observation during which they implemented personal goals related to the intended session outcome.

First Session Activities

There were five steps in Session 1: (1) introductions and setting-up, (2) problem identification, (3) overall study goal presentation, (4) presentation of the specific day's goal (done through role-playing), and (5) presentation of the overnight assignment.

Introductions and Setting-Up (2 minutes). To begin the session, name tags were distributed and I introduced myself to the subjects (I conducted all six sessions personally.) I reviewed the format of the study (i.e., number and length of sessions, entering and exiting procedures for students coming to the intervention activities from other rooms, etc.). Subjects received answers to their questions.

Problem Identification (5 minutes). Problem identification involved four steps: (1) subjects shared two pieces of information about themselves, (2) were presented with one major concept, (3) brainstormed examples of how the concept applied in their lives, and (4) wrote personal examples.

The problem was identified when, by a show of hands, subjects acknowledged having had upsets at school and wanting fewer of them. They were told that two common upset feelings at school were hurt and anger. The researcher shared three personal experiences of being hurt and angry at school and listed them on the chalk board. By a show of hands, subjects acknowledged having had similar things upset them. They brainstormed several more upsetting outcomes, which were also listed on the chalkboard. Finally, on individual worksheets (see figure 9.1), subjects listed three things that made them angry and three things that made them feel hurt at school.

WHAT MAKES ME ANGRY?

1. _____

_____

2. _____

_____

3. _____

_____

1. _____

_____

2. _____

_____

3. _____

_____

WHAT HURTS MY FEELINGS?

1. _____

_____

2. _____

_____

3. _____

_____

1. _____

_____

2. _____

_____

3. _____

_____

Fig. 9.1

Presentation of the Overall Study Goal (10 minutes). The overall study goal was presented through an activity called the "grapes game." There were two intended outcomes in this game: To recognize that achieving any goal requires certain actions (defined as ground rules), and to define ground rules as those actions necessary and sufficient to achieve a goal. The stated objective of the grapes game was that subjects each eat a grape they had been given. One grape was placed upon a napkin on each of their desks. The stated rules of the game made achieving the objective impossible. Subjects were not to move any part of their bodies nor could the grape be moved. Subjects could only talk and make suggestions. As soon as the subjects noted the impossibility, an analogy was drawn between ground rules (i.e., the necessary actions) for eating a grape and ground rules for having fewer upsets. Subjects were told that the goals in the five remaining training sessions were to find out what the ground rules were for having fewer upsets at school and to experiment with acting on them.

Presentation of Specific Session Goal Through Role-Playing (5 minutes). Subjects were told that the first essential step in having fewer upsets was to recognize when they or someone else was upset. In a group circle formation, the researcher and the subjects demonstrated angry and hurt body stances and facial expressions for each other. They also practiced identifying emotions demonstrated.

Presentation of the Overnight Assignment (3 minutes). Subjects were given three overnight assignments: (1) to observe and identify when others were feeling hurt or angry, (2) to observe and identify what others did when they were hurt or angry, and (3) to guess what the ground rules for having fewer upsets might be. Subjects were asked to be prepared to share their guesses and what they had observed at the next day's session. They were also cautioned to just observe and nothing more.

Session Two Activities

There were three intended outcomes in this session. Subjects were to (1) acknowledge having aggressed against others in ways similar to those others had used to aggress against them, (2) identify similarities between their own and others' motives for aggressing, and (3) recognize that they and others usually explained their aggression as defensive (i.e., due to external and uncontrollable causes) rather than offensive (i.e., due to internal and controllable causes).

Reporting Back and Journal Writing (5 minutes). The researcher shared personal results from doing the assignment. By a show of hands, subjects acknowledged having done or not done the assignment. Several subjects who had not done the assignment told why. The researcher listened to the reasons with an attitude of acceptance. The primary reason given was forgetting. Subjects were told that forgetting was natural and were encouraged to think of some way to help themselves remember to do the coming night's assignment. One or two of the subjects who had done the observation reported what they noticed. Verbal probes were used to elicit what happened, how the angry and/or hurt persons looked, and how the persons behaved. One report was, "Somebody teased my best friend about his shirt. I could tell he felt hurt because he got quiet after that and didn't talk or play much." Each report was followed by the question, "How many of you have ever felt and acted like the person _____ [reporter's name] observed?" The response was a show of hands. In all sessions, a show of hands were used to promote self-other identification (i.e., seeing oneself as similar to others).

Role-Playing (7 minutes). Pairs of subjects participated in a two-line, two-person skit (see figure 9.2). The skit was about a student who, upon accidentally dropping a book, was called a dummy by a classmate. The skit was chosen because the majority items reported in the subjects' anger/hurt lists from the first session involved someone teasing them or saying something mean.

Concept Presentation (10 minutes). The session concept was as follows: Responding aggressively to hurt and anger often yields more hurt and anger. Two perspective-taking activities were used to present it: the Hurt/Anger Checklist (see figure 9.3) and the Upset Chain Diagram (see figure 9.4). Things the subjects had indicated on their previous day's worksheet as those that hurt them were listed on one side of the Hurt/Anger Checklist, and things they said made them feel angry were listed on the other side. Each item listed had a blank space be-

---

Skit 1 (Making it safe for difference and mistakes)

"YOU DUMMY!"

SCENE: STUDENTS A AND B ARE TALKING. STUDENT A
HAS AN OBJECT.

STUDENT A: (ACCIDENTALLY DROPPING THE OBJECT)
OOPS!

STUDENT B: YOU DUMMY!

Fig. 9.2

fore and after it. I read aloud the first four or five items on the list and pointed out those I had personally experienced. Next I read each item of the list while the subjects followed along silently, putting a check mark in the space in front of each item for which something similar had been done to them. Finally, while I reread the list, subjects went back over it and put a check behind each thing they had done to others. The purpose of the checklist was for subjects to hold two simultaneous self-observation perspectives: one as the victim and one as the perpetrator.

In the second activity, subjects were introduced to the Upset Chain Diagram. Its purpose was to help subjects recognize that most people see their own aggression as being a justifiable defense, not an offense, and that retaliating against someone who is defending themselves often elicits more defensiveness. The activity went as follows: I and several subjects reported something we had each done when angry of hurt (e.g., shouted at or hit someone). They then identified how the other person might have felt, what the other person did in response, how that response made the subject feel, and how the subject responded in return. This sequence of actions and responses was labeled a chain. A chain generated by one subject was, "I shouted at my friend. My friend felt angry and called me name. I got angrier and called my friend a name back. My friend called me a name again. . . ." The point of the chain was to create for the subjects a clear image of how they were often all feeling the same way (hurt or angry) and trying to do the same thing (defend).

THINGS THAT HURT MY FEELINGS

_____ people telling others to beat me up   _____

_____ people not being my friend   _____

_____ being called names like dumb or stupid
      when I make a mistake   _____

_____ people talking behind my back   _____

_____ people making fun of my last name   _____

_____ people picking on me   _____

_____ people lying about me   _____

_____ people teaming up against me   _____

_____ my friends abandoning me   _____

_____ being left by a friend   _____

_____ friends not wanting to be my friend any more   _____

_____ people treating me unfairly   _____

_____ people laughing when I don't play the game well   _____

_____ people giving me the silent treatment   _____

_____ my friends leaving me out   _____

_____ getting teased about the way I dress   _____

_____ being called bad names   _____

_____ not being able to get help   _____

_____ people making fun of personal things like being
      Black or Mexican   _____

_____ people making fun of my different language
      or accent   _____

_____ people telling others about something I am
      embarassed about   _____

Fig. 9.3
Hurt/anger checklist.

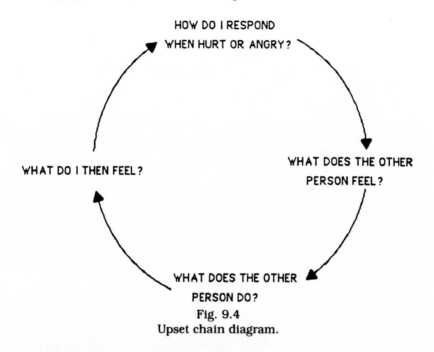

Fig. 9.4
Upset chain diagram.

Presentation of the Ground Rule (3 minutes). Subjects received a Ground Rules Sheet (see figure 9.5). On it were written two ground rules with space for a third. Below each ground rule was a space in which each subject could write. Subjects were reminded of how easy it was to feel defensive and act aggressively. They were told that each person needed to stop fueling the other's defensiveness if upsets were to decrease. The first ground rule was, "Make it safe for differences and mistakes." I shared two things I had done as a student to make it unsafe for others' differences and mistakes: I told about poking fun at one schoolmate who had acne and about teasing another schoolmate when she lost an important contest. I also shared about realizing how hurt those people felt, about deciding never to tease again, and about having found it difficult not to ever tease.

Presentation of the Overnight Assignment (5 minutes). In the space below Ground Rule 1, subjects wrote one thing they would do as an experiment for twenty-four hours to make it safe for someone else's differences and or/mistakes. They were asked to notice how hard or easy it was to do. One of two subjects shared what they had written. Examples of things subjects wrote were: "Ignore the differences and mistakes,"

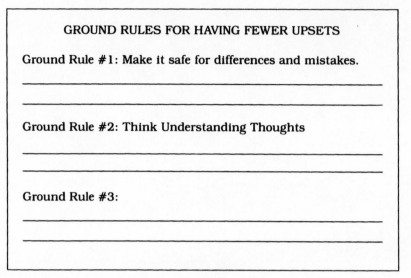

Fig. 9.5
Ground rules sheet #1.

"Stop talking behind their backs," and "Stop calling people names." All written materials were given the subjects' numbers instead of their names, were placed in individual folders with the same number, and were collected and kept with me between sessions.

The Last 4 Sessions

The last four (and the first two) sessions were conducted using some variation of the following five general steps: (1) reporting back and journal writing, (2) concept presentation, (3) role-playing, (4) ground rule presentation, and (5) overnight assignment presentation. In the reporting back and journal writing step, the researcher and subjects reported on the overnight assignment and noted the results in their journals. The sequence for reporting journal writing was always as follows: In a sentence or two, the researcher summarized the previous days' outcomes, reminded the subjects of the overnight assignment, shared personal results, took volunteered reports from one or two subjects about their results, and had subjects write about their results in their journals. The objectives of the journal writing step were to have the subjects relate to each other's personal experiences and establish a comfortable group atmosphere.

The concept presentation step, as implied, presented the major points of the session. The usual mode of presentation was a story, skit, or demonstration. The role-playing step was accomplished through a seven-step skit procedure as follows:

1. The researcher read the skit aloud and acted out both parts while the subjects followed along silently.
2. The subjects and the researcher together did a high-spirited reading of the skit. (Steps 1 and 2 were intended to familiarize the subjects with the skit vocabulary and allow them to role-play in nonthreatening anonymity.)
3. The researcher and a subject volunteer demonstrated the skit twice, each playing both parts.
4. Subjects paired off and each practiced both skit parts at their seats. In the case of an odd number the researcher worked with the unpaired subject.
5. Pairs of subjects volunteered to perform before the group.
6. In the large group, the subjects told how it felt to be the victim in a similar real-life situation in school.
7. Subjects acknowledged having been the perpetrator in similar situations and one or two subjects disclosed actual experiences.

Each skit was approximately fifteen seconds in length and presented the targeted concept in an aggressor/victim situation. Each subject played both roles.

In the ground rule presentation step, the major concept was related to a necessary action (i.e., ground rule) and subjects set personal goals for taking that action. During the presentation of overnight assignments, subjects were asked to implement their personal goals. Each session was closed with a thank you and the collecting of all name tags and written materials.

Results

There were both predicted and surprising results in this study. Both will be discussed here. Because of the limited numbers of subjects in the other ethnic groups, only results for Asian- and Hispanic-American students will be reported.

Expected Results Related to Study Hypotheses

Results from this study demonstrate that, in a three-week period, perspective-taking effectively changed many subjects' attributions. As predicted, these subjects were significantly less likely after the treatment than before to interpret a perpetrator's behavior as due to controllable causes. In keeping with decreases in controllability attributions, when the vignettes involved personal aggression these subjects reported feeling significantly less angry and less motivated to respond aggressively after the intervention.

Surprising Results Related to Study Hypotheses

The most surprising result was that no subjects were significantly more likely to interpret a perpetrator's behavior as being due to uncontrollable causes in correspondence to significant decreases in their controllability attributions. Other unexpected results were related to differing cultural group responses to the intervention. First, only for Hispanic-American subjects did decreases in controllability attributions influence decreases in their anger as well as in their reported desire to aggress, and only when personal aggression was involved. Second, before the intervention, for the personal and property aggression conditions, Asian-American subjects' controllability attributions, anger, reported desire to act aggressively, and predicted actual aggressive response ratings were significantly lower than ratings for Hispanic-American subjects. For vignettes involving verbal aggression, only the Asian-American subjects' ratings of anger, reported desire to act aggressively, and predicted likelihood to actually act aggressively were significantly lower than those of the Hispanic-American subjects. Third, after the intervention there were slight, though not significant, increases in Asian-American subjects' anger ratings in the personal and property aggression conditions. Fourth, only for vignettes involving personal aggression did Hispanic-American subjects' controllability attributions, anger, and desired aggression ratings decrease significantly. For the vignettes involving property and verbal aggression, only their controllability attributions decreased. These selective responses to certain types of aggression were not expected. Finally, after the intervention, Hispanic-American subjects' ratings of their reported desire to respond aggressively and pre-

TABLE 9.1 MEANS & STANDARD DEVIATIONS FOR THE PRE- AND POST INTERVENTION ASSESSMENT PERIODS BY CULTURAL GROUP

PERSONAL AGGRESSION CONDITION

	Intervention Assessment Period						
	Pre			Post			
Subject Responses:	N	M	SD	N	M	SD	t
Control.							
Asian	24	13.08	(3.54)	23	12.00	(3.15)	1.06
Hispanic	64	16.62	(4.30)	64	11.64	(4.18)	7.73**
t test		*t*(86)	= 3.93**		*t*(82)	= .43	
Uncontrol.							
Asian	24	12.08	(3.37)	23	12.43	(3.19)	.18
Hispanic	64	11.09	(2.99)	43	12.03	(3.72)	1.62
t test		*t*(86)	= 1.26		*t*(82)	= .49	
Anger							
Asian	24	7.92	(2.30)	24	8.13	(2.24)	.56
Hispanic	64	9.38	(2.33)	64	8.51	(2.59)	2.20*
t test		*t*(86)	= 2.64**		*t*(82)	= .66	
Desired Aggression							
Asian	24	15.58	(6.83)	23	16.40	(6.00)	1.13
Hispanic	64	25.27	(9.65)	60	21.62	(9.24)	2.77**
t test		*t*(86)	= 5.25**		*t*(81)	= 2.55**	
Act. Resp.							
Asian	23	6.52	(1.78)	22	7.00	(2.51)	.60
Hispanic	60	8.87	(3.57)	57	8.09	(3.82)	.94
t test		*t*(86)	= 3.00**		*t*(77)	= 1.48	
VERBAL AGGRESSION CONDITION							
Control.							
Asian	24	13.38	(3.49)	23	12.22	(3.73)	1.11
Hispanic	65	14.66	(5.39)	60	12.40	(4.92)	3.08*
t test		*t*(87)	= 1.32		*t*(81)	= .18	
Uncontrol.							
Asian	24	10.75	(3.80)	23	12.09	(3.16)	1.84
Hispanic	65	11.72	(3.87)	60	11.98	(4.10)	.59
t test		*t*(87)	= 1.05		*t*(81)	= .12	
Anger							
Asian	24	7.75	(2.05)	23	7.57	(2.17)	.54
Hispanic	65	8.86	(2.51)	60	8.28	(2.71)	1.39
t test		*t*(87)	= 1.94*		*t*(81)	= 1.25	
Desired Aggression							
Asian	24	16.58	(6.88)	23	16.87	(6.22)	.80
Hispanic	65	25.69	(10.56)	58	23.02	(9.60)	1.71
t test		*t*(87)	= 3.92**		*t*(79)	= 2.84**	

	Intervention Assessment Period						
Subject	Pre			Post			
Responses:	N	M	SD	N	M	SD	t
Act. Resp.							
Asian	21	7.57	(2.18)	21	7.71	(2.03)	.21
Hispanic	58	8.83	(2.90)	55	9.42	(2.64)	1.92
t test		*t*(77)	= 1.85		*t*(74)	= 2.67**	
PROPERTY AGGRESSION CONDITION							
Control.							
Asian	24	10.61	(2.83)	23	11.01	(3.50)	1.05
Hispanic	65	13.68	(4.70)	60	11.57	(4.57)	3.39**
t test		*t*(87)	= 2.99**		*t*(81)	= .52	
Uncontrol.							
Asian	24	12.53	(3.87)	23	12.90	(3.24)	.40
Hispanic	65	12.42	(3.53)	60	13.01	(4.08)	1.71
t test		*t*(87)	= .12		*t*(82)	= .13	
Anger							
Asian	24	7.78	(1.70)	23	7.97	(1.91)	.74
Hispanic	65	9.11	(2.20)	60	8.74	(2.52)	1.36
t test		*t*(87)	= 2.68**		*t*(81)	= 1.50	
Desired Aggression							
Asian	24	14.58	(6.96)	23	13.73	(5.05)	2.55
Hispanic	65	21.81	(9.76)	59	19.80	(9.78)	.08
t test		*t*(87)	= 3.32**		*t*(80)	= 2.85**	
Act. Resp.							
Asian	22	6.97	(2.22)	22	7.12	(1.98)	1.29
Hispanic	56	9.01	(3.01)	56	8.84	(3.12)	.65
t test		*t*(76)	= 2.89*		*t*(76)	= 2.41*	

*$p < .05$, **$p < .01$

dicted likelihood of actually responding aggressively were still significantly higher than those for Asian-American subjects in the property and verbal aggression conditions. This was also true for differences in their reported desire to act aggressively in personal aggression conditions.

Discussion of Differences in Group Responses to Intervention

Asian-American students' controllability attributions, anger, reported desire to respond aggressively, and predicted actual aggressive responses were less intense than those of Hispanic-American students. There are several possible explanations. Asian-American children may characteristically be less likely to respond with intense emotion and desire to retaliate aggressively than Hispanic-American children. On the other hand, Hispanic-American students may have more freely expressed their true feelings than Asian-American students. It may also have been that the vignette content depicted incidents which, culturally, were different from the incidents that are arousing to Asian-American children.

The study shows that different types of aggression elicit different responses from children. Children's attributions, anger, desire to respond aggressively, and probable actual responses varied significantly for the three aggression conditions presented in this study. Acts of personal aggression (i.e., being hit or having things spilled on them) and verbal aggression seemed to elicit the highest controllability and desired aggression responses. These conditions also elicited the lowest uncontrollability responses. The Hispanic-American students in this study seemed to be more intensely aroused by personal aggression.

While true differences in children's responses to different types of aggression seem probable and logical, there are problems that threaten the validity of such a conclusion, at least in this study. At least three problems with instrumentation may have influenced the results. Items designed to be similar in the three forms of the NORA may not have been truly comparable, thereby eliciting very different responses from the subjects. Some of the response options may not have provided subjects with viable choices. The uncontrollability attribution response, "has an injured leg and couldn't move fast enough," for example, consistently received low ratings. This was not, therefore, a viable item. Finally, combining ratings for four different types of aggressive response items into one aggression score may also have caused a problem. The combination of very low with very high ratings could have resulted in scores that weren't sensitive to subject differences. Instead of determining mean scores based on a combination of several types of aggression, it might have been better to use frequencies as units of analysis. Frequencies might have given clear evidence of the differences in subjects' initial and final responses.

Educational Implications

Several implications for education can be drawn from this study. First, perspective-taking was shown to be a viable alternative to behavior modification for reducing children's anger and their motivation to retaliate through aggression. It was particularly effective with Hispanic-American subjects in this study. It is recommended as a potentially valuable addition to the classroom teacher's behavior management repertoire. Second, cultural differences in children's responses to different types of aggression need greater consideration when evaluating children's behavior. Teachers, psychologists, and other clinicians may get much clearer information about how to intervene in children's aggressive behavior if there is clarity about the specific types of aggression serving as stimuli. Third, cultural group responses to different types of intervention procedures need to be considered in daily classroom management routines and in formal aggression intervention programs. A given approach may have very different effects on children from different cultural backgrounds, more positive on some than on others. The overall implication of this study is that, in order for educators to "be able to counter social forces that mitigate against culturally and linguistically diverse students talking together and solving problems cooperatively" (DeVillar and Faltis 1991: 27), they need to give greater attention to cultural group differences in the way children respond to each other and to classroom discipline and management strategies.

Note

1. Name has been modified.

References

Atkin, E. L. (1957). *Aggressiveness in children.* New York: Child Study of America.

Benson, S. S. (1979). The responsibility training. In B. Clark *Growing Up Gifted.* Columbus, Ohio: Charles E. Merrill.

Benson, S. S. (1978). School Enrichment-Parent Education (S. E. - P. E.) program. In B. Clark. *Growing up Gifted. Columbus, Ohio: Charles E. Merrill.*

DeVillar, R. A. and C. J. Faltis (1991). *Computers and cultural diversity: Restructuring for school success.* Albany, N.Y.: State University New York Press.

Dodge, K. A. (1981). *Social competence and aggressive behavior in children.* Paper presented at the meeting of the Midwestern Psychological Association, Detroit, Mich.

Feshbach, N. D. (1984). Empathy, empathy training, and the regulation of aggression in elementary school children. In R. M. Kaplan, V. J. Koneci, and R. W. Novaco, (Eds.), *Aggression in Children and Youth.* Boston: Martinus Nijhoff Publisher, 192–208.

———. (1983). Learning to care: A positive approach to child training and discipline. *Journal of Clinical Psychology,* 12(3), 266–71.

Feshbach, S. (1979). *Aggression and behavior change.* In S. Feshbach and Adam Fraczek (Eds.). New York; Praeger.

Goldstein, A. P., S. J. Apter, and B. Harootunian (1984) *School violence.* Englewood Cliffs, N.J.. Prentice-Hall, Inc.

Higgins, T. E. (1984). Role taking and social judgment: alternative developmental perspectives and processes. I. J. Flavell and L. Ross (Eds.) Social Cognitive Development. New York: Cambridge University Press, 119–153.

Kaplan, R. M. (1984). Measurement of human aggression. In R. M. Kaplan, V. J. Koneci, and R. W. Novaco (Eds.), *Aggression in Children and Youth. Boston: Martinus Nijhoff Publisher, 192–208.*

Korndant, H. J. (1984). In R. M. Kaplan, V. J. Koneci, and R. W. Novaco (Eds.) *Aggression in Children and Youth. Boston: Martinus Nijhoff Publisher, 192–208.*

Laemmell, M. S. (1985). Examination of the self-perceptions and social competencies of popular, rejected, and neglected fifth and sixth grade children. Unpublished doctoral dissertation, University of California, Los Angeles.

Lochman, W. M., W. M. Nelson, and J. P. Sims (1981). A cognitive behavioral program for use with aggressive children. *Journal of Clinical Child Psychology, 10*(3), 146–48.

Pastore, N. (1950). A neglected factor in the frustration-aggression hypothesis: A comment. *Journal of Psychology, 29,* 271–79.

Rule, B. G., and T. M. Ferguson (1984). Developmental issues in attritution, moral judgement and aggression. In R. M. Kaplan, V. J. Koneci, and R. W. Novaco (Eds.), *Aggression in Children and Youth. Boston: Martinus Ninjhoff Publisher,* 138–61.

Sparling, S. S. (1988). Modifying Attributions to Reduce Anger and Motivation to Aggress. Unpublished doctoral dissertation. University of California, Los Angeles/California State University, Los Angeles.

———.(1986). The shared responsibility model. In B. Clark. Optimizing Learning. In B. Clark. *Growing Up Gifted.* Columbus Ohio: Charles E. Merrill.

Storms, M. D. (1973). Videotape and the attribution process: Reversing actors' and observers' points of view. *Journal of Personal and Social Psychology, 27*(2), 165–75.

Weiner, B. (1986). *Attribution, a theory of motivation and emotion.* New York: Springer-Verlag.

————. (1984). Principles for a theory of student motivation and their implications within an attributional framework. In. R. Ames & C. Ames (Eds.) *Student Motivation, Vol. 1.* New York: Academic Press., 15–38.

————. (1980a). May I borrow your class notes? An attributional analysis of judgements of helpgiving. *Journal of Educational Psychology, 72,* 676–81.

————. (1980b). A cognitive (attribution)-emotion-action model of motivated behavior: An analysis of help-giving. *Journal of Personality and Social Psychology, 39,* 186–200.

————. (1979). A theory of motivation for some classroom experiences. *Journal of Educational Psychology, 39,* 186–200.

Weiner, B., Anderson, A. L, and Prawat, R. S. (1983). Affective experience in a classroom. Unpublished paper, University of California at Los Angeles.

Weiner, B., Graham, S., Stern, P., and Lawson, M. E. (1982) Using affective cue to infer causal thoughts. *Developmental Psychology Bulletin, 18*(2), 278–86.

▼ 10 ▼
Effectiveness Of Bilingual Education in an Elementary School District

LINDA GONZALES

The effectiveness of bilingual education has been discussed throughout the United States for decades. There is hardly an educator who does not have an opinion about the merits of "bilingual" education. Most of the opinions are often colored by the program or approach that has been taken in a particular school district or school where they have taught. Unfortunately, few opportunities have been available to look at the "textbook" approaches to bilingual programs and their effectiveness. This paper will explore how those "textbook" approaches worked in a mid-sized K–8 school district in a rural section of southern California.

Background

In 1980, a group of parents complained that the program they were receiving was not qualitatively effective in meeting the needs of their children academically. Their oral complaint became a state-level written complaint. Most of their children were being taught in English-only classrooms with little opportunity to benefit from Spanish instruction that was usually provided by an instructional aide on a pull-out basis. Children appeared to do well during the early years, but fell behind as they progressed in school. By junior high and high school the students were below the performance level of their nonbilingual peers. In their complaint, parents stated that more bilingual (Spanish/English) staff, an organized curriculum, a training program for all teachers, and Spanish language instruction provided in the traditional classroom were needed.

In the fall of 1981, a consultant was hired for the district at the recommendation of the San Diego County Office of Education. The consultant had worked as a bilingual teacher in elementary and secondary schools, held a master's degree in Multicultural Education, and was credentialled as a Bilingual Cross-Cultural Specialist by California. In addition to teaching experience, she had also served as a site administrator, district office administrator, and teacher trainer.

The first step taken by the consultant was a meeting with the district level staff, who indicated a concern to appease the community and a willingness to provide resources, time, and commitment to design a better academic program for the students. There was private acknowledgement that the academic program provided for the limited-English-proficient (LEP) students was not comparable to the one offered English-only (EO) students. The district also recognized the need for bilingual teachers and training for all teachers.

After meeting with the district staff, the consultant met with parents, bilingual teachers, principals, and the English-only teacher leadership identified by site administrators. The consultant visited each district classroom and conducted an assessment of the district's service to ethnically and linguistically diverse students. The visits to the schools confirmed the legitimacy of the parents' complaint. A program needed to be developed to better address the needs of Spanish speaking students.

There was strong resistance to the use of Spanish on all campuses except one. The principal of the campus where Spanish was widely used and a bilingual program was prospering was interviewed in-depth to determine what components had contributed to his success. He identified these areas as critical: (1) all teachers need to understand the concept of bilingual education and language acquisition; (2) English-only students need to be included and taught Spanish as a second language; (3) the principal needs to support the program; (4) Spanish speaking parents need to feel welcome at the school; (5) the bilingual teachers need to be good teachers and get along well with other teachers; (6) the English speaking parents need to be educated about the benefits of learning a second language early; (7) parallel textbooks need to be available in Spanish; (8) English as a second language instruction and materials should not only lead to English fluency, but learning in English; (9) students who participate in the bilingual program should be continuously enrolled for more than six years; and (10) students, both English-only and Spanish-proficient, should be exposed to a wide range of role models who were bilingual and actualizing their potential.

When the information was shared with the district staff, there was agreement that the findings of the needs assessment were accurate. The district staff were also angry with the one successful school's staff, because they believed that teachers from the school had encouraged the parents to file the complaint. Although there was wide acknowledgement that the program was successful, there were strong statements of mistrust expressed on the part of the district staff toward the faculty of the school that was implementing a modified bilingual program.

In the spring of 1982, training was organized for the English-only teacher leaders identified by the principals. The training included second language acquisition and research-based information about the advantages of bilingual education to all students. During that semester, a Title VII proposal was developed to provide seed monies to implement a bilingual program at three of the six elementary schools. These schools were selected because they had the largest representation of LEP students. The grant was funded. Prior to June 1982, thirteen fully certified teachers were hired. These teachers joined the eight teachers that were already working as bilingual teachers in the school district. The principal with the successful program participated on all of the hiring committees with the consultant and the associate superintendent.

During the summer of 1982, extensive training was conducted with the bilingual staff. By the end of 1983, curricula and a bilingual resource guide were developed for the twenty-one bilingual classrooms. Each of the ten points made by the principal of the successful school was addressed. The following summarizes the activities that took place in each of the ten areas identified as essential to program success in this community:

1. *All teachers need to understand the concept of bilingual education and language acquisition.* A thirty hour workshop was held for the teacher leaders identified by the principals. The leaders became a support network for the bilingual teachers and became team partners with the bilingual teachers. Following the workshop, similar training was conducted at each of the schools.

2. *English-only students need to be included and taught Spanish as a second language.* A Spanish as a second language curriculum was developed by the teachers. Most of the English-only students participated in the team-taught classrooms. After four years, there was a waiting list of English-only students.

3. *The principal needs to support the program.* Two of three principals were transferred to other district schools. The principal who had successfully developed a program at his school was transferred to a school where there was the most resistance to change. That school became a California Distinguished and Nationally Distinguished School. The staff and principal attributed the awards to the success of the bilingual program.

4. *Spanish speaking parents need to feel welcome at the school.* Bilingual clerks were hired for schools with more than 20 percent Hispanic enrollment. Parent activities and events were translated. A literary magazine, previously published only in English, included student work in Spanish. All communication to the homes was bilingual.

5. *The bilingual teachers need to be good teachers and get along well with other teachers.* During the selection of teachers, interview panels searched for candidates with interpersonal skills and bilingual certification. Questions were drafted that would elicit responses that would indicating good social interaction skills.

6. *The English speaking parents need to be educated about the benefits of learning a second language early.* A videotaped presentation with an informal brochure was developed for a community relations program. The project director spoke at all service clubs in the community. A presentation was made for all parent groups sponsored by the community and school district. Articles were in the local newspaper about the pros and cons of the bilingual approaches.

7. *Parallel textbooks need to be available in Spanish.* Parallel textbooks were purchased for mathematics, science and social studies. A Spanish reading series was adopted by the board of education.

8. *English as a second language instruction and materials should develop English fluency for subject area learning.* Strategies were tested and developed in the class rooms to provide mathematics, science, music, physical education and computer education in English. Second language development became a natural part of schooling.

9. *Students should be continuously enrolled.* During parent conferences, the goals of the program were explained. Most parents to enroll their children for a minimum of four years complied with the request.

10. *Students need role models.* Career fairs were held at each of the project schools. Community leaders who were bilingual participated. Their interaction with the students assisted them to understand the value of bilingualism. The number of Latino teachers and administrators at the program sites increased.

The most important element of the project evaluation of student success came seven years after the initial parent complaint. After five years of project participation, a study was conducted comparing the performance of the Spanish-proficient students to students that had proceeded them.

Major Findings

There were six major findings that resulted from the study. First, extensive bilingual education improves the acquisition of English. The second major finding was that bilingual instruction is academically and linguistically beneficial for students. The study's third major finding was that assistance through English as a Second Language instruction resulted in improved academic performance in reading achievement but only on a limited basis. The fourth major conclusion is that bilingual instruction has a very positive effect on the reading achievement of students who received this instruction. The fifth major finding was pressure to move students into English is pervasive and difficult to overcome. The final major finding was that more extensive bilingual experiences result in improved academic performance.

Procedures

Subjects

To identify the subjects, the cumulative folders of all 474 students identified and listed by the district as LEP were reviewed. The criteria for selection of students to participate in the study were (a) the student had been continuously enrolled in the school district (the cumulative folder of the student indicates if the folder has ever been sent to or requested by another district); (b) the student had been identified as LEP by the district under study, and (c) the student had completed four years of schooling in district programs.

Of the 474 students, 132 students met the selection criteria, having started kindergarten in the district between 1977 and 1982 and completed four years of schooling in district programs. The students were at different grade levels because of age differences.

In the group of students who entered kindergarten in the 1977–78 year, 5.6 percent were receiving Aid to Families with Dependent Children (AFDC). Of the total group of children, 4.3 percent were reported as Limited English or Non-English Speaking (LES/NES).

In the group of students who entered kindergarten in the 1980–81 year, 5.2 percent were receiving AFDC. Of the total group of children, approximately 14.7 percent were reported as LES/NES, due to increased awareness of and efforts to identify bilingual students within the district.

While the percentage of children receiving AFDC did not change dramatically over these intervening years, reflecting the steady state socioeconomic ranking of the district reported as part of the California Assessment Program results, there was a large shift in the number of students reported as LES/NES. This increase was due primarily to the increased efforts in the district to identify LEP students. Concurrently, this shift in identified LES/NES students also impacted teachers' awareness of LEP students and district efforts to assist these language diverse students.

Type of Programs

There were three types of educational programs that had been offered LEP students. These programs were *bilingual, team-*

taught, and English-only. According to district audit reports, all of the students in all three strands received 54,910 minutes of instruction annually, 1,445 minutes weekly or 289 minutes daily. The district had one curriculum, with parallel English and Spanish textbooks, for mathematics, social studies, and science. In reading, the district adopted a Spanish reading series that included the same objectives for comprehension as those of the English basal.

In the *bilingual program*, students, in a self-contained classroom, received their instruction in the core curriculum (reading, mathematics, language arts, science, and social studies) in their native language. The bilingual program provided 145 minutes, or approximately 50 percent, daily of primary-language instruction. This program used a parallel curriculum, in Spanish, to the English-only curriculum. The textbooks and materials were Spanish versions of English texts for mathematics, science, and social studies. In reading, a comparable Spanish language program was used that included all of the comprehension skills of the English basal program. Teachers in the bilingual program were bilingually certified/credentialled in accordance with California state requirements.

In the *team-teaching program*, the students were grouped for language of instruction. In the team-taught classroom, only the basic skills (reading, mathematics, and language arts) were taught in the primary language. Elective subjects, science, and social studies were taught in English. In this program, all first and second grade students received 90 minutes, or approximately 30 percent, of instruction from a bilingually credentialled/certified teacher in their native language using the same texts and curriculum from the self-contained bilingual classroom for reading, mathematics and language arts. Third and fourth graders received 50 minutes, or approximately 17 percent, of instruction from a bilingually credentialled/certified teacher in their native language using the same texts and curriculum from the self-contained bilingual classroom for reading and language arts. During the third and fourth grade, students in the team-taught setting received their mathematics instruction in English and Spanish. New concepts were taught in Spanish, but review lessons were taught in English. The remainder of the day, approximately 200 minutes for first and second grades and 240 minutes for third and fourth grades 70 percent to 80 percent respectively of the time, was English-only instruction. The materials and methods used during English instruction were the same as texts and instruction used in the English-only classroom. The English-only teaching team partner of the bilingual teacher had participated in thirty hours of special training in the areas of second language methods and culture provided by the district.

In the *English-only program*, the students were placed in a self-contained classroom. The teacher taught all subjects in English and LEP students were expected to maintain their academic progress without other assistance, such as ESL. In this program, 100 percent of the instruction was in the second language (English). The teacher did not have any special training.

ESL

There were also three types of ESL programs. These were *in-class, team-taught, and pull-out/none*. Those students who participated in the in-class and team-taught programs received 30 minutes of ESL instruction daily. Both of these programs used the same materials for ESL instruction.

In the *in-class program* offered to students in the bilingual classroom, the LEP students received a comprehensive lesson in their classroom for the purposes of English-language acquisition. This training was offered by the classroom teacher.

In the *team-taught ESL programs*, the LEP students received a comprehensive English language development lesson and content area instruction in a manner to assist their comprehension of the subject content. In this ESL program, the English language training was not just for the sake of learning English but to assist in the mastery of academic content. The English-only team partner of the bilingually certified teacher provided ESL instruction.

In the *pull-out program*, LEP students in an English-only classroom received sporadic services outside their classroom from an instructional aide. Due to the fact that there was a limited amount of training and a limited number of LEP students receiving these services, these students and those students not receiving services were placed together for statistical purposes. This decision was made not only for statistical reasons but also because it was very difficult to determine whether the ESL services for these LEP students were merely sporadic or nonexistent.

Instrumentation

This study used two primary instruments. The academic performance of the students was established by the administration of the Comprehensive Test of Basic Skills (CTBS), which is published by CTB/McGraw-Hill (1975, 1981). The second instrument was the Data Collection Survey (DCS), developed by the author to systematically collect data on language-minority students.

Data Collection Survey

The Data Collection Survey (DCS) is a data collection instrument for systematically collecting data on LEP, FEP, and NEP students. This survey was divided into three major categories. In the first category, information about the background of the student was entered. The category contained a number of areas for detailing information on the student:

1. student's birthdate,
2. school at entry,
3. date of enrollment
4. language proficiency at entry
5. English proficiency (BSM score)
6. Sex
7. Reclassification date
8. Date of transfer to English reading
9. Retentions
10. Special education eligibility
11. Attendance
12. Eligibility for free/reduced lunch

It should also be noted that the attendance category was based on an estimate by the teachers of the attendance of the students. This estimate was divided into three major categories: high, average, or low attendance.

The second category consisted of program treatment factors such as the program, type of teacher, language of instruction, and type of ESL instruction. This information differentiated student participation by grade level in different types of programs (bilingual, team-taught, and English-only) within the groups.

The third category was composed of the academic scores that the student attained in reading and mathematics by grade level while in school. The scores from mathematics and reading were recorded in standard scores to allow comparisons between differing years and groups of students. Scores were collected for both English and Spanish tests where available.

Data Collection

The data were collected by two bilingual resource specialists over a three month period from September 1987, through November 1987 by reviewing the cumulative folders at every school. The results on the CTBS in English for the students' scores from kindergarten through eighth grade were collected. For this study, the results from kindergarten through fifth grade were collected on the Spanish CTBS. Data were gathered on the reading and mathematic achievement of the participating students on both the CTBS English and Spanish forms. Scores for the students were also collected as standard scores or converted from scaled scores to standard scores.

To cross-reference the accuracy of the information collected, the cumulative folders of each child were inspected and data entered directly onto the DCS. The two specialists entered data from five identical student forms to ensure that they were consistent in their interpretation and application of the data necessary to complete the forms.

Students sometimes shifted between bilingual and team teaching depending on their grade level and the respective staffing patterns at particular grade levels. Students in the bilingual strand moved primarily between bilingual and team teaching groups. Students in the English-only group either remained in that program or were moved to the EO classroom, but were never returned to either the bilingual or team-taught conditions.

Data Analysis

The four research hypotheses were evaluated by the following statistical procedures. For the purpose of data analysis, a student was classified as being in an English-only (EO), team-taught (TT), or bilingual (BIL) classroom if the student was in that type of program during a particular school year. This means that a student was classified as EO as a second grader or as TT during the third grade as detailed in the Data Collection Survey. Likewise, the type of ESL program was also classified by the type of program the student experienced during a specific year of schooling.

The accumulated data were analyzed in the following manner. For the first research hypothesis, a *t* test was used to compare the differences in lengths of time required to achieve English proficiency. The independent variable was program type (bilingual, team-taught, and English-only). The dependent variable was the amount of time required to achieve English proficiency. In order to support the research hypothesis, a .05 level of significance was set, indicating that there are significant differences in the amounts of time to master English between LEP students in bilingual education (bilingual and team-taught) and those in English-only classrooms.

The second and fourth research hypotheses were evaluated by using a one-way analysis of variance. The independent variable was the type of program (bilingual, team-taught, and English-only); the dependent variables were achievement in mathematics and reading as measured by the CTBS.

In order to support the research hypothesis, a .05 level of significance was set indicating that there are significant differences in mathematical and reading achievement among the three program types (bilingual, team-taught, and English-only). In order to determine which of the three program types significantly differed from the others, a Tukey least significant difference (LSD) a posteriori procedure was calculated. The .05 level of significance was used to identify the significant differences among the groups.

The third research hypothesis was also evaluated with a one-way analysis of variance. The independent variable was type of ESL instruction (in-class instruction, team teaching, pull-out ESL and/or no ESL); the dependent variable was reading achievement as measured by the CTBS.

A .05 level of significance was set to support the research hypothesis, indicating that there are significant differences in the reading achievement among the three types of ESL instruction. In order to determine which of the three program types significantly differed from the others, a Tukey least significant difference (LSD) a posteriori procedure was calculated. The .05 level of significance was used to identify any significant differences among the groups.

Demographic Characteristics

A total of 132 LEP students constituted the sample, consisting of 57 males and 75 females. In examining the demographic characteristics of the students used in this study, the numbers of boys and girls who were retained one grade level, were in special education, or received free lunches were compared. Nearly 67 percent of the males and nearly 79 percent of the females had not been retained. There was no significant difference (chi-square = 1.81, df = 1, p>.05 between the retention percentages.

The students were also compared in terms of the type of special education they received. Nearly 79 percent of the males and 87 percent of the females did not receive any special education assistance. Very similar percentages of males and females (11 percent each, respectively) were receiving Resource Special Program (RSP) assistance. Three males (5 percent) were in full day Special Education (SDC) classes while three males (5 percent) and two females (2 percent) were in Speech classes.

The numbers of students with good, average, and poor attendance rates were analyzed. Over 40 percent of the males and 44 percent of the females had good attendance. Another 56 percent of the boys and 55 percent of the girls had average attendance. Only 4 percent of the males had poor attendance compared to 1 percent of the females. There was no significant difference (chi-square = 0.78, df = 2, p>.05) in the rates of attendance by boys and girls.

Finally, the numbers of LEP boys and girls receiving free lunch were compared. Thirty-two percent of the males and 31 percent of the females were receiving free lunches. There was no significant difference (chi-square = 0.00, df = 1, p >.05) in the two groups use of this social service.

Analyses of the Hypotheses

Hypothesis One

The first hypothesis was that there is a significant difference in the length of time necessary for mastery of English proficiency for those LEP students who participate in bilingual education and those LEP students who do not participate in bilingual education as measured by the time between entry into school and

TABLE 10.1 COMPARISONS OF THE AMOUNT OF TIME REQUIRED TO ACHIEVE ENGLISH LANGUAGE MASTERY FOR STUDENTS IN BILINGUAL AND ENGLISH-ONLY PROGRAMS

Group	M	$s.d.$	t Ratio	df
English-only	46.6	1.15		
			3.04*	41
Bilingual Education	44.8	0.92		

*$p<.001$

mastery of English proficiency as determined by the district procedures.

At the end of five years of instruction, there were 36 bilingual students (bilingual or team-taught LEP students) who had intact records and 7 English-only students. To compare the two groups, a t test was computed, the results of which appear in Table 10.1. The bilingual program students took 44.8 months to master English while the nonbilingual program students took 46.6 months. As reflected by Table 1, there was a significant difference ($t[41]=3.04$, $p<.001$) in the two time lengths. Thus, the nonbilingual students required significantly more time to achieve English mastery.

Hypothesis Two

The second hypothesis predicted a significant difference in the mathematical achievement of those LEP students who participate in bilingual education and those LEP students who do not participate in bilingual education based on performance on the Comprehensive Test of Basic Skills. This hypothesis was analyzed by examining the mathematics performance of the students at four separate grade levels.

Grade One

Since the children in this study frequently started in Spanish and then, over a period of years, moved into English, the language of instruction changed as these individuals matured. The bulk of the Spanish speaking students in this group (89 percent) were taught in Spanish, either in a self-contained classroom or in a team-teaching setting.

The majority of the students in English instruction (67 percent) were in self-contained, English-only classrooms. Be-

TABLE 10.2 TUKEY A POSTERIORI TESTS COMPARING THE MATH-
EMATICAL ACHIEVEMENT OF THE STUDENTS IN THE THREE
TYPES OF PROGRAMS AT GRADE ONE

Program	MEANS		
	EO	TT	BIL
	1	2	3
1. English-only (EO)76.4			
2. Team-taught (TT)96.3			
3. Bilingual (BIL)104.2	*		

$*p < .05$

cause the majority of Spanish-speaking students were either
receiving instruction in Spanish or were in a self-contained,
English-only classroom, the analysis of the first-grade data examines only the type of program, without consideration of the
language of instruction.

In order to determine differences among the types of programs, the mathematics scores of the 113 students, who were
tested on the CTBS (English) and the CTBS-Spanish, were
converted to standard scores. This conversion allowed direct
comparison of the students in each of the programs. The results of the comparisons of the three types of programs for the
children bilingual program, team-taught bilingual program,
and English-only were analyzed. There was a significant difference $(F[2,109] = 15.18, p<.0001)$ among the three types of programs, indicating that the three types of programs did not have
the same impact on the mathematical achievement of the students. A Tukey LSD a posteriori procedure was computed. The
results of this computation indicate that the students within
the self-contained bilingual (BIL) program (mean = 104.2) performed significantly higher than the English-only (EO) classroom (mean = 76.4). Additionally, the students in the team
teaching (TT) environment (mean = 96.3) did not statistically
differ from the students in the English-only classroom.

The matrix format of Table 2 allows comparisons of the
groups. The asterisk under the EO group indicates that the EO
group (mean = 76.4, $n = 8$) performed significantly different
than the BIL (bilingual group), which averaged 104.2 in mathematics achievement ($n = 101$). The lack of any figure under the
TT column indicated that the team-taught group ($n = 4$) did not
significantly differ in mathematic performance from either
group.

TABLE 10.3 TUKEY A POSTERIORI TESTS COMPARING THE MATH-
EMATICAL ACHIEVEMENT OF THE STUDENTS IN THE THREE
TYPES OF PROGRAMS AT GRADE TWO

Program	MEANS	EO	TT	BIL
		1	2	3
1. English-only	70.9			
2. Team-taught	97.6			
3. Bilingual	100.1	*		

*$p < .05$

Grade Two

At the second grade level, most Spanish-speaking students
were either in the self-contained program (89 percent) or in the
team-teaching bilingual program (11 percent). The Spanish-
speaking students being instructed in English were in a self-
contained, English-only classroom (67 percent). Because the
bulk of students were in appropriate programs, the analysis of
mathematical achievement at the second grade level compared
differences among the programs.

There was a significant difference $(F[2,123] = 18.62,$
$p<.0001)$ among the three programs on the mathematical
achievement of the 126 students at the second grade level. The
results of the Tukey LSD demonstrated that students in the bilingual instructional environment (mean = 100.1) and those in
the team-taught bilingual classrooms (mean = 97.6) scored significantly higher mathematics scores than did the students in
the English-only classroom (mean = 70.9). The results, represented in Table 3, indicate the EO group ($n = 6$) performed significantly differently ($p<.05$) than the bilingual (BIL) group
($n = 104$). Likewise, the lack of an asterisk in the TT column indicates that the TT group ($n = 16$) did not significantly differ
from the EO group nor the bilingual (BIL) students. Thus, the
significant difference reported in Table 3 was primarily due to
the higher achievement of the bilingual (BIL) group.

Grade Three

The distribution of the students across the language of instruction and type of program at the third grade were divided
across English (67 percent of the total students in English) and

Spanish (91 percent of the total in Spanish). Nine percent of students in English and Spanish were in team-taught classrooms. Finally, only 24 percent of all the students receiving English instruction were in English-only, self-contained classrooms. Because there were so few students in English-only classrooms, in the analysis of mathematical achievement at the third grade, the students in the English-only classroom were combined with those students in the team-taught program. In this analysis, the differences among the groups were examined not only from the position of the impact of the program but also from the language of instruction. There was a significant difference ($F[1,83] = 119.49$, $p<.0001$) in the mathematical achievement of students being taught in English and those being taught in Spanish.

The mean for students in Spanish instruction ($n = 62$) averaged 110.5, which is significantly higher than students being taught in English ($n = 25$), who averaged 88.5. The mathematical performance of students in Spanish corresponds to approximately the seventieth percentile, compared to the twentieth percentile for students taught in English.

There was no significant difference between the types of programs ($F[1,83] = 1.14$, $p>.05$), suggesting that the type of program alone did not result in significant differences in mathematical achievement. Finally, there was no significant interaction ($F[1,83] = 0.95$, $p>.05$) between the type of program and the language of instruction, suggesting that both type of program and language of instruction had very consistent effects. This implies that the LEP students in the two types of programs and in the two languages of instruction responded consistently within each group.

Grade Four

Due to the similarity of the distribution of fourth grade students between language of instruction and type of program, the evaluation for the fourth graders also examined the impact of language and type of program as in previous grades. There was a significant difference ($F[1,46] = 10.24$, $p<01$) in the mathematical achievement of the 50 students in English and in Spanish instruction. There was no significant difference between types of programs ($F[1,46] = 0.69$, $p>.05$), nor was there a significant interaction between the language of instruction and the type of program ($F[1,46] = 0.20$, $p>.05$).

The students in the English instruction program (mean = 76.6, n = 31)) scored significantly below the students taught in Spanish (mean = 98.6, n = 19). The impact of the bilingual program (mean = 86.6, n = 36) was higher, but not significantly, than that of the non-bilingual program (mean = 78.0, n = 14).

In the four analyses reported as part of the second research hypothesis, the students in the bilingual program performed significantly higher in mathematics achievement in the first and second grades than those students in the English-only program. At the third and fourth grades, while the students who were in the bilingual program did not score significantly higher than the students in the nonbilingual program, the students receiving Spanish instruction did outperform those students who had English-only instruction. These results indicate that LEP students who were taught in Spanish scored significantly higher in mathematics than those taught primarily in English, thus supporting the second research hypothesis.

Hypothesis Three

The third research hypothesis predicted a significant difference in reading achievement among LEP students who experience different programs of ESL, based on their performance on the Comprehensive Test of Basic Skills. These results appear by grade level.

Grade One

To examine the impact of ESL programs, a comparison was made between in-class programs, team-taught and pull-out and/or none. The analysis of the reading achievement of the 113 first graders receiving ESL instruction identified a significant difference (F[2,110] = 49.10, p<.0001) in the reading scores of the three types of ESL programs. In order to identify which ESL program outperformed the other, a Tukey LSD procedure was computed. The in-class ESL program (mean = 116.5, n = 86) and the team-taught ESL program (mean = 18.4, n = 16) scored significantly higher than the students who had pull-out or no ESL instruction (mean = 68.7, n = 11). Thus, the students in in-class ESL and team-taught ESL programs performed at a superior level in reading achieve-

TABLE 10.4 MEANS IN READING ACHIEVEMENT OF THE STU-
DENTS IN THE THREE TYPES OF ESL PROGRAMS AT GRADE ONE

	MEANS			
Program		NO	IC	TT
		1	2	3
1. Pull-out/No	68.7			
2. In-Class	116.5	*		
3. Team-taught	118.4	*		

*p < .05

ment to those students who received ESL on a pull-out basis or
who did not have ESL instruction.

This is illustrated in Table 10.4 by the use of the asterisks.
At the top of this table, the three types of programs are represented by NO (pull-out or no program), IC (in-class ESL program), and TT (team-taught ESL program). In this table, the
two asterisks in the NO column indicate that the NO group
(mean = 68.7) significantly differed from the IC group
(mean = 116.5) and the TT group (mean = 118.4). The lack of an
asterisk in the IC column reflects that the IC group and the TT
group do not significantly differ in this academic area.

Grade Two

There was a significant difference $(F[2,123] = 79.76, p<.0001)$
by program for the 126 students in terms of their reading
achievement. In order to determine where the groups were
significantly different, a Tukey a posteriori procedure was
calculated. The results of the Tukey LSD are presented in
Table 10.5. As is shown in this table, the in-class ESL
group (mean = 105.1) and the team-taught ESL group
(mean = 106.8) scored significantly higher in reading than

TABLE 10.5 MEANS IN READING ACHIEVEMENT OF THE STU-
DENTS IN THE THREE TYPES OF ESL PROGRAMS AT GRADE TWO

	MEANS			
Program		NO	IC	TT
		1	2	3
1. Pull-out/No	68.7			
2. In-Class	105.1	*		
3. Team-taught	106.8	*		

*p < .05

those students who did not have ESL assistance or who were in ESL pull-out programs.

Grade Three

The performance of third graders who received differing levels of ESL instruction was compared among the three groups. There were no significant differences ($F[2,82]=0.40$, $p>05$) in the performances of the 86 students. This means that students with in-class ESL instruction ($n=66$), those with team-taught ESL ($n=15$), and those students with pull-out or who received no ESL ($n=4$) scored statistically the same in reading achievement. In terms of reading achievement, the in-class ESL group averaged a standard score 90.7, while the team-taught group averaged 84.5, and the students with no ESL averaged 84.3.

Grade Four

The analysis of variance for the groups of students receiving ESL instruction was calculated. There were only two types of ESL instruction: team-taught ($n=47$) and no ESL instruction ($n=3$). There was no significant difference ($F[1,48]=2.62$, $p>.05$) between the two types of students. The team-taught ESL students had a mean standard score of 89.2 while the students with pull-out/no ESL instruction averaged 105.7 in reading achievement.

In these analyses, the students receiving ESL instruction scored significantly higher than students without ESL instruction at the first-grade and second-grade levels. At the third-grade and fourth-grade level, there were no significant differences among the students receiving various types of ESL instruction. Because the third research hypothesis stated that there would be differences in reading achievement of the students experiencing differing levels of ESL instruction, the third research hypothesis is not supported.

Hypothesis Four

The fourth research hypothesis predicted a significant difference in the reading achievement of LEP students who have participated in bilingual education and LEP students who have not participated in bilingual education, and measured by performance on the CTBS. The analyses appear by grade level.

TABLE 10.6 TUKEY A POSTERIORI PROCEDURE AND MEANS FOR
READING ACHIEVEMENT OF THE STUDENTS IN THE THREE
TYPES OF BILINGUAL PROGRAMS AT GRADE ONE

	MEANS	EO	TT	BIL
Program		1	2	3
1. English-only	65.7			
2. Team-taught	88.1	*		
3. Bilingual	106.8	*	*	

*$p<.05$

Grade One

The analysis of variance of the reading achievement of the
three programs compared at the first-grade level was made. As
stated in the analysis of the mathematical achievement of the
113 students in the first grade, the reading achievement of
three groups (bilingual, team-taught, English-only), was compared due to the distribution of the LEP students at this grade
level. There was a significant difference ($F[2,110]=44.18$,
$p<.0001$) in reading achievement at the first grade level among
the three groups of students. A Tukey a posteriori procedure
was calculated and is presented in Table 10.6. As this table dis-
plays, the students in the bilingual program had an average
standard score of 106.7 ($n=101$) while those students in the
team-taught bilingual program ($n=4$) averaged 88.1. Finally,
the students in the English-only program ($n=8$) had an average of 65.7. This group performed significantly below the students in the bilingual classroom. Furthermore, the students in
the full bilingual program performed significantly better
($p<.05$) in reading achievement than the students in the team-
taught bilingual program.

Grade Two

The comparison of the three programs was made for the 126
students in the second grade. As is reflected in Table 10.7,
there was a significant difference ($F[2,123]=47.45$, $p<.0001$)
in the reading performances of the three groups. A Tukey a
posteriori procedure demonstrated that the bilingual only students (mean = 105.7, $n=104$) scored significantly higher than
the students in the team-taught bilingual program
(mean = 89.5, $n=16$), and the students in the English-only

TABLE 10.7 TUKEY A POSTERIORI AND MEANS FOR READING ACHIEVEMENT OF THE STUDENTS IN THE THREE TYPES OF BILINGUAL PROGRAMS AT GRADE TWO

Program	MEANS	EO	TT	BIL
		1	2	3
1. English-only	63.5			
2. Team-taught	89.5	*		
3. Bilingual	105.7	*	*	

*$p < .05$

program (mean = 63.5 $n = 6$). Furthermore, the students in the team-taught bilingual program (mean = 89.5) scored significantly higher in reading achievement than the students in English-only classrooms.

Grade Three

An analysis of variance comparing the reading achievement of students receiving instruction either in English or in Spanish and comparing those in bilingual and those not in bilingual programs was made. There was a significant difference ($F[1,81] = 117.58$, $p < .0001$) in reading achievement for the 85 students who were instructed in English or in Spanish. There was no significant difference ($F[1,81] = 0.24$, $p > .05$) between students in bilingual or not in bilingual programs. Finally, there was no significant interaction ($F[1,81] = 1.69$, $p > .05$) between the language of instruction and the type of program.

The students receiving Spanish instruction (mean = 101.9, $n = 61$) scored significantly higher in reading achievement than students receiving English-only instruction (mean = 87.2, $n = 24$). Furthermore, there was no significant difference between students in the bilingual program (mean = 98.0, $n = 71$) and the students not in the bilingual program (mean-96.6, $n = 4$). Nevertheless, students in the bilingual program outperformed student in the English-only program.

Grade Four

The reading performance of the LEP students who received Spanish language or English language instruction, and those in bilingual education (bilingual and/or team-taught) and in English-only programs were compared. There was a significant difference $(FR[1,46] = 14.70, p<.0001)$ in the CTBS reading achievement scores of the 50 students who had Spanish or English instruction. There was no significant difference $(F[1,46] = 1.30, p>.05)$ between students who had bilingual education and those who did not. Finally, there was no significant interaction $(F[1,46] = 0.03, p>.05)$ between the language of instruction and the type of bilingual experience.

The means for reading achievement from the groups receiving English and Spanish instruction as well as bilingual program experience were analyzed. The students who received Spanish instruction (mean = 97.4, $n = 19$) scored significantly higher in reading achievement than did students who received English instruction (mean = 82.9, $n = 31$). While the reading achievement of students in bilingual classes (mean = 91.5, $n = 36$) was higher than those students who did not receive bilingual instruction (mean = 80.7, $n = 14$), these differences, as reported previously, were not significant ($p>.05$).

In terms of the fourth hypothesis, the students in the bilingual program scored significantly higher than the students receiving team-taught bilingual instruction and no bilingual instruction at both the first-grade and second-grade levels. Concurrently, the students receiving the team-taught bilingual instruction scored significantly higher than those students not receiving bilingual instruction. At the third-grade and fourth-grade levels, the students who had received instruction in Spanish outperformed the students who had been taught in English.

These results support the notion that bilingual instruction does have a significant impact on the reading achievement of LEP students. Because the data support this conclusion, the fourth hypothesis is supported.

Discussion

In reviewing the data and literature for this study, it is clear that often the major concern of educators is not the academic performance of LEP students but rather how quickly students will be mainstreamed. The central concern should be how well students are achieving academically, regardless of language. Evidence, supported by the finding that students in bilingual instruction became proficient in English two months prior to students in the English-only program, indicates that the main concern should be academic achievement, not English proficiency.

Positive Benefits

This study has shown that students who receive extensive bilingual education do perform better academically than their peers who do not receive it. This result parallels those of Ramírez (1986) and Burnham and Peña (1986) who also reported that intensive native-language instruction did result in positive academic achievement. This current study, additionally, indicates that not only do these students perform better academically, they also achieve English proficiency sooner than students who receive instruction only English.

The results clearly delineate the effects of *submersion*. Submersion, as Cohen (1975) defined it, means placing an NEP student or LEP student in an English-only classroom without resources and support. Academically, the students in the English-only program scored very low. At the first and second grades, these students averaged between the fifth and tenth percentiles in both reading and mathematics. At the third-grade and fourth-grade levels, their performance rose to approximately the fifteenth through the twentieth percentiles, but, academically, these students continued to achieve in the lowest quartile.

The students receiving native-language instruction, on the other hand, were never overwhelmed by the learning experience. Academically, they scored as one would expect: average. This result is very similar to that reported by Krashen and Biber (1988), who found that students receiving strong native-language instruction or who participated in late-exit bilingual programs were at or above the national and district norms in reading and mathematics by the fifth grade.

Interestingly, the students in this current study had attained the same level of academic performance cited by Krashen and Biber by the fourth-grade level. Furthermore, in this study, LEP students in the bilingual program maintained average academic growth throughout the four years they were evaluated.

Affective Gains

The fact that the LEP students did not experience extended academic difficulties is very important for several reasons. First, as suggested by Curtain and Pesola (1988), the affective experiences of students were critical in comprehending why certain students achieved well in school and others did not. The causation for this seems obvious. If a student continued to fail in the school setting, sooner or later the individual branded the educational experience as awful, and decided, consciously or unconsciously, to just quit.

Second, one of the most difficult problems to address within Hispanic youth has been the high dropout rate. With 30 to 40 percent of Hispanic youth leaving school, it would appear that we have a national tragedy in the making (Watson, Northcutt and Rydell, 1989). Language diverse students who do well in their elementary educational experiences, as the students in this study have, will not only be better prepared academically, they will also feel more positive toward learning and studying. This means that they would be less likely to leave during their high school years. The solution to the dropout problem for Hispanics may be, then, providing them with good bilingual programs that allow them to make normal academic progress.

ESL Instruction

One of the most interesting outcomes of this study was the effect of ESL instruction. As cited earlier, LEP students receiving ESL instruction had significantly higher academic performances in reading in the first and second grades when compared to students who did not have this instruction. This benefit, however, was not noticeable at the third and fourth grade levels.

The positive benefits during the first years of the academic experience appears to be a very solid demonstration of the Common Underlying Proficiency (CUP) model identified by Cummins (1986). In this model, when one learns information, this knowledge assists the learner in better comprehending the educational experience. Specifically, by having ESL instruction, the students were assisted in reading.

At the third-grade and fourth-grade levels, there was minimal difference between those students receiving ESL instruction and those not receiving ESL instruction, without consideration of the type of educational program. This difference could be due to several factors. One of these issues is a procedural one. During these two years, students are being shifted at a much higher rate into English-only classrooms. As a result, decisions about providing ESL instruction to LEP students may have been on a case-by-case basis. That is, ESL instruction would probably be offered to those students, no matter the program, who appeared to have greater need for further instruction in English.

The data further support the fact that the more academically or cognitively capable students were exited earlier from primary-language instruction programs. While the differences between the no ESL students and the students receiving ESL instruction are not statistically significant (mean = 105.7 versus 89.2, respectively), it is obvious that those students not receiving ESL instruction at the third-grade level were performing at higher levels (roughly the sixtieth percentile versus the fortieth percentile) in their reading achievement.

The second reason for the lack of differences is discussed in greater depth in the next section. However, summarizing quickly, it appears that very different students remained in the primary language program than those who were exited at an earlier moment.

Program Effect

The research by Baker (1987) and Willig (1987) clearly called for further research examining the performance of students in early exit and late-exit programs in relation to the performance of students who have not received bilingual education. This study presents findings that relate to all three types of programs (bilingual, team-taught, and English-only). Examining the performance of these students, one can see that the students who remained in primary language instruction scored significantly higher, in reading and mathematics, than those students who were instructed in English. This higher academic performance was also maintained in the fourth grade. It is worthwhile to note that students in the primary-language had a fully certified teacher for core instruction for a longer period of time and had been frequently exposed to more information in their native language than students who were moved into an English learning environment.

One would expect, however, that students who had a strong academic training (in Spanish) should perform better at the third-grade and fourth-grade levels. This might be true once the students have mastered English reading skills. But, these early-exit LEP students were suddenly competing with students whose primary language was English and were tested in English. As a result, their academic performance was not as strong as those students who had stayed in the Spanish-language classroom (late-exit). In fact, these students did perform better academically than those students who had only English as the language of instruction. Generally, the early-exit students had higher academic scores than their counterparts who had only English. These differences, however, were not significant. This result indicates that late-exit students do achieve significantly higher than students who are exited early from the Spanish instructional program. This result is what would have been predicted by Ramírez (1986) and Krashen and Biber (1988).

Overall, this study provides one more link in educational research demonstrating the efficacy of maintaining the native-language capabilities of students. While authors like Danoff (1978b), Danoff et al. (1977a, 1977b, 1978a), and Baker (1987) have argued that bilingual education is not a sound educational practice, the present results support the contentions of Willig (1985, 1987), Burnham and Peña (1986), and Krashen and Biber (1988) that native-language instruction provides the best education for LEP students.

This study, as others, posits that the major issue to be addressed is that of exiting LEP students too early from native-language instruction. The data from this study suggest that LEP students who left the bilingual program early seemed to revert to performing, at the level of students who had never had native-language instruction. The challenge, then, is to strengthen bilingual instructional programs, to work to ensure that LEP students receive the educational support they need to make academic progress, and to systematically follow the academic progress of LEP students to clarify what impact native-language and ESL instruction has on their academic performance and dropout rates.

References

Baker, K. (1987) Comment on Willig's: metaanalysis of selected studies of bilingual education. *Review of Educational Research, 57,* (3), 351–362.

Burnham, L and M. Peña (1986). *Effects of bilingual instruction on English academic achievement of LEP students.* Baldwin Park, Calif.: Baldwin Park Unified School District.

Cohen, A. D. (1975). A Sociolinguistic Approach to bilingual education. Rowley, MA: Newburg House.

CTB/McGraw-Hill. (1975). *The comprehensive test of basic skills - Espanol.* New York: CTB/McGraw-Hill.

———.(1981). *The comprehensive test of basic skills: Third edition.* New York: CTB/McGraw-Hill.

Cummins, J. (1986). Empowering minority students: A framework for intervention. *Harvard Educational Review, 56,* 18,36.

Curtain, H. and Pesola, C. (1988). *Languages and children: Making the match.* Reading, MA: Addison-Wesley.

Danoff, M. N. (1978b). *Evaluation of the impact of ESEA Title VII Spanish/English education program: Overview of Study and Findings.* Palo Alto, CA: American Institute for Research.

Danoff, M. N. Coles, G. J., McLaughlin, D. H., & Reynolds, D. J. (1977a). *Evaluation of the impact of ESEA Title VII Spanish/English Bilingual Education Programs, Volume I: Study design and interim findings.* Palo Alto, Calif.: American Institute for Research.

———.(1977b). *Evaluation of the impact of ESEA Title VII Spanish/English Bilingual Education Programs, Volume II: Project Findings.* Palo Alto, CA: American Institute for Research.

———.(1978a). *Evaluation of the impact of ESEA Title VII Spanish/English Bilingual Education Programs, Volume III: Year two impact data, educational processes, and in-depth analyses.* Palo Alto, CA: American Institute for Research.

Krashen, S. and D. Biber (1988). *On course: Bilingual education's success in California.* Sacramento, CA: California Association for Bilingual Education.

O'Malley, J. M. (1987). *Academic growth of high school age Hispanic students in the United States.* (Report No. CS-87-359c). Washington, D.C.: U.S. Government Printing Office.

Ramírez, J. D. (1986). Comparing structured English immersion and Bilingual Education: First-year results of a national study. *American Journal of Education,* September, 122–148.

Watson, D., L. Northcutt and L. Rydell (1989) Teaching bilingual children successfully. *Educational Leadership, 46,* 59–62.

Willig, A. (1985). A meta-analysis of selected studies on the effectiveness of bilingual education. *Review of Educational Research, 55,* 269–317.

———.(1987). Examining bilingual education research through meta-analysis and narrative review: A response to Baker. *Review of Educational Research, 57,* 363–376.

▼ Part IV ▼
Cultural Diversity
and Technology

▼ 11 ▼
A Communicative Computer Environment for the Acquisition of ESL

NIDIA GONZALEZ-EDFELT

While readily acknowledged as an effective educational tool in several areas of the curriculum, the use of the computer for the acquisition of a second language has been controversial. Its conception as a taskmaster—capable only of teaching language in isolated, discrete parts through drill-and-practice activities—has been greatly responsible for this. However, as the capabilities of both software and hardware continue to develops a growing number of practitioners and researchers see the machine as a viable second-language learning/teaching medium. A research area of increasing interest has been the ability of the computer to create an environment conducive to authentic and purposeful verbal interaction between and among students.

Several studies have attempted to test this ability by looking at the linguistic behavior of students working in pairs or groups at the computer (DeVillar 1987; Edfelt 1989; Webb, Ender, and Lewis 1986; Young 1988). As knowledge of this behavior expands, it has become evident that student dyadic or group work does not automatically result in creative and purposeful communication. The manner in which language learners approach communicative tasks at computers seems to depend on several factors that either engender or not the authentic use of the target language (DeVillar 1991). Because a setting that offers communicative opportunities for the natural acquisition of language has enormous potential for second-language learning, there is a pressing need to increase our knowledge about these elements.

The first part of this paper identifies and briefly discusses these factors. Although each will be examined separately, it should be kept in mind that they do not operate in isolation but are highly interdependent and interrelated. The second part of the paper explores one of these factors in greater depth: the degree of cooperative learning embedded in the structure of the setting and its effects on the role of the student as collaborator. Most of the discussion will be conducted with reference to the computer setting in a study (Edfelt 1989) in which I looked at the oral interaction of students of different degrees of language proficiency. Because reference to this study is made throughout this chapter, information about it is presented below.

The Study and Its Results

In this study, sixteen fifth-grade Hispanic male students were videotaped and audiorecorded working in pairs at the computer for a total of forty fifteen-minute sessions. Their speech was transcribed, tabulated, and analyzed quantitatively (descriptive and inferential statistics) and qualitatively (discourse analyses). The students, representing four different levels of language proficiencies: non-English-proficient (NEP), limited-English-proficient (LEP), fluent-English-proficient (FEP) and monolingual-English-speaker (ME), were paired alternatively with different partners in such a way that all possible combinations of language proficiencies were represented.

The questions in the study centered around two main areas. The first of these looked at the students' verbal collaborative behavior about the language presented by the software program (i.e., oral interactions regarding the meaning of the text displayed on the screen). This behavior was operationalized as requests for help (i.e., asking for information regarding the meaning of the text on the screen), comprehension checks (i.e., requesting feedback as to whether the text had been understood by a partner), explanations (giving the meaning or interpretation of the text), and translations (i.e., interpreting into Spanish the text on the screen).

The second area looked at the amount of negotiations of meaning, defined, after Varonis and Gass (1985: 151), as "those exchanges in which there is some overt indication that understanding between participants has not been complete." That is, the focus here was on exchanges derived from lack of understanding in the human dyadic interaction. This question was motivated by the prominent position that negotiations of meaning occupy in first- and second-language acquisition research. Language acquisition is hypothesized as a product of meaningful interaction, which is in turn made possible by the interlocutors—both learners and native speakers—negotiating the understanding of the message. This negotiation permits them to receive comprehensible input and transmit comprehensible output, and thus provides a necessary condition for acquisition (Gass and Varonis 1985; Long 1985; Swain 1985).

The results of the study indicated that the students, in general, produced a great deal of collaborative verbal behavior—they gave each other help through explanations and translations, checked each other's comprehension, and requested assistance. The number of negotiations of meaning engendered by their interaction, however, was low. The apparent contradiction of students producing a great deal of collaborative behavior but a low amount of negotiations of meaning may be explained by the fact that, except for the ME speakers, all the subjects could speak Spanish in different degrees of proficiency. As a result, excepting dyad combinations with ME speakers, all others could choose the language of interaction, either English or Spanish, according to their comfort level. The NEP and LEP students, consequently, tended to use Spanish when working with Spanish-speaking partners. This diminished their opportunities to have to understand, and make themselves understood in, their second language, English.

Furthermore, the least amount of collaborative work in dyads with either an NEP or LEP student occurred when the partner was an ME speaker, in which case the conversation occurred totally in English. This low collaborative production is believed to have been caused in great part by the asymmetry of power in the dyadic oral interaction, most sharply seen in the ME–NEP dyad combination.

These results suggest that while the setting offered students the opportunity to collaborate in their most proficient language, it did not provide NEP and LEP students with an optimal environment for negotiation work in the target language. The grouping strategies in this setting and the resulting unequal balance of power in the interaction seem to have contributed to these findings. There were, however, several additional elements at play that directly affected the study's results. Such elements are the subject of the following section.

Determining the Communicative
Potential of a Computer Environment

The challenge of determining the features that configure an ideal computer setting for providing limited-English-proficient students with a stimulating environment for acquiring ESL has begun to be addressed by researchers. DeVillar (1991) identified three contextual variables capable of making or breaking the potential for authentic communication at the computer: software program, student task assignment, and formal training in cooperative learning. In addition, three elements pertaining to grouping strategies also appear to influence the nature of student communication. These include the number of peers at the computer, the learning structure and the composition of the dyad or group regarding student first language and degree of English language proficiency. The five elements are discussed below.

Number of Students at the Computer

Intuitively, it would seem that working in pairs, rather than triads or larger groups, would increase student opportunity and time to talk. Although, to my knowledge, little research has been conducted that specifically investigates group-size effects on the amount and kind of student talk at the computer, some researchers have addressed this issue. Hare (cited by Dickson and Vereen 1983), for instance, recommended the placement of only two students at the computer to obtain maximum opportunities for verbalization and tutoring. Bork (1985), in a study of junior high school students working with science and mathematics programs in groups of different sizes (one to four), found that the groups of two or three were the most desirable for student interaction. Results of a study by Trowbridge and Durnin (1984) indicated that the frequency of peer tutoring and correctness of answers as well as the incidences of cooperation were higher when students worked in dyads than in triads. An additional consideration in favor of dyads is the possibility that triads might create a setting favorable to the development of two-member partnerships that leave one student out of the interaction.

More research is needed to determine the ideal number of students and how this number interacts with other elements in the communicative setting, such as task interdependence, type of instructional activity (determined by the software program), and student language proficiency.

Composition of Dyad or Group

The manner in which students are paired or grouped regarding both their first language and their degree of English language proficiency can be a significant factor in determining their language choice. The latter, in turn, will affect their degree of opportunity to practice the target language, English. The intuitive assumption is that dyads formed by students who do not share the same first language will use English as the medium of communication, regardless of their degree of English proficiency. Likewise, speech in dyads where at least one member is an ME speaker will occur in English, even if his or her partner is NEP. On the other hand, when paired students of differing English proficiency levels share the same linguistic background, their language choice will be influenced by their degree of proficiency in both languages. In my study, as expected, students more proficient in Spanish than in English tended to choose Spanish when paired with bilingual partners. This was especially true when at least one of the interlocutors was very limited in English, in which case the oral interaction was mostly in Spanish.

The results of my study indicated that there was a great deal of English language *learning* taking place when the students interacted in their first language, as this interaction gave them the opportunity to give, and listen to, explanations *about* the language on the screen (i.e., English). However, the opportunity to communicate in their first language reduced the amount of time spent trying to communicate in English. If the motive for placing students at the computer is target language *acquisition* (through oral interaction *in* the language) it is evident that, under certain conditions, this opportunity could only be assured by pairing NEP and LEP students with ME speakers or with partners of a different language background from their own. The study's results did, in effect, indicate that the NEP–ME combination produced the highest number of negotiations of meaning ($M = 10.75$). However, this number was lower than intuitively expected, given the fact that these students represented monolinguals (one in Spanish and another in English) communicating in English. Such verbal interaction would be expected to produce a great deal of misunderstanding or lack of understanding, and, consequently, of negotiations of meaning. That this was not the case seems to indicate that elements more powerful than language proficiency were directly influencing the subjects' oral interaction.

Software Program

The software program is a critical element that influences the linguistic behavior of the students at the computer. Among the different types of programs—such as drill-and practice, tutorials, text manipulation, text generation, and so on—several researchers, based mostly on anecdotal evidence, have argued that simulations offer the most potential for generating conversations among students (Higgins and Johns 1984; Kenning and Kenning 1983; Wyatt 1984). The results of a study that attempted to test empirically the effects of two types of software programs on student language production seemed to confirm the superiority of simulations over at least one other program type. In this study, Young (1988) investigated the amount and kind of conversational discourse produced by two groups of students, one working with text-reconstruction programs (which included activities such as jumbled words, fill-in-the-blanks, and cloze exercises) and the other with simulation and adventure games. The results indicated significant differences in the students' oral interaction. Because in the first type of programs the outcome (i.e., the "right" answer) was predetermined, most of the resulting student speech was noncreative and the product of direct readings from the screen. The second type of programs, on the other hand, allowed for the negotiation of outcome and, consequently, the production of creative language and longer conversational turns.

These anecdotal and empirical findings, as well as other positive characteristics of simulations (e.g., they can be played repeatedly, are enjoyed by students, and can be used by speakers of different levels of English language proficiency), influenced the choice of the program *The Oregon Trail* (1986) for my study. In this simulation, the students are presented with life-and-death decisions as they travel by covered wagon across the United States. In spite of the obvious enjoyment on the part of the subjects, the study uncovered shortcomings of this kind of program as an ideal generator of oral interaction between its users. The finding that NEP students working with ME partners tended to become passive and to relinquish the decision-making power to the latter, is, for example, one of these shortcomings. That this was a construct of the context rather than of the subjects' personality is shown by the great deal of collaborative behavior in which the same NEP students engaged when working with bilingual peers. In this case, being able to communicate (in Spanish) allowed them to become active participants in the interaction; because they were able to present and defend their choices they could contribute to the decision-making process, and thus have a much greater degree of participation in the conversation.

The fact that when paired with ME partners and confronted with the necessity to communicate in English, NEP students could "get by" without much oral participation points to an inability on the part of the activities in the simulation to create a need for real exchange of information. The body of research looking at the relationship between task and verbal interaction has significant application here. Hatch (1983), for instance, found that conversations in which the exchange of information was crucial resulted in more intense negotiations of meaning. Similarly, research comparing several types of tasks (Long 1981; Pica and Doughty 1985) found that tasks in which each interlocutor needed to transmit to and receive information from the other resulted in a two-way exchange. This, in turn, generated not only increased oral interaction between students, but also authentic and purposeful communication. Two-way activities, defined as exchanges in which both participants have information they must share in order to complete the task (Long 1981), have the ability to create positive interdependence between the students. Positive interdependence, called by Johnson and Johnson (1984) "the essence of cooperative learning," has been defined as the perception on the part of each student that she or he is linked with others in a way so that she or he cannot succeed unless the others do. The relationship between two-way communication and cooperative learning has been discussed by DeVillar (1991). A significant aspect of this relationship is that, because in two-way tasks each interlocutor in a dialog depends on information that the other has, interdependence is a fundamental characteristic of these tasks.

Different types of software programs have been selected for research investigating the oral production of students at the computer. For instance, the subjects in DeVillar's (1987) study used the *Bank Street Writer* (1984), a word-processing applica-

tion through which the students wrote electronically the creative product of their conversational exchange; Chávez (1990)
used *Writing to Read*, a reading and writing program for kindergarten and first-grade children (Martin 1986); Webb, Ender
and Lewis (1986) looked at the oral production of students
learning BASIC. Although these and several other studies investigated group or dyadic oral interaction variables, these
variables represented a wide range of differing research questions. The lack of a common focus in these investigative efforts
makes any cross-study—based conclusions or implications regarding software program effects inherently difficult. To clarify,
if studies using word-processing programs (such as, for instance, DeVillar's and Chávez's) had found a high production
of negotiations of meaning, such finding could suggest that
programs of this type have a more positive effect than others
(e.g., simulations) on this aspect of student interaction. None
of these studies, however, investigated student production of
negotiations of meaning; consequently, software program effects on this variable remain unknown. Moreover, when the
interaction of other contextual elements comprising the computer environment of the different studies is considered, comparisons of results from one study to another are even more
problematic. More studies that focus on one particular variable
(e.g., effects of type of software program on student interaction)
while controlling all other variables in the context (e.g., number of students at the computer, learning structure, student
language combination, etc.), are needed to answer more fully
questions about the effects of different contextual elements in
the computer environment.

Meanwhile, second-language—acquisition software programs need to be developed along the lines of the two-way
model. The potential of this type of activity seems significant.
Apart from increasing communication, these programs, by
making students positively dependent on their peers regardless of their target proficiency level, would result in more equitable verbal interactions. One ramification of this relationship
would be to give less-proficient students equal access to the
keyboard, an important element of the computer context and
the subject of the following section.

Student Task Assignment

Student task assignment refers to the division of labor at the
computer, including student roles assignment, work distribu-

tion, and keyboard use. This component is thus highly intertwined with the type of learning structure at the computer (i.e., individualistic, competitive, or cooperative), a contextual element discussed in the next section. Role assignment (e.g., keyboarder, reader, etc.) can be a means of achieving task interdependence between students, as these roles determine how students share the work and the keyboard.

The question of whether a student has greater access to the keyboard than his or her partner is significant, as keyboard control could result in control over the computer and its input. Control over the activity on the part of one student, in turn, diminishes the dyad's opportunities and/or need for interaction. In this setting, unequal access may result as a consequence of inequalities in student status, which, in turn, are in great measure determined by student differences in language proficiency.

Several strategies attempt to neutralize the effects of this status inequity by increasing the likelihood of equal access to the computer. The subjects in my study were required to alternate each turn at the keyboard, make joint decisions, and reach a consensus before pressing the key. However, as discussed above, the finding indicated that when working with ME speakers, less-proficient students in the dyad (especially NEP students) had much less decision-making control. This suggests that stronger elements in the setting rendered these strategies ineffectual. It appears that unless this and other structural elements associated with the learning activity guarantee equal student participation and power, such as the two-way tasks described above, the computer will not produce an optimal environment for oral interaction and language acquisition.

The task assigned to the students at the computer cannot be divorced from the type of activity in the software program. In DeVillar's (1987) study, where the subjects used a word-processing program, task interdependence was created by assigning each student in the dyad a task—one student responsible for the keyboard and the other for the screen. While the former keyboarded what his partner dictated, the latter read and verified the text appearing on the screen. In this way, the power was equally divided; although one student had absolute control of the keyboard for 10 minutes, he was constrained to only entering either what his peer had dictated or the negotiated result of this dictation. Consequently, control of the keyboard was not here synonymous with control of the activity. This role was reversed at the end of ten minutes, which marked the session midpoint, so that each partner had the opportunity to engage in each task for the same amount of time. This system, feasible with the type of software program used for that study, assured both students equitable access to the keyboard. A question that remains to be investigated is whether the effects of equal keyboard access trickles down to the type and amount of conversational exchange between students of different degrees of English language proficiency.

Learning Structure

"Learning structure" refers to the nature of student-to-student interaction in instructional situations. Research on three types of structures—individualistic, competitive and cooperative—has supported the intuitive assumption that cooperative settings lead to greater communication and exchange of information between students (see Johnson and Johnson 1984 for a review of this research). Similarly, studies of computer settings have found evidence that oral interaction and collaborative acts are greatly increased if the students are not merely assigned to work in pairs but placed in cooperatively structured computer activities. One study, for instance (Johnson, Johnson, and Stanne 1986), compared the effects of computer-assisted cooperative, competitive, and individualistic instruction and found that the oral interaction produced by the students working in the first of these conditions was significantly greater and more task related than that of students working in the other two types of settings.

In my study, a cooperative structure was created in the computer setting by integrating elements of cooperative learning, including positive interdependence and individual accountability. Positive interdependence was structured through (a) goal interdependence (i.e., students worked toward the mutual goal of arriving to Oregon safely); (b) resource interdependence (i.e., students shared the same computer and software program); (c) task interdependence (i.e., students took turns at the keyboard); and (d) reward interdependence (i.e., students received joint recognition points based on their ability to work together at the computer). Individual accountability was structured by giving students individual recognition points for making sure that (a) each dyad member participated in equal measure; (b) no one member dominated the group;

and (c) members asked for and gave explanations and help when needed.

An additional element of cooperative learning—training in collaborative skills, which has been also identified as an integral component of a communicative computer environment—is discussed in the following section.

Cooperative Learning Training

In spite of inroads made by cooperative learning in the last decade, most teaching and learning in the elementary schools continues to take place in competitive classroom structures (Kagan 1989). As a result of this competitive socialization, the majority of students lack the skills to work collaboratively. It is not surprising, then, that youngsters do not automatically start cooperating when simply encouraged to do so. Although not all scholars in this area believe that the teaching of cooperative skills is necessary (see Graves and Graves 1989 for a discussion on this controversy), most researchers and educators (e.g., Johnson and Johnson 1986; Kagan 1990) believe that, just as students need to be taught the skills of reading and math, they need to be taught the skills of cooperation in order to be able to cooperate.

Before the videotaped computer sessions, the subjects in my study were trained in cooperative-learning techniques. This training consisted of two one-hour treatment and practice sessions delivered on consecutive days in the rooms where the videotaping would take place. Although the training served to give the subjects an opportunity to work together and to become familiar and comfortable with the videotaping situation, its main objective was the learning of basic cooperative skills.

The training sessions in the study followed the three main steps delineated in the Learning Together approach, developed by Johnson and Johnson (1975), as follows:

Explaining the learning task and interdependence

A discussion was first held with the students in which the objectives of the computer simulation were reviewed (all subjects had previous experience using the computer program) and the group goals were set. The goal interdependence of the activity was emphasized by asking the students to work together in each decision they had to make, reach a consensus

before keyboarding their answers, contribute their own opinions, ask their peers for theirs, listen carefully, and state the
reasons for their choices. They were also given specific examples of these and other collaborative behavior and they were informed that they would earn joint and individual points for
working cooperatively.

Monitoring and intervening

The students then sat down at the computer in pairs and
started working with the simulation while being videotaped
and monitored. The monitoring consisted of my observing how
effectively they were working together. An observation instrument (see Figure 11.1), where I recorded instances of collaborative behavior, was used for this purpose. When deemed
necessary, I intervened in order to clarify instructions, answer
questions, reinforce particularly effective behaviors, and give
specific examples of collaborative skills in need of improvement.

Evaluation and processing

A follow-up discussion was then held in order to process the
observation. During this session, the students, after filling out
a self-evaluation form, received feedback as to how well they
were using cooperative skills and shared with me their own
feelings about and reactions to their teamwork at the computer. Because these processing sessions were audiorecorded,
it was possible to examine their content in detail. Their analysis supplied information that was especially significant because it provided insight into the learners' perspective, an
important source of knowledge that tends to be neglected in education research. The next part of this paper presents and discusses these data.

The Student as Collaborator
in the Computer Environment

After each computer session, the subjects were given the opportunity to describe, discuss, and reflect on how they had
worked together as a team. As a first step, students were asked
to fill out a self-evaluation instrument, after which the processing discussion began. The results of the data from these two
sources are presented below.

Collaborative Skills			.		
Took turns at the Keyboard					
Asked for reasons behind decisions Gave discussed reasons					
Reached agreement					
Listened to classmate					
Asked for help					
Asked partner if he understood					
Explained to classmate					

Fig. 11.1
Observation Sheet: General   From Male et al., 1986, p. 162

Student Self-Evaluation

The Student Self-Evaluation Form, which the subjects could fill out either in English or Spanish (see Figures 11.2 and 11.3), contained five statements (1) I asked my partner for the reason behind his ideas; (2) I listened to my partner's responses; (3) We got agreement before the keyboarder typed; (4) I asked my partner for help when I did not understand; (5) I explained the best I could when my partner did not understand. The students reacted to these statements by checking one among three answers in a multiple choice format: All of the time, Some of the time, Very little of the time. The purpose of the questions was (a) to encourage students to reflect on their collaborative behavior, (b) to obtain information regarding the students' perception of their behavior, and (c) to serve as a springboard for processing.

Although the students were not asked to discuss with each other their responses to the self-evaluation form, on occasion spontaneous conversations emerged in which they talked about the questions, pondered their answers, discussed what their collaborative behavior had been, and solicited and gave each other examples of this behavior. These conversations, inadvertently recorded, provided me with additional information. One interesting finding from these serendipitous data was how candidly the students reacted to and answered the questions on this form, an honesty that was confirmed by existing data. The answers given by the students on the form were tabulated and analyzed, and the results compared with the findings from the videotaped student oral interaction during the computer sessions. The comparison revealed that the students' perceptions of their collaborative behavior paralleled their actual behavior. This positive association suggests not only that the students were quite perceptive about their own collaborative behavior but extremely candid when reporting on it as well.

Thus, the results of the analysis of student responses to the statement "I asked my partner for help when I did not understand" indicated that the more-English-proficient partner in the dyad tended to respond "Very little of the time" (see Table 1). For example, FEP students working with NEP peers checked this category with 75 percent frequency. However, there was a marked change in this behavior when paired with students of higher proficiency level than their own; thus, after working

	All of the time	Some of the time	Very little of the time
1. I asked my partner for the reason behind his/her ideas.	☐	☐	☐
2. I listened to my partner's responses.	☐	☐	☐
3. We got agreement before the keyboarder typed.	☐	☐	☐
4. I asked my partner for help when I did not understand.	☐	☐	☐
5. I explained the best I could when my partner did not understand.	☐	☐	☐

Fig. 11.2

Student self-evaluation form * *Adapted from Male et al., 1986, p. 66.

	Todas las veces	Algunas veces	Muy pocas veces
1. Le pregunté a mi compañero la razón de sus decisiones.			
2. Escuché las respuestas de mi compañero.			
3. Nos pusimos de acuerdo antes de escribir la respuesta.			
4. Le pedí ayuda a mi compañero cuando no entendí algo.			
5. Le expliqué a mi compañero lo mejor que pude cuando él no entendió.			

Fig. 11.3
Formulario de auto-evaluación del estudiante

TABLE 11.1 PERCENTAGE OF RESPONSES TO THE QUESTION "I ASKED MY PARTNER FOR HELP WHEN I DID NOT UNDERSTAND" AS A FUNCTION OF PARTNER PROFICIENCY*

Target Speaker	Partner	All of the time	Some of the time	Very Little of the time
NEP	NEP	0	75	25
NEP	LEP	100	0	0
NEP	FEP	100	0	0
NEP	ME	0	50	50
LEP	NEP	0	75	25
LEP	LEP	0	25	75
LEP	FEP	75	25	0
LEP	ME	100	0	0
FEP	NEP	0	25	75
FEP	LEP	0	75	25
FEP	FEP	0	75	25
FEP	ME	50	25	25
ME	NEP	0	25	75
ME	LEP	0	50	50
ME	FEP	25	50	25
ME	ME	0	50	50

*Percentages are based on 4 responses

with ME partners, 50 percent of the FEP students' responses indicated they had asked for help "All of the time" and 25 percent, "Some of the time." Data on requests for help from the videotaped sessions confirm this was the case—students of any level of English proficiency working with peers of a lower proficiency level than themselves produced few or no requests for help, but increased this behavior when working with partners of a higher proficiency level than themselves. Continuing with the example of FEP students, the videotaped data show that the latter asked for no help at all when working with NEP and LEP partners, but averaged 1.25 requests for help when working with ME peers.

Following a similar pattern, when LEP students worked with NEP peers, 75 percent of their responses indicated having asked for help "Some of the time." However, when working with FEP partners, 75 percent of their responses indicated having asked for help "All of the time." This again parallels the results

TABLE 11.2 PERCENTAGE OF RESPONSES TO THE QUESTION "I EXPLAINED THE BEST I COULD WHEN MY PARTNER DID NOT UNDERSTAND" AS A FUNCTION OF PARTNER PROFICIENCY*

Target Speaker	Partner	All of the time	Some of the time	Very Little of the time
NEP	NEP	25	25	50
NEP	LEP	0	50	50
NEP	FEP	0	25	75
NEP	ME	0	25	75
LEP	NEP	100	0	0
LEP	LEP	0	25	75
LEP	FEP	0	50	50
LEP	ME	0	75	25
FEP	NEP	100	0	0
FEP	LEP	100	0	0
FEP	FEP	25	50	25
FEP	ME	25	50	25
ME	NEP	100	0	0
ME	LEP	100	0	0
ME	FEP	25	50	25
ME	ME	0	25	75

*Percentages are based on 4 responses

in the data from the videotaped sessions, which indicated that the LEP students averaged .50 requests for help when working with NEP peers, 2.00 when working with students of their own proficiency level, and 5.00 when working with FEP partners. This behavior is consistent with the helper role the more-English-proficient students in the dyad automatically assumed when working with less-proficient peers. This self-assigned role reflects student awareness (whether conscious or not) of their degree of English proficiency vis-à-vis their peers.

In the same vein, when the subjects' responses regarding their giving of help are analyzed, it is clear that the more-English-proficient students in the dyad consistently answered "All of the time" to the statement "I explained the best I could when my partner did not understand" (see Table 2). For example, when working with NEP peers, both LEP and FEP students so responded 100 percent of the time. Data from the videotaped student interaction confirmed that, in effect, LEP and FEP students gave a tremendous amount of help in the form of explanations and translations to their NEP peers. Conversely, when working with LEP and FEP students, the NEP students' answers indicated they gave explanations to their peers "Very little of the time" with 50 and 75 percent frequency, respectively. However, 100 percent of their answers indicated to have asked their partner for help "All of the time."

Thus, self-disclosure by the students suggests that they were aware of their relative place in the dyad's conversational hierarchy, essentially characterized by the less-English-proficient students depending on their more-proficient partners to a degree determined by their own proficiency, with no reciprocal dependency on the part of the latter. All the available data sources, including the student self-evaluation, seem to indicate that dependence went mostly in one direction. Although this condition is to a great degree intrinsic in any peer tutoring situation, in a language-learning environment there is a greater need to empower the language learner so as to bring a greater degree of communicative equity. This equity, in turn, will affect the limited-English-proficient student's degree of language acquisition.

As Tables 1 and 2 show, patterns of low collaborative behavior were also exhibited by NEP students working with ME peers as well as by dyads formed by students of the same proficiency level. The first of these cases will be discussed in greater detail below. As one example of the second case, when ME students were paired with their ME counterparts, they tended to check the lowest category ("Very little of the time") for both "I asked my partner for help when I did not understand" (50 percent of responses) and "I explained the best I could when my partner did not understand" (75 percent of responses). Data from the videotaped sessions showed that, in effect, there were very few instances of explanations ($M = .75$) and requests for help $M = 1.2$) in this dyad combination. During processing time, the ME students were asked whether they had the chance to collaborate with each other. Their response is typified by Alex's comment: "No, we knew the words." That is, they felt that discussions and explanations were not needed because each student in the dyad understood the messages on the screen.

Similarly, 75 percent of responses on the part of LEP students working with their matched LEP counterparts indicated that they had asked for help or explained to their partners "Very little of the time." Results from the videotaped sessions again confirmed this to have been the case—the LEP students exhibited very low collaborative behavior when working with other LEP students (an average of 2.0 requests for help and .5 explanations). These data suggest that students at the same English proficiency level felt they had little to negotiate with respect to meaning, in all probability due to their assumption of shared knowledge. In this case, the status equity conferred by the students' similar degree of proficiency resulted in neither equal nor unequal interdependence but in the absence of it. Again, the computer environment failed to create the type of reciprocal dependence and two-way communication that would have made it truly communicative.

Processing

The processing of the collaborative aspects of the computer session started with a discussion of the students' responses to the statements posed in the self-evaluation form. The conversation then continued with questions and/or comments either from the students or myself. Students were encouraged to express their feelings and impressions about working collaboratively and any other aspect of the computer session. In addition, the positive collaborative behaviors I observed were mentioned and praised and the negative or missing ones were brought up for discussion. In this manner, students were provided with feedback from their peers and myself about how effectively they had collaborated and, at the same time, with the opportunity to express their views about the session.

The processing activities, therefore, introduced to the students the notion of authentic communication with their peers and an adult (myself) in an instructional setting, and provided them with concrete examples of the verbal behavior that characterizes this kind of communication. In view of the general lack of opportunities for authentic communication in classrooms (Mehan 1979; Schinke-Llano 1983), processing was thus a significant component of this study; it not only served as a source of data but, in providing the students with positive practice, was an essential part of their collaborative experience.

The processing sessions varied in length, ranging from five to fifteen minutes, and were informally conducted. Throughout the discussion, students were asked several questions that focussed on how they contributed to each other's learning. The same candid behavior observed by the students when filling

out their self-evaluation forms was evident during these discussions. The questions I asked and some of the students'
most frequent answers are discussed below.

Question #1: How do you think the session went?

The students answered positively to this question[2] (e.g.,
"Good"; "Very good!"; "Right"; "I liked it!") without further
elaboration. The follow-up request, "Tell me what you think
went well," usually brought a discussion about how the simulation had progressed, what they had done correctly or incorrectly toward the goal of reaching Oregon, and what they would
do differently next time. This discussion was welcome, as it
created a relaxed atmosphere for the processing. A second
follow-up question, "How do you think you worked together?"
served to focus the children's attention and the discussion on
their collaborative behavior. Some common answers to this
question were: "We worked well," "We worked together good
[sic]," "We are a good group." These answers suggest that the
students, in general, enjoyed the sessions and had a positive
feeling about them.

Question #2: What do you think you did well as a team?

This question also frequently brought answers having to do
with successes regarding the simulation, such as: "None of us
died," "We stopped to rest, so we didn't get sick," "We didn't
drown," "When we went to the lake," "Crossing the river with
the raft," "I liked it when we got to Oregon." A brief discussion
on this particular achievement then followed.

If the conversation took this turn, the topic was redirected
to that of collaboration with the follow-up question: "What do
you think you did well working together?" The most common
answers referred to reaching an agreement before keyboarding
(e.g., "That we decided together how much food to buy and
other things," "When we discussed how deep it was to take the
ferry and we made it"), taking turns at the keyboard (e.g. "We
did not hoard the keyboard"), explaining to each other (e.g.,
"We explained the words we didn't know"), and asking for and
giving help (e.g., "I asked when I didn't understand something," "I liked it best when I was helping him," "That I helped
him and he helped me"). Less common were answers having to
do with working harmoniously (e.g. "We did not argue"),

checking comprehension (e.g., "When I asked him if he was understanding what I was saying so I could help him"), sharing (e.g., "I liked sharing the work"), and listening to their partners (e.g., "When I listened to him and we agreed to do something, like see a landscape").

One striking aspect of these responses is the preponderant use of the pronoun "we" as opposed to "I," which reflects the students' developing collaborative attitude and skills. The responses also seem to show enjoyment of the cooperative structure in which they were working and a high degree of awareness of their collaborative behavior.

Question #3: How did you try to help each other?

The purpose of this question was to elicit from the students concrete instances of collaboration; however, it proved difficult for them to do so. Most of their answers continued to describe behaviors of a general nature, such as: "We talked things over," "When he needed help I told him everything," "Like he didn't understand an English word and I told him in Spanish what it is." A few students were able to produce concrete examples: "I told him what 'ferry' was," "We explained to each other the words 'measles' and 'fort'," "One time that it was his turn, I told him [because] he forgot."

This question was also used as a bridge to give students my own feedback regarding the session. When the students failed to mention particularly effective behaviors, I would say, for example: "Also, Tomás, I noticed that when the message on the screen said that your party had found an abandoned wagon, you realized that Pablo did not understand and you explained it very clearly to him." Or: "You collaborated very nicely when you stated your opinion and then listened, Stewart. For instance, when you and Joseph had to decide how many days you were going to rest, and you told Joseph, who wanted to input nine days: 'Well; maybe I don't agree. Did we discuss it?' You stated how you felt and then listened to what Joseph had to say." Any observed uncooperative behavior was also mentioned in a nonthreatening manner and the students were encouraged to engage in the opposite and desired way. For instance, I would say: "I noticed that when you were ready to cross the river, Tony was so involved in the simulation that he pressed the keyboard two or three times in a row without asking Alberto for an opinion. Remember that working as a team means that all the decisions are taken together, as you frequently did during the simulation. Can any of you remember an occasion in which you decided together about what to do?" The students would then contribute their own examples.

Question #4: Did you ask your partner for the reasons behind his responses?

In an attempt to transmit the message to the students that conversation between them was welcome and to emphasize the collaborative nature of their work at the computer, they were encouraged to find out the reasons behind their partners' choices as to the course of action to follow in the simulation. The students' responses both to this question during processing and to a very similar statement on the self-evaluation form (i.e., "I asked my partner for the reasons behind his ideas") shows that they felt they had done so frequently. In the self-evaluation form, 62 percent of the responses indicated "All of the time"; 33 percent "Some of the time"; and only 5 percent "Very little of the time." Although the analysis of the data from the videotaped interaction showed that student did, in fact, engage in this practice, the strategy did not always work as expected. One difficulty was that students tended to interpret their peers' questioning as criticism. It was not infrequent for a student to change his choice when asked by his peer why he had made it rather than to explain the reasons behind it. This is clearly examplified in the following exchange, where the NEP student, upon being asked by his LEP partner for the reasons behind his particular choice, item #3, changed it to item #2:

NEP: Tre' Three
LEP: ¿Por qué quieres tres? Why do you want three?
NEP: ¿Do'? Two?
LEP: ¿Eh? Eh?
NEP: No answer; just looks at the screen)
LEP: ¿Por que quieres tres? Why do you want three?
NEP: Do', entonces Two, then
LEP: ¿Dos? Two?
NEP: Mhm (affirm.) Mhm
LEP: O.K. (types)

   This behavior suggests that requesting students to engage in a particular speech act (in this case, finding out the reasons

behind what their partners chose to do) created, in some instances, a forced, artificial conversational exchange. The analysis of the students' discourse showed that although, on many
occasions, they were genuinely curious as to why their partner
desired, for example, to pay a guide to take the wagon across
the river rather than cross it by themselves, on other occasions
they asked for reasons without a real curiosity to find out. This
was especially evident in a few conversations where the asking
of "why" became repetitive and ritualistic, and thus occurred
on occasions when reasons for a particular course of action
were obvious and, consequently, needed no explication.

*Question #5: In what way could you collaborate even more
next time?*

The responses given to this question generally expressed the
intention of increasing the amount of collaborative behavior
students were already exhibiting, such as "Help each other
more," "Asking my partner the meaning of the words I don't
know," "Not monopolizing the keyboard," and so on.

    As in the use of "we" as opposed to "I," discussed under
question #2, other words used in these responses reflect the
developing collaborative attitudes and skills on the part of the
students. Words such as "help" and "ask" were frequent in
these conversations. Furthermore, the students integrated
into their active vocabulary new words that relate to the cooperative environment in which they worked. For instance, the
words "monopolize" and "contribute," new for most of the subjects at the beginning of the study, were used with ease by all of
them at the end of it.

Question #6: Anything else you would like to add?

This question usually brought no additional comments. On
two occasions there was a reaffirmation of a positive feeling toward collaboration: "I'd just say we work very well" and "I liked
working with Joseph."

    Thus, constant monitoring (during the computer sessions)
and feedback (during processing), which constitute integral elements of the Learning Together approach, were also part of
the computer-based cooperative structure in my study. In general, the students' answers, comments, and feedback reflect
the behaviors stressed in their cooperative-learning training.

Both their engaging in, and awareness of, these desired behaviors would seem to suggest that the cooperative training they received for the study was generally effective. The question remains, however, as to how much of the collaborative behavior the dyads exhibited during these sessions would carry over to situations where they worked without being observed. Such data exist. At the end of each "official" fifteen-minute videotaped session, the students were allowed to continue working for ten more minutes or until the simulation was finished, whichever came first. Because during this extra time I was not present and the students did not know the camcorder was still on, they worked under the impression of being unobserved. Although their oral interaction during these additional computer taperecordings has not been formally examined (transcribed, tabulated, and statistically analyzed), a careful viewing and listening of these tapes seem to indicate that students continued the same degree and type of collaborative behavior they had exhibited while being observed. A more formal analysis, however, is needed to corroborate this impression.

Other student comments and input shed light on additional aspects of their collaborative relationship. These are discussed in the following section.

Non-English-Proficient Students Working at the Computer with Monolingual English Speakers

Data from the processing of the computer sessions between NEP and ME students provided significant insight into some characteristics of the oral interaction produced by this dyad combination while working at the computer. The main aspects of interest focused on the NEP students' passive behavior, the amount of comprehensible input they were able to receive, and how pervasively they had feigned comprehension of their ME partner's speech. The student's comments regarding these issues and the insights gained from these comments are discussed below.

NEP students' passive behavior

It will be recalled that the data from the videotaped computer sessions revealed that the verbal exchange in the NEP–ME dyad combination approached the characteristics of a monologue (i.e., the ME speakers did most of the talking and the

NEP partner assumed a passive, risk-avoiding role). This non-reciprocal dyadic relationship resulted in an average of .75 acts of collaborative behavior for NEP students and 14.75 for ME students. The analysis of the students' responses to the self-evaluation statements showed that they were aware of their degree of participation. As Table 1 shows, to the statement "I asked my partner for help when I did not understand," 50 percent of the NEP student responses indicated they had done so "Very little of the time," 50 per cent "Some of the time," and not once "All of the time." A clue to the NEP children's feelings about their respective roles was given while processing the last computer session between Daniel (NEP) and Joseph (ME). The former, upon being asked why he had been so quiet during the session, responded that Joseph did not speak Spanish nor himself English, so he could not communicate with him.[3]

Although apparently simple, this response suggests a disturbing condition in these students' classrooms—the belief on the part of NEP students that they cannot work with ME classmates because they do not speak a common language. This might explain in great part their passivity when working with ME peers. The lack of physical and academic integration between these students in the classroom seems to communicate the clear message that it is impossible or undesirable for them to work together. Even though this message might not be consciously articulated by the teacher, it is given de facto by not creating a learning structure where students could work together. That this was occurring in my subjects' classrooms is further confirmed by the fact that the study gave at least one of the four NEP subjects, Ricardo, his first opportunity to work with an ME speaking classmate. In spite of having been in his classroom for three months prior to the study, he was puzzled when told he would be paired with Alex, an ME speaker, asking me with astonishment: "¿Yo voy a trabajar con Alex?" ("I am going to work with Alex?"). He made a point of wondering aloud how he could work with this student when he could not speak English; it was obvious that they had not worked together before. During his first computer sessions with Alex, Ricardo seemed somewhat intimidated and ill at ease; he resorted to a great number of facial expressions, played nervously with his jacket and sat rigidly in his chair, behaviors that he did not exhibit when working with bilingual peers. In spite of the collaborative elements in this computer setting, his psychological distance and high affective filter when working with an ME classmate obviously prevailed.

Comprehensible input.

The topic of comprehensible input was spontaneously brought up by Alex (ME) during the processing of his first computer session with Ricardo (NEP).[4] When asked what they thought they had done well as a team, Alex answered: "I was always trying to understand what he was telling me. Some of the time I did, but not all the time." Ricardo, in turn, said: "Sometimes I understood the words he said and sometimes I didn't. . . . [Today] I understood him all but three times. When he told me the first time that we had to rest nine days, I could not understand him. . . . But the second time [he told me] I did. That's why when he talked to me I paid a lot of attention to see if I could understand something." this comment suggests that Ricardo actively attempted to figure out what his ME classmate was saying, a learner strategy which leads to language acquisition (Long 1981; Wong-Fillmore 1985). Similarly, in their second processing session, when asked if he had been able to understand Alex, he responded: "Yes, because I heard him once and now I heard him again. One time that I did not understand him was when he told me that he wanted me to press the number for 'food,' *that* I could not understand. I understood only half of it. Later he told me [again] . . . and I remember what 'food' was."

In the comment above, Ricardo is very clearly expressing his belief that hearing his ME peer convey a similar message on multiple linguistic occasions gave him the opportunity to predict or guess the content of the native-speaker's speech, a strategy identified as one employed by the "good language learner" (Rubin 1975). Similarly, in her study on effective classroom strategies for second-language acquisition, Wong-Fillmore (1985) found that efficient teachers tended to use language that was repetitive, consistent, and familiar. These teachers did this by adopting routines for their lessons (which permitted them to present new material in a familiar format) and by giving students the opportunity to hear repeatedly practically the same sentence with small changes in them. In fact, these repetitions resembled pattern-substitution drills, but, unlike the latter, were used in situations that provided students with context and understanding. Another effective teaching strategy found by Wong-Fillmore was the use of paraphrases; hearing the same message in different linguistic forms gave students the opportunity to figure out its meaning.

This condition closely resembles the circumstances in my study, where the computer situation allowed the NEP and LEP students a greater opportunity to understand the spoken language through familiar verbal routines engendered by the simulation program. The students heard unknown words in known contexts and used words they had just learned in new situations. Although the NEP students could not understand every word uttered by their ME peers, the familiarity and predictability of the situation permitted them the use of their prior knowledge to figure out the meaning of their ME partner's speech.

During processing, Ricardo also expressed repeatedly the belief that his comprehension in English was greatly facilitated by hearing a message in Spanish before hearing it in English. For instance, after his first computer session with Alex, he said: "[Today] I understood almost everything because when I was working with Pablo, he explained everything in Spanish and in English to me, and then we both said it in English. [I understood also] because Pablo first read in English, and then he explained to me in Spanish." These words described very aptly Ricardo's session with Pablo (LEP), in which the latter frequently read the message on the screen in English, then translated the content into Spanish for Ricardo's benefit, and finally discussed the meaning with him. On another occasion, in response to the question of whether he preferred to work with bilingual or ME partners, he said: "Both. I like [to work] with Pablo because he tells me everything in Spanish, and with Alex because he tells me everything in English. And when that one tells me in Spanish, and this one tells me in English, I more or less know the words that Pablo already explained to me, so that when Alex tells me I already know."

The above comments strongly suggest the NEP student's belief that his learning and comprehension of English as well as of the subject matter content (in this case, the situations in the simulation) was facilitated by the sequence that first provided him with support in his first language (when paired with bilingual peers), and then with the opportunity to hear the same content in English (when paired with an ME partner). This model thus appears effective for developing academic and second-language skills simultaneously, and serves as a strong argument for dyad combinations that give NEP and LEP students first the opportunity to work with FEP bilingual peers and then with ME partners.

The question of feigning comprehension

My observations of the computer sessions between NEP and ME students led me to believe that the former had frequently resorted to the risk-avoiding strategy of feigning comprehension of their ME partner's speech. I was therefore particularly interested in the students' comments and reflection about this issue, and brought the topic up during processing. To my very direct question, "When you did not understand Alex, did you let him know so that he could tell you again?," Ricardo replied: "No, because when he told me something, I understood about half of it and about half I didn't. I more or less knew what he was telling me." Ricardo is here referring again to the effective learning strategy of making educated guesses as to the meaning of the native-speaker's speech.

Although no student ever "confessed" to pretending that they understood when they didn't, one FEP student, Tomás, stated that he had witnessed some of his peers doing it. "I tell them 'Do you know what that means?' and they say, 'Yes!' and I tell 'em 'What does it mean' and they say 'I don't know.' They just want one to believe that they do." During the same conversation, Pablo (LEP) presented the perspective of the LEP student: "One time in the classroom, when I did not know the meaning of a word in English, and I told Roy, 'What does that mean,' and then Tomás said (with exaggerated tone): 'Oh, you don't know what that means!! Ahh!' And then he laughed. I think it was a word that almost everyone knew the meaning of."

The above exchange illustrates how unmerciful the politics of language can be in nonsupportive environments, where students with little or no proficiency in the English language can be made to feel very vulnerable. Recent arrivals frequently have to contend not only with difficult situations at home and the hardships of adjusting to a new culture but with the hostile attitudes of some classmates as well. This was vividly exposed during a conversation in which Pablo and Alex revealed to me that when Ricardo first arrived from Mexico he was ridiculed and taunted by many classmates. According to the students, because of Ricardo's dark circles around his eyes, caused by his not getting much sleep, one classmate had called him "Beat up Karate Kid." Soon everyone started calling him by this name.

On the other hand, a setting that encourages students to share their linguistic knowledge with less-proficient peers in a generous and open way would decrease this vulnerability. A warm, compassionate environment where students are taught to welcome their recently arrived peers and take pride and pleasure in helping them would provide those who are not proficient in English with increased confidence and the feeling that they can take risks in their verbal exchanges. The communicative potential of this setting could be enhanced even further by making it possible for NEP and LEP students to contribute to the exchange as much as their English-proficient-speaking peers, by means of activities along the lines of the two-way communicative model.

The Student as Collaborator

The high number of explanations and other cooperative behavior in which the subjects of my study engaged suggests that students, when the appropriate environment is created, like working collaboratively. The input received from my subjects during processing confirmed this. On several occasions, they expressed spontaneously their enjoyment of specific collaborative aspects of the computer sessions (e.g., "I liked sharing the keyboard," said by an especially shy student) or volunteered expressions of pleasure to work with a specific partner. For example, after a session in which Joseph (ME) had been especially successful at refraining from his impulse to monopolize the keyboard, Stewart (ME) said: "I like working with Joseph!" to which the latter replied emphatically: "so do I!"

This feeling seemed to extend into those settings where students worked with peers less-proficient in English than themselves. In general, they responded enthusiastically when asked if they liked working with Ricardo or Daniel, the NEP target subjects in my study. Students seemed to enjoy the role of tutor, although, as is to be expected, they revealed differences in their teaching styles. While some of them proved to be "natural teachers," giving themselves to the tutoring task with obvious gusto, others kept a guarded attitude; while some seemed to rely heavily on translating, others preferred to explain meanings in English; while some were constantly checking their partner's comprehension, others waited to be asked for an explanation.

As noted above, LEP students became more assertive and self-assured when they were helping peers who were less English proficient than themselves. Research on peer tutoring has confirmed that tutoring not only helps students cognitively (Webb 1985) but confers status and increases their self-esteem (Cohen 1986). In a recent study, for instance, Pease-Alvarez and Vásquez (1990) found that tutoring first graders was associated with significant positive academic and social changes in the fifth-grade tutors' behaviors, such as taking more risks in their oral and written interactions and exhibiting increased confidence. Unfortunately, peer tutoring is not yet a widely used instructional strategy in schools. The subjects in my study invariably responded negatively to the question whether they had the chance to help and tutor their non-English-speaking classmates. Working at the computer in dyads or triads, although a common occurrence in elementary schools, is not necessarily regarded as an opportunity to tutor less-proficient peers or to work cooperatively.

Consulting with their partners and reaching a consensus before keyboarding was one of the cooperative skills stressed during the student training and directly addressed by one of the statements on the self-evaluation form (i.e., "We got agreement before the keyboarder typed"). The students, in general, were able to adjust to this new working modality. This was reflected by the fact that 87 percent of their responses to the statement indicated that they had done so "All of the time." However, as has been discussed above, although the students usually reached a consensus, the decision-making process in some dyads, especially the NEP–ME combination, was heavily weighed in favor of the more-proficient student. In addition, some youngsters had to constantly fight their tendency to try to be the first to input their answer. This could be interpreted as a result of the competitive socialization students receive in schools as well as in society at large. On more than one occasion, processing would start with the students asking "Who won?" or "Did Luis beat me?" My taking notes during their work at the computer led them to assume I was assigning points in a competitive mode. This suggests how difficult to eradicate from these sessions was the spirit of competition the students brought with them.

Summary and Conclusions

The first part of this chapter looked at the elements of a computer setting that determine the communicative potential such a setting offers to second-language learners. The two factors first discussed had to do with grouping strategies, including number of students at the computer and the combination of students according to both their first language and their target-language proficiency. A third element, student task assignment, was considered critical, as it affects student access to the keyboard, which in turn directly influences their contribution to the conversational exchange. A fourth element, software program, was found to be the single most important component, having an overriding influence over the others, as it determines, in a pervasive way, the interactional task of the students at the computer. Among the different types of instructional activities in software programs, tasks developed along the two-way model were described as offering the greatest potential for second-language acquisition. This is because two-way activities, by creating positive interdependence through the need to exchange information, seem more capable of generating egalitarian and authentic communication between the participants. Furthermore, because natural conversation derives spontaneously from the activity, the responsibility for generating authentic and purposeful communication appears to lie in the software program.

Finally, cooperative training and learning structure were discussed as additional significant elements of the computer environment. Training in cooperative learning is believed to be necessary because students are significantly influenced by a competitive society and schooling. In addition to experiential learning of social skills, a cooperative computer structure is essential to provide students with an environment in which they feel at ease in either a tutor or a tutee role.

The second part of the chapter focused in greater depth on these latter elements of the communicative setting (i.e., experiential collaborative learning and cooperative structure). The analysis of data from student self-evaluation and feedback during the processing of the computer sessions conducted in the study suggests the following conclusions:

1. The students had no previous experience either working collaboratively or peer tutoring.

2. It appears that the classroom did not offer NEP students the opportunity to integrate physically and academically with their ME speaking classmates. Physical distance appeared to have exacerbated the psychological distance that the NEP students seemed to feel toward ME classmates.

3. Feigning comprehension might be interpreted as a non-risk strategy on the part of NEP students to protect themselves in a nonsupportive environment.

4. The students were aware of their degree of participation and power in the interaction, and, in some cases, felt they had little to contribute to it. Software program activities are needed that confer more status to students with less language so that they can participate in a more egalitarian fashion.

5. The students enjoyed working in a collaborative setting and tutoring, and being tutored by, peers. This enjoyment needs to be fostered toward the goal of creating a more humanistic learning environment for nonnative as well as native-English speakers in the classroom.

The analysis of the students' own reflections and feedback added a significant perspective to the existing data—that of the learner's. These data not only revealed the students' feelings, opinions, likes, dislikes, and reactions to the computer setting in which they worked but also their ability to perceive their own learning behavior and to reflect honestly about it. The collection of these data was based on the belief that asking for, and listening to, the students' perceptions of the environment in which they learn, will give researchers and other educators important practical and theoretical insights into the learning process, particularly within culturally and linguistically diverse learning settings. Above all, it will permit us to extend to our students the collaborative spirit and two-way communication needed for their successful socioacademic achievement.

Notes

1. All the subjects' names have been changed.
2. Here and throughout this paper, all students' answers in Spanish have been translated into English. All translations are mine.

3. This exchange took place in Spanish.

4. Because of the presence of two monolinguals of different language backgrounds (Spanish and English) in this discussion, the conversation was conducted in both languages, in a concurrent mode (i.e., what was said in one language was immediately interpreted by me into the other language).

References

The Bank Street Writer [Computer program] (1984). NY: Scholastic.

Bork, A. (1985). Children and interactive learning environments. In M. Chen and W. Paisley (Eds.). *Children and microcomputers.* Beverly Hills: Sage, 267–275.

Chávez, R. Ch. (1990). The development of story writing within an IBM Writing to Read program lab among language minority students: Preliminary findings of a naturalistic study. In C. Faltis and R. DeVillar (Eds.), *Language minority students and computers.* N.Y.: The Haworth Press, 121–144.

Cohen, E. G. (1986). *Designing groupwork. Strategies for the heterogeneous classroom.* N.Y.: Teachers College Press.

Cohen, E. G. and J. K. Intili. (1981) *Interdependence and management in bilingual classrooms.* Final Report to NIE: Grant #G–80-0217. California: Stanford University, Center for Educational Research at Stanford.

DeVillar, R. A. (1987). *Variation in the language use of peer dyads within a bilingual, cooperative, computer-assisted instructional setting.* Unpublished doctoral dissertation, Stanford University.

———(1991). Cooperative principles, computers, and classroom language. In M. E. McGroarty and C. J. Faltis (Eds.), *Languages in school and society.* Berlin, Mouton de Gruyter.

Dickson, W. P. and M. A. Vereen (1983). Two students at one microcomputer. *Theory into Practice, 22*(4), 296–300.

Edfelt, N. M. (1989). *Computer assisted second language acquisition: The oral discourse of children at the computer in a cooperative learning context.* Unpublished doctoral dissertation, Stanford University.

Gass, S. M. and E. M. Varonis (1985). Task variation and nonnative/nonnative negotiation of meaning. In S. Gass and C. Madden (Eds.), *Input in second language acquisition.* Rowley, MA: Newbury House, 149–161.

Graves, N. and T. Graves (1989). Should we teach cooperative skills as a part of each cooperative lesson? *Cooperative Learning, 10*(2), 19–20.

Hatch, E. (1983). Simplified input and second language acquisition. In R. Andersen (Ed.), *Pidginization and creolization as language acquisition.* Rowley, MA: Newbury House, 64–86.

Higgins, J. and T. Johns (1984). *Computers in language learning.* Collins ELT and Addison-Wesley.

Johnson, D. W. and R. T. Johnson (1975). *Learning together and alone. Cooperation, competition, and individualization.* Englewood Cliffs, N.J.: Prentice-Hall.

————. (1984). *Cooperation in the classroom.* New Brighton, MN: Interaction Book Company.

Johnson, R. T., D. W. Johnson, and M. B. Stanne (1986). Comparison of computer-assisted cooperative, competitive, and individualistic learning. *American Educational Research Journal, 23,* 382–392.

Kagan, S. (1989). *Cooperative learning. Resources for teachers.* San Juan Capistrano, CA: Resources for Teachers.

————. (1990). A "structured natural approach" to social skill acquisition. *Cooperative Learning, 10*(3), 20–21.

Kenning, M. J. and M-M. Kenning (1983). *An introduction to computer assisted language teaching.* Oxford: Oxford University Press.

Long, M. H. (1981). Input, interaction and second language acquisition. In H. Winitz (Ed.), *Annals of the New York Academy of Sciences: Vol. 379. Native language and foreign language acquisition.* New York, 259–278.

Male, M., Johnson, R., Johnson, D. and Anderson, M. (1986). *Cooperative learning and computers: An activity guide for teachers.* Los Gatos, CA: Educational Apple-cations.

Martin, J. H. (1986). *Writing to read teacher's manual.* International Business Machines.

Mehan. H. (1979). *Learning lessons: Social organization in the classroom.* Cambridge, MA: Harvard University Press.

The Oregon Trail [Computer program] (1986). St. Paul, MN: Minnesota Educational Computing Corporation.

Pease-Alvarez, L. and O. A. Vásquez (1990). Sharing language and technical expertise around the computer. In C. J. Faltis and R. A. DeVillar, *Language minority students and computers.* N.Y.: The Haworth Press, 91–107.

Pica, T. and C. Doughty (1985). Input and interaction in the communicative language classroom: A comparison of teacher-fronted and group activities. In S. M. Gass and C. G. Madden (Eds.), *Input in second language acquisition.* Rowley, MA: Newbury House, 115–132.

Rubin, J. (1975). What the "good language learner" can teach us. *TESOL Quarterly, 9*, 41–51.

Schinke-Llano, L. A. (1983). Foreigner talk in content classrooms. In H. W. Seliger and M. H. Long (Eds.), *Classroom oriented research in second language acquisition.* Rowley, MA: Newbury House, 146–165.

Swain. M. (1985). Communicative competence: Some roles of comprehensible input and comprehensible output in its development. In S. M. Gass and C. G. Madden (Eds.), *Input in second language acquisition.* Rowley, MA: Newbury House, 235–253.

Trowbridge, D. and R. Durnin (1984). *Results from an investigation of groups working at the computer.* Unpublished manuscript. Irvine: University of California, Educational Technology Center.

Varonis, E. M. and S. M. Gass (1985). Non-native/non-native conversations: A model for negotiation of meaning. *Applied Linguistics, 6*, 71–90.

Webb, N. M. (1984). Microcomputer learning in small groups: Cognitive requirements and group processes. *Journal of Educational Psychology, 76*, 1076–1088.

———. (1985). Student interaction and learning in small groups. In R. Slavin, S. Sharan, S. Kagan, R. H. Lazarowitz, C. Webb and R. Schmuck (Eds.), *Learning to cooperate, cooperating to learn.* N.Y.: Plenum Press.

Webb, N. M., P. Ender and S. Lewis (1986). Problem-solving strategies and group processes in small groups learning computer programming. *American Educational Research Journal, 23*, 243–261.

Wong-Fillmore, L. (1985). When does teacher talk work as input? In S. M. Gass and C. G. Madden (Eds.), *Input in second language acquisition.* Rowley, MA: Newbury House, 17–50.

Wyatt, D. H. (1984). *Computers and ESL.* NY: Harcourt Brace Jovanovich.

Young, R. (1988). Computer-assisted language learning conversations: Negotiating an outcome. *CALICO Journal, 5*(3), 65–83.

▼ 12 ▼
Bilingual Team-Teaching Partnerships over Long Distances: A Technology-Mediated Context for Intragroup Language Attitude Change

DENNIS SAYERS

ORILLAS is a computer-based collaborative teaching network coordinated by two Schools of Education, the first at Brooklyn College of the City University of New York, and the second at the University of Puerto Rico. Briefly, ORILLAS uses technology to form long-distance team-teaching partnerships. The network's name is taken from its full title, *De Orilla a Orilla*, which is Spanish for 'From Shore to Shore', and was chosen to reflect the reality of teacher collaborations that span oceans and continents. As a consequence of the ORILLAS project, team-teaching partnerships have been formed between educators in Puerto Rico, Quèbec, and the United States, principally, but also include teachers in English-speaking Canada, Costa Rica, France, Japan, Mexico, and several French- and English-speaking islands in the South Pacific.

ORILLAS's four-fold goal has been to employ various classroom technologies—especially computer-based telecommunications—to (1) increase the mother tongue and English language proficiency of ethnic and linguistic minority students; (2) improve both their self-esteem *and* their academic achievement; (3) reduce prejudice by promoting positive intergroup relations between "majority students" and their linguistic minority schoolmates; and (4) promote acquisition of foreign languages and cross-cultural knowledge. To accomplish these ends, ORILLAS has employed an educational networking model first developed by the French pedagogue Célestin Freinet in 1924 (Clandfield and Sivell 1990; Lee 1980, 1983; Sayers 1990b).

299

Following Freinet's model, ORILLAS is *not* a student-to-student penpal project, but rather a class-to-class collaboration designed by partner teachers who have been matched according to common teaching interests and their students' grade level. Partner teachers plan and implement jointly executed, collaborative teaching projects between their classes. Typical projects have included: (1) shared student journalism and publishing; (2) comparative investigations, including dual community surveys, joint science investigations, and contrastive geography projects; and (3) both traditional and modern folklore compendia, extending from oral histories and collections of proverbs to children's rhymes and riddles, lullabies, and game songs, as well as fables and folktales. ORILLAS has been described as a model project for bilingual education, English as a Second Language (ESL), and foreign language programs (Cazden 1985; Cummins 1986a, 1988, 1989; Cummins and Sayers 1990; Faltis and DeVillar 1990; Figueroa, Sayers, and Brown (1990); Sayers and Brown, 1987). DeVillar and Faltis (1991) judged ORILLAS "certainly one of the more, if not the most, innovative and pedagogically complete computer-supported writing project involving students across distances" (116). The network was also cited as an exemplary project for linguistic minority students by the U.S. Congress Office of Technology Assessment (Roberts and staff 1987).

The country with by far the largest number of ORILLAS teachers is Puerto Rico, where thirty of the one hundred schools presently participating in the network are located. This reality reflects both the origin of ORILLAS in Puerto Rico in 1985 and the enthusiastic support among Puerto Rican teachers and researchers, which the network has enjoyed from its inception. Among the principal goals of the Puerto Rican component of ORILLAS has been the construction of "cross-cultural" knowledge between the school-age children of Puerto Ricans who, as U.S. citizens, have moved to the mainland, and their distant peers who are studying in Puerto Rico's schools (Sayers 1991). This chapter details a study of eighty-six Puerto Rican students in four upper-elementary bilingual classrooms in a New England urban school district, classrooms which were paired with a partner class in Puerto Rico (Sayers 1990a). It examines, in the context of a technology-mediated partner class exchange, how the language attitudes of these young students changed toward speakers of Spanish in general, and toward their Spanish-speaking classmates in particular.[1]

Students' Language Attitudes
and Bilingual Education Programs

Bilingual educational programs are frequently misrepresented by the popular press as promoting the mother tongue of minority-language children at the expense of their mastery of the dominant language of the society. The reality is another story altogether. In the overwhelming majority of school districts that offer mother-tongue—based instructional programs for minority-language students, the most common program model is that of Transitional Bilingual Education (TBE). TBE has as its stated goal an insistent emphasis on the teaching of English, providing content-area instruction in the child's first language *only* until such time as the student can function in an all-English classroom *and no longer*. This limited goal is consonant with the requirements of both state legislation and federal regulations. Because of its assimilationist objectives, TBE has been negatively characterized by some educational researchers as a rationale for

- "language substitution" programs which "subtract" the home language while "replacing" the majority language (Lambert 1977); and
- "language inoculation" programs which provide students with small doses of their home language in instructional contexts with a view toward preventing future "contamination" in wider academic settings (Cummins 1985).

These are clearly partisan characterizations of Transitional Bilingual Education by researchers who favor a balanced and more fully bilingual language development for minority-language children. These and other advocates of fully bilingual education fear that as students participate in TBE programs, they are doing more than unlearning their first language while learning a second language; unwittingly, minority-language students may also be acquiring negative attitudes toward the culture and values of their parents and their community.

Unfortunately, this concern appears to be well-founded, as shown by many students revealing negative attitudes toward speakers of minority languages. Most research into language attitudes has been conducted with adults, with the largest subgroup focusing on teachers at all levels, from preschool to higher education (Edwards 1982). Day (1982) reviewed the much smaller body of research that centers on the development of language attitudes in children.

The research literature on young students' language attitudes and ethnic socialization suggests that children speaking a minority language variety begin schooling with a positive attitude (or at worst, a neutral one) toward the speech variety of their home, but before long they adopt a negative attitude toward their home language; indeed, in some cases, they come to value the larger society's dominant language variety more highly. Of course, Transitional Bilingual Education programs, by design and by legislative mandate, will do little to counteract this lopsided development of language attitudes in minority-language children. It is more likely that TBE's unabashedly anti-home-language bias will only exacerbate the negative attitudes which these students are acquiring toward their home language from an early age.

ORILLAS in the Bilingual Classroom: A Context for Intragroup Language Contact

Another common misconception about bilingual educational programs is that students in bilingual classrooms are homogenous in terms of language skills and cultural background. The high mobility rates of minority-language children, especially notable among those of Puerto Rican heritage, are among the factors that make for the heterogeneous mix of language skills and cultural backgrounds found in TBE programs. Any teacher or researcher familiar with the mobility patterns of minority-language children will attest to the difficulty of completing a school year with an intact class. This is particularly true in the case of Puerto Rican students such as those who participated in the present study, since the territorial and, some would argue, colonial status of Puerto Rico with respect to the United States confers on Puerto Rican parents all the rights and obligations of American citizens, including the right to travel without passport restrictions between Puerto Rico and the continental United States. Two studies concur that "return migrant" students (that is, pupils of Puerto Rican descent who have been raised and/or schooled in the United States and who are dominant in English) make up between 10 and 12 percent of enrollees in Puerto Rican schools and that these students are highly mobile, with a significant number returning with their families to the United States in a pattern of "circular migration" (Curran 1986; Vázquez-Brunet 1979). These highly mobile students, as United States citizens, are entitled by law to a public-funded instructional program suitable to their learning needs, which in most cases means a program of bilingual education.

Three qualitative studies (Sayers 1989, 1988a; Sayers and Brown, in press), conducted in the New England school district where the present research also took place, have demonstrated the heterogeneous character of bilingual classes. In this city the typical composition of a fourth- or fifth-grade bilingual class is 25 percent Spanish-dominant new arrivals and 75 percent bilingual and English-dominant students in their second or third, frequently last, year of bilingual schooling. The Spanish-dominant children were all born in Puerto Rico, while most of the English-dominant children were born in the United States. All students in the pilot studies, regardless of their language dominance, were from Puerto Rican families and spoke Spanish in their homes.

The qualitative studies also revealed that instructional delivery in "bilingual" classrooms at this level was predominantly in English, which placed the Spanish-dominant students at a marked disadvantage vis-á-vis their bilingual and English-dominant classmates. Spanish was principally used by bilingual teachers for quick summaries and to ask for questions on material previously covered in English. The negative language attitudes of the English-dominant students toward their Spanish-dominant classmates was revealed in direct commands ("Talk English!"), deprecatory comments ("I can't understand you when you talk that Spanish"), and through critical remarks upon hearing Spanish spoken by Spanish-dominant classmates ("I wish they wouldn't talk so fast that way"). Negative attitudes toward Puerto Rican culture were exemplified by one U.S.-born Puerto Rican student (who was English-dominant) when the topic was raised of "personas ilustres puertorriqueñas" (famous Puerto Rican historical figures): "What she talkin' about? We don' got none of those 'round here" (Sayers 1988).

Thus, bilingual program students display a variety of cultural experiences as well as a spectrum of language skills (ranging from Spanish to English dominance, and including full and competent bilingualism), owing to individual differences in length and degree of contact with the society of the "mother culture" (Matute-Bianchi 1986). Students in bilingual classrooms are *not* homogeneous in their language abilities and cultural background. Of course, after minority-language students are exited from bilingual classrooms they must face challenging intergroup learning situations with "majority" students, where many learn to reject and deny their linguistic and cultural heritage. But, as starkly shown by the examples above of some students' negative attitudes toward classmates who spoke *their own home language,* these challenges will be nothing new to pupils in TBE programs. Indeed, long before minority-language students are "mainstreamed," they have already confronted extremely complex intragroup dynamics through which they are likely to internalize the at times subtle, but quite often painfully direct, denigration of their language and culture.

In an ORILLAS exchange, the prestige of the Spanish-dominant new arrivals is enhanced as they become "cultural experts" who are in a particularly advantaged position to help interpret and clarify messages from their Puerto Rican partner class, while the balanced bilinguals play a special role as translators, in the most profound sense, of both linguistical and cultural knowledge, working to mediate communications between English-dominant classmates, on the one hand, and both their Spanish-dominant classmates and the distant students in Puerto Rico, on the other. In this fashion, ORILLAS provided the students in this research study with multiple opportunities to display and share their changing linguistic competencies and varied cultural experiences within their classrooms, thus fostering genuine bilingualism and the creation of authentic "cross-cultural" knowledge between distinct subgroups of Puerto Rican language-minority students.

Testing Allport's "Contact Theory": Long-Distance Teacher Partnerships

The principal research questions that guided this study were: (1) Is there change in bilingual program students' attitudes toward speakers of Spanish in the context of ORILLAS activities that require high levels of linguistic skill in two languages? and (2) Which of two contact situations is more predictive of change in these students' language attitudes toward Spanish speakers, *(a)* a student-directed, small groupwork (SG) contact situation, or *(b)* a teacher-mediated exchange that stressed whole groupwork (WG) contact situation? However, before detailing the outcomes of this exploratory research into intragroup contact and attitude change, it is crucial to establish its relationship to the large body of research on intergroup attitude change.

Some of the earliest research in the emerging field of social psychology identified cooperation and competition as key factors affecting social relationships between ethnic groups (Allport 1954; Cook 1960, 1978; Williams 1947). Gordon Allport's classic formulation off what has been termed 'contact theory' or the 'contact hypothesis' has guided the research agenda of several generations of researchers concerned with the reduction of prejudice through meaningful contact between groups, usually when engaged in cooperative, interdependent activities. Prejudice, Allport maintained, may be reduced by equal status contact between majority and minority groups in the pursuit of common goals. The effect is greatly enhanced if this contact is sanctioned by institutional supports (i.e., by law, custom, or local atmosphere), and provided it is of a sort that leads to the perception of common interests and common humanity between members of the two groups (1954: 281). To test this hypothesis, research has been conducted in many settings. However, since schooling provides the setting of principal interest to the concerns of this study, and as the extensive research literature focusing on school contexts has been reviewed (Amir 1969, 1976; Ben Ari and Amir 1986; DeVillar and Faltis 1991, Schwarzwald and Amir 1984), the discussion which follows will survey only the research and findings of particular relevance to this study's research hypotheses, that is, attitude change within whole group and small group learning contexts.

Much of the outpouring of contact-theory-related research centered on cross-racial contact situations, stimulated by the landmark *Brown v. Board of Education* ruling by the Supreme Court (1954). Studies conducted by Katz (1955), for example, concluded that replacement of cooperative interaction patterns with more competitive relationships in interracial recreational groups of African-American and Anglo-American adolescents led to increased prejudice. Another investigation conducted by Singer (cited in Lindzey and Aronson 1969) found that Anglo-American fifth graders, in the context of an interracial school that stressed cooperative learning techniques, had favorable attitudes toward African-American students and toward future social contact with African-Americans. In this same vein, a study by Cohen (1973) found that cooperative classroom experiences between Anglo-American and African-American teenagers resulted in lower prejudice on the part of Anglo-Americans.

Weigel, Wiser, and Cook (1975) compared patterns of interethnic contact between African-American, Mexican-American, and Anglo-American high school students in cooperative and regular instructional programs and found that interethnic group instruction was favored by teachers, resulted in significantly increased cross-ethnic helping behaviors, and led to a favorable change in Anglo-Americans' attitudes toward Mexican-American classmates. Investigations published as part of the research program of Johns Hopkins University's Center for the Social Organization of Schools (DeVries and Edwards 1973, 1974; DeVries, Edwards, and Slavin 1978; DeVries, Edwards, and Wells 1974; Edwards and DeVries 1974; Slavin 1977a, 1977b, 1979; Slavin and Oickle 1975) have further documented the value of interdependent biracial learning groups in promoting favorable attitude change between members of different ethnic groups.

An investigation by Johnson, Johnson, and Stanne (1986) compared the impact of computer-assisted cooperative, competitive, and individualistic instructional models on eighth graders' achievement, pupil–pupil interaction, and student attitudes toward their colleagues. They reported that the cooperative model of computer-assisted instruction resulted in increased achievement, more task-related interactions, and higher perceived levels of status female students. Finally, Johnson, Johnson, and Maruyama (1983) conducted a meta-analysis of the research to compare cooperative, competitive and, individualistic learning, in which they also analyzed the effects of intergroup contact on individuals. They found that within cross-racial, cross-ethnic, cross-sex, and other cross-group contexts, cooperation and the absence of intergroup competition produced the greatest gains in "interpersonal attraction" in contact situations (p. 5).

Clearly, there is a long tradition of research which suggests that, under specialized conditions such as those first posited by Allport, cross-group contact to achieve interdependent goals will promote positive intergroup attitude change. The present research, while part of this tradition, attempted to break new ground. First, this study sought to test aspects of Allport's hypothesis in an intragroup contact situation. The ORILLAS partner teaching network, which was designed to heighten the status of speakers of a low-prestige language, namely, Spanish—a world language that is low in prestige only in the context of most U.S. school systems. Second, change in students' language attitudes is an outcome variable that had never been studied in research relating to Allport's Contact Theory.[2] Third, this study compared the effects of two kinds of contact activity structures with special relevance for intragroup attitude change. Student-directed small groupwork (SG) projects consisted of "editorial committees" for a curriculum unit on student journalism carried out jointly with the distant Puerto Rican partner class. The second activity structure was characterized by whole groupwork (WG) processes that focused on the production of teacher-coordinated slide-tape presentations to be exchanged between partner classes (after Jonas 1969, 1972). If student-directed SG processes were found to play a more decisive role in activating positive language-attitude change toward Spanish speakers, then it could be argued that an SG process creates a context for meaningful contact between students from different language-dominance groups, leading to students' language-attitude change. On the other hand, if the teacher-directed WG process were to prove more effective in encouraging positive changes toward Spanish speakers, credence would be lent to the supposition that teachers need to play a more central role in organizing WG interactions that increase the status of minority-language students. Within this setting, the teachers serve, in effect, as cross-cultural interlocutors who shape the process through which the initial low status of these Spanish speakers is heightened.

To summarize, my research questions led me to form three hypotheses. First, I anticipated that the relative brevity of the ORILLAS project, less than five months, would not preclude the measurement of significant change in language attitude. Secondly, I hypothesized that as a result of ORILLAS exchanges there would be evidence in all classrooms of change in language attitudes among English-dominant, Spanish-dominant, and balanced-bilingual students in the form of increased favorable evaluations toward speakers of Spanish. Finally, I predicted that the degree of change in students' language attitudes toward Spanish speakers would be greater for those classes employing the SG process, due to the greater opportunity provided for students to interact directly with Spanish-dominant and bilingual classmates around specific cultural and linguistic issues.

The Bilingual Program Students
and How Their Language Attitudes
were Measured

There were two classes, a fourth-grade and a fifth-grade class, which were involved in the SG ORILLAS activities; similarly, WG ORILLAS activities were carried out in two other classes at the fourth- and fifth-grade levels. The SG fourth grade and WG fifth grade classes were drawn from Loma Central Elementary School, and the remaining two classes were selected from King, another elementary school. These schools were chosen for several reasons. They are located six blocks apart; thus, students assigned to King and Loma Central are drawn from geographically contiguous areas of the city. Pupils who attended both schools identified themselves as living in the same neighborhood, referred to as the "Loma Section" of the city, and known as the poorest neighborhood in a city that is consistently rated as having among the highest proportions of families living below the poverty level in the nation. I assumed that students at these schools, which had the largest populations of Latino students in bilingual programs of all the district's schools, would be comparable in terms of socioeconomic status, linguistic background, and educational experience within North American schools.

Student's language dominance group (LDG), whether Spanish-dominant (SpLDG), English-dominant (EngLDG), or bilingual (BiLG) was initially determined by their performance on translation tasks (from Spanish to English, and vice versa). For each student, this initial assignment to language-dominance groups was checked against (a) self-assessments by students; (b) teacher assessments of each student according to a 3-point scale of relative proficiency in English and Spanish comprehension, speaking, reading, and writing; and (c) comparisons of performance on English and Spanish versions of standardized reading comprehension tests[3]. The LDGs of the SG and WG classes are summarized in table 12.1.

Measures of change in students' language attitudes included pre- and posttest forms of a group-administered task

TABLE 12.1 LANGUAGE DOMINANCE GROUPS (LDGS) IN SMALL GROUPWORK AND WHOLE GROUPWORK CLASSES BY GRADES

| | Grade | | | |
| | 4th | | 5th | |
Group	N	%	N	%
Small Groupwork Classes				
Spanish-Dominant	5	19 %	5	31 %
Balanced Bilingual	11	42 %	6	38 %
English-Dominant	10	39 %	5	31 %
Whole Groupwork Classes				
Spanish-Dominant	7	32 %	9	37 %
Balanced Bilingual	10	46 %	10	42 %
English-Dominant	5	23 %	5	21 %

and an individually administered task. A group-administered "Matched Guise" task was given as a pre- and posttest measure of language attitude change toward speakers of English and Spanish. The individually administered measure was a sorting task in which photographs of classmates were selected to complete an Inventory of Cross-Language-Dominance-Group Respect (Cross-LDG) toward each student's classmates. The Cross-LDG inventory and the Matched Guise task were administered as pretests between December 1988 and January 1989 by trained bilingual interviewers who were unaware of the LDG of the pupils; posttests were given in May 1989. As the following description of these two measures indicate, each instrument is designed to tap different components of language attitude.

The Matched Guise

For over thirty years, studies of language attitude have relied almost exclusively on the Matched Guise procedure, first developed by Wallace Lambert (1960) to assess the attitudes of English and French Canadian listeners toward speakers of ingroup and outgroup language varieties. For the present study, the Matched Guise language attitude measure was an adaptation of the CERAS Bilingual Attitude Measure developed by the Stanford Program on Teaching and Linguistic Pluralism (Ramírez et al. 1978; Ramírez 1981). Two "guises" (a Spanish and an English version of a short narrative about a girl whose younger brother hid her clothes as a joke) were read onto an audiotape by a single twelve-year-old bilingual Puerto Rican girl student unknown to any of the research project students. When the Matched Guise task was administered, students first listened in groups to the tape of one of the versions (Spanish or English). Students then responded on test sheets to the interviewer, who prompted the listeners to rate the speaker of that guise at one of four levels for each of four constructs:

1. Correctness ("How well does she speak English/ Spanish?" and "When she speaks English/Spanish, does she make a lot of mistakes?")
2. The listener's "solidarity" or personal identification with the speaker ("How friendly do you think she is?" and "How often do you talk like this with your friends?")
3. Appropriateness for school ("Do you think the way she talks is good for school?" and "If she needs help with her work, do other students help her?")
4. Likelihood of achievement ("How do you think this girl does in school?" and "When she takes tests, how do you think she does on them?")

Before the second guise was played for students, the tester explained that they would now listen to another child; of course, this information was false, since both guises had been produced by the same bilingual student. The rating procedure was repeated for this second guise. Difference scores were constructed based on the results of the Matched Guise pre- and posttests[4], and formed the basis of the data analysis.

The Cross-LDG

Since the Matched Guise had been used nearly exclusively with adolescents and adults, this research project endeavored to evaluate the appropriateness of the Matched Guise tasks with elementary-school-age students by taking Edwards's (1982) advice and comparing the results of the Matched Guise with another measure. To this end, the Cross-LDG was designed by combining elements of an attitude scale developed by Weigel, Wiser, and Cook (1975) in prejudice-reduction research and of a sociometric measure used by Triviz (1987) to evaluate awareness of gender socialization among elementary-school students.

The Cross-LDG was administered individually, with photographs of classmates used as "markers." Each student rated on a 4-point continuum all of his or her classmates on these five personal attributes: *(a)* how hard-working they are, *(b)* how friendly they are, *(c)* how easy they are to work with, *(d)* how helpful they are to the evaluating student, and *(e)* how helpful they are to the teacher. Specifically, after the test administrator determined that an adjective (for example, "helpful to you") was comprehended, the student was asked to rank photos of her or his classmates in bins stacked at four different levels. After the test administrator recorded the letter code of the ranked students' photos, the next adjective was explained and the student ranked his or her classmates according to the new criterion. When each student's ratings were later recoded according to the LDG of his or her classmates, the Cross-LDG provided an index of that student's relative appreciation for his or her own LDG vis-à-vis the other LDGs in the class. Once pre- and post-tests had been administered and recoded, I constructed difference scores that measured the change in each student's perception of the three LDG after the ORILLAS intervention. Because there are three language groups to be evaluated and five constructs on which they were evaluated, each student had 15 difference scores. These scores form the basis of the data analysis.

Data Analysis of the Results of the Matched Guise and Cross-LDG Tasks

I utilized ANOVA by regression to analyze the results of the Matched Guise and Cross-LDG measures. ANOVA by regression performs the same analyses as ANOVA, but it is statistically stronger in its ability to analyze unbalanced cell counts such as those encountered in the present research (see table 12.1). It is also more convenient since, in a single operation, it allows a researcher to find not only main effects but also to specify in which category of the variable the effect is occurring. Most importantly, because the value of regression model intercepts are difference scores of the base group[5], I was able to examine the effect of the ORILLAS intervention for each LDG my variables delineate. All models in which the effect shown had a 10 percent chance or greater of being due to error ($p > .10$)[6] were discarded.

Results, Conclusions, and Discussion
in Terms of the DeVillar and Faltis
Socioacademic Achievement Framework

Preliminary Baseline Analyses and
Correlations of Measures

To establish a baseline of language-attitude ratings, I conducted an analysis of pretest differences in students' evaluations for both the Cross-LDG Inventory and the Matched Guise
task. For the Cross-LDG Inventory, the mean pretest ratings
given by evaluating students overall was highest for bilingual
classmates (3.04), lower for Spanish-dominant classmates
(2.64), and lowest for English-dominant classmates (2.52). Differences between the mean pretest scores were examined for
these variables. These differences in respect were statistically
significant; evaluations of bilingual classmates were more favorable as compared with evaluations of Spanish-dominant
classmates ($p = .0001$) or with evaluations of English-
dominant classmates ($p = .0001$), and Spanish-dominant
classmates were viewed more positively than were English-
dominant classmates ($p = .0068$).

Interestingly, these results stand in sharp contrast to the
mean pretest scores for the Matched Guise task, where ratings
given by evaluating students were higher for the English tape
than were those given for the Spanish tape ($p = .0276$). Given
these very different pretest mean scores for the two measures,
it is not surprising that, when correlations of the Matched
Guise and the Cross-LDG were calculated, no association was
found between pretest measures toward English speakers
($r = .099$, $p = .3675$), and there was only a weak to moderate
correlation between pretest measures of attitude toward Spanish speakers ($r = .257$, $p = .0181$). Moreover, when change in
pre- and posttest scores was assessed over the course of the
ORILLAS intervention, no association was found between
these two measures of language attitude, neither toward English speakers ($r = .033$, $p = .7662$) nor toward Spanish
speakers ($r = .122$, $p = .2679$).

Therefore, even before considering the specific results provided by the Matched Guise and Cross-LDG, these initial analyses of the pretest mean scores and the correlations between
the two tasks suggest that each measure may tap into a very

different component of language attitude. Put another way, if it is assumed that the Cross-LDG Inventory and the Matched Guise measure similar components of language attitude, then the results yielded by these instruments appear to be contradictory. However, a more plausible interpretation may be based on the assumption that the Cross-LDG Inventory (a sociometric measure of attitudes toward known colleagues that is based on actual interactions) and the Matched Guise (a stereotypic measure of attitudes toward an unknown and unknowable speaker based on general impressions acquired in many social contexts) assess very different components of language-attitude variation.

Results and Discussion

The Presence of Measurable Effects of Change in Language Attitudes

The first prediction—that even over the relatively short period of five months there would be measurable effects of change in language attitudes among these bilingual-program students engaged in ORILLAS projects—was borne out by the results of the ANOVA by regression analyses for the Cross-LDG Inventory and the Matched Guise. For the Cross-LDG measure there were 7 main effects, 1 interaction effect, and 20 intercept effects (see Tables 2–5 for a summary of a number of these effects), while for the Matched Guise task, 5 main effects and 1 interaction effect resulted. The fact that there were so many effects in the analyses of these two measures of young minority-language students is extremely interesting.

As noted previously in the review of the literature on language attitude measurement, there are few studies of children's language attitudes as compared with investigations of secondary-school students and adults. Moreover, investigations which consider *change* in language attitudes as an outcome variable are rarely conducted for any age group (Lambert, personal communication, 1988); those few studies which have sought to measure children's language attitudes over time as a dependent variable have focused on attitude change among majority-language students learning a second language (Jonas 1969, 1972; Genesee, Tucker, and Lambert 1978), rather than on minority-language students. Thus, the results of the present study suggest that language attitude change among linguistic-

TABLE 12.2 CROSS-LANGUAGE DOMINANCE GROUP INVENTORY
INDEPENDENT VARIABLE NAMES FOR TABLES 3–5

Variable Name	Level	Description
CLASSROOM	C1	5th grade class/small groupwork
	C2	4th grade class/small groupwork
	C3	4th grade class/whole groupwork
	C4	5th grade class/whole groupwork
GROUP	0	whole groupwork
	1	small groupwork
LDG	L1	Spanish-dominant pupils
	L2	Bilingual pupils
	L3	English-dominant pupils

minority children is measurable using both "stereotypic" and "sociometric" instruments.

Evidence of Increased Favorable Evaluations toward Speakers of Spanish after ORILLAS Interventions

My second hypothesis was that there would be evidence of change in language attitudes among English-dominant, Spanish- dominant, and bilingual students in the form of increased favorable evaluations toward speakers of Spanish as a result of the ORILLAS exchanges in all classes. Several results from the Cross-LDG Inventory support this hypothesis. A univariate analysis of all fifteen of the dependent variables on the Cross-LDG showed that on the construct "Helpfulness of Spanish-dominant students to the evaluating student" all evaluating students, whether Spanish-dominant, bilingual, or English-dominant and regardless of their participation in SG or WG classes, perceived their Spanish-dominant classmates as more helpful to them personally ($p = .0370$).

The Cross-LDG measure also showed that, across all SG and WG classes, Spanish-dominant students evaluated pupils from their own LDG as more helpful to the teacher ($p = .0752$) and more helpful to the evaluator ($p = .0835$) after the ORILLAS intervention than before. Moreover, bilingual students viewed other bilingual students as working harder after the ORILLAS intervention ($p = .0139$). Finally, students in SG classes viewed Spanish-dominant students as more helpful after participating in ORILLAS project work ($p = .0831$).

TABLE 12.3 MAIN EFFECTS MODELS RELATING TO LANGUAGE ATTITUDES TOWARD SPANISH SPEAKERS (CROSS-LANGUAGE DOMINANCE GROUP INVENTORY)

Variable	Intercept	L2	L3	GROUP	Model	Model
	$\beta 0$, se(β)	β, se(β)	$\beta 0$, se(β)	$\beta 0$, se(β)	P(F)	R-2
Bilinguals seen as hard-working	−.138*, .064	.276**, .084	.134, .090		.0061	.1182
Bilinguals seen as helpful to the evaluator	−.129, .091			.219~, .127	.0879	.0351
Spanish-dominants seen as helpful to the teacher	.177, .119			−.320~, .167	.0584	.0430

****p.0001 ***p.001 **p.01 *p.05 ~p.10 ns = not significant

TABLE 12.4 INTERCEPT EFFECTS ON CROSS-LANGUAGE DOMI-
NANCE GROUP INVENTORY

Effect	Model P (F)	Model R-squared
Spanish-dominant students come to see Spanish-dominant classmates as more helpful to the evaluator	$\beta0 = +.242$,	p=.0835
Spanish-dominant students come to see Spanish-dominant classmates as more helpful to teacher	$\beta0 = +.275$,	p=.0752
Spanish-dominant students come to see English-dominant classmates as more helpful to teacher	$\beta0 = +.291$,	p=.0684
Spanish-dominant students come to see English-dominant classmates as easier to work with	$\beta0 = +.273$,	p=.0574
Bilingual students come to see Bilingual classmates as working harder	$\beta0 = +.138$,	p=.0139
Spanish-dominant students come to see Bilingual classmates as working less hard	$\beta0 = -.138$,	p=.0335
Small group students come to see Spanish-dominant classmates as more helpful to the evaluator	$\beta0 = +.184$,	p=.0831

While the Cross-LDG generally provided results that supported the second hypothesis, there were a few contradictory findings. For example, bilingual students' perceptions of other bilingual classmates as being hard-working improved more ($p = .0061$) than Spanish-dominant pupils' perceptions of bilingual classmates as working hard; however, this result does little to weaken the preponderance of supportive evidence from the Cross-LDG, since it merely states that one subgroup of Spanish-speaking classmates, namely, the balanced-bilingual students, developed a more positive opinion of their own LDG than did another subgroup of Spanish speakers, that is, the Spanish-dominant students.

More interestingly, the Cross-LDG offered a mixed picture with regard to the SG and WG categories on the two "helpfulness" constructs. Evaluating students in SG classes saw bilingual classmates as being more helpful to them than WG classroom students saw bilingual students as helpful to the evaluator ($p = .0879$); and WG students' perception of Spanish-dominant classmates as being helpful to the teacher improved more than did the perception of SG students toward Spanish-dominant classmates as helpful to the teacher ($p = .0584$). While contradicting this hypothesis, these findings do seem to offer an accurate portrayal of important differences between SG and WG processes in the context of an ORILLAS exchange. In an SG class, it will be the bilingual students who most directly mediate the communication between Spanish-dominant and English-dominant classmates; hence, it is likely that they would be seen as more helpful to evaluating students in general. Yet in a WG class it is probable that Spanish-dominant students would be viewed as more helpful to the teacher, since the teacher plays a larger mediating role in interpreting the cultural and linguistic communications from the distant ORILLAS class in Puerto Rico, and the Spanish-dominant students—as recent arrivals from Puerto Rico—are specifically recognized by the teacher as the "local experts" on the distant culture.

Small vs. Whole Groupwork as Predictive
of Change in Language Attitudes

Third, I had anticipated that the degree of positive change in students' language attitudes toward Spanish speakers would be greater for those classes employing SG processes as compared with the classes utilizing WG processes, owing to the greater opportunity provided for students to interact directly with Spanish-dominant classmates around specific cultural and linguistic issues.

There were two findings that supported this hypothesis. On the Cross-LDG, the construct "Helpfulness of bilingual students toward the evaluating student" showed both a main effect of GROUP and an interaction effect of GROUP with the LDG of the evaluating student (see table 12.5). The perception of students in SG classrooms of their bilingual classmates as being helpful to them personally was greater than that of students in WG classes ($p = .0879$). The interaction effect revealed that in the SG classes it was the English-dominant students who demonstrated the greatest gains in improved perceptions of bilingual classmates as being helpful to them personally ($p = .0240$).

One finding from the Cross-LDG Inventory, centering on the construct "Helpfulness of Spanish-dominant students to

TABLE 12.5 INTERACTION MODELS FOR "HELPFULNESS OF BILINGUAL CLASSMATES TO THE EVALUATING STUDENT" ON CROSS-LANGUAGE DOMINANCE GROUP INVENTORY

Model	Intercept		L2		L3		GROUP		LG2		LG3		Model	Model
	β0,	se(β)	β0,	se(β)	β0,	se(β)	β0,	se(β)	β0,	se(β)	β0,	se(β)	P(F)	R-2
I	-.121,	.118	.143,	.155									.5790	.0134
II	-.129,	.091			.153,	.167	.219~,	.127					.0879	.0351
III	-.202,	.128	.117,	.155	.112,	.167	.203,	.129					.3148	.0431
IV	-.107,	.145	.142,	.202	-.315,	.230	-.033,	.230	.012,	.300	.791*,	.325	.0423	.1345

****p.0001 ***p.001 **p.01 *p.05 ~p.10 ns = not significant

the teacher", did not support the research hypothesis. Students in SG classrooms had a negative change in perception of Spanish-dominant classmates as being helpful to the teacher as compared with the positive change in perception of students in WG classes toward classmates who were Spanish-dominant in terms of their helpfulness to the teacher ($p = .0584$). However, this result does not decisively offset the supporting evidence of both a main and an interaction effect reported in the previous paragraph. As noted in the discussion of the second hypothesis, this outcome may simply represent a faithful rendering of expected differences in the nature of SG and WG processes within the context of ORILLAS cross-cultural exchanges.

The Matched Guise measure, on the other hand, appears to offer evidence against accepting the third research hypothesis. When using means of aggregated scores for students in each LDG, the data suggested that participating in WG classes had a positive impact on students' attitudes toward Spanish in terms of their posttest evaluations of the Spanish-speaker's tape. The relationship was found to be statistically significant ($p < .0016$). Moreover, these results were corroborated when mean difference scores were used as the basis of analysis. The results indicated that, across all LDGs, WG students showed more improvement in their evaluation of the Spanish cassette ($p = .0577$) than SG students showed improvment in favorability ratings toward the Spanish tape; however, both SG and WG gave improved ratings pre- to posttest.

Additionally, the interaction effect between the mean difference scores for the English tape and GROUP did not support this research hypothesis. The evaluation by the SG students of the English tape demonstrated a greater positive change from pre- to posttest than their evaluation of the Spanish tape ($p = .0743$), while the evaluation of the WG students toward the English tape showed the same rate of positve change as their evaluation of the Spanish tape.

The results of the Cross-LDG Inventory and the Matched Guise appear contradictory; but are they? Perhaps our earlier discussion of differences between the two language-attitude measures is relevant in interpreting these apparently discrepant data. The Matched Guise measure, presumably, is more sensitive to those components of language attitudes that are acquired from wide-ranging interaction with the larger society. Because such components are acquired over extended periods of time and from a full spectrum of social settings, they are likely to prove less susceptible to short-term change stemming from interactions in a single setting, such as a school context. The Cross-LDG Inventory, on the other hand, may be viewed as more responsive to variables that center upon ongoing group processes around specific, interdependent activity. Sociometric measures of language attitudes such as the Cross-LDG are therefore less likely to be responsive to more generalized, enduring, and stereotypical impressions of language speakers. The present research offers some support of this general view. Although there were significant effects measured by both instruments, no correlation was found between these measures of changed perceptions toward English or toward Spanish speakers. The Matched Guise and the Cross-LDG Inventory appear to respond to differing components of language-attitude change.

Using a similar line of reasoning, it is possible that these measures vary in their sensitivity to language-attitude change as a function of small- vs whole-group processes. That is, the Matched Guise may detect changes in attitudes that are produced by wider-ranging social interactions, like those occurring in WG projects, more readily than would the Cross-LDG Inventory. The Cross-LDG measure, on the other hand, may be more responsive than the Matched Guise to language-attitude variation produced through focused interdependent activity, such as that occurring in SG projects. Confirmation of this view is offered by the results presented in support of the second hypothesis, since *all* of the evidence showing improvement in the SG classrooms is drawn from the Cross-LDG Inventory, while the Matched Guise is the *sole* measure which indicates positive change within the WG classes.

A more plausible and coherent interpretation of what appears at first to be a pattern of contradictory outcomes thus emerges from the above considerations. Initially, the Matched Guise revealed more positive attitudes toward English speakers among all students, a result consistent with the status accorded English speakers in the larger society and the school system as a whole. After the ORILLAS intervention, the Matched Guise disclosed evidence of improved perceptions of Spanish speakers *only* in the classes where larger social dynamics were central to the intervention, that is, in the WG classrooms. On the other hand, the Cross-LDG Inventory initially showed the highest favorability ratings toward bilingual classmates over all classrooms, a result consistent with the perception of these students as most able to function productively, both in classrooms where two languages are the means of instruction, as well as in the context of a project like ORILLAS that demanded their skills as cultural and linguistic mediators between Spanish- and English-dominant classmates.

Conclusions

This study of ORILLAS long-distance partnerships has special implications for language-attitude research. First, the results support the view that change in language attitude is a measurable dependent variable that may prove useful in describing the effects of educational interventions. This is a significant implication because it refocuses attention on language attitudes as an outcome variable of interest to educational researchers, along with those studied more frequently in recent investigations that have centered on language-minority students, such as improvement in standardized test scores or on reading comprehension measures.

Secondly, the study forcefully suggests that research into change in language attitudes need not be limited to studies involving older school-age students and adults, or to investigations that center on speakers of majority languages who are learning a second language, but may also include younger students, at least at the upper-elementary level, as well as minority-language students.

Finally, the present research has implications for the measurement of change in attitudes toward language variation, both at the "micro" level of intragroup contact within school settings and at the "macro" level of cross-linguistic group contact within speech communities. The study supports the view expressed by Edwards (1982), who argued that evidence provided by the "traditional" measure of language attitudes—the Matched Guise—should not be dismissed as decontextualized and stereotypic; more appropriately, these results should be confirmed or disconfirmed through comparison with other measures.

Aside from its contribution to language-attitude research, however, the study has important implications for the tradition of research into cross-group contact as a vehicle for encouraging positive intergroup relations. It is in this area that the study validates the principal elements of the DeVillar and

Faltis socioacademic achievement framework (1991), while raising intriguing questions that may be tested in future qualitative and quantitative research.

The enormous value of the DeVillar and Faltis framework is that it is grounded in a thorough critique of contemporary approaches to computer-based learning that carefully avoids the vague, one-sided polemics so characteristic of discussions of classroom computing. Moreover, the framework puts forth an integrated model of teaching and learning that is derived from an analysis of three extensive research literatures: (1) the relationship between classroom talk and student learning, with a special focus on second-language acquisition; (2) interactions between students in racially and ethnically heterogeneous schools and classrooms; and (3) the impact of structured cooperative learning activities on intergroup *and intragroup* relations. DeVillar and Faltis assert that

> in arguing that social interaction is at the heart of classroom learning, that integration is required for social interaction to occur, and that cooperative learning is a formal means to social integration in the classroom, we are presenting what we consider to be the three *minimal necessary conditions* for effective learning in computer-integrated classrooms. (28)

Especially interesting is the detailed discussion by DeVillar and Faltis of the important implications for their framework found in the research on intragroup contact by Milk (1980), Matute-Bianchi (1986) and Fordham (1988), since far too often minority groups are treated as homogeneous and undifferentiated "black boxes" in discussions that center exclusively on contact between groups. The present study falls within this emerging tradition of intragroup research, which DeVillar and Faltis correctly recognized as central to any attempt to develop a socioacademic framework that is sensitive to cultural diversity.

In a narrow sense, this research of ORILLAS teacher partnerships has significance for the DeVillar and Faltis framework since the study offers the refinement of another useful category (namely, language-dominance groups among minority-language speakers) to the cross-group categories which they review and which center on interactions between racial and ethnic groups, across genders, between speakers of majority and minority languages, and between students with handicaps and those with no evident handicapping condition.

Yet there is a larger sense in which this investigation into ORILLAS partnerships corroborates the DeVillar and Faltis framework and its major components of communication, integration, and—in the broadest terms—cooperation. With respect to social interactions, the study suggests that long-distance collaborations promote new patterns of student–teacher and student–student interactions, since unanticipated linguistic and cultural communications were negotiated among teachers and their students who, although all of Puerto Rican heritage, have differing language skills and cultural knowledge. The classroom integration of the students from these three intra-group categories (that is, the Spanish-dominant, bilingual and English-dominant pupils) played a major role in promoting these new patterns of social interaction, since only through collective activity that relied on students' differing linguistic skills and cultural experiences could the long-distance projects be completed successfully.

"As Jim Cummins (1991) notes in his foreword to *Computers and Cultural Diversity*, "in order to make use of the power of the computer as a communicative and discovery tool, students must have some non-trivial reasons for communicating with others and motivation to search out and interpret various forms of communication" (p. viii). I would maintain that for these students of differing bilingual skills and cultural experiences, long-distance partnerships such as ORILLAS create just such a motivating context for *interpretation, both generally and in the literal sense of linguistic and cultural mediation*. ORILLAS, in effect, helped define a highly structured activity which implicitly guided cooperative work at the classroom level. In this sense, then, the present research validates cooperation as a minimal necessary condition for effective computer- based learning.

There is, however, one area where this ORILLAS study appears to contradict an aspect of the argument advanced by DeVillar and Faltis in their discussion of cooperative learning approaches and the improvement of intergroup relations. Recently, an interesting debate has emerged concerning the need for research that looks beyond cooperative activity leading to short-term improvement in intergroup relations, and emphasizes instead the development of more enduring attitude change that generalizes beyond the structured contact situation. One position, advanced by Miller et al. (1985) and supported by DeVillar and Faltis (1991: 64–66) argues that longer lasting attitude change between groups will occur when cooperative activities stress personalized as opposed to category-based communications.

A very different view is taken by Hewstone and Brown (1986) and Pettigrew (1986). These researchers assert that the almost exclusively interpersonal focus of much of the research on the Contact Hypothesis places an overemphasis on heightening the awareness of similarities between individuals while deemphasizing the perception of differences between groups. They argue that frequently, when prejudicial attitudes are challenged by positive interpersonal contact, a psychological mechanism that Allport referred to as "fence-mending" (1954: 23) may be invoked to maintain the prejudice. In fence-mending (encapsulated in the remark "Some of my best friends are. . ."), the positive interpersonal experience is viewed as an exception, and effectively dismissed in future contact situations. These researchers stress the need for research into cooperative cross-group interactions that are designed to heighten rather than mask *the salience of group membership*, presumably leading to positive and enduring intergroup attitude change that will generalize beyond merely interpersonal encounters.

The present research evaluated one such effort to make the subgroup identity of Spanish-dominant, balanced bilingual, and English-dominant students more salient through an interdependent activity in which Spanish language proficiency and cultural knowledge of Puerto Rico was explicitly valued in attaining a superordinate goal. While the study did not evaluate how the resulting attitude change generalized to noncontact situations, the number and magnitude of the effects that were measured, as well as their rapid rate of change, suggests a robust improvement in intragroup attitude with a potential to generalize beyond the intervention. Clearly, there is a need for future research to test the claims of these alternate hypotheses in terms of the DeVillar and Faltis framework.

Notes

1. I gratefully acknowledge support for this research from CLEAR (the Center for Language Education and Research) at Yale University, as well as the encouragement and counsel of its principal investigator, Dr. Kenji Hakuta, presently of Stanford University. Anne Chase and Zeynep Beykont of Harvard Graduate School of Education ably assisted in the interpretation of complex language attitude datasets

through advanced statistical techniques. I am especially indebted to Catherine Riess, CLEAR Research Associate, for her remarkable efforts toward achieving the study's goals, and to Kristin Brown and Enid Figueroa, fellow Coordinators of the ORILLAS network.

2. A possible exception to the first two points is Sharan and Shachar's study (1988) comparing language outcomes (including instances of "cooperative language" that could be construed as reflecting changed language attitudes) with learning outcomes. The classrooms they studied were comprised of Israeli students whose families were originally from Western European and Middle Eastern countries. The authors, however, describe their research as involving intergroup, not intragroup, contact.

3. The translation tasks were designed by Hakuta (1988a, 1988b) for CLEAR's psycholinguistic research agenda into translation ability among elementary school Spanish—English bilingual-program students. However, the concept of employing the results of these holistically scored tasks to ascertain relative language dominance is that of the present researcher. This approach should not be misinterpreted as providing anything other than an indicator that may prove useful in comparing proficiencies. I am not asserting, for example, that bilinguals actually interpret their thoughts from one language to another when speaking, nor that their writing abilities depend on their ability to translate the "source code" of their ideas into a "target code" on paper. The accurate assessment of bilingual proficiency remains among the top research priorities for bilingual education (Harley, Allen, Cummins, and Swain 1990).

4. A Principal Component Analysis of the four constructs revealed that six of the eight items could be summed into a single composite variable that would measure the overall perception of each language. Two of the items showed no intercorrelation. Further inspection revealed poorly constructed items involving, for example, reversed directionality of the attitude scale.

5. The base group is the group not specified in the regression model. Taking a model that looks at the relationship between LDG and difference scores, only two of the three LDGs are included in the model. The intercept parameter is the difference score of the LDG not included in the model and the parameters of the other two LDGs are their respective differences from the LDG specified by the intercept. Because CLASSROOM and GROUP were heavily confounded (each class, of which there were four, worked entirely through whole group process or small group process during the ORILLAS intervention) no attempt was made to untangle any joint relationship of these two variables to the difference score.

6. While the customary *alpha* level for statistical analyses in social science research is $p < .05$, I have employed a wider latitude of possible interesting effects ($p < .10$), specifying the p value in each case. The present exploratory research may thus offer guideposts for

investigations of issues which have been little studied in previous studies of language attitudes, such as intragroup (as opposed to inter-group) attitude change; attitude change among elementary-school-age linguistic-minority children; the use of holistically rated translation tasks to determine language dominance among bilinguals; the development of sociometric—as compared with stereotypic—measures of language attitudes; and language-attitude change as an outcome variable in studies on SG vs. WG process (a subset of cooperative learning research in contact situations). A greater latitude in the customary *alpha* level permits the reporting of a wider range of effects from this exploratory research, which may serve as guideposts for future research.

Finally, it is reasonable to conclude from this research that *team-teaching via technology* holds promise for promoting positive attitude change among speakers of minority languages. Of course, it would be ingenuous to infer that ORILLAS exchanges, in isolation, can counteract the negative effects of the prejudice which, in some school settings, borders on xenophobia and against which language-minority students must continually struggle to maintain a positive self-concept while developing their academic potential. However, by making possible daily contact, using computers and other technologies, with fellow students from the countries that were the birthplaces of their parents, teacher partnerships like ORILLAS work to foster full bilingualism and biculturalism among language-minority students. This is an outcome that stands in sharp contrast to the stated objectives of English-centered or Transitional Bilingual Education programs, in which the linguistic and cultural heritage of language-minority students is eradicated and replaced by the language and culture of the dominant society.

References

Allport, G. (1954). *The nature of prejudice.* Cambridge, MA: Addison-Wesley.

Amir, Y. (1969). Contact hypothesis in ethnic relations. *Psychological Bulletin, 71,* 319–42.

Amir, Y. (1976). The role of intergroup contact in change of prejudice and ethnic relations. In P. A. Katz (ed.), *Towards the elimination of racism.* Elmsford, NY: Pergamon Press.

Ben Ari, R. and Amir, Y. (1986). Contact between Arab and Jewish youth in Israel. In M. Hewstone and R. Brown (eds.), *Contact and Conflict in Intergroup Encounters.* New York: Basil Blackwell.

Brown v. Board of Education, 347 U.S. 483 (1954).

Cazden, C. (1985, April). *The ESL teacher as advocate.* Plenary presentation to the TESOL Conference, New York.

Clandfield, D. & Sivell, J. (1990). *Cooperative Learning & Social Change: Selected Writings of Celestin Freinet.* Toronto: Our Schools/Our Selves.

Cohen, E. (1973). Modifying the effects of social structure. *American Behavioral Scientist, 16,* 861–79.

Cook, S. (1960). The systematic analysis of socially significant events: A strategy for social research. *Journal of Social Issues, 18* (2), 66–84.

Cook, S. (1978). Interpersonal and attitudinal outcomes in cooperating interracial groups. *Journal of Research and Development in Education, 12* (1), 98–113.

Cummins, J. (1985). *Blessed with bilingual brains: A videotape interview.* Hartford, Toronto: University of Hartford-Ontario Institute for Studies in Education.

Cummins, J. (1986). Cultures in contact: Using classroom microcomputers for cultural exchange and reinforcement. *TESL Canada Journal/Revue TESL du Canada. 3* (2), 13–31.

Cummins, J. (1988). From the inner city to the global village: The microcomputer as a catalyst for collaborative learning and cultural interchange. *Language, Culture and Curriculum, 1,* 1–13.

Cummins, J. (1989). *Empowering minority students.* Sacramento: California Association for Bilingual Education.

Cummins, J. (1991). Foreword for R. DeVillar & C. Faltis, *Computers and cultural diversity: Restructuring for school success.* Albany NY; State University of New York Press.

Cummins, J. & Sayers, D. (1990). Education 2001: Learning networks and educational reform. In C. Faltis & R. DeVillar (Eds.) *Language minority students and computers, Special Edition, Computers and the Schools, 7* (1-2), 1-29.

Curran, M. (1986). *Toward understanding interactions in high school classes containing return migrants in Puerto Rico.* Unpublished Doctoral dissertation, Teachers College. New York: Columbia University.

Day, R. (1980). The development of linguistic attitudes and preferences. *TESOL Quarterly, 14,* 27–37.

Day, R. (1982). Children's attitudes toward language. In E. Ryan and H. Giles (Eds.), *Attitudes towards Language Variation: Social and applied contexts.* London: Edward Arnold.

DeVillar, R. & Faltis, C. (1991). *Computers and cultural diversity: Restructuring for school success.* Albany NY; State University of New York Press.

DeVries, D. & Edwards, K. (1973). Learning games and student teams: Their effect on classrooms process. *American Journal of Educational Research, 10* (4), 307–318.

DeVries, D. & Edwards, K. (1974). Student teams and learning games: Their effects on cross-race and cross-sex interaction. *Journal of Educational Psychology, 66* (5), 741–749.

DeVries, D., Edwards, K. & Slavin, R. (1978). Biracial learning teams and race relations in the classroom: four field experiments on teams-games-tournaments. *Journal of Educational Psychology, 70,* 356–362.

DeVries, D., Edwards, K. & Wells, E. (1974). *Team competition effects on classroom group process.* Baltimore: Center for Social Organization of Schools, Johns Hopkins University.

Edwards, J. R. (1982). Language attitudes and their implications among English speakers. In E. Ryan and H. Giles (Eds.), *Attitudes towards language variation: Social and applied contexts.* London: Edward Arnold.

Edwards, K. & DeVries, D. (1974). *The effects of teams-games-tournaments and two instructional variations on classroom process, students' attitudes, and student achievement.* Baltimore: Center for Social Organization of Schools, Johns Hopkins University.

Faltis, C. & DeVillar, R. (1990). Computer uses for teaching Spanish to bilingual native speakers. In C. Faltis & R. DeVillar (Eds.) *Language minority students and computers.* New York: The Haworth Press.

Figueroa, E., Sayers, D. & Brown, K. (1990). Red multilingüe para el aprendizaje: De Orilla a Orilla. [multilingual learning network: From Shore to Shore]. *Micro Aula: El maestro y la computadora [Micro-classroom: The teacher and the computer], 8,* 27–30.

Fordham, S. (1988). Racelessness as a factor in Black students' success: Pragmatic strategy or Pyrrhic victory? *Harvard Educational Review, 58* (1), 54–84.

Genesee, F., Tucker, G.R., & Lambert W.E. (1978). The development of ethnic identity and ethnic role taking skills in children from different school settings. *International Journal of Psychology, 13* (1), 39–57.

Hakuta, K. (1984). *The causal relationship between the development of bilingualism, cognitive flexibility, and social-cognitive skills in Hispanic elementary school children.* Final Report. Rosslyn, VA.; National Clearinghouse for Bilingual Education, and New Haven CT.; Yale University Psychology Department.

Hakuta, K. (1988a). *El Gato: An English to Spanish translation task.* Unpublished typescript. New Haven CT.; Yale University Psychology Department.

Hakuta, K. (1988b). *The Three Boys: A Spanish to English translation Task.* Unpublished typescript. New Haven CT.; Yale University Psychology Department.

Harley, B., Allen, P., Cummins, J. & Swain, M. (1990). *The develop-ment of second language proficiency.* New York: Cambridge University Press.

Hewstone, M. and Brown, R., Editors. (1986). *Contact and conflict in intergroup encounters.* New York: Basil Blackwell.

Johnson, D., Johnson, R. & Maruyama, G. (1983). Interdependence and interpersonal attraction among heterogeneous and homogeneous individuals: A theoretical formulation and a meta-analysis of the research. *Review of Educational Research, 53* (1), 5–54.

Johnson, R., Johnson, D. & Stanne, M. (1986). Comparison of computer-assisted cooperative, competitive, and individualistic learning. *American Educational Research Journal, 23* (3), 382–92.

Jonas, R. (1969). The twinned classroom approach to FLES. *Modern Language Journal, 53,* (5), 342–346.

Jonas, R. (1972). African studies in French for the elementary grades: Phase II of a twinned classroom approach to the teaching of French in the elementary grades. ED 066 944. Washington, DC: Institute for International Studies.

Katz, I. (1955). *Conflict and harmony in an adolescent interracial group.* New York: New York University Press.

Lambert, W.E. (1960). Evaluational reactions to spoken languages. *Journal of Abnormal and Social Psychology, 2,* 84–90.

Lambert, W.E. (1977). The effects of bilingualism on the individual: Cognitive and sociocultural consequences. In P.A. Hornby (Ed.), *Bilingualism: Psychological, social, and educational implications.* New York: Academic Press.

Lee, W. B. (1980). Ecole moderne pedagogie Freinet: Educational bonesetters. *Phi Delta Kappan, 61* (5), 341–45.

Lee, W. B. (1983). Celestin Freinet, the unknown reformer. *Educational Forum, 48* (1), 97–114.

Lindzey, G. & Aronson, E., Editors. (1969). *Handbook of social psychology: Volume 5.* Reading, MA: Addison-Wesley.

Matute-Bianchi, M.E. (1986). Ethnic identities and patterns of school success and failure among Mexican-descent and Japanese-American students in a California high school: An ethnographic analysis. In M. B. Arias (Ed.), The education of Hispanic Americans: A challenge for the future, *American Journal of Education, 58* (3), 265–279.

Milk, R. (1980). Variations in language use patterns across different group settings in two bilingual second grade classrooms. Unpublished doctoral dissertation, Stanford University.

Miller, N., Brewer, M.B. & Edwards, K. (1985). Cooperative interaction in desegregated settings: A laboratory analogue. *Journal of Social Issues, 41* (3), 63–79.

Pettigrew, T.F. (1986). The intergroup contact hypothesis reconsidered. In M. Hewstone and R. Brown (Eds.), *Contact and conflict in intergroup encounters*. New York: Basil Blackwell.

Ramírez, A. (1981). Language attitudes and the speech of Spanish-English bilingual pupils. In R. Durán (Ed.), *Latino Language and Communicative Behavior*. Norwood, NJ: Ablex.

Ramírez, A., Arce-Torres, E. & Politzer, R. (1978). Language attitudes and achievement of bilingual pupils in English language arts. *The Bilingual Review/La Revista Bilingue, 5*, 169–206.

Roberts, Linda & staff. (1987). *Trends and status of computers in schools: Use in Chapter 1 programs and use with limited English proficient students*. Washington: US Congress Office of Technology Assessment.

Sayers, D. (1989). Bilingual sister classes in computer writing networks. In D. Johnson & D. Roen (Eds.), *Richness in writing: Empowering ESL writers*. New York: Longman's.

Sayers, D. (1988a). Editorial boards between sister classes. Unpublished typescript for Qualitative Research Methods, Harvard Graduate School of Education.

Sayers, D. (1990a). Language attitude change among bilingual program students in technology-based Sister Class exchanges. Unpublished Doctoral Dissertation. Harvard Graduate School of Education. Cambridge, MA: Gutman Library.

Sayers, D. (1990b). Interscholastic correspondence exchanges in Celestin Freinet's Modern School Movement: Implications for computer-mediated student writing networks. Keynote Address, November 17, 1990. First North American Freinet Congress, St. Catharines, Ontario.

Sayers, D. (1991). Cross-Cultural exchanges between students from the same culture: A portrait of an emerging relationship mediated by technology. *The Canadian Modern Language Review/La Revue Canadienne des langues vivantes*, Theme issue on "Heritage Languages", J. Cummins (ed.), *47, (4)*, 678–696.

Sayers, D. & Brown, K. (1987). Bilingual education and telecommunications: A perfect fit. *The Computing Teacher, 17*, 23–24.

Sayers, D. & Brown, K. (In press). Putting a human face on educational technology: Intergenerational bilingual literacy through parent-child partnerships in long-distance networks. In David Spener (Ed.), *Bilingual Literacy: A National Clearinghouse for Literacy Education Forum*. Englewood Cliffs, NJ: Prentice Hall.

Schwarzwald, J. and Amir, Y. (1984). Interethnic relations and education: an Israeli perspective. In N. Miller and M. B. Brewer (eds.), *Groups in contact: The psychology of desegregation*. New York: Academic Press.

Sharan, S. & Shachar, H. (1988). *Language and learning in the cooperative classroom.* New York: Springer-Verlag New York, Inc.

Slavin, R. (1977a). How student learning teams can integrate the desegregated classroom. *Integrated Education, 15,* 56–58.

Slavin, R. (1977b). *Using student learning teams to desegregate the classroom.* Baltimore: Center for Social Organization of Schools, Johns Hopkins University.

Slavin, R. (1979). Effects of biracial learning teams on cross-racial friendships. *Journal of Educational Psychology, 71,* 381–387.

Slaving, R. & Oickle, E. (1975). Effects of cooperative learning teams on student achievement and race relations: Treatment by race interactions. *Sociology of Education, 54,* 174–180.

Triviz, R. (1987). Gender's salience over ethnicity in first graders' identifications. Unpublished doctoral dissertation. Cambridge, MA: Harvard Graduate School of Education.

Weigel, R., Wiser, P. & Cook. S. (1975). The impact of cooperative learning experiences on cross-ethnic relations and attitudes. *Journal of Social Issues, 31,* (1), 219–244.

Werner, N. E. and Idella, M.E. (1968). Perception of prejudice in Mexican American preschool children. *Perceptual and Moter Skills, 27,* 1039–46.

Williams, R. (1947). *The reduction of intergroup tensions: A survey of research on problems of ethnic, racial and religious group relations.* New York: Social Science Research Council.

Vázquez-Brunet, I. (1978). *Estudio sobre los estudiantes procedentes de EEUU.* Bayamon, Puerto Rico: Departamento de Instrucción Pública.

Yager, S., Johnson, R., Johnson, D. & Snider, B. (1985). The effect of cooperative and individualistic learning experiences on positive and negative cross-handicap relationships. *Contemporary Educational Psychology, 10,* 127–138.

▼ 13 ▼
Teaching Teachers about Computers and Collaborative Problem-Solving

HOWARD BUDIN

This paper reports on a collaborative project of the Teachers College Program in Computing and Education and two New York City public elementary schools. Begun in September 1989 with support from the Fund for the Improvement of Post-secondary Education (FIPSE) of the U.S. Department of Education[1] and a donation of 15 Apple IIGS workstations from Apple Computer, the three-year project's main goal was to develop a model for long-term teacher education, in collaboration with inner-city public schools, for integrating computing into elementary curricula in ways that emphasized problem solving and cooperative learning.

Our motivation for exploring new approaches to teacher education stemmed partly from fifteen years' experience working with teachers and computer coordinators, locally and nationally. This experience made it clear to us that the usual practice of offering teachers brief in-service courses or workshops on (typically) the easiest kinds of software applications, or those which fit most easily into existing curricula, was inadequate for two reasons—it ignored both the potential of the technology in itself and its potential for helping to transform curricula. These potentials are discussed below, following an outline of the project.

The project, Teacher Training for Using Computers in Minority Education, began with a year and a half of intensive work with a core of three teachers from each of two inner-city elementary schools. The second year and a half added a number of other teachers from each school to the group. Our only criteria for selecting teachers were that they had little or no prior experience using computers and that they were interested in exploring how computers could facilitate collaborative problem solving.

Each half of the project consisted of three phases:

- *First semester:* Teachers took their Apple IIGS's and printers to their homes and spent one day a month at Teachers College working with project personnel to learn how to use them. This included learning to set the computers up, to troubleshoot problems in their operations, and to use different software applications such as databases, simulations, word processors, and desktop publishing programs. It also included readings and discussions on computers and collaborative learning.
- *Second semester:* Teachers took their computers to their classrooms and tried out various applications with their students. Project personnel were available for help in schools—assisting teachers, modeling lessons with students and sometimes working with groups of students, and meeting with teachers to discuss progress.
- *Third semester:* After a year of becoming familiar with computers, teachers designed their own curriculum projects for use with their students. Project personnel remained available for assistance.

The second half of the project followed the same pattern as the first for the newly added group of teachers, with the original core group of teachers available for support within the school. During the second half, project personnel continued to work with core teachers as they extended and deepened their knowledge about computing in the classroom and developed new and more comprehensive curriculum projects.

This brief description of project activities is fleshed out in the next section with a discussion of the background thinking that informed this organization. The project's goals were complex in that they aimed to investigate teacher education not only in workshops but also in the real classroom context, thus testing teachers' learning in practice. The following section outlines several examples of projects that we and the teachers developed to encourage collaborative work with computers. The final section summarizes preliminary findings of the project.

Background: Computers, Classrooms, and Teacher Education

Equity

Throughout most of the 1980s, the number of computers in United States schools nearly doubled each year (Office of Technology Assessment 1988). Early in this growth a disparity between richer and poorer school districts became noticable—richer districts had more access to certain kinds of funding, more connections with the computer industry, and possibly more financial support from parents (Zakariya 1984). Equity, in terms of equal access to computers for all students, became an important issue, grounded in the longstanding American belief in equal opportunity in schooling (Lazerson et. al. 1985).

Equity, however, involves not only how many computers are in schools, but what they are used for (DeVillar and Faltis 1987). Recent studies have shown that in poorer districts student use of computers, when it occurs, involves mostly drill work, while in richer districts students often use spreadsheets, databases, simulations, programming, and other computer applications designed to enhance their creativity or research skills (Cole and Griffin 1987). Educators' rationale for this dichotomy is usually that poorer students tend to lack "basic skills" in reading and math, and that computer-assisted instruction can provide tutoring in these areas. The problem with this rationale is that the same poorer students who get basic drill-and-practice remedial work in the lower grades are typically doing the same kind of activity in later years, if they are still in school. In fact, the belief that so-called "lower-level" thinking skills can be totally separated from "higher-order" thinking is a fallacy that serves to perpetuate the dichotomy in educators' thinking about poorer and richer students (Resnick 1987). In reality, all students can think, and do so all the time, normally combining "higher" and "lower" skills. (Smith 1990).

The different computer applications mentioned above also typically involve students in different ways of working together. Whereas the more creative applications often lend themselves to student interaction, drill and practice is usually seen as individual or even competitive work—microcomputers or larger systems with terminals deliver drill work to individual stu-

dents whose progress is measured and reported (Budin 1991).
Researchers have found that any use of computers tends to
motivate students to interact spontaneously (Laboratory of
Comparative Human Cognition 1989; Budin et. al. 1989). Nevertheless, without conscious teacher attention to, and structuring of, such interaction it can be relatively worthless; and in
the context of drill work especially, teachers tend to discourage
any interaction (DeVillar and Faltis 1991).

At the present, in the beginning of the 1990s, the disparity
in numbers of computers seems to be diminishing, and many
educators believe that through a combination of public and
private donations the number of students per computer will
tend to equalize throughout all districts. The question of how
different students will use computers remains, however, and is
crucial. The present dichotomy of use, if continued, will serve
only to exacerbate further the inequality of education between
rich and poor districts. Computers are potentially powerful
and empowering tools, but using them only as remedial tools
will result only in extending the differences in schooling for
rich and poor.

Teachers' Decision Making

While the ultimate focus of education efforts is the student, a
necessary condition for success is, of course, the preparation
of teachers. It follows that if we want students to become collaborative problem-solvers, teachers must be prepared to facilitate this development. Teachers, however, have two kinds of
difficulty with collaborative problem-solving. First, teachers
generally teach as they were taught, and their own school experiences did not usually emphasize cooperative learning or
meaningful problem-solving. Second, teachers are not often
enough collaborative solvers of significant problems in their
own working situations.

Throughout this century one historical trend has reduced
teachers' decision-making authority over how and what students learn. Movements of scientific curriculum-building and
school efficiency have combined to place this authority increasingly in the hands of outside experts and administrators. The
result has been the growth of programmed learning in which
teachers are seen as implementers of materials developed elsewhere. One characteristic of such programming is the effort to
make curriculum materials "teacher-proof" in the sense that

any teacher could implement them—instructions often specify not only what teachers should say to students but how they should say it (Smith 1986; Apple 1982).

Computer-assisted drill-and-practice software is in some ways an extension and refinement of programmed learning. It essentially does away with the necessity for a teacher by "individualizing" the computer's responses to student input. Although for most teachers and schools this software is not a substantial part of the instructional program, its logical extension represents a systematic mechanical "delivery" of instruction to students, and all such use represents a further removal of curricular decision-making from teachers. Programmatic learning, whether through software or printed materials, is deficient in several respects: it dehumanizes instruction by eliminating the face-to-face communication between teacher and student; it breaks instruction into discrete skills which can presumably be taught sequentially and uniformly; and it treats the entire range of students alike by presenting the same material to them in the same way (Budin, 1991).

At the basis of our project is the assumption that if teachers are to make a difference they must have the authority to make decisions about curriculum, to tailor it to the needs of their students and schools, and to create their own curricula. The teacher's voice has long been denigrated in decisions about pedagogy, research, and policy (McDonald 1988). Recent reform efforts have begun to involve teachers in school-based management and shared decision-making. While these welcome efforts are focusing on all aspects of school life, special attention must be paid to curriculum decisions, and especially to the use of technology within them.

Making Teachers Technologically Adept

We want teachers to see, and to use, technology's potential to empower students to think critically and creatively and to work together. This is a complex task, for the magnitude of change necessary to accomplish it is greater than it may appear. The traditional approach to implementing innovations—namely, providing teachers with implementation directions—has been shown ineffective in the case of technology (as well as in other kinds of innovation). A simplistic approach to training teachers has simply not resulted in a revolution in learning (Tucker 1985).

Many educators believe that technology necessarily implies certain changes for schools. It may, for instance, change the role of the teacher from didactic lecturer to facilitator of learning (Budin et. al. 1989). It may change the kind of access students have to information (Budin et. al. 1987). It may alter the space configurations and time schedules of schools (Taylor 1987). Some degree of change may occur inevitably, regardless of what teachers and administrators do, but the prospects for deep and lasting changes in learning with technology are not great unless educators devote their attention to making these changes happen.

Thus, becoming technologically adept implies an interrelated set of learnings for teachers:

1. Teachers must become familiar enough with hardware setup and aspects of troubleshooting so they will feel confident about having a computer in their classroom.
2. Teachers must be experts at using any software application they intend to use with their students.
3. Teachers must understand the theoretical and practical backgrounds of problem solving and cooperative learning, and how software best relates to them.

Details of this project were planned to help teachers through these kinds of learning. To provide an opportunity for unpressured learning, teachers take computers home and meet periodically with project experts to discuss and learn about software. The number of teachers involved in the original core group was kept small so that their progress and problems could be monitored closely. Teachers were introduced gradually to more complex software applications. The sequence of three semester phases described above was designed to involve teachers step by step in making their own informed decisions about integrating computing, based on their experiences, reflections, and conversations. To enhance teachers' involvement with and participation in students' learning, computers were placed in teachers' classrooms instead of in computer labs. All of these project details were intended to facilitate a blend of learning, thinking, and practice in which teachers gradually assume more responsibility, based on increased learning, for making curriculum decisions that were sound for their own classrooms and schools.

A final aspect of project organization involves the nature of teacher collaboration. An often-cited problem in teacher planning is teachers' isolation from one another, both in terms of learning about what other teachers are doing and in working with other teachers (Cleveland 1986). Too often teachers in adjacent classrooms are ignorant about how their colleagues teach. This project tried to overcome teacher isolation in several ways. Workshop meetings provided opportunities for discussion between teachers in two schools. Work with project personnel, in workshops and in their classrooms, provided teachers support and ongoing discussion. Finally, an electronic bulletin board that we operate was available to teachers for communication not only with others in the project but with teachers from around the country. Thus, a variety of methods of adult learning was facilitated by several kinds of collaborative work among adults.

Models of Collaborative Software Use

As discussed above, this project attempted to combine various kinds of theoretical and practical learning for teachers. Having had an opportunity to learn software thoroughly outside of the classroom, and having planned with project personnel for its use in the classroom, the next step was for teachers to test different applications and methods with their students.

In workshop sessions with teachers we discussed several models of cooperative learning, mostly variants on peer tutoring and group investigation, and how different software applications could best use them. Following are descriptions of two models of use that we designed and tested in classroom situations.

Cartooning

Several relatively new programs allow children to make their own animated cartoons. The one we used included many ready-to-use characters, each with predesigned actions, various background scenes, and music. Speech balloons with different styles, colors, and sizes of texts could be added and moved along with characters. With these elements and more, children could create cartoons of up to two thousand frames.

As one might imagine, this activity was immensely popular, since it offered a kind of capability not previously available to children. Cartooning was attractive enough that the first and second graders who used it were not daunted by the relative complexity of the menus and dialogue boxes. To the contrary, we found that the second graders quickly became software experts, while the first graders generally needed the second graders' help but gradually became competent.

We divided the activity into two parts. The first involved making children competent at using the software. Here adults at first scaffolded students' learning, supporting them where they needed it. As the children learned, especially the second graders, they supported other children, often holding first graders' hands while they learned to manipulate a mouse. This kind of peer tutoring quickly spread software knowledge and expertise through the class.

The second part involved collaborative design of cartoons. Group of four or six children met and worked out ideas for cartoons with several scenes, sketching their ideas on specially prepared screen design sheets. After the groups had agreed on the cartoons' theme, characters, and scenes, pairs of children worked on implementing each scene. Finally the whole group reviewed the cartoon and edited it.

Databases

The merits of database work for enhancing thinking have been rehearsed fairly extensively (Hunter 1987; Budin 1988). We consider a database a good collaborative tool for the same reason cartooning is—both are examples of software that is complex enough that meaningful tasks can be divided among group members and the parts combined to achieve a goal. With cartooning, the software provides a structure whose goal is to create a certain kind of product. A database is more open-ended in the sense that any kind of information can be included; it provides only a set of procedures for entering and manipulating data.

For this reason the collaborative framework we used with databases more closely resembles group investigation than peer tutoring. In group investigation students have a degree of initiative in deciding exactly what to investigate, how to go about it, and what to do with the information (Sharan and Sharan 1989/90). Tasks within a database project can be divided in different ways: horizontally, so that all group members are doing the same kind of research; or vertically, so that one member gathers data, another enters it, while a third formats it, and so on. Although members do different jobs, they have a common goal: to organize and manipulate the data by sorting and selecting from it so as to help them make decisions, particularly as a group.

Several classes in our project have used databases in this group investigative manner. One researched facts about animals, deciding to investigate the relationship between herbivores, carnivores, and omnivores. This extended to off-computer activities such as drawing murals of animal habitats. Another class made a database of all the rooms in the school, investigating relative dimensions and areas. Other projects have involved data on countries of the world. In all these projects, groups have helped define the topic, decide what information to gather, and decide how to divide the tasks. Sometimes certain group members became more expert than others in using the software, and sometimes all shared equally in software tasks. In all cases, groups met to discuss how to use the data they had collected and entered to show what they wanted to show, and how to format and present their results.

These examples illustrate only two ways to use computers to support collaborative learning. They were chosen partly because of their differences, but also because of the ways in which they are alike. One important similarity is in the opportunities they provide for structuring cooperative tasks. Any kind of task can be structured for collaboration, of course, but the two kinds of software used here were themselves structured in such a way as to make it easy for teachers to see how tasks could be divided within them. The most commonly used software for cooperative purposes in schools is probably word processing, but in many cases we have found that teachers often simply tell students to write together, believing that they will naturally collaborate (New York City Board of Education 1990). Structuring writing experiences for collaboration is of course possible, but using a word processor does not in itself ensure meaningful collaboration. This laissez-faire approach extends to other computer-supported learning contexts as well, and to learning settings in general (DeVillar and Faltis 1991). Applications such as databases and cartoon production programs clearly highlight the complexity of their tasks and thus, we feel, they make it easier for teachers to begin to think of how collaboration can be structured within them.

These software activities helped create a kind of classroom laboratory where teachers could integrate theoretical with practical learning. One aspect was teachers' testing of different configurations for student learning: students learned from adults and from each other, either within small groups or in peer-tutoring settings. Another aspect was the variety of ways for teachers to learn in this situation: from working directly with students, from watching student groups work, and from watching other adults (e.g., project personnel) model working with students.

Another area of learning for teachers involved classroom organization and structure. We made an initial decision to place computers in classrooms partly because we had only one to give to each teacher. Beyond this, though, we felt that the usual effect of placing computers in lab settings was to remove them from classroom teachers' knowledge of what their students were doing with them and from a decision-making context for teachers. Placing them in classrooms provided teachers an opportunity to see them in operation, and in fact made teachers think about how to organize and schedule their use. Thus teachers experimented with furniture arrangements and with time schedules in trying to maximize ease and effectiveness of computer use.

We have presented examples of software use not only to illustrate ways computers might be used collaboratively but also to highlight ways for teachers to learn about such use. Teacher learning should be a process that is informed not only by workshops but by the opportunity to experiment and to observe results. We propose that the organization of this project facilitates a kind of learning in which teachers will continue to experiment and learn from actual classroom situations in defining how they integrate computers into their own curriculum.

Implications for Teacher Learning

Learning about collaborative problem-solving in itself is new to many teachers, and so is learning about computers. If giving teachers lesson plans for using software in collaborative modes were all that was necessary, our project's task would have been simple. But in reality many elements were involved, including learning about the multifaceted potential of relatively sophisticated software to facilitate kinds of learning, relating adult learning to student learning, and others discussed above. From our experience, we can draw some preliminary implications for teacher education programs in general, and collaborative problem solving situations in particular. The following implications address what works, and what may be necessary, both for teachers to learn about collaborative use of technology and for infusing such use into classrooms and schools.

Stages of Teacher Learning

Like other kinds of learning, the learning of software proceeds in stages. Trying to "teach" computer-naive teachers to use sophisticated applications is usually doomed to failure. A certain period of time to integrate new experiences at one level is necessary for teachers. Beginning with an easy desktop publishing program, for instance, will increase teachers' confidence and, once they run up against its limitations, will whet their appetites for software that does more. Most teacher training programs avoid this problem by sticking to easy-to-learn applications. Evidence from our studies with project teachers, however, indicates that by the end of one year most teachers were beginning to feel comfortable with computers and software and to believe that they could learn new software by themselves. This is not to say that teachers were completely at ease, only that they now felt ready to proceed on their own to a more complex word processor or database program. They had, that is, become more confident and self-directed learners.

Collaboration in Teacher Learning

One clear implication of our work is that, at least in a new and different area like software, learning together is often much easier than learning alone. Supported by project personnel (in workshop sessions, on the telephone and bulletin board, and in classrooms) and by their colleagues (who are available daily for help and discussion), teachers have not only ready support but also motivation to think about and keep using software. Teachers need more support in the beginning stages of learning about computers and software, and as they become more confident (as noted above) learning alone becomes more practical and often more productive. In a larger sense, though, teachers need a structure of ongoing support and networking with other teachers and outside experts that they rarely experience. We need to build as much adult collaboration as possible into teacher education and teachers' work in school, for continuous learning, discussion, and planning, and also so that in their own practice they learn to model what they expect of students.

Transfer from Personal Learning to Teaching

This project assumed that a good way to build teachers' technological expertise was to send computers to their homes for a period of time. If this is true, the question remains whether, and how well, this learning transfers to using computers in classrooms. Based on observations, questionnaires, and in-depth interviews we have conducted with teachers, it seems that the confidence built during the time teachers had to learn at home did help equip them for bringing their computers to school. Problems with hardware and software of course arose, but teachers now either knew how to handle them or knew how to look for help. An implication here is that teacher education programs should provide teachers not only sufficient time to learn but also some kind of easy access to computers so that teachers will use them outside of the classroom.

Varieties of Learning

A variety of ways to learn often facilitates acquisition and integration of new concepts, for adults as well as children. This project provided not only different forms of collaboration between adults, but also, as described above, several ways for teachers to learn within the classroom. The assumption was that theoretical learning (in this case learning to use software at home, and thinking about using it with students) should be linked with the more practical learning that comes from actually trying out software in class. Because in-service is usually offered as courses, if often has difficulty connecting teacher learning to actual practice. This project combined laboratory learning and discussion with supported practice in teachers' classrooms. Ongoing discussions with project teachers indicate the benefits of tying together many kinds of learning. Not only do theoretical and practical learning continually reinforce one another, but both should be ongoing—our teachers see themselves as learners as well as teachers, learning from students as well as other adults. Though they feel a degree of competence, continuous discussion and experimentation continue to give them a personal sense of growth and discovery.

Diffusion of Interest

One condition of this project was to include teachers who were interested in it and wanted to be involved. When we reached the second half of the project, in which we were to expand the group within each school, we found that there were more teachers interested in joining than we anticipated. This resulted from knowledge that spread around the school about what our core group was doing (and perhaps also from the desire to have a computer at home). We are still working out methods of relating to a larger group than we originally anticipated, but the fact of such interest suggests a number of points. First, teachers are naturally interested in a project that works. Second, the voluntary nature of a project—the opportunity to see or hear about it without feeling compelled to be part of it—can engender interest and enthusiasm. Third, and possibly most crucial, a necessary element may be the long-range partnership with an outside agency like a school of education, which can help teachers learn in an unthreatening way and continue to support them and help them develop. Our commitment to each school runs for three years, but we will most likely continue the relationship in some form after the official project concludes.

Different School and Classroom Cultures

Finally, we want to emphasize the uniqueness of each school, and even each particular classroom, in planning activities. The small number of core teachers in this project allowed us to relate personally and intensively to each, in discussions, workshops, and visiting and working in their classrooms. From this experience we found confirmation of what should be an obvious principle of educational planning but is often ignored—that each classroom is a unique cultural and educational setting, created and influenced by factors within and without the classroom.

These few examples begin to illustrate the remarkable diversity of teachers and classrooms, and offer implications for working with teachers. Beyond providing alternative ways for teachers to learn about technology, we must provide opportunities for individual (as well as collaborative) development of curriculum materials and planning for how to integrate technology into curriculum. In terms of developing a model for working with teachers, the implication is that while some lessons, such as those sketched above, may be generic, a model can never be completely replicable. Aspects of interaction with teachers—planning, individual discussion, different needs—cannot be completely specifiable in advance.

In summary, this project has provided us rich opportunities for investigating factors involved in working with teachers in the collaborative use of technology. The collaborations extended from that between a teachers college and public schools, to those between teachers in the project, and ultimately to those between students. The insights gained so far from this investigation, I believe, strengthen our contention that one kind of collaboration depends to a large degree on the others, and that they are mutually reinforcing. Teachers' unfamiliarity with computers, as well as their lack of experience with collaboration, made it necessary to search for and develop, with teachers and students, appropriate software applications and learning situations. These factors alone justified the in-depth and long-term nature of the project. Technology offers unique opportunities and potentials for collaborative work, the nature of which we are just beginning to discover. In a larger sense, however, many of the insights elaborated here about helping teachers learn about collaboration are most likely not limited to working with technology, but equally applicable to other areas of teachers' work.

Note

1. FIPSE Project Number P116B91293, Teacher Training for Using Computers in Minority Education.

References

Apple, M. (1982). Curricular form and the logic of technical control: building the possessive individual. In M. Apple (Ed.), *Cultural and Economic Reproduction in Education*. London: Routledge & Kegan Paul.

Budin, H., R. P. Taylor, and D. S. Kendall. (1987). Computers and Social Studies: Trends and Directions. *The Social Studies*, 78 (1), 7–12.

Budin, H. (1988). Teacher Training for Using Databases. *Outlook*, 20 (1). New York: Association for Computing Machinery.

Budin, H., J. Eisler, F. Guerrero, and J. Schoener (1989). Changing Roles of Teachers and Students in the Computer Lab. A paper presented at the American Educational Research Association's Annual Meeting, San Francisco, March 1989.

Budin, H. (1991). Technology and the Teacher's Role. *Computers in the Schools*, 8 (1/2/3), 15–26.

Cleveland, H. (1986). Educating Citizens and Leaders for an Information-Based Society. *Educational Leadership*, 43 (6), 62–64.

Cole, M. and Griffin, P. (1987). *Contextual Factors in Education*. Madison, WI: University of Wisconsin Center for Education Research.

DeVillar, R. A. and Faltis, C. J. (1991). *Computers and Cultural Diversity, Restructuring for School Success*. New York: SUNY Press.

DeVillar, R. A. and Faltis, C. J. (1987). Computers and Educational Equity in American Public Schools. *Capstone Journal of Education*, 7 (4), 3–10.

Hunter, B. (1987). Knowledge-Creative Learning with Data Bases. *Social Education*, 51, (1), 38–43.

Laboratory of Comparative Human Cognition (1989). Kids and Computers: A Positive Vision of the Future. *Harvard Educational Review*, 59, (1), 73–86.

Lazerson, M., McLaughlin, J. B., McPherson, B., and Bailey, S. K. (1985). *An Education of Value: The Purposes and Practices of Schools*. Cambridge: Cambridge University Press.

McDonald, J. P. (1988). The Emergence of the Teacher's Voice. *Teachers College Record*, 89, (4), 471–486.

Office of Technology Assessment, United States Congress (1988). *Power On! New Tools for Teaching and Learning*. Washington, DC: U.S. Government Printing Office.

New York City Board of Education, Office of Research, Evaluation, and Assessment (1990). *Collaborative Learning and Computers: What Some New York City Teachers are Doing, 1988–89*. New York: NYC Board of Education.

Resnick, L. (1987). *Education and Learning to Think*. Washington, D.C.: National Academy Press.

Sharan, Y. and Sharan, S. (1989/90). Group Investigation Expands Cooperative Learning. *Educational Leadership*, (47), 4, 17–21.

Smith, F. (1986). *Insult to Intelligence: The Bureaucratic Invasion of our Classrooms*. New York: Arbor House.

Smith, F. (1990). *to think.* New York: Teachers College Press.

Taylor, R. P. (1987). How will computing change education? *Education and Computing, 3,* 101–105.

Tucker, M. S. (1985). Computers in the Schools: What Revolution? *Journal of Communication, 34,* (4), 12–23.

Zakariya, S. B. (1984). In school (as elsewhere), the rich get computers: the poor get poorer. *The American School Board Journal,* 29–32, 54.

▼ 14 ▼
Pedagogical and Research Uses of Computer-Mediated Conferencing

ARMANDO A. ARIAS
and
BERYL BELLMAN

The philosopher Abraham Kaplan, in a 1989 interview on the future of computer-mediated conferencing and education, stated that the technology will have such an impact that the university of the future will be radically transformed. He predicted that in the future the campus will be used for lab sessions and similar work that involves actual presence, but that the majority of education can and will be done at a distance, utilizing the new technologies. Likewise, others predict that K–12 education will also be transformed (DeVillar and Faltis 1991). Still others argue that much of the educational process will take place at home or in special learning centers where students progress at individual paces (Mason and Kaye 1990). The schoolhouse of the future will, as with the campus of the future, be used only for those tasks that necessitate actual rather than virtual interaction (Arias, in press).

In the case of K–12 this will strongly entail face-to-face encounters important for socialization. However, rather than children necessarily being at the school physical plant for six hours each day, the time can be reduced to only those periods where actual encounter is required. Such programs, of course, suggest greater equity and access to technologies by all social classes, which may be more optimistic than realistic for the immediate future. Although such potential for educational transformation exists, it is important to inquire as to what the driving forces are behind such potential changes.

Why should education shift from being primarily face-to-face to virtual or electronic? The mere possibilities afforded by media are not enough. Rather, the media proffer possibilities as potential solutions to current problems (Brand 1988). The demographics of our society have changed radically in recent years, albeit independently of developments in new technologies. The United States is a diversity of cultures that mostly reside in ethnically and culturally distinct city neighborhoods and rural townships, and share a national culture through participation in public institutions, business, industry, and the media (Blake, Saufley, Porter, and Melodia 1990). Because this national culture is associated with the social and economic benefits of postindustrial society, it is most strongly represented in White or Anglo communities and in the lives of the upper-income classes of all ethnic groups. Many minority ethnic-group members, however, have had only limited access because of a history of discrimination and the resulting lack of social and economic resources (Arias and Bellman 1990). Consequently, there are different perceptions of American national culture associated with each ethnic group's respective culture and relative economic position in society.

Since the turn of century, the "melting pot" image became a slogan of American culture and was assumed to be a necessary condition for equal opportunity and success in our democratic society. Yet many immigrants, who were expected to give up traditional customs, instead succeeded only by supporting their respective ethnic group's culturally conscious religious, occupational, and political organizations. These were often in the form of ethnically dominated churches, clubs, fraternal associations, business societies, and political interest groups.

Thus, contrary to the ideal of the melting pot, cultural identity has been essential for both success and survival in a multicultural, multilingual, and multiethnic society where access to the "national culture" has been historically limited. Over the past several decades many previously underrepresented groups from all parts of Latin America, Africa, Asia, the Middle East, the Caribbean, and Oceana have added to the cultural diversity of American society. This influx, along with increased migrations from already-represented cultures, has significantly changed the demographic shape of the country. It has forced a recognition of the unique kinds of community needs and problems relevant to different cultures and their mixing with others.

This mix of cultures in the educational environment co-occurs with demands for individualized attention and mass teaching methods and, with the increase in classroom size, led to the recognition that students need individualized attention. The use of new technologies suggests possible solutions by providing self-paced instructional programs as well as the ability to organize groups of learners in new ways through computer-mediated communication (Arias and Bellman, 1993). This chapter describes an experiment that demonstrates such an application, BESTNET, which initially was an acronym for the Binational English and Spanish Telecommunications Network, but has since been expanded to include students and faculty representing an even greater diversity of languages. These users are involved in frequent interaction with one another in a series of course-related conferences and computer communications-supported collaborative work projects.

Computer-Mediated Conferencing

Within the past few years a number of institutions have introduced computer-mediated conferencing on a regular basis to augment existing classroom instruction (cf. Arias 1992; Arias and Bellman 1993, 1987; FIPSE Technology Study Group 1988; Feenberg 1987; Harasim 1986; Hiltz 1984; Kaye 1987; Zimmerer 1988). For example, in 1984, the University of Guelph (in Canada) developed its own conferencing system to use in seminars in the School of Extension Education. Since that time the University has extensively developed its conferencing software and introduced it to a number of other universities in the United States and Europe.

Also, during the past four years the Ontario Institute for Studies in Education (OISE) has operated a program whereby OISE students take graduate-level seminars in virtual (while interacting over the computer) and actual (face-to-face) settings. In some of the latter contexts, students are asked to engage in both face-to-face and online projects in groups of various sizes. The objective is to create a multiple of settings surrounding the same seminar in order to give the students what Steve Erhman (personal communication), Program Officer at the Annenberg/CPB Project, describes as a "distributed learning environment, an environment for teaching and learning characterized by great flexibility of time, place, resources and learning/teaching style." The New York Institute of Technology's Open University and the British Open University have also used computer-mediated conferencing to supplement existing media programs (cf. Kaye 1987).

In 1984, we drew upon several of these experiments in the writing of our first proposal focusing on the use of computer-mediated conferencing. Upon receiving funding by the Fund for the Improvement of Post Secondary Education (FIPSE), and supplemental resources from the Western Behavioral Sciences Institute (WBSI), BESTNET (Binational English/Spanish Telecommunications Network) was created. At that time, we started with computer-mediated conferencing and electronic mail as an interactive component to bilingual (English/Spanish) video lectures or telecourses aired on both sides of the U.S.–Mexico border via the local cable television educational channel we coordinated. BESTNET originally involved our production of a series of Spanish-language/English-transition distance education video courses, which we made interactive using computer conferencing in the sciences, mathematics, engineering, and computer/information fields. In our evaluation of the project we learned that students were particularly responsive to the computer-conferencing interactions, and that they did not need as much presentation of formal lecture materials in video lectures as we had originally designed. As a result, we began to rely more heavily on the computer-conferencing interactions for both the presentation and discussion of materials, and used video and other materials to present or supplement data for those discussions.

Finding conferencing to be so effective that it could be used as the dominant and/or standalone form of course delivery, we wrote and were funded for a second FIPSE proposal to explore various applications of computer conferencing for a range of different kinds of courses (e.g., writing composition, anthropology, sociology, psychology, and communications). At the same time, Digital Equipment Corporation (DEC) provided a major grant to provide multiple VAXmate workstations for each of the project sites (see below). Additionally, BESTNET participants were able to acquire equipment at their respective campuses that could be integrated into the network.

In addition to providing the hardware and computer-conferencing software *VAX Notes*, the BESTNET faculty and staff provide ongoing hands-on computer communications training and administrative support, travel to professional meetings and to biannual project meetings, and absorb various computer communications costs (when necessary). Participants also have access to Internet, which is considered to be the "electronic highway of highways," linking over 200,000 servers worldwide.

We feel that the foremost contribution BESTNET has made, however, is twofold: introducing the concept of computer-mediated conferencing to participating institutions, together with the pedagogical insight with respect to how we use the medium for teaching, researching, and learning. BESTNET faculty's focus of research, for example, has included the study of how various participants interact with one another, including faculty-to-faculty, faculty-to-student, as individuals, and as groups. Several related publications have resulted (see references) and the lessons learned from these studies have assisted us in developing a methodology for training teachers, as well as researchers, for working collaboratively while using the medium of computer-mediated conferencing.

Presently, the BESTNET institutions that are participating in the research program include California State University in Los Angeles; San Diego State University; Imperial Valley Campus of San Diego State University; California State University at Sonoma; Texas A&I University; University of New Mexico; the University of California at Irvine; Centro de Enseñanza Técnica y Superior en Tijuana and Mexicali; Instituto Tecnológico en Tijuana and also with participation of national system; Centro de Investigación Científica y Estudios Superiores en Ensenada; and the Universidad Autónoma de Baja California. In addition we have faculty participation from Arizona State University, California State University at Long Beach, California State University at Sacramento, California State University at Bakersfield, Icana in Argentina; University of California at Riverside; University of Colorado, Boulder; Indiana University–Purdue University at Indianapolis; University of Nairobi in Kenya; and the University Zimbabwe. The latter African universities are coordinated by the African Academy of Sciences, who are using BESTNET to network African scientific organizations.

Together these institutions constitute our electronic educational and research network, or BESTNET, whose focus is multi-fold:

1. to recognize that computer conferencing itself involves social psychological factors which must be taken into account by both course and human/social network designers;

2. to recognize that computer-mediated conferencing systems must be specifically tailored such that their features not only permit but also explicitly suggest new
social forms and the development of new pedagogical
methods;

3. to recognize that conferencing software must incorporate a variety of media to expand the information server,
including videotext, graphics, E-mail, phone, video/au-
dio, and the like; and lastly,

4. to understand the integration of the above communication tools, within the context of multiple institutions
and over public data networks, as it presents in light of
the significant organizational, social, and human factors, and the technical challenges they represent. We are
basically working with what we call "intermediate technologies" (Arias and Bellman 1991), while researching
enhanced forms of teaching and learning; hence, the
examination of what we call "electronic pedagogical
behavior."

Much more strategic thinking surrounding access to and
use of the new technologies is needed. Too many administrators focus only on the acquisition of computer hardware as the
cure-all to their technological deprivation. In our years of experience with computer technology in the educational setting
(at all levels and in a multitude of educational programs), we
have learned that the quantity (or lack thereof) of computers in
an institution is not the primary obstacle. The obstacle lies in
the limited vision faculty and administrators have about what
computer communications can provide. Most particularly,
with the advent of and basically free access to any number of
mainframes via the Internet, students, faculty, staff, and administrators have unlimited access to endless amounts of technological opportunity (e.g., databases, software, and networks);
if only they used them. Rooms full of computers are nice, but
not necessary.

What faculty and administration want throughout elementary, secondary, and postsecondary is to readily assemble the
hardware needed to provide students and teachers a new path-
way for accessing information throughout their region, nationally, and internationally. One computer made readily available
and connected to a mainframe (and perhaps with the ability to
connect to other mainframes) can take the place of a room full

of computers, once the student, teacher, or administrator develops the strategic thinking that directs them to seek beyond their institution to gain access to sorely needed software and other relevant materials.

In our BESTNET sites, our formula for access is one computer (connected to a mainframe) per seventy-five students. This ratio works because students are very creative about gaining access to the mainframe (once they have learned the method) from home, work, the library, the computer center, and the computer we have set aside for them. Subsequently, students develop a much different felt sense towards gaining access to computers and software. They soon realize that they can sign on from almost anywhere, including other cities (should they be away from their campus), to continue learning. This is not a "band-aid" approach to solving one's institutional problems at a technologically undeserved campus; rather, it is a cognitive shift towards computers that must take place and that also is indicative of where we as a society are currently headed. The fact is, campuses that have not yet experienced large acquisitions of computer hardware need not plan to do so. Instead they should "short-circuit" their "technological woes" by adopting a BESTNET paradigm, which recommends that a campus design for fewer computers (perhaps no "computer centers"), strategically locate the computers they can configure, connect these to modems, and teach individuals how to configure and use existing technologies to communicate via Internet (cost free), again for the purposes of teaching/researching and learning.

In the spring semester of 1990, BESTNET expanded to incorporate Texas A&I University, a minority institution (primarily Hispanic-Americans), to encourage regular practice and use of computers and telecommunications technologies to reach monolingual, bilingual, or ESL (English as a second language) Hispanic/Latino students. Moreover, the educational courses delivered were to have ethnic-group interest and satisfy general university liberal-studies requirements. (The latter function facilitates matriculation into regular degree programs.) Instructional delivery and interaction were realized through computer conferencing in the areas of intercultural communications, access to the new technologies, and teaching in the bilingual classroom. Students from three BESTNET sites (California State University–Los Angeles, San Diego State University, and Texas A&I University) participated in these classes, carrying out a dynamic interchange of electronically mediated ideas concerning the issues raised in each computer conference. Members of the BESTNET environment (around one hundred members for the spring semester of 1990) generated approximately ten thousand electronic interchanges during that time period, utilizing three nodes installed with *VAX Notes* computer conferencing software. The same course generated 35 percent more interactions during the fall semester of 1991.

Such success resulted in several professors at Texas A&I University, Corpus Christi State University, and Laredo State University forming a consortium and submitting a major proposal to the Annenberg/CPB Project for funding the collaborative teaching of basic composition courses via the BESTNET model. While these campuses are all part of the Texas A&M University system, they share similar technological needs that are complemented by the use of the newly installed Texas A&M University System Interactive Video/Graphics/Data/ Voice/Facsimile Network. The BESTNET model provides a pedagogically- and research-based approach to the uses of these new technologies, of which the network may take advantage before embarking on technologically-only—focused designs—a mistake that many institutions fail to avoid.

Consequently, BESTNET provides both on-campus students/faculty and off-campus distance learners, at different sites, with environments that enable regular practice with computer, telecommunications, writing, and literacy skills. This is especially important because each of our participating institutions has an institutional focus on developing Hispanic-American and other minority scientists and engineers, as well as those who will continue work towards a doctorate across disciplines.

As a result of seven years of continuous successful experimentation with computer-mediated conferencing, we have found the following positive results:

A. Curricular Enhancements
  1. Having involved over three thousand students in sixteen different institutions in the United States and Mexico, we have found that the technology greatly augments regular classroom instruction and is a viable technology for off-campus or distant education.
  2. Computer conferencing serves as a viable interactive component to video or instructional television courses

by providing individualized attention to student needs and requirements that cannot be obtained using traditional methods of audio and video feedback.

3. This technology facilitates writing across the curriculum and greatly improves student writing, editorial, and logical skills.

4. Online terminal mode activity is important for developing positive attitudes or connectivity with users' diversified electronic groups—both for computer phone online office hours and for asychronous terminal mode writing in conferences.

5. This technology, when used with video presentations of lectures, permits students to move faster than the televised segments. Where at first we used computer communications to augment and supplement video instruction, we now use video to supplement computer-communications-delivered instruction.

6. Students are able to master the basics of *VAX Notes* computer conferencing software in a single training/lab session and immediately begin communicating online. However, user-consultant assistance is required for troubleshooting during the first two weeks of instruction. The basics include: accessing server, entering user name and password, opening notes, reading topics and replies, writing a topic and writing a reply, leaving notes, and logging off the system.

7. The computer phone utility facilitates the development of asychronous conferencing skills, and is useful for online user-consultant assistance and electronic office hours.

8. A fully distributed, multimodality (e.g., multiapplication), multi-institutional communications environment served by a public communication network such as BESTNET provides a setting for institutions to not only learn from but to also model their own institutions after.

B. Pedagogical Benefits
1. Computer conferencing supports a Socratic method of instruction, whereby students are much more actively involved in the learning process rather than passive recipients.

2. This technology is particularly useful for facilitating group discussion and constructive criticism in virtually all areas of the curriculum.

3. The medium is viable for reaching culturally and linguistically diverse learners, and has been positively received by students.

4. Computer-naive students learn with facility equal to those more sophisticated with the technology.

5. Social science and humanities students having some word-processing skills learn and accept the technology at an level equivalent to students taking computer sciences courses (e.g., Pascal, C, and data structures courses).

6. Students adapt particularly well to the technology when interacting with students from distant locations and campuses.

7. Group reading of conference notes in a class promotes discussion with students on distant campuses and international locations.

8. Thinking textually is sufficient to improve literacy even when a liberal attitude is taken toward grammar, syntax, and spelling.

9. Writing skills improve with active participation in computer conferences.

C. Social Psychological Impact

1. Computer-mediated conferencing and supportive technologies (E-mail and computer phone) promote participation and learning in traditionally communicative apprehensive learners. This is especially the case with shy students, students whose first language is not English, and women who are not apt to verbally confront men. In each of the latter three categories, individuals willingly express themselves when interacting online.

2. This technology greatly augments student interaction and promotes attitudes that such learning is a legitimate and necessary part of the pedagogical process. In traditional classroom situations, students are often reluctant or not given the opportunity to interact with others except the instructors; computer communications as discussed here promote student-to-student interaction.

3. The anonymity of the technology promotes discussion that might otherwise be inhibited out of concern for student face-to-face negative feedback.

4. The anonymity of the medium is sufficient to promote critical discussion, and is as effective as anonymity of identity in conferences.

5. The connectivity of the medium promotes friendly attitudes toward those engaged in discussion, and promotes
   more critical than hostile competitive discussion.
6. Conferencing promotes stronger group attitudes and
   participation than E-mail distribution-list-organized
   conferences.

By the end of 1992, project BESTNET has as its primary
technological goals and objectives the creation of a fully functional computer-mediated conferencing system over a network
that is collaboratively integrated with other computer communication technologies, in the following ways:

1. Development of a multicampus information management system for computer conferences and other shared
   files on distributed notes that will allow for the remote
   systems management for multi-institutional computer
   conferences, course enrollments, expeditious translations of asynchronous computer conferences and interpretations of synchronous computer phone, and
   systems security (provide protection of Internet connections from unauthorized access using DECNET nodes)
2. Integrate VAX Notes into Internet/NSF-NET scientific,
   database library, regional supercomputers, and schol-
   arly services; development of system backup and conference libraries for an international and multi-
   institutional distributed university network
3. Automation of all features of notes for different kinds of
   course conferences—hide, search, send, etc.; continued
   development of hypertext for conference-management
   programs and integrating conference and other data
   bases across distributed nodes; integration of Videotext
   (VTX) for database access and interface with notes conferences; integration of collaborative technologies and
   compound document architecture into conferences
4. Establishment of a fully distributed media lab for experimenting with collaborative technologies and compound documents.

In order to create a fully distributed computer-conferencing
network, each BESTNET member institution will install the
same computer-conferencing-based information server on
their host computers. The servers will integrate computer con-

ferencing and electronic mail for asynchronous communication, computer phone for real time interaction, and VTX/videotext for accessing course material databases at different nodes. In addition, students will be provided with interactive videodisc materials developed by the Integrated Research Group at the University of California at Riverside and by Centro de Investigación Científica y Estudios Superiores en Ensenada, which will permit rapid search of a considerable amount of visual data. These resources will also be expanded upon by faculty participating in the project on each of our other university campuses.

Faculty at each BESTNET institution will teach online university credit courses in humanities and biological, natural, and social sciences at their local nodes. These course conferences will be open for students enrolled at all institutions. In this manner students interact with each other and other participating faculty across the eight institutions as a regular part of each class. They will do so by signing on to their local university VAX computers that are connected to Internet. The list of conferences that appear on their computer screens will be distributed among the participating institutions. However, students will enter any given conference from their local node and DECNET will interconnect to the distant node where it is housed. Thus, from the user's point of view the distributed network will appear seamless.

In addition to the conference, faculty will put scientific databases on the VAXes and make them available to other participating faculty and their students. These databases will be accessed using distributed VTX/videotext. When students and faculty log on to their local host, they will encounter a videotext front-end that gives them a choice between using computer conferencing, videotext, data bases, electronic mail, or computer phone (for synchronous interaction).

BESTNET is a research-based organization that grapples with electronic pedagogical behavior as it contributes to the in-class socioacademic achievement model presented by DeVillar and Faltis in this text. Our ability to achieve successful cultural diversity in the classroom has largely been a result of experimenting with the learning process in the electronic environment as it combines integration, communication, and cooperation in both the virtual and face-to-face classroom.

Technically, until this year BESTNET was not a computer communications network (e.g., BITNET, EIES, and Internet).

Rather, BESTNET was a paradigm for looking at how to conduct successful computer-mediated communications. Today, BESTNET is a select group of scholars and students networked over eight Micro Vax mainframes donated by Digital Equipment Corporation for the purpose of carrying out collaborative efforts ranging from team research (i.e., writing a book/paper/grant) to team-teaching classes between universities. In addition to having coordinated over forty existing special-interest groups, all performing research on pedagogy (in their areas of specialization) and/or the use of intermediate technologies, we have coordinated and continue to coordinate private networks (by invitation only) with similar purposes for the Fund for the Improvement of Postsecondary Education; the Lilly Endowment, Inc.; the Fulbright Scholars Program; the Latin American Scholarship Program affiliated with Harvard University; the Diversity Electronic Network at the University of Colorado, Boulder; the Kellogg Foundation; Indiana University–Purdue University at Indianapolis; and Digital Equipment Corporation.

References

Annenberg/CPB Project (1991). *New Pathways To A Degree*. A report on funded programs. Washington, D.C.

Arias, A. (forthcoming). *Virtual Interactions: Mediated Interactions and Everyday Life.*

Arias, A., and Bellman, B. (1993). Understanding Intermediate Technologies Research: The BESTNET Research Program. *The Journal of Sponsored Research* (forthcoming).

Arias, A., and Bellman, B. (1990). Computer-mediated classrooms for "Culturally and linguistically diverse learners. *Computers in the Schools*, 7 (1&2). Reprinted in *Language Minority Students and Computers*, eds. Faltis and DeVillar (1990: 227–243).

Arias, B., and Bellman, B. (1987a). BESTNET: International cooperation through interactive Spanish/English transition telecourses. *Technology and Learning*, 1(3), 6–8.

Blake, H., R. Saufley, O. Porter, and A. Melodia. (1990). The Challenge of Diversity. *Ethics in Higher Education*, W. May (ed.), McMillan Press.

Brand, S. (1988). *The Media Lab: Inventing the Future at M.I.T.* New York, NY: Penguin Books.

DeVillar, R. A. and C. J. Faltis (1991). *Computer and Cultural Diversity: Restructuring for School Success*. Albany, New York: State University of New York Press.

Feenberg, A. (1987). *The planetary classroom: International applications of advanced communications.* Unpublished manuscript, Western Behavioral Science Institute, Boulder, CO.

FIPSE Technology Study Group, including Arias, A. A. and Bellman, B. L. as collaborative authors (1988). *Ivory Towers, Silicon Basements: Learner-Centered Computing in Postsecondary Education.* Texas: Academic Computing Publications.

Galegher, R. E. (1990). *Intellectual Teamwork: The Social and Technological Foundations of Cooperative Work.* Lawrence Erlbaum Associates.

Harasim, L. (1986). Computer learning networks: Educational applications of computer conferencing. *Journal of Distance Education.*

Hickman, L. A. (1990). *Technology as a Human Affair.* New York, NY: McGraw-Hill.

Hiltz, S. R. (1984). *Online Communities: A Case Study of the Office of the Future.* Norwood, NJ: Ablex.

Johnson-Laird, P. N. (1988). *The Computer and the Mind: An Introduction to Cognitive Science.* Cambridge, MA: Harvard University Press.

Kaplan, A. (1989). Video interview conducted at the Western Behavioral Sciences Institute, La Jolla, CA.

Kaye, T. (1987). Introducing computer-mediated communication into a distance education system. *Canadian Journal of Educational Communications,* 16(1), 78–97.

Mason, R. and A. Kaye (1990). *Mindweave: Communication, Computers and Distance Education.* Elmsford, NY: Pergamon Press.

Scientific American. (1991). (Special Issue.) *Communications, Computers and Networks,* Vol. 265, no. 3.

Zimmerer, J. (1988). Computer conferencing: A medium for facilitating interaction in distance education. *Educational Media and Technology Yearbook,* 14.

▼ 15 ▼

The Socioacademic Achievement Model in the Context of Coercive and Collaborative Relations of Power

JIM CUMMINS

The socioacademic achievement model outlined by DeVillar and Faltis in this volume (Introduction) and in DeVillar and Faltis (1991) represents an extremely useful synthesis of research and theory relating to the educational development of culturally diverse students. The three key components of the model—*integration, communication,* and *cooperation*—provide a framework that helps elucidate the academic difficulties that many such students have experienced in racist and competitively oriented school systems and also points clearly to the modifications in educational structures and interactions that are required to reverse this pattern and attain equity in schooling outcomes.

My goal in this paper is to explore linkages between their model and other theoretical approaches that address similar issues. In particular, I want to explore how the dimensions of integration, communication, and cooperation relate to the ways that power is negotiated in both the *macrointeractions* between dominant and subordinated groups in the society at large and the *microinteractions* between educators and students in school settings. I have argued that students from subordinated groups are disempowered educationally in very much the same way that their communities are disempowered in their interactions with societal institutions. The converse of this is that these students will succeed educationally to the extent that the patterns of interaction in school reverse and challenge those that prevail in the society at large. The microinteractions between educators and students in school are strongly influenced by the ways in which educators define their roles in relation to societal power structures. When educators adopt role definitions that implicitly or explicitly accept the societal status quo, then their interactions with culturally diverse students are likely to reflect and reinforce the coercive relations of power that exist in the broader society. However, when educators adopt role definitions that challenge coercive relations of power, then their interactions with culturally diverse students will reflect a vision of society that strives to establish collaborative and equitable relations of power among groups.

I will suggest that the dimensions of integration, communication, and cooperation describe particular patterns of microinteractions between educators and students and reflect both educational structures and educator role definitions which, in turn, reflect the broader relations of power in the society at large. While relations of power (at both macro- and microinteractional levels) are not explicitly elaborated in the socioacademic model, I believe that these relations are clearly implied by the model. In a similar way, I believe that the model can profitably be extended at the level of microinteractions to take account of the fact that not only are knowledge and thinking abilities being negotiated within the *zone of proximal development* (ZPD) (Vygotsky 1978), student and educator identities are also being negotiated in these interactions. I will suggest that it is crucial to take account of the ways in which identities are negotiated in the interactions between educators and students, since considerable research suggests that the formation of identity is a crucial determinant of academic success for culturally diverse students (e.g. Fordham 1990).

I will suggest one additional extension to the socioacademic model as formulated by DeVillar and Faltis (1991, this volume). The model emphasizes the importance of particular kinds of interactions between educators and students as determinants of educational success. However, little is said about curriculum content as reflected in materials and textbooks nor about the development of critical thinking abilities required to deconstruct systematic disinformation used to bolster coercive relations of power. From the present perspective, content is not neutral with respect to the power relations between societal groups as played out both in school and in the broader society. Thus, both curricular content and critical inquiry are relevant to the academic success of culturally diverse students and should be incorporated explicitly into any framework that aspires to account for patterns of school success and failure.

In summary, the present paper attempts to elaborate the dimensions of the socioacademic model to take account of (a) the relevance of societal power relations to the educational development of culturally diverse students, (b) the crucial role that negotiation of identity between educators and students plays in student success, and (c) the importance of curriculum content and the promotion of critical inquiry, in addition to the interactional processes of integration, communication, and cooperation, in determining success or failure for culturally diverse students.

In the next section, I present a general framework for exploring these issues and try to outline how the socioacademic dimensions relate to both the macro- and microinteractions that culturally diverse students and communities experience.

A Framework for Integrating Socioacademic Development with Societal Power Relations

In the proposed framework, macrointeractions between subordinated communities and societal institutions established and controlled by the dominant group, represent a primary determinant of school success or failure for culturally diverse students. These macrointeractions give rise to particular forms of educational structures that are designed to reproduce the relations of power in the broader society. They also influence the ways in which educators define their roles in relation to culturally diverse students and communities; in other words, they influence the mindset of assumptions and expectations that educators bring to the task of educating students. The microinteractions between educators and students constitute the most immediate determinant of student academic success or failure, and these microinteractions are a function of the role definitions that educators assume and the educational structures within which they operate. These microinteractions can be described in relation to DeVillar and Faltis's dimensions of integration, communication, and cooperation, which determine the shape or boundaries of the zone of proximal development (ZPD). Not only are knowledge and thinking abilities generated within the ZPD but student and teacher identities are also actively negotiated in the interpersonal space that the ZPD forms. At a general level, the patterns of macro- and microinteractions can be described in terms of the extent to which they reflect and contribute to either coercive or collaborative relations of power. Each of these components of the framework is considered in more detail below.

Coercive and Collaborative Relations of Power

Coercive relations of power refer to the exercise of power by a dominant group (or individual) to the detriment of a subordinated group (or individual). The assumption is that there is a fixed quantity of power that operates according to a balance effect; in other words, the more power one group has, the less is left for other groups. Coercive relations of power have constituted the predominant mode of intergroup contact since the beginnings of human history, at the level of both international and domestic relations.

Collaborative relations of power, on the other hand, operate on the assumption that power is not a fixed predetermined quantity but rather can be *generated* in interpersonal and intergroup relations, thereby becoming "additive" rather than "subtractive." In other words, participants in the relationship are *empowered* through their collaboration such that each is more affirmed in her or his identity and has a greater sense of efficacy to effect change in their lives or social situations. Thus, power is created in the relationship and shared among participants.

A fundamental assumption of the present chapter (and, I believe, of the socioacademic model) is that real change in the education of culturally diverse students is likely to occur only when competitive and coercive social structures shift towards cooperative ones. The history of humanity does not augur well for the imminence of such a paradigm shift, but environmental and social deterioration has reached a point where there may be little alternative if our species is to survive. The reality is that in the world of winners and losers, the "winner" ultimately joins the loser. Witness how the overdeveloped world is threatened by the destruction of the rainforests in the developing countries; or how poverty in the inner cities impacts on the wealthier sectors of society through increased crime, drugs, or costs associated with incarceration or on upgrading of literacy levels. The challenge is to change the structure of power relations such that they become additive through collaboration rather than subtractive through coercion; in other words, the structure of macro- and microinteractions needs to shift so that these interactions generate power for all participants rather than increase the disparities of power.

The operation of coercive and collaborative relations of power is manifest in intimate personal relationships (Laing 1969), as it is in international relations (Chomsky 1987). In educational contexts, the benefits of collaborative relations of power are clearly seen in the outcomes of cooperative learning activities in classroom or teacher training activities (Johnson and Johnson, this volume; Calderón, this volume). Reciprocal or additive empowerment is also very clearly an outcome of the sister class networks documented by Sayers (this volume).

In short, a shift from coercive to collaborative relations of power between dominant and subordinated groups has the potential to empower both groups, whereas coercive relations of power will, in the long term, result in disempowerment of both. This implies that the continuation of structures that create educational failure and impoverishment among subordinated groups will disempower not only the subordinated group but also the dominant group. The dominant group increasingly needs to invest in social and physical structures (e.g., prisons) to protect itself from what it has created through the exercise of coercive relations of power. The riots in Los Angeles in the spring of 1992 vividly illustrate the mutually destructive potential of long-term coercive relations of power.

Social and fiscal policy in the United States during the 1980s represented a dramatic escalation of coercive relations of power (see Barlett and Steele 1992; Hodgkinson 1991). This is clearly illustrated in some of the data presented by Hodgkinson:

- 23 percent of preschool children (birth to age 5) in the United States live in poverty, the highest rate of any industrialized nation
- About 350,000 children annually are born to mothers who were addicted to cocaine during pregnancy
- The United States ranked 22d in global rankings for infant mortality, with a rate of 10 deaths per 1,000 live births (1988 statistics)
- The number of reports of child abuse or neglect received annually by child protection agencies tripled between 1976 and 1987 to 2.2. million

- Young males in the United States are five times as likely to be murdered as are their counterparts in other nations
- A Black male in the United States was about five times as likely to be in prison as a Black male in South Africa (1988 statistics)
- More than 80 percent of America's one million prisoners are high school drop-outs, and each prisoner costs taxpayers upwards of $20,000 a year

Hodgkinson points out that while America's best students are on a par with the world's best, "ours is undoubtedly the worst 'bottom third' of any of the industrialized democracies." He summarizes the situation as follows: "about one-third of preschool children are destined for school failure because of poverty, neglect, sickness, handicapping conditions, and lack of adult protection and nurturance. There is no point in trying to teach hungry or sick children" (1991: 10). He goes on to point to the strong correlations among educational levels, income, and crime reduction. He notes, for example, that "every dollar spent on a Head Start child will save taxpayers $7 in later services that the child will not need" (p. 15) (see Schweinhart, Weikart, and Larney 1986). Despite the fact that education is a far better public investment than prisons, the level of K–12 educational expenditures of the United States is considerably lower than that of other industrialized countries (4.1 percent of gross domestic product compared to a non-United States average of 4.6 percent).

In summary, the policies of government and business have significantly increased the gap between the wealthy and impoverished in the United States during the 1980s, thereby contributing directly to the numbers of students who experience educational failure and drop out of school prematurely. The costs of more adequate social and economic programs designed to combat poverty and educational failure are usually viewed as "prohibitive" by the same politicians who, with minimal dissent or even debate, bailed out $157 billion of taxpayers' money to "resolve" the Savings and Loan scandal (Waldman 1990) and whose trillions of dollars of wasted military expenditures never required justification. This escalation of coercive relations of power has reached a point of diminishing returns for the economically dominant group in the sense that the costs of maintaining the status quo (e.g., the need to incarcerate more and more people) have outstripped the costs of shifting to a more collaborative sharing of power through investment in education and social programs.

Macro-Interactions between Dominant and Subordinated Groups

The long-term effects of coercive relations of power are evident in the educational performance of groups that have been subordinated in the wider society over generations. Several theorists (e.g., Cummins 1989; Ogbu 1978) have pointed to the fact that minority groups that fail academically tend to be characterized by a sense of ambivalence about the value of their cultural identity and powerlessness in relation to the dominant group. This is what Ogbu refers to as "castelike" status, and its educational effects are strikingly evident in many situations where formerly subjugated or colonized groups are still in a subordinated relationship to the dominant group.

The rules of the social mobility (or educational achievement) game reflect the status of subordinated groups as "internal colonies" (Blauner 1969). Dominant-group institutions and representatives of those institutions (e.g., teachers) require that subordinated groups deny their cultural identity as a necessary condition for success in the "mainstream" society where the gatekeepers are invariably representatives of the dominant group or, at lower levels, compliant subordinated-group members who have accepted the rules of the game. Many students resist this process of subordination through "disruptive" behaviour, often culminating in dropping out of school (Fordham 1990; Willis 1977). Others modify their cultural identity by "acting white" (Fordham 1990), often buying educational success at the expense of rejection by their peers and ambivalence about their identity. Still others are never given the opportunity in school to gain either academic confidence or pride in identity and, over time, internalize the negative attributions of the dominant group and live down to their teachers' expectations.

The phenomenon of "internal colonies" is exemplified by the fact that the three groups in the United States context that experience the most pronounced educational difficulty (African-American, Latino/Latina, and Native-American students) have each been subordinated for centuries by the dominant group. Similar patterns exist in Scandinavia, where Finnish minority students in Sweden are reported to experience severe academic difficulties, a phenomenon not unrelated to the fact that Finland was colonized by Sweden for several hundred years (Skutnabb-Kangas 1984).

Similarly, within the Canadian context, aboriginal and minority francophone students have experienced long-term devaluation of their cultural identity and languages both in the school and in wider society. In Ontario, for example, Regulation 17, passed in 1912, eliminated for more than 50 years the possibility for francophones to be educated in their own language. Ambivalence in regard to cultural identity still emerges in debates about the proportion of French that should be included in French-language schools. Wagner and Grenier (1991), for example, point out that in a context of societal oppression, education is often devalued, and this can persist even when the minority controls its own schools.

> It can happen that the minority group devalues its own schools or refuses to have them because the group is ashamed of itself and its culture as a result of internalizing the critical or scornful views of the majority group. The fiercest adversaries of the "French school" in Saskatchewan are francophones themselves. (p. 41, my translation).

This feeling of insecurity and sometimes even shame in regard to one's own cultural identity is strikingly apparent among minority groups around the world that experience persistent school failure and marginal levels of literacy (for reviews see Ogbu 1978; Cummins 1989). The ambivalence about identity results from internalizing the negative attributions of the dominant group at both the macro- and microinteractional level. When students enter school, the pattern of macrointeractions in the broader society is usually reflected and reinforced in the microinteractions they experience with educators. Students are rendered "voiceless" (Giroux 1991) or silenced (Fine 1987; Walsh 1991) in very much the same way that their communities have been disempowered (often for centuries) through their macrointeractions with societal institutions. The converse of this proposition is that students from communities that have historically been subordinated will succeed educationally and amplify their "voice" or their expression of personal identity to the extent that the microinteractions in school reverse the macrointeractions that prevail in the society at large. The ways in which educators attempt to orchestrate the pattern of interactions with students will reflect the role definitions that they have assumed with respect to societal power relations.

Resistance to the pattern of macrointeractions in the society may require educators to challenge educational structures operative in their schools or school systems, since many forms of educational structures are designed to place limits on the extent to which the microinteractions can deviate from the established pattern of macrointeractions.

Educational Structures

Educational structures refer to the organization of schooling in a broad sense that includes policies, programs, curriculum, and assessment. This organization is established to achieve the goals of education as defined by the dominant group in the society. For example, the historical patterns of educational apartheid in the United States, South Africa, and many other countries were designed to limit the opportunities that subordinated groups might have for educational and social advancement. As documented by Kozol (1991) for African-American students and by Berman et al. (1992) for recent immigrants, similar patterns of segregation still characterize the education of many subordinated groups (see Skutnabb-Kangas 1984 for a discussion of similar phenomena in the European context). Olsen and Minicucci (1992) discuss the implications of the Berman et al. (1992) findings with respect to the degree of integration/segregation of culturally diverse students in twenty-seven California secondary schools:

> On an integration/segregation continuum, the majority of the schools in our study are moving increasingly towards the use of sheltered English classes with a resultant formal curricular separation of limited English proficient students. Despite calling the LEP program "transitional," and despite recurring and persistent rhetoric about preparing the students to enter the mainstream, the evidence appears to run contrary to an integration orientation. LEP students are tracked into separate classes, spend the great percentage of the school day in these LEP classes, and appear to rarely be reclassified into the mainstream. Thus, it appears that through the use of English as a language of instruction students are being channelled away from their native language and culture, and they are simultaneously also being kept separate from their En-

glish speaking peers and denied access to the track which houses mainstream English speaking students. We would conclude from our small sample that secondary school LEP programs are thus segregatory. (1992: 18).

Other examples of educational structures that might systematically discriminate against culturally diverse students are:

- The medical model of special education that uncritically locates the source of academic difficulties within students rather than within the pattern of interactions that students experience in school (see Cummins 1984, 1989)
- Ability grouping and tracking practices that deny students in low-ability groups access to quality instruction (Oakes 1985)
- The use of culturally and linguistically biased IQ tests to give culturally diverse students a one-way ticket to special education or low-track programs (see Cummins 1984)
- Teacher education institutions that continue to treat issues related to culturally diverse students as marginal and that send new teachers into the classroom with minimal information regarding patterns of language and emotional development among such students and few pedagogical strategies for helping students learn (see Henley and Young 1989)
- Curriculum that reflects only the experiences and values of middle-class English-speaking students and effectively suppresses the experiences and values of culturally diverse students
- The absence from most schools of professionals capable of communicating in the languages of culturally diverse students and their parents; such professionals could assist in such functions as primary language instruction, primary language assessment for purposes of placement and intervention, and parent/school liaison
- Criteria for promotion to positions of responsibility (e.g., principals) that take no account of the individual's experience with or potential for leadership in the education of culturally diverse students

These educational structures constitute a frame that sets limits on the kinds of microinteractions that are likely to occur between educators and students. The macrointeractions and educational structures also influence but do not completely determine the ways in which educators define their roles in relation to culturally diverse students and communities.

Educator Role Definitions

The notion of *educator role definitions* has been proposed as a central explanatory construct in the "empowerment framework" elaborated in Cummins (1989). This framework argued that culturally-diverse students

> are "empowered" or "disabled" as a direct result of their interactions with educators in the schools. These interactions are mediated by the implicit or explicit role definitions that educators assume in relation to four institutional characteristics of schools. These characteristics reflect the extent to which:
> 1. minority students' language and culture are incorporated into the school program;
> 2. minority community participation is encouraged as an integral component of children's education;
> 3. the pedagogy promotes intrinsic motivation on the part of students to use language actively in order to generate their own knowledge; and
> 4. professionals involved in assessment become advocates for minority students by focusing primarily on the ways in which students' academic difficulty is a function of interactions within the school context rather than legitimizing the location of the "problem" within students (1989: 58)

These four dimensions—namely, language/culture incorporation, community participation, pedagogy, and assessment—represent sets of educational structures that will affect, but can also be influenced by, educators' role definitions.

Thus, the construct of *educator role definition* refers to the mindset of assumptions, expectations, and goals that educators bring to the task of educating culturally diverse students. The role definitions adopted by educators will determine the ways in which they attempt to orchestrate patterns of microinteractions with students in the school context. These microinteractions are also limited by the educational structures that are in place at national and local levels. For example, the requirement to administer standardized achievement tests that do not reflect teachers' curriculum objectives (e.g., appreciation of literature, creative writing, critical thinking, etc.) may inhibit teachers' pursuit of these objectives. In other cases, the contradiction between the test and the educational objectives will provoke educators to actively challenge the assessment structure.[1]

The ways in which educators define their roles will also be influenced by patterns of dominant/subordinated macrointeractions. For example, attitudes towards cultural diversity in the broader society and the reflections of these attitudes in the media (e.g., "immigrants are taking our jobs") are likely to influence the orientation of many teachers towards teaching culturally diverse students. Negative societal attitudes may also be reinforced through discriminatory structures in the school. For example, culturally diverse students may perform more poorly on biased IQ and achievement measures, thereby reinforcing prior expectations of some educators regarding these students' inherent inferiority. Failure to address issues related to cultural diversity in preservice or inservice courses also represents a set of structures that reflect broader societal priorities and are likely to influence educator role definitions.

However, educators, both individually and collectively, have opportunities to become aware of patterns of disinformation and of the effects of discriminatory structures and thus to challenge the process of "manufacturing consent" (Chomsky 1987) within the educational system. There are many examples of this process of challenging racist educational practices and structures (e.g., Ada 1988b; Lindholm, this volume; Shannon 1989). Thus, while educational structures will tend to influence the ways in which educators define their roles, educator role definitions can also affect specific educational structures, at least in local contexts.

Similarly, students and communities have the possibility to actively resist the operation of the societal power structure as it is manifested in educational settings (see, e.g., Skutnabb-Kangas 1988). While for some students resistance may contribute to academic development (see Zanger, in press), in many situations resistance has severe costs with respect to academic success and upward mobility (e.g., Fordham 1990; Willis 1977).

In short, the ways in which educators define their roles with respect to culturally diverse students and communities will strongly influence the kinds of microinteractions they engage in with students, which, in turn, will constrict or expand students' options for identity formation and knowledge generation. The individual and collective role definitions of educators occupy a central place in mediating, and potentially transforming, the relation between the macro- and microinteractions that culturally diverse students and communities experience. When educators define their roles in such a way that the division of resources and power in the society is not problematized or called into question in any way, then their microinteractions with students will simply reproduce the coercive relations of power in the broader society. However, when educators define their roles in terms of promoting social justice and equality of opportunity, then their microinteractions with culturally diverse students will embody a transformative potential by challenging coercive relations of power as they are manifested in the school context.

In general, the framework explicitly posits that all participants (e.g. students, communities, and educators) in micro- and macrointeractions have the potential to resist and challenge coercive relations of power and to transform these into collaborative relations of power, thereby undermining oppressive structures. The microinteractions between educators and students not only reflect the relations of culture and power in the society, they *constitute* these relations and thereby embody a transformative potential.

Microinteractions and the Zone of Proximal Development

The micro-interactions between educators and students can be described in terms of the degree of integration/segregation, communication/silencing, and cooperation/competition that they embody. According to DeVillar and Faltis (1991, this volume) in culturally diverse educational contexts, individual student success is directly related to the social interaction activities that students experience during the learning process. The academic success of culturally diverse students will be maximized when they have opportunities to develop and exchange ideas through active use of language in cooperative and socially integrated settings. The overwhelming predominance of teacher-centered whole-classroom learning environments in U.S. schools and the presistence of segregated school environments (Kozol 1991; Olsen and Minicucci 1992) means that culturally diverse students typically are denied access to communication with their teachers and peers; in Fine's (1987) terms, they are silenced. The orientation of microinteractions in U.S. schools towards segregation, silencing, and competition represents the combined effect of particular educator role definitions and educational structures, both of which reflect coercive relations of power in the broader society.

The microinteractions between educators and students form a zone of proximal development (ZPD) in which possibilities for the generation of knowledge and formation of identity are negotiated. Vygotsky viewed the ZPD as the distance between children's developmental level as determined by individual problem solving without adult guidance and the level of potential development as determined by children's problem solving under the influence of, or in collaboration with, more capable adults or peers. Expressed simply, the ZPD is the interpersonal space where minds meet and new understandings can arise through collaborative interaction and inquiry. Newman, Griffin, and Cole (1989) label this interpersonal space *the construction zone*. Moll (1989: 59) points out that central to Vygotsky's notion of the ZPD are "the specific ways that adults (or peers) socially mediate or interactionally create circumstances for learning," and he emphasizes that the child is not passive but "an active organism helping create the very circumstances for his or her own learning." In other words, the ZPD is actively constituted by both students and educators.

The present chapter argues that in addition to mediating the learning process, the interactions within the ZPD script an image of the envisaged relations of culture and power within the society. The microinteractions that constitute the ZPD can either reinforce or challenge particular educational structures within the school or school system and by implication the power structure in the wider society.

The historical pattern of dominant/subordinated group interactions has been one where educators have constricted the ZPD in an attempt to sanitize deviant cultural identities. For educators to become partners in the transmission of "knowledge," culturally diverse students were required to acquiesce in the subordination of their identities and to celebrate as "truth" the "cultural literacy" of the dominant group. The constriction of the ZPD by educators reflected a process whereby they defined their role as "civilizing," "saving," "assimilating," or "educating" students whose culture and values they viewed as inherently deficient. Through this exercise of coercive power they reproduced the pattern of societal macrointeractions and limited students' possibilities to define and interpret their own realities and identities.

One of the most blatant and criminal examples of this process concerns the treatment of aboriginal students in residential schools in North America. The following account (from the *Globe & Mail,* Canada's most widely circulated newspaper), illustrates how identities have been negotiated on very unequal terms in such schools. While this kind of sexual, physical, and psychological abuse no longer occurs in the same overt manner, the example illustrates a broader process of identity negotiation that continues to operate between educators and culturally diverse students in all schools.

> A representative of four British Columbia native bands said yesterday that they intend to call churches and governments to account—morally and financially—for the damage done to their communities through the religious residential school system. . . . [T]he council of four Shuswap Indian bands decided to mount the conference after the community started to conquer widespread alcoholism and social problems in recent years and realized that the self-destructive behaviour had been masking the pain of the residential school experience.
>
> Most children in the bands were forced to attend the St. Joseph's Mission, a residential school operated by the Roman Catholic Oblate order, until it was closed 10 years ago. Two former officials of the school have been convicted of sexually abusing male students, and its former principal, Bishop Hugh O'Connor of Prince George, is scheduled to go to a preliminary hearing next month on charges of abusing female students. . . .
>
> Bev Sellars, chief of the Soda Creek Indian band of the Cariboo region, said aside from incidents of sexual abuse, residential school children were brutally strapped, sometimes "until they were black and blue" and permanently scarred. She said they were treated "like dirt" and made to feel like "part of a weak, defective race." "That to me is not training for success, it is training for self-destruction," she said. "And thousands did self-destruct. If they didn't commit suicide, they became addicted to anything that could numb or distract the pain, and the addictions unfortunately only became another thing to be ashamed of." (Wilson 1991: A4)

A psychologist, Roland Chrisjohn from the University of Guelph, reported on extensive interviews he had carried out with 187 individuals from the bands, two-thirds of whom had attended residential schools. He found that residential school students were subjected to far more verbal and physical mistreatment than students at nonresidential schools. Those who had attended residential schools said they felt the experience had affected their sexual relations, their ability as parents, their feelings about religion and non-Indians, and their use of alcohol. In addition, those whose fathers had attended residential school said their fathers were stricter and less affectionate with their children, and more frequently beat their wives (Wilson 1991).

The volume of consistent reports from across Canada would indicate that this process of destruction of identity was the norm rather than the exception in residential schools. It is not unreasonable to suggest that a central goal of such schools was to prepare children of subordinated groups for their status in life by rekindling shame from one generation to the next.

The process of identity negotiation in schools is a reciprocal one between educators and students. For example, in the case of aboriginal students in residential schools, for educators to define their role as dispensers of "salvation" and "civilization," aboriginal students had to be defined as "heathen" and "savage." The same process is interwoven into all educator-student interactions and is usually nonproblematic when there is a cultural and class match between educator and student, but often highly problematic when there is a cultural and class mismatch (see, for example, Fordham 1990).

A second example further illustrates the relationship between academic success and identity negotiation in the school context. Isidro Lucas (1981), in describing a research study he carried out in the early 1970s with Puerto Rican students in Chicago to explore the reasons for student dropout, highlighted issues related to identity as more critical for student success or failure than proficiency in English. Although he prepared questionnaires in both Spanish and English, he never had to use the Spanish version. The reason was that

All my dropout respondents spoke good understandable English. They hadn't learned math, or social sciences, or natural sciences, unfortunately. But they had learned English. . . . No dropout mentioned lack of English as the reason for quitting. As it evolved through questionnaires and interviews, theirs was a more subtle story—of alienation, of not belonging, of being "push-outs." . . . To my surprise, dropouts expressed more confidence in their ability to speak English than did the stay-ins (seniors in high school). For their part, stay-ins showed more confidence in their Spanish than did dropouts. . . . I had to conclude that identity, expressed in one's confidence and acceptance of the native culture, was more a determinant of school stay-in power than the mere acquisition of the coding-decoding skills involved in a different language, English." (p. 19)

Zanger (in press) has also described very clearly the dynamics of identity negotiation from the perspective of Latino/Latina high school students. Students see very clearly the ways in which teachers and peers ignore their contributions and attempt to define them as inferior. In the words of one student describing what happens to many of her Spanish-speaking peers:

They just feel left out, they feel like if no one loves them, no one cares, so why should they care? No one wants to hear what they have to say, so they don't say anything." (Zanger, in press: 13 [ms])

It is clear from the examples cited by Zanger that the process of identity negotiation is closely tied to academic success. Although the students interviewed by Zanger managed to develop academically despite devaluation of identity by teachers and peers, they represent a minority. One gets the impression that their insights into the process of identity devaluation to which they were being subjected was an important factor in helping them resist the devaluation without sacrificing academic development. In fact, it is possible that for these students, academic development represented a form of resistance, a way of refusing to live down to their teachers' expectations.

A starting point in constructing an alternative interactional process is to recognize that educator–student interactions constitute a process of negotiating identities. Through our interactions with students (and colleagues) we are constantly sketching an image not just of our own identities and those we envisage for our students, but also of the society we hope our students will form. Our actions and interactions reflect our identities and also contribute to their formation. This implies that identity is not a static and fixed construct but rather encompasses multiple facets striving toward integration. Identity is constantly being shaped through experiences and interactions, and different aspects of identity find differential possibilities for expression depending on the institutional and interpersonal context (Laing 1969; Simon 1987; Walsh 1991).

In short, the ZPD represents a useful metaphor for describing the dual process of reciprocal negotiation of identity and collaborative generation of knowledge. Educators whose role definition encompasses challenging discriminatory institutional structures will attempt to create conditions for interaction that expand students' possibilities for identity formation and critical inquiry (knowledge generation). Rather than constricting the ZPD such that students' voices are silenced, educators who adopt this type of role definition will attempt initially to constitute the ZPD in such a way that students' voices can be expressed, shared, and amplified within the interactional process. Under these conditions, the ZPD will then be co-constructed by students and educators as, through their interactions, they script their own identities and that of the society they envisage.

The relevance of the socioacademic dimensions of integration, communication, and cooperation to this account of identity negotiation within the ZPD is obvious. Very different possibilities for identity formation (as well as knowledge generation) are afforded to culturally diverse students when they are in learning contexts where expression of their experience is encouraged and their contributions to cooperative projects are valued, in contrast to learning contexts where their experience and expression of self are suppressed and their only role is the internalization of inert information.

The present framework extends the scope of Vygotskian learning theory (and the socioacademic model) to the negotiation of identity, which is regarded as equally or more important for the academic achievement of culturally diverse students as the development of thinking. According to Vygotskian learning theory, interaction within the ZPD is designed to lead students from other-regulated (interpsychological) to self-regulated (intrapsychological) learning and thinking, or in DeVillar and Faltis's terms "the goal of interaction within the zone is to enable the child, through guided verbal exchange of ideas, to take on the role of knower" (1991: 12). In a similar way, I am suggesting that an equally significant goal of interaction within the zone is to enable students to use language actively to express, share and collaboratively interpret their experience, thereby defining their identities. The defining of self (identity) moves from other-regulated to self-regulated as students progressively develop self-respect and confidence as a result of their interactions with educators and peers.

The socioacademic framework is also extended by arguing that the interactional dynamics that constitute the ZPD are always either reinforcing of, or oppositional to, the pattern of coercive power relations between dominant and subordinated groups in the wider society. In other words, educator/student microinteractions always reflect an image of society and of the roles that educators envisage for culturally diverse students within that society. Interactions within the ZPD that are mutually empowering are, by definition, oppositional to coercive relations of power in the wider society.

As outlined above, one additional aspect of the socioacademic framework that might be elaborated more extensively is the relevance of curricular content and critical inquiry for the academic success of culturally diverse students. The argument elaborated in the next section is that the processes of integration, communication and cooperation must be oriented towards critical inquiry on issues relevant to societal power relations if they are to address fully the roots of culturally diverse students' academic difficulty.

Curricular Content and Critical Inquiry

Curricular content and its mode of presentation represents one aspect of the way education is structured. In the not-so-distant past, much of the curriculum in North American schools was unashamedly Eurocentric and in many cases explicitly racist. Analyses of curricular accounts of Columbus' "discovery" of America (e.g., Bigelow 1991) show very clearly how such accounts legitimate genocide and the continuation of coercive relations of power. Particular conceptions of dominant and subordinated group identity are reinforced in curricular materials which present the dominant group version of "truth" and "cultural literacy" (Hirsch 1987). The predominant transmission model of instruction (DeVillar and Faltis, this volume) in North American schools ensures that the lies of official histories are celebrated rather than critically analyzed.

The framework elaborates the dimensions of educator role definitions and educational structures previously discussed in order to highlight the importance of collaborative critical inquiry for both knowledge generation and identity formation. Conservative approaches to education that are reflected in much of the current focus on "educational reform" in North America tend to combine a transmission orientation to pedagogy with a social control orientation to curricular topics and student outcomes. The patterns of classroom interaction and their social implications are similar to those described by Sirotnik (1983) in discussing the predominant transmission orientation evident in Goodlad's (1984) major study of American classrooms (see DeVillar and Faltis, this volume). Sirotnik argues that the predominance of total-class instructional configurations in virtually affectless environments suggests that "we are implicitly teaching dependence upon authority, linear thinking, social apathy, passive involvement and hands-off learning" (1983: 29).

Within a transmission orientation to pedagogy, task analysis is typically used to break language down to its component parts (e.g. phonics, vocabulary, grammatical rules) and transmit these parts in isolation from each other. Knowledge is viewed as static or inert, to be internalized and re-produced when required. Approaches to learning associated with a transmission orientation reflect these views of language and knowledge in that learning is assumed to progress in a hierarchical manner from simple content to complex.

By contrast, within a critical pedagogical orientation, educators encourage the development of student voice through critical reflection on experiential and social issues. Language and meaning are viewed as inseparable and knowledge is seen as a catalyst for further inquiry and action. This is consistent with a Vygotskian view of learning that emphasizes the centrality of the ZPD, where knowledge is generated through collaborative interaction and critical inquiry. Language use and interaction in the classroom reflect and elaborate on students' experience and are focused on *generating* knowledge rather than on the transmission and consumption of socially sanitized information more typical of most North American classrooms.

With respect to social outcomes of schooling and ways of achieving these outcomes, conservative approaches aim to (re)produce compliant and uncritical students and, to this end, they ensure that all curricular content that might challenge the view of reality favored by the societal power structure is expunged. By contrast, critical educators are focused on creating conditions that open possibilities for student empowerment and transformation of oppressive social structures. Thus, they attempt to select curricular topics that relate directly to societal power relations and encourage students to analyze these topics/issues from multiple perspectives.[2]

As one example of the very different pedagogical implications of conservative versus critical approaches, consider the ways in which the issue of Columbus' "discovery" of America might be treated. Traditional curricula have celebrated Columbus as a hero whose arrival brought "civilization" and "salvation" to the indigenous population. In fact, as Bigelow (1991) points out, few North American texts mention that Columbus initiated the slave trade and cut off the hands of any indigenous people who failed to bring him sufficient gold. The "discovery" of America resulted within a few years in the genocide of the indigenous populations in the islands where Spanish rule was established. Critical educators would encourage students to explore the reality omitted form the sanitized accounts in traditional texts, critically inquire as to why the texts present the type of picture they do and ask what the parallels are with current issues relating to power in our society. They would also explore the possibilities for taking action in relation to the issues raised through critical inquiry, as outlined by Bigelow.

One framework that elaborates a critical literacy approach to the education of culturally diverse students is presented by Ada (1988a, 1988b) on the basis of Paulo Freire's work. Ada's framework outlines how zones of proximal development can be created that encourage culturally diverse students to share and amplify their experience within a collaborative process of critical inquiry. She distinguishes four phases in what she terms "the creative reading act."[3] Each of the phases distinguished by Ada is characterized by an interactional process (either between the teacher and students or among peers) that progressively opens up possibilities for the articulation and amplification of student voice. The "texts" that are the focus of the interaction can derive from any curricular area or from newspapers or current events. The process is equally applicable to students at any grade level. Ada (1988a: 103) stresses that although the phases are discussed separately, "in a creative reading act they may happen concurrently and be interwoven."

- *Descriptive Phase.* In this phase the focus of interaction is on the information contained in the text. Typical questions at this level might be: Where, when, how did it happen? Who did it? Why? These are the type of questions for which answers can be found in the text itself. Ada points out that these are the usual reading comprehension questions and that "a discussion that stays at this level suggests that reading is a passive, receptive, and in a sense, domesticating process" (1988a: 104). When the process is arrested at this level, the focus remains on internalization of inert information and/or the practice of "reading skills" in an experiential and motivational vacuum.

- *Personal Interpretive Phase.* After the basic information in the text has been discussed, students are encouraged to relate it to their own experiences and feelings. Questions that might be asked by the teacher at this phase are: Have you ever seen (felt, experienced) something like this? Have you ever wanted something similar? How did what you read make you feel? Did you like it? Did it make you happy? Frighten you? What about your family? Ada (1988a) points out that this process helps develop children's self-esteem by showing that their experiences and feelings are valued by the teacher and classmates. It also helps children understand that "true learning occurs only when the information received is analyzed in the light of one's own experiences and emotions" (104). An atmosphere of acceptance and trust in the classroom is a prerequisite for students (and teachers) to risk sharing their feelings, emotions, and experiences. It is clear how this process of sharing and critically reflecting on their own and other students' experiences opens up identity options for culturally diverse students that are typically suppressed within a transmission approach to pedagogy where the interpretation of texts is nonnegotiable and reflective of the dominant group's notions of cultural literacy. The personal interpretive phase deepens students' comprehension of the text or issues by grounding the knowledge in the personal and collective narratives that make up their histories.

- *Critical Analysis Phase.* After children have compared and contrasted what is presented in the text with their personal experiences, they are ready to engage in a more abstract process of critically analyzing the issues or problems that are raised in the text. This process involves drawing inferences and exploring what generalizations can be made. Appropriate questions might be: Is it valid? Always? When? Does it benefit everyone alike? Are there any alternatives to this situation? Would people of different cultures (classes, genders) have acted differently? How? Why? Ada emphasizes that school children of all ages can engage in this type of critical process, although the analysis will always reflect children's experiences and level of maturity. This phase further extends students' comprehension of the text or issues by encouraging them to examine both the internal logical coherence of the information or propositions and their consistency with other knowledge or perspectives. When students pursue guided research and critical reflection, they are clearly engaged in a process of knowledge generation; however, they are equally engaged in a process of self-definition; as they gain the power to think through issues that affect their lives, they simultaneously gain the power to resist external definitions of who they are and to deconstruct the sociopolitical purposes of such external definitions.

• *Creative Action Phase.* This is a stage translating the results of the previous phases into concrete action. The dialogue is oriented towards discovering what changes individuals can make to improve their lives or resolve the problem that has been presented. Let us suppose that students have been researching (in the local newspaper, in periodicals such as *National Geographic*, the Greenpeace magazine, etc.) problems relating to environmental pollution. After relating the issues to their own experience, critically analyzing causes and possible solutions, they might decide to write letters to congressional representatives or members of parliament, highlight the issue in their class/school newsletter in order to sensitize other students, write and circulate a petition in the neighborhood, write and perform a play that analyzes the issue, etc. Once again, this phase can be seen as extending the process of comprehension insofar as when we act to transform aspects of our social realities we gain a deeper understanding of those realities.

The processes described in Ada's framework are clearly compatible with the socioacademic model and with Vygotskian approaches to learning. A context (or ZPD) is created where students can voice their experience, meaningful and socially relevant content is integrated with active use of language in written and oral modalities, and students are challenged to use their developing language skills for higher-order thinking.

There is also a clear relationship with the *experience-text-relationship* (ETR) method (Au 1979, cited in DeVillar and Faltis 1991) insofar as each scheme focuses on relating culturally diverse students' experiences to the text. The ETR scheme makes the valid point that it is often useful to elicit students' experience prior to engaging in reading the text but it fails to highlight the importance of critical inquiry or creative action which are central to Ada's scheme.

Conclusion

I have argued that while the socioacademic model highlights a core set of dimensions critical to restructuring schools for promoting the academic success of culturally diverse students, it can usefully be extended to make explicit some of the relationships that are implied by the dimensions of *integration, communication,* and *cooperation.* In particular, the model implies (but does not make explicit) that the microinteractions between educators and students must challenge the pattern of coercive power relations in the wider society and strive towards establishing collaborative relations of power if culturally diverse students are to succeed in school.

I have also suggested that these microinteractions within the ZPD constitute a process of negotiating identities in addition to generation of knowledge. The social construction of both knowledge and identity is jointly constituted by students and educators within the zone of proximal development. The ways in which educators define their roles with respect to culturally diverse students and communities will determine the extent to which they constrict the ZPD to limit students' possibilities for identity development and knowledge generation or, alternatively, expand the ZPD to ground the curriculum in students' experiences such that a much broader range of possibilities for identity formation and knowledge generation are available to students.

Finally, I have suggested that curricular content is not neutral with respect to the power relations between societal groups as played out both in school and in the broader society, and thus interaction within the ZPD must also focus on development of the critical thinking abilities required to deconstruct systematic disinformation used to bolster coercive relations of power. Students engaged in the critical literacy processes outlined by Ada have the possibility of actively voicing their own realities and their analyses of issues rather than being constricted to the identity definitions and constructions of "truth" implicitly or explicitly transmitted in the prescribed curriculum.

In short, the goal of interaction within the ZPD is collaborative empowerment for both students and educators. A socioacademic model oriented towards *empowerment* requires that educators actively challenge the societal power structure that historically and currently has disempowered culturally diverse students. In other words, the racism woven into the fabric of schooling and inadvertently (or intentionally) communicated by educators in their interactions with culturally diverse students must be exposed as a reflection of similar forms of racism in the institutions of society at large. Viewed from this perspective, the ZPD is as much a sociopolitical construct as a psychological construct.

Notes

1. This has happened at Garfield School in the Milwaukee Public Schools, where the contradictions between test content and classroom objectives prompted the school to develop alternative portfolio-based assessment systems. In the words of the principal (Kery Kafka):

> We stressed having the children work in cooperative groups, but we were rated on how well students did independently on standardized tests. . . . We replaced basal readers and workbooks with quality literature and children's writing, but we were rated on how well the children filled in circles on tests. We were becoming schizophrenic. (Miner 1992: 8)

2. I have slightly modified the labels given by Ada for the four phases in order to try to highlight certain aspects of the process. Although presented here in a linear format, the phases should not be thought of as requiring a linear or sequential approach. In other words, the process of collaborative critical inquiry can begin at any of the four phases and be incorporated in any manner into the instructional process. For example, as suggested in the *experience-text-relationship* method elaborated by Au (1979, cited in DeVillar and

388   CUMMINS

Faltis 1991) and her colleagues (e.g., Mason and Au 1986), an experi-
ental or personal interpretive phase, in which the teacher elicits students' personal experiences relevant to the text or topic, can precede
the descriptive phase. Ada's scheme is not in any sense formulaic but
should be reinvented by individual teachers according to their perceptions and circumstances. The essential components are that students' experience and critical inquiry constitute the curriculum as
much as any "text" since in the absence of students' experience and
critical inquiry no text can become truly meaningful.

References

Ada, A. F. (1988a). Creative reading: A relevant methodology for language minority children. In L. M. Malave (Ed.), *NABE '87. Theory,
research and application: Selected Papers.* Buffalo: State University of New York.

Ada, A. F. (1988b). The Pajaro Valley experience: Working with
Spanish-speaking parents to develop children's reading and writ-
ing skills in the home through the use of children's literature. In
T. Skutnabb-Kangas and J. Cummins (Ed.), *Minority education:
From shame to struggle.* Clevedon, England: Multilingual
Matters.

Au, K. H. (1979). Using the experience-text-relationship method with
minority children. *Reading Teacher, 32,* 677–679.

Barlett, D. L. and Steele, J. B. (1992). *America: What went wrong?*
Kansas: Andrews and McMeel.

Berman, P., Chambers, J., Gandara, P., et al. (1992). *Meeting the challenge of linguistic diversity: An evaluation of programs for pupils
with limited proficiency in English.* Berkeley: BW Associates.

Bigelow, B. (1991). Discovering Columbus: Re-reading the past. *Our
Schools, Our Selves, 3*(1), 22–38.

Blauner, R. (1969). Internal colonialism and ghetto revolt. *Social
Problems, 16,* 393–408.

Chomsky, N. (1987). The manufacture of consent. In J. Peck (Ed.) *The
Chomsky reader.* New York: Pantheon Books, 121–136.

Cummins, J. (1984). *Bilingualism and special education: Issues in
assessment and pedagogy.* Clevedon, England: Multilingual
Matters.

Cummins, J. (1989). *Empowering Minority Students.* Sacramento:
California Association for Bilingual Education.

Delpit, L. (1988). The silenced dialogue: Power and pedagogy in educating other peoples's children. *Harvard Educational Review, 58,*
280–298.

DeVillar, R. A. and Faltis, C. J. (1991). *Computers and cultural diversity: Restructuring for school success.* Albany: SUNY Press.

Fine, M. (1987). Silence and nurturing voice in an improbable context: Urban adolescents in public school. *Language Arts, 64*(2), 157–174.

Fordham, S. (1990). Racelessness as a factor in Black students' school success: Pragmatic strategy or pyrrhic victory? In N. M. Hidalgo, C. L. McDowell, and E. V. Siddle (Eds.), *Facing racism in education.* Reprint series No. 21, Harvard Educational Review, 232–262.

Galtung, J. (1980). *The true worlds: A transnational perspective.* New York: The Free Press.

Giroux, H. A. (1991). Series introduction: Rethinking the pedagogy of voice, difference and cultural struggle. In C. E. Walsh, *Pedagogy and the struggle for voice: Issues of language, power, and schooling for Puerto Ricans.* Toronto: OISE Press, xv–xxvii.

Goodlad, J. I. (1984). *A place called school: Prospects for the future.* New York: McGraw Hill.

Harry, B. (1992). *Cultural diversity, families, and the special education system: Communication and empowerment.* New York: Teachers College Press.

Henley, R. and Young, J. (1989). Multicultural teacher education, Part 4: Revitalizing faculties of education. *Multiculturalism, 12*(3), 40–41.

Hirsch, E. D., Jr. (1987). *Cultural literacy: What every American needs to know.* Boston: Houghton Mifflin Co.

Hodgkinson, H. (1991). Reform versus reality. *Phi Delta Kappan,* September, 1991, 9–16.

Kozol, J. (1991). *Savage inequalities: Children in America's schools.* New York: Crown Publishers.

Laing, R. D. (1969). *Self and others.* London: Tavistock Publications.

Lucas, I. (1981). Bilingual education and the melting pot: Getting burned. *Illinois Issues Humanities Essay No. 5.* Champaign, IL: Illinois Humanities Council.

Mason, J. M. and Au, K. H. (1986). *Reading instruction for today.* Glenview: Scott, Foresman and Company.

Miner, B. (1992). Experimenting with assessment: Milwaukee school says "No" to standardized tests. *Rethinking Schools, 6*(3), pp. 8 and 23.

Moll, L. (1989). Teaching second language students: A Vygotskian perspective. In D. Johnston and D. Roen (Eds.) *Richness in writing: Empowering ESL students.* New York: Longman, 55–69.

Newman, D., Griffin, P., and Cole, M. (1989). *The construction zone.* Cambridge: Cambridge University Press.

Oakes, J. (1985). *Keeping track: How high schools structure inequality.* New Haven: Yale University Press.

Olsen, L. and Minicucci, C. (1992). Educating limited English proficient students in secondary schools: Critical issues emerging from research in California schools. Paper presented at the American Educational Research Association annual conference, San Francisco, April.

Ogbu, J. (1978). *Minority education and caste.* New York: Academic Press.

Schweinhart, L. J., Weikart, D. P. and Larney, M. B. (1986). Consequences of three preschool curriculum models through age 15. *Early Childhood Research Quarterly, 1,* 15–45.

Shannon, P. (1989). *Broken promises: Reading instruction in 20th century America.* South Hadley, MA: Bergin and Garvey.

Simon, R. (1987). Empowerment as a pedagogy of possibility. *Language Arts, 64,* 370–380.

Sirotnik, K. A. (1983). What you see is what you get—consistency, persistency, and mediocrity in classrooms. *Harvard Educational Review, 53,* 16–31.

Skutnabb-Kangas, T. (1984). *Bilingualism or not: The education of minorities.* Clevedon, England: Multilingual Matters.

Skutnabb-Kangas, T. (1988). Resource power and autonomy through discourse in conflict—a Finnish migrant school strike in Sweden. In T. Skutnabb-Kangas and J. Cummins (Eds.) *Minority education: From shame to struggle.* Clevedon, England: Multilingual Matters, 251–277.

Vygotsky, L. S. (1978). *Mind in society: The development of higher psychological processes.* (Eds. M. Cole, V. John-Steiner, S. Scibner, and E. Souberman). Cambridge, MA: Harvard University Press.

Wagner, S. and Grenier, P. (1991). *Analphabétisme de minorité et alphabétisme d'affirmation nationale á propos de l'Ontario français. Volume I: Synthèse théoretique et historique.* Toronto: Ministère de l'Éducation.

Waldman, M. (1990). *Who robbed America? A citizen's guide to the Savings and Loan Scandal.* New York: Random House.

Walsh, C. E. (1991). *Pedagogy and the struggle for voice: Issues of language, power, and schooling for Puerto Ricans.* Toronto: OISE Press.

Willis, P. (1977). *Learning to labor: How working class kids get working class jobs.* Lexington: D.C. Heath.

Wilson, D. (1991). Native bands demand action on school's abuse of children. *The Globe and Mail,* Wednesday, June 19, 1991, p. A4.

Zanger, V. V. (in press). "Not joined in": Intergroup relations and access to English literacy for Hispanic youth. In B. M. Ferdman, R. M. Weber, and A. Ramírez (Eds.) *Literacy across languages and cultures.* Albany: SUNY Press.

▼ Author Index ▼

Aclán, Z. and Lindholm, 204
Acosta-Belén, E. and Sjostrom, 43
Ada, A. F., 119, 374, 383–86, 387
Allen, P., 325
Allport, G., 4, 8, 12–3, 15, 17, 192, 305, 324
Allport, G. and Vygotsky, 12–3
Amastae, J, 164
Amaya-Williams, M. and Díaz, 9
Amaya-Williams, M. and Neal, 9
American Council on Education, 102
Amir, Y., 305
Amir, Y. and Ben Ari, 305
Amir, Y. and Schwarzwald, 305
Ammon, P., 163, 174
Anderson, A. L., 209
Apple, M., 337
Applebee, A. and Langer, 161
Applebee, A., et al., 162
Apter, S. J., 231
Arce-Torres, E., 309
Arias, A. A., 349, 351
Arias, A. A. and Bellman, 349–62, 350, 351
Arias, M. B., 1, 32
Arias, M. B. and Cohen, 1
Aronson, E. and Lindzey, 305–6
Arvizu, S. F., 75–97, 82, 88, 95
Arvizu, S. F. and Saravia-Shore, 76, 77, 78
Ashkinaze, C. and Orfield, 1
Atkin, E. L., 213, 215
Au, K. H., 9, 386, 388
Au, K. H. and Kawakami, 9, 10
Au, K. H. and Mason, 9, 388

Bailey, S. K., 325
Baker, K., 257
Banton, M., 27
Baral, D. P., 182
Barlett, D. L. and Steele, 367
Barrera, M., 43
Bell, Andrew, 61
Bellman, B. and Arias, 349–62, 350, 151
Ben Ari, R. and Amir, 305
Bennett, K. P. and LeCompte, 2
Benson, S. S., 216
Bents, R. and Howey, 117
Berman, P., et al., 371–72
Biber, D. and Krashen, 255, 258
Bigelow, B., 381, 383
Bilingual Education Act, 39
Bird and Little, 126
Blake, H., et al., 350
Blauner, R., 369
Boas, F., 78
Bolam, R., et al, 117
Borgas, G. J. and Tienda, 1
Bork, A., 266
Bouvier, L. F. and Gardner, 1
Braun, C. and Klassen, 165, 182
Brewer, M. and Edwards, 16
Brewer, M. and Miller, 16
Brizzi, E., 119
Brooks, R. L., 29, 43
Brewer, M., 324
Brown v. Board of Education, 347, U.S. 483 (1954), 326
Brown, A. and Campione, 11
Brown, A. and Palincsar, 11
Brown, K., 300

Brown, K. and Sayers, 303
Brown, R. and Hewstone, 324
Bruce, B. and Michaels, 11
Bruce, B. and Watson-Gageo, 11
Bruce, M. G., 2
Budin, H., 333–48, 337, 340
Budin, H., et al. (1987), 338
Budin, H., et al. (1989), 336, 338
Burnham, L. and Peña, 255
Bush, 118

Calathes, W., 1
Calderón, M., 117–41, 118, 119, 121, 367
Calderón, M. and Houston, 117
Calderón, M. and Marak, 118
Calderón, M. and Mata, 118
Calderón, M., et al., 145
Campione, J. and Brown, 11
Campione, J. and Palincsar, 11
Carlisle, R. S., 161–87, 168–72, 175
Castañeda, A. and Ramírez, 34
Catterall, J. and Cota-Robles, 1
Cazden, C., 300
Cazden, C. and Forman, 173
Center for Bilingual Education & Research, 108
Chambers, J., 371–72
Chan, S., 43
Chapala, C., et al., 119
Chávez, R. Ch., 270
Child, I and Whiting, 78
Chomsky, N., 367, 374
Christie, M., 166, 175
Clandfield, D. and Sivell, 299
Clark, E. and Milk, 119
Cleveland, H., 339
Cohen, A. D., 255
Cohen, E. G., 293, 306
Cohen, E. G. and Arias, 1
Cole, M., 376
Cole, M. and Griffin, 335
Cole, M. and Scribner, 148, 161
Coles, G. J., 258
Comenius, Johann Amos, 60–1
Commission on Work, Family and Citizenship, 1
Compton, R. S., 118
Cook, S., 305, 306, 310
Cook-Gumperz, J. and Gumperz, 163

Cortes, C. E., 78, 102
Cota-Robles, E. and Catterall, 1
Cronnell, B., 164
CTB/McGraw-Hill, 241
Cuban, L., 2, 150
Cuevas, J. and Lindholm, 195
Cummins, J., 11, 18, 103, 105, 119, 150, 172, 180, 256, 300, 301, 323, 325, 363–91, 369, 370, 372, 373
Cummins, J. and Sayers, 300
Curran, M., 303
Curtain, H. and Pesola, 256
Cziko, G. A., 41

Daedalus, 43
Daniels, R., 28, 29, 43
Daniels, R.and Kitano, 43
Danoff, M. N., 258
Danoff, M. N., et al., 258
Davis, C. and Haub, 1
Davis, C. and Willette, 1
Day, R., 302
Delpit, L., 388
Deutsch, M., 34, 65
DeVillar, R. A., 1, 2, 3, 18, 25–6, 263, 266, 269–70, 271
DeVillar, R. A. and Faltis, 1–22, 3, 6, 8, 9, 10, 11, 14, 15, 16, 17, 30, 34, 36, 75, 90, 95, 105, 145, 163, 207, 230, 300, 305, 312, 321–25, 335, 336, 341, 349, 363, 364, 365, 375, 380, 381, 382, 386, 388
DeVries, D. and Edwards, 306
DeVries, D., et al. (1974), 306
DeVries, D., et al. (1978), 306
Dewey, J., 61
Díaz, R. C. and Amaya-Williams, 9
Díaz, R. C. and Neal, 9
Dickson, W. P. and Vereen, 266
Dobzhansky, T., 27
Dodge, K. A., 208, 210
Doughty, C. and Pica, 269
Dukes, R. L. and Martínez, 191
Dunn, L. 32–4
Durán, R. P., 145–57, 145, 152–53
Durnin, R. and Trowbridge, 266

Ecclesiastes, 60, 67
Eddy, E., 82

Edelsky, C., 163, 164
Edfelt, N. M. (See González-Edfelt, N.), 263, 264
Edwards, J. R., 302
Edwards, K., 306, 321, 324
Edwards, K. and Brewer, 16
Edwards, K. and DeVries, 306
Edwards, K. and Miller, 16
Edwards, J. R. 310
Ender, P., 263, 270
Erickson, F., 85
Ewen, E. and Gipps, 164

Faigley, L. and Witte, 161, 162
Faltis, C. J., 108
Faltis, C. J. and DeVillar, 1–22, 3, 6, 8, 9, 10, 11, 14, 15, 16, 17, 30, 34, 36, 75, 90, 95, 105, 145, 163, 207, 230, 300, 305, 312, 321–25, 335, 336, 341, 349, 363, 364, 365, 375, 380, 381, 382, 386, 388
Farella, M. and Rosier, 180
Federal Register, 40
Fennberg, A., 351
Ferguson, T. M. and Rule, 210
Fernández, R. R., 27, 32, 33
Fernández, R. R. and Shu, 1
Ferris, M. R. and Politzer, 167–68, 175, 182
Feshbach, N. D., 209, 210, 211–12, 213–14, 215, 216
Fetterman, D., 76
Figueroa, E., et al., 300
Fine, M. 6, 370, 376
FIPSE Technology Study Group, 351
Flower, L. and Hayes, 161
Foley, D., 83
Ford, E., 151
Fordham, S., 1, 35, 322, 364, 369, 374, 378
Forman, E. and Cazden, 173
Franklin, Benjamin, 28
Franklin, J. H., 28, 29
Freinet, C., 299–300

Gaies, S., 12
Gales, K., et al., 166, 172, 175
Gallimore, R., 82, 154
Gallimore, R. and Goldenberg, 1

Gallimore, R. and Weisner, 11
Gallimore, R. and Jordan, 11
Gallimore, R. and Tharp, 137, 151–52
Gálvez-Hjornevik, D., 118
Gandara, P., 371, 372
García, E., 173
García, R., 145
Gardner, R. C., 196, 203
Gardner, R. C. and Lambert, 191
Gardner, R. W. and Bouvier, 1
Gass, S. M. and Varonis, 264, 265
Gaddes, M., et al., 109
Genesee, F., et al. (1978), 313
Gilbert, R. and Grabe, 170
Gibbs, C. and Ewen, 164
Giroux, H. A., 370
Goldenberg, C., 154
Goldenberg, C. and Gallimore, 1
Goldstein, A. P., et al., 214, 215
Gonzales, Linda, 233–59
González-Edfelt, N., 263–98
Goodlad, J., 2, 5, 150, 382
Gordon, M., 45
Grabe, W. and Gilbert, 170
Graham, S., 209
Grant, C. and Zeichner, 117
Graves, N. and T. Graves, 273
Grenier, P. and Wagner, 370
Griffin, P., 376
Griffin, P. and Cole, 335
Gumperz, J. and Cook-Gumperz, 163
Gumperz, J. and Hymes, 82
Gutiérrez, K., 148, 149

Hakuta, K., 325
Harasim, L., 351
Harley, B., et al, 325
Harootunian, B., 231
Harris, M. 95
Harris, S., 166, 175
Harry, 372
Harter, 191, 195, 199
Hatch, E. 269
Haub, C. and Davis, 1
Haub, C. and Willette, 1
Hawkins, B., 12
Hayes, J. and Flower, 161
Henley, R. and Young, 372

Henry, J., 82
Hernández-Chávez, E., 191, 201
Hertz-Lazarowitz, R., 138, 145
Hewstone, M. and Brown, 324
Higgins, J. and Johns, 268
Higgins, T. E., 216
Hill-Burnett, J., 85
Hiltz, S. R., 351
Hirsch, E. D., 381
Hodgkinson, H., 367–68
Holm, W. and Rosier, 180
Holmes Group, The, 2
Holubec, E. J. and Johnson, D. W.,
    14–5, 61, 62, 63, 64, 145, 192
Holubec, E. J. and Johnson, R. T.,
    14–5, 61, 62, 63, 64, 145, 192
Houston, W. R. and Calderón, 117
Howey, K. and Bents, 117
Hudelson, S., 163, 164
Huling-Austin, L. and Murphy,
    117, 118
Hunter, B., 340
Hymes, D., 148
Hymes, D. and Gumperz, 82

Jefferson, Thomas, 28
Jensen, A. R., 32, 34
Johns, T. and Higgins, 268
Johnson, D. W., 64, 272, 306
Johnson, D. W. and Holubec, 14–5,
    61, 62, 63, 64, 145, 192
Johnson, D. W. and Johnson, F., 64
Johnson, D. W. and Johnson, R. T.,
    4, 8, 14–5, 16, 57–73, 57, 60,
    65, 66, 67, 68, 69, 70, 269, 272,
    273, 367
Johnson, D. W., et al. (1983), 306
Johnson, F. and Johnson, D. W., 64
Johnson, R. T., 306
Johnson, R. T. and Holubec, 14–5,
    61, 62, 63, 64, 145, 192
Johnson, R. T. and Johnson, D. W.,
    4, 8, 14–5, 16, 57–73, 57, 60, 65,
    66, 67, 68, 69, 770, 269, 272, 273
Johnson, R. T., et al. (1986),
    272, 306
Jonas, R., 313
Jones, S and Tetroe, 162
Jordan, K and Gallimore, 11
Jordan, K. and Weisner, 11

Kagan, S., 145, 192, 273
Kaplan, R. M., 210
Katz, I., 3305
Kawakami, A. and Au, 9, 10
Kaye, A. and Mason, 349
Kaye, T., 351, 352
Kendall, D. S., 338
Kenning, M. J. and M-M Kenning,
    268
Kirst, M. W., 2
Kitano, H. and Daniels, 43
Klassen, B. and Braun, 165, 182
Kliebard, H., 4
Kohn, A., 15
Korndant, H. J., 210
Kozal, J., 371, 376
Krashen, S. and Biber, 255, 258
Kwiat, J., 109

Laboratory of Comparative Human
    Cognition, 336
Laing, R. D., 367, 380
Lambert, W. E., 190, 192, 201, 203,
    301, 309, 313
Lambert, W. E. and Gardner, 191
Lancaster, Joseph, 61
Langer, J., 162
Langer, J. and Applebee, 161
Larney, M. B., 368
Lawson, M. E., 209
Lazarus, E., 25
Lazerson, M., et al., 335
LeCompte, M. D. and Bennett, 2
Lee, W. B., 299
Levin, H., 1
Lewin, K., 65
Lewis, S., 263, 270
Liberty, P., 113
Lincoln, Abraham, 28
Lindholm, K. J., 187–206, 193–94,
    195, 201, 204, 374
Lindholm, K. J. and Aclán, 204
Lindholm, K. J. and Cuevas, 195
Lindholm, K. J. and Padilla, 203
Lindzey, G. and Aronson, 305–6
Lipkin, J., 3
Little, L. W., 118, 126
Little and Bird, 126
Lochman, W. M., et al., 209, 210,
    214, 215

Long, M. H., 265, 269, 289
Long, M. H. and Porter, 173
Lorhre, D., 118
Lucas, I., 378–79

McCaleb, J. L., 117
McClay, D., 166, 175
McDonald, F., 117
McDonald, J. P., 337
McGroarty, M., 12
McLaughlin, B., 325
McLaughlin, D. H., 258
McPherson, B., 325
Marak and Calderón, 118
Markstrom-Adams, C. and Spencer, 191
Martin, J. H., 270
Martínez, R. and Dukes, 191
Maruyama, G., 306
Mason, J. and Au, 9, 388
Mason, R. and Kaye, 349
Mata, S., 119
Mata, S. and Calderón, 118
Matthews, F., 102
Matute-Bianchi, M. E., 35, 304, 322
Matute-Bianchi, M. E. and Ogbu, 147
Mead, M., 78
Mehan, H., 282
Melodia, A., 350
Merino, B. and Ramírez, 2, 6, 173
Michaels, S. and Bruce, 11
Michaels, S. and Watson-Gageo, 11
Milk, R. D., 12, 101–15, 111, 322
Milk, R. D. and Clark, 119
Miller, N. and Brewer, 16
Miller, N. and Edwards, 16
Miller, N., et al., 324
Miner, B., 387
Minicucci, C. and Olsen, 371, 376
Modiano, N. 180
Moll, L. 106, 376
Montagu, A., 27
Moore, J. and Pachón, 1, 37, 43
Moynihan, D., 34
Mullis, I. 162
Murphy, S. C. and Huling-Austin, 117, 118
Myrdal, G., 28, 43

National Council of La Raza, 108
Navarro, R. A., 1
Neal, C. and Amaya-Williams, 9
Neal, C. and Díaz, 9
Nelson, W. M., 209
Neves, A., 12
New York City Board of Education, 341
Newberry, J. M., 117, 118
Newman, D., et al., 376
Northcutt, L. (See Gonzales, L.), 256
Novak, M., 44

Oakes, J., 372
Office of Technology Assessment, 335
Ogbu, J., 83, 85, 91, 95, 369, 370
Ogbu, J. and Matute-Bianchi, 147
O'Hare, W. P., 1
Oickle, E., 306
Olsen, L. and Minicucci, 371, 376
Orfield, G. and Ashkinaze, 1

Pachón, H. and Moore, 1, 37, 43
Padilla, A. M. and Lindholm, 203
Palinscar, A., 11
Palinscar, A. and Brown, 11
Palinscar, A. and Campione, 11
Parker, Francis (Colonel), 61
Pastore, N., 209
Pease-Alvarez, L. and Vásquez, 293
Peña, M. and Burnham, 255
Perkins, K., 170
Perle, S., 161, 162, 163
Pesola, C. and Curtain, 256
Pettigrew, T. F., 324
Philips, S. U., 164
Pianko, S., 161
Pica, T. and Doughty, 269
Pienemann, M., 173
Politzer, R. L., 309
Politzer, R. L. and Ferris, 167–68, 175, 182
Porter, O., 350
Porter, P. and Long, 173
Porter, R., 173
Potter, L., 164
Prado-Olmos, P., et al., 145
Prawat, R. S., 209

Quintillion, 60

Rainer, A., 162
Ramey, D., 172, 174, 180
Ramírez, A. G., 150, 258, 309
Ramírez, A. G., et al., 309
Ramírez, J. D., 255
Ramírez, J. D., et al., 38, 41, 172, 174, 180
Ramírez, J. D. and Merino, 2, 6, 173
Ramírez, M. and Castañeda, 34
Report on Education Research, 147
Resnick, L., 335
Reynolds, D. J., 258
Rivera, C. and Zehler, 103, 106
Roberts, L. and staff, 300
Rodrigues, R., 165, 172, 175, 181
Rose, M., 161
Rosenberg, M., 190
Rosier, P. and Farella, 180
Rosier, P and Holm, 180
Rubin, J. , 289
Rueda, R., et al., 154
Rule, B. G. and Ferguson, 210
Ryan, K., 117
Rydell, L., 256

Salinas, G., 32
Samway, K., 164
Saravia-Shore, M. and Arvizu, 76, 77, 78
Saufley, R., 350
Sayers, D., 299–331, 300, 303, 367
Sayers, D. and Brown, 303
Sayers, D. and Cummins, 300
Schwarzwald, J. and Amir, 305
Schinke-Llano, L. A., 35, 174, 282
Schweinhart, L. J., et al, 368
Scribner, S. and Cole, 148, 161
Scruton, R., 27
Seneca, 60
Shannon, P., 374, 387
Sharan, S. and Shachar, H., 325
Sharan, Y. and Sharan, S., 340
Shu, G. and Fernández, 1
Simon, R., 380
Sims, J. P., 209
Sirotnik, K., 5, 6, 382
Sivell, J. and Clandfield, 299

Sjostrom, B. R. and Acosta-Belén, 43
Skutnabb-Kangas, T., 370, 371, 374
Slavin, R., 14, 16, 145, 146, 191, 192, 306
Smith, F., 335, 337
Sommers, N., 161, 162
Sparling, S. S., 207–32, 216
Spencer, M. B. and Markstrom-Adams, 191
Sperlich, H. K., 65
Spindler, G., 79, 85
Stallard, C., 161
Stanne, M. B., 272, 306
Steele, J. B., 367
Steller, 125
Stern, P., 209
Storms, M. D., 216
Suárez-Orozco, M. M., 35
Swain, M., 12, 166, 181–82, 182, 265, 325

Takaki, R., 43
Taylor, R. P., 338
Tenhula, J., 43
Tetroe, J. and Jones, 162
Tharp, R. G. and Gallimore, 137, 151–52
Tienda, M. and Borjas, 1
Tinajero, J., 145
Tisher, R., 117
Triviz, R., 310
Troike, R., 180
Trowbridge, D. and Durnin, 266
Trueba, H., 27, 32, 85, 95
Tucker, G. R., 313
Tudge, J., 9
Tucker, M. S., 337

Urzua, C., 164

Valadez, C., 119
Valdez, C. M., 164
Valencia, A., 86
Van Gennep, A., 88
Varonis, E. M. and Gass, 264, 265
Vasquez-Brunet, I., 303
Vásquez, O. A. and Pease-Alvarez, 293

Veenman, S., 117
Veltman, C., 37
Vereen, M. A. and Dickson, 266
Vygotsky, L. S., 4, 8, 9, 13–4, 137,
    150–51, 364, 376
Vygotsky, L. S. and Allport, 13

Wagner, S. and Grenier, 370
Walberg, H., 173
Waldman, M., 368
Walker, C. L., 34
Walsh, C. E., 370, 380
Washington, George, 28
Watson, D., et al., 256
Watson-Gages, K. and Bruce, 11
Watson-Gages and Michaels, 11
Webb, N. M., 293
Webb, N. M., et al., 263, 270
Weigel, R., 14, 16
Weigel, R., et al., 306, 310
Weikart, D. P., 368
Weiner, B., 209–10, 215
Weiner, B., et al. (1982), 209, 212
Weiner, B., et al. (1983), 209
Weinreich, U., 35
Weisner, T. and Gallimore, 11
Weisner, T. and Jordan, 11
Wells, E.,306
White, M. I., 2
Whiting, J. and Child, 78

Willette, J. and Davis, 1
Willette, J. and Haub, 1
William T. Grant Foundation, 1
Williams, R., 305
Willig, A. C., 33, 38, 191, 257
Willis, P., 369, 374
Wilson, D., 377–78
Wiser, P., 306, 310
Witte, S. and Faigley, 161, 162
Wolcott, H., 77, 82–3, 85
Wollenberg, C. M., 30, 32, 34, 43
Wong-Fillmore, L., 12, 156, 174,
    289–90
Woods, D., 162
Wyatt, D. H., 268
Wylie, R., 190

Young, J. and Henley, 372
Young, R., 263, 268
Yuen, S., 172, 174, 180

Zakariya, S. B., 335
Zamel, V., 162
Zanger, V. V., 374, 379
Zangwill, I., 25, 43–4
Zehler, A. and Rivera, 103, 106
Zeichner, K., 117
Zeichner, K. and Grant, 117
Zimmerer, J., 351

▼ SUBJECT INDEX ▼

African Americans in U.S. schools, 28–31

Anglo conformity model of national unity, 45, 49 *See also.* Socialization and resocialization, 46

Anthropology, defined, 76–77; and education, 79; contribution to educational practice, 83–85; future of educational research, 88, 89

Asian Americans in U.S. schools, 42

Beginning minority/bilingual teachers: first year experiences of, 121–23; induction of, 118; mentoring and coaching of, 127–29; training of, 124–24; what practices work best, 119; study of, 120–22

BESTNET (Binational English and Spanish Telecommunications Network), 351–53; courses taught on, 360; focus of, 353–54; participating institutions of, 353, 355; positive results of, 356–59

Bilingual Education: and affective gains, 255–56; and amount of time need to achieve English mastery, 245; as an English dominant program, 38; early-exit, late-exit, and transitional programs, 6, 7; effectiveness of, 223, 256–58; and mathematical achievement, 245–48; positive benefits of, 255; and reading achievement, 249–52; and rhetoric, 38; and students' attitudes toward, 301; talk in bi-

lingual classrooms, 6, 7; as structured immersion, 6

Bilingual Education Act, 39

Bilingual immersion education, 189, 193; features of, 194; types of instruction in, 238–39; critical components of, 234–37

Brown v. Board of Education, 30, 31, 36, 305

CIRC (Cooperative Integrated Reading and Composition), 153

Cisneros v. Corpus Christi Independent School District, 32

Coercive relations of power, 366–70; and microinteraction, 377

Collaborative relations of power, 366–68

Communication as two way exchanges, 105

Communicative competence, 148

Computers: and collaborative work with, 334, 343; and equity issues, 335; and teachers' decision making, 337; teaching teachers about, 333, 337

Computer-mediated conferencing, 349; *See also* BESTNET

Computer environments: and collaborative behavior, 264, 292; and the division of labor, 270–71; and English acquisition, 263; features of, 266; and how students are paired or grouped, 267; and learning structures, 272

Computer software: collaborative uses of, 339–42; and language behavior, 268; types of, 269–70

Contact theory, 304, 324; and Orillas, 304–306; and prejudice, 305; *See also* Orillas

Cooperative learning, defined 57, 146; and achievement, 66; basic elements of, 15, 62–65; and crosscultural attitudes, 193; effects of, 65, 70; distinguished from collaborative learning, 145–46; elements of, 15; evaluation of at the computer, 276–78; and implications for diversity, 70; and interpersonal relations, 67; and language minority children, 145–47; as a minimal requirement for computer based learning, 323; and prejudice, 306; and psychological health and social competencies, 69; and self esteem, 129–30, 193; and the socioacademic framework, 15; and the computer, 272; topics arising from, 154–55; training for at the computer, 273–74. *See also* Socioacademic framework.

Cooperative learning groups, as discourse communities, 149, 151; learning helping strategies, 152, 153

Creative reading act, phases of, 383–85

Critical pedagogy, 382

Cross Cultural Language Attitudes Scale, 195

Cross cultural approaches to education, 81–82

Cross cultural leadership, 78, 79

Cross cultural literacy, 77

Cross Cultural Resource Center at California State University, Sacramento, 82; Cross-Language-Dominance-Group-Respect (Cross-LDG), 309, 310–12, 319, 320

Council of Anthropology and Education, 79

Cultural diversity and rhetoric, 25; and socialization, 25, 26

Cultural literacy, 381

Culturally diverse classrooms management of, 207

Culture, defined, 78; within a cross cultural context, 80, 81

Curricular content, and critical inquiry, 381–83

Democratic nation, melting pot model, 48

DeVillar and Faltis Framework. *See* Socioacademic framework/model

Diversity, defined, 76; anthropological contributions to, 75; as strength, 58; *See also* Stellar cohesion of cultures

Dropping out as being pushed out, 378–79

Educational reform efforts and the achievement gap for minority students, 102; at the classroom level, 103; as test driven, 102

Educational structures, 371–72; and discrimination, 372

Educator role definitions, 373–74; and microinteractions with students, 375

Empowerment and education, 94, 95

Empowerment framework dimensions of, 373

Enculturation, 46

English as a second language (ESL) effectiveness of, 256–57; types of programs, 240, 241

Equal status in groupwork, 17

Equity, defined, 3; as assess, 3; and equality, 2

Ethnography, defined, 77; and life history, 91

Ethnicity, confused with race, 31

Exclusion and school failure, 32

Experience-text-relationship, 386; method, 9–11, 14; as a Vygotskian approach, 9

Face-to-face promotion of interaction, 63

Feigning comprehension, 291; during collaborative learning, 295
Friendship patterns, 16
Funds of knowledge, 106

Gaps between wealthy and poor, 368
Groupwork small vs. large and language attitudes, 317
Group investigation, 14
Group process, 64

Hispanic Americans in schools, 31
Holistic education, 104

Individual accountability, 64
Influences of L1 writing on L2 writing, 164; studies of, 165–68
Innovative Approaches Research Project (IARP), 106
Integration, see Socioacademic framework, 3
Intelligence and Hispanic Americans, 32, 33; used to explain genetic inferiority, 34
Interactive journal uses with beginning minority bilingual teachers, 135–36
Interdependence hypothesis, 172
Internal colonies, 369

Jigsaw I, II, 14

Kamahameha Project, 82; See also Experience-, Text-Relationship

Language education social contexts of, 190
Language and schooling, 37
Life history: uses of in educational anthropology research, 84–85
Literacy as social practice, 148

Macrointeractions, 363; between dominant and subordinate groups, 369–71; and power relations, 365

Matched guise test, 309, 319, 321
Melting pot, 350; myth of, 27
Mendez v. Westminster, 32
Mentoring and coaching beginning minority/bilingual teachers, 127–28
Mexican American Education Project, 82
Mexican descent students categories of, 35
Microinteractions and the Zone of Proximal Development. See, 375; also Zone of Proximal Development.

Negotiation of Meaning, 264; among students of differing English language proficiency; 287–89; and computer use, 265; and language acquisition, 264

Orillas, (also de orilla a orilla), 299–304; in bilingual classrooms, 302–4; and favorable attitudes toward Spanish speakers, 314, 315; and Freinet's model, 300; goals of, 299; and language attitudes, 321; and the promotion of Spanish, 307

Peabody Picture Vocabulary Test Series, 32
Peer coaching: teacher feelings and perceptions of, 133–34
Perspective taking activities, 213
Plessy v. Ferguson, 30
Pluralism, defined, 78; operationalizing pluralism, 92–94
Positive interdependence, defined, 63
Preparation of teachers for culturally diverse schools: coursework needed, 109; dealing with cultural diversity, 107; field experiences, 112; innovative strategies, 110, 111
Prosocial behaviors, 16

Race: notions and social consequences of, 27, 28; confused with ethnicity, 31

Racially based exclusion, philosophy of, 28

Reconceptualizing instruction for language minority students, 104

Rhetoric: adjusting the imbalance between rhetoric and practice, 42; national vs. national practice, 45; shifts in, 38, 41

Roberto Alvarez v. the Board of Trustees of the Lemon Grove School District, 32

Second language acquisition and communicative principles, 11

Segregation in the classroom, 17; as the norm, 30

Self-esteem, 189; and bilingual education, 191

Socioacademic achievement model 363, 364. See Socioacademic Framework

Socioacademic Framework, 3, 90, 163, 189, 312, 322, 323, 324, 360; applied to school, 14–18; components of, 3, 12, 363; explained, 3; related to power, 363–65, 386

Socialization and resocialization, 46; resocialization as an alternative to Anglo Conformity model, 47

Sociohistorical school of learning and cognitive development, 150–51

Stellar cohesion of cultures, 52

Student anger and aggression, 208; attributions of, 210; definition of, 210; and empathy, 211, 216

Student-Teams-Achievement-Divisions (STAD), 14

Teaching writing, in different educational programs, 164; instructional practices of teachers, 174–76; studies of, 169

Team-Assisted-Individualization, 14

Teams-Games-Tournaments, 14

Title VII. See Bilingual Education Act

Upset chain, 223

U.S. classrooms, current practices in, 4–7; whole class instruction, 5; bilingual instruction, 6

Vygotskian principles, 8–11; as applied to classroom learning, 9, 10; and the socioacademic framework, 13; and the zone of proximal development, 9

Writing processes: differences between more- and less- proficient writers, 161; similarities between first and second language writing, 162

Zone of proximal development (ZPD), 151, 156, 364, 365, 380, 382; as the construction zone, 376; and culturally diverse schools, 383; defined, 383